the 2006 Gamer's Tome of Ultimate Wisdom

An Almanac of Pimps, Orcs, and Lightsabers

William Abner

800 East 96th Street, Indianapolis, Indiana 46240 USA

The 2006 Gamer's Tome of Ultimate Wisdom

Copyright© 2006 by Que Publishing

International Standard Book Number: 0-7897-3465-6

Library of Congress Catalog Card Number: 2005933312

Printed in the United States of America

First Printing: December 2005

08   07   06   05   4   3   2   1

Trademarks

All terms mentioned in this book that are known to be trademarks or service marks have been appropriately capitalized. Que Publishing cannot attest to the accuracy of this information. Use of a term in this book should not be regarded as affecting the validity of any trademark or service mark.

Warning and Disclaimer

Every effort has been made to make this book as complete and as accurate as possible, but no warranty or fitness is implied. The information provided is on an "as is" basis. The author and the publisher shall have neither liability nor responsibility to any person or entity with respect to any loss or damages arising from the information contained in this book.

Bulk Sales

Que Publishing offers excellent discounts on this book when ordered in quantity for bulk purchases or special sales. For more information, please contact

> **U.S. Corporate and Government Sales**
> **1-800-382-3419**
> **corpsales@pearsontechgroup.com**

For sales outside the United States, please contact

> **International Sales**
> **international@pearsoned.com**

Associate Publisher
Greg Wiegand

Executive Editor
Rick Kughen

Development Editor
Todd Brakke

Managing Editor
Charlotte Clapp

Project Editor
Tonya Simpson

Copy Editor
Mike Henry

Indexer
Ken Johnson

Publishing Coordinator
Sharry Lee Gregory

Interior Designer
Anne Jones

Cover Designer
Anne Jones

Contents at a Glance

Table of Contents

About the Author

William Abner is a graduate of The Ohio State University and has been an avid gamer since the days of Space Invaders and Pong. He has worked in the gaming industry as a member of the media since 1996, first as the founder of The Gaming Nexus website and then as managing editor for GamePen.com. He then served as an associate editor for *Computer Games* magazine until the birth of his daughter, Ashley, in the fall of 2000. Since then, he has worked out of his home near Columbus, Ohio as a freelance writer for *Computer Games* magazine, GameSpy, and GameShark.com. He also helps run a sports-gaming blog at http://www.sportsgamer.blogspot.com. His most rewarding job, however, is being a dad.

Photo Credits

Most images printed in this book are provided courtesy of GameSpy (www.gamespy.com). However, all game screenshots and product photos used in this book are ultimately owned by the respective manufacturers and publishers, including, but not limited to: 3D Media Labs, 3DO, 4Players, Acclaim Entertainment, Activision Publishing, Advanced Micro Devices, Alienware, Ambrosia Software, Antec, Apex Digital, Apple, Atari, Atlus Software, BAWLS Guarana, Beermat Software, Bethesda Softworks, Blizzard Entertainment, Borderbrund, Buena Vista Interactive, Bungie Software, CDV Software, Capcom, Carada, Cisco Systems, Inc., Code Junkies, CodeMasters, Concept Lab, Crave Entertainment, Creative, Cy-Visor, Decal Girl, Dell, Disney Interactive, DreamCatcher Interactive, ESPN Video Games, eDimensional, Eidos Interactive, Electronic Arts, eMobile, Firaxis, Fisher-Price, Freeverse Software, GT Interactive, Gathering of Developers, Global Star, Gravis, HPS Simulations, Hip Interactive, Hypersonic, I-O Display Systems, id Software, Infinium Labs, InFocus, Infogrames Entertainment, Inkplosion Gamer Store, Intec, Interplay, Io Interactive, Ionside, Jakks TV Games, Jamdat, Jolt, Kensington, Klipsch, Koei, Konami Computer Entertainment, Kuma Games, Laminar Research, LavaMind, Learning Company (The), Logitech, LucasArts, Ltd., MGM Interactive, MadCatz, Magnavox, Majesco Games, Master Replicas, Mattel, *Maximum PC Magazine*, McFarlane Toys, Microprose, Microsoft, Midway Games, Mindscape, Monster Cable, Muse Software, Mystique, NCSoft, Naki International, Namco Hometek, Natsume, Nintendo Corporation, Nyko, PAN Vision, PalmOne, Inc., PalmSource, Inc., Pangea Software, Pazzazz Games, Philips, PopCap Games, Razor 3D, Red Orb Entertainment, Ripcord Games, Rockstar Games, Sega of America, Sicuro, Sierra Online, Skinsane, Sony Corporation, Sorrent, Spiderweb Software, Square Enix Company, Tapwave, TDK, Tecmo Ltd., THQ, Inc., Titus Software, Tripp Lite, U.S. Army, Ubisoft Entertainment, Via, Victorinox, Vivendi Universal, VoodooPC, Wisdom Tree, Xen Games, Xfire, and XTZ.

Dedication

To Mary, for seven wonderful years of marriage.
To my daughter, Ashley, for the best five years of my life.

Acknowledgments

I should start off by thanking my wife, Mary, for being the most understanding woman in the world. You leave every morning to deal with the rat race of life while I stay at home with our daughter to play video games and watch cartoons. Mary, the fact that you haven't killed me in my sleep means a lot.

Even though she's only five, I need to thank my daughter Ashley for allowing me to work during the day on this book even when she wanted dad to play a game or watch a movie. I could not have asked for a better child.

I'd also like to thank my parents for taking me to the arcades when I was a kid and spending untold amounts of money so that I could play Track and Field and Donkey Kong. Also, thanks for buying me that Atari 2600, Intellivision, Commodore 64, Commodore 128, Amiga 500, and my first 486 PC. When you think about it, it's your fault that I'm not a doctor.

Huge thanks go out to the people at GameSpy.com, specifically John Keefer, for giving us the green light to use the vast majority of screenshots you see in this book. I'm also grateful to Bill Harris, Sean "Elysium" Sands, Sean Carton, Jared Medina, and Mur Lafferty for their helpful suggestions and kind words about the book.

I also tip my hat to three of the best editors I have ever had the pleasure of working with: Steve Bauman of CGM, Sal Accardo of GameSpy, and James Fudge of GameShark—thanks for understanding that my freelance schedule was out of whack due to the book, and also thanks for being friends as well as colleagues. You guys helped me more than you know.

Finally, I want to extend an enormous thank you to all the fine people at Que Publishing, beginning with executive editor Rick Kughen for believing in this project. I personally want to thank my editor and long-time friend Todd Brakke for having faith in me to write this book and for holding this first-time author's hand through the entire process. Todd is living proof that even a Michigan fan can be a standup guy. I'd also like to thank copy editor Mike Henry not only for his hard work but also for catching some of my more obscure references to music and movies. Shine on, you crazy diamond. Finally, thanks to project editor Tonya Simpson and everyone else who had a hand in putting this all into print.

We Want to Hear from You!

As the reader of this book, *you* are our most important critic and commentator. We value your opinion and want to know what we're doing right, what we could do better, what areas you'd like to see us publish in, and any other words of wisdom you're willing to pass our way.

As an associate publisher for Que Publishing, I welcome your comments. You can email or write me directly to let me know what you did or didn't like about this book—as well as what we can do to make our books better.

Please note that I cannot help you with technical problems related to the topic of this book. We do have a User Services group, however, where I will forward specific technical questions related to the book.

When you write, please be sure to include this book's title and author as well as your name, email address, and phone number. I will carefully review your comments and share them with the author and editors who worked on the book.

Email: feedback@quepublishing.com

Mail: Greg Wiegand
           Associate Publisher
           Que Publishing
           800 East 96th Street
           Indianapolis, IN 46240 USA

For more information about this book or another Que title, visit our website at www.quepublishing.com. Type the ISBN (excluding hyphens) or the title of a book in the Search field to find the page you're looking for.

Introduction

Welcome to the *2006 Gamer's Tome of Ultimate Wisdom*!

Writing a book about gaming is a tricky endeavor. We live in a fast-food culture. We want everything RIGHT NOW. The gaming industry is no different. Websites race to get reviews posted as quickly as possible and news flows like a swift stream on a daily basis. If you miss a day, your information is obsolete.

This presented a problem. Gaming magazines are usually a month behind the times in terms of game reviews and news, so how could a book on gaming stay topical in such a speed-loving climate?

The answer was to take a different tack and not to attempt to compete with the daily news and review websites that crank out exclusive info on a daily basis, but rather to focus on providing a unique collection of gaming information that you won't find anywhere else.

The *2006 Gamer's Tome of Ultimate Wisdom* is the perfect book for the busy gamer who doesn't have the time to read about games every single day. If you love to play computer and videogames, but also have a life outside of your monitor or TV, this book is for you.

Even if you are a hardcore gamer, there should be some nuggets and pearls of wisdom inside this book that you can use—be it a mod for your favorite game or an under-the-radar indie game that you haven't heard of—there is a little something for everyone in the *2006 Gamer's Tome of Ultimate Wisdom*.

How This Book Is Organized

This book is part 2005 retrospective and part 2006 preview guide. It covers games on nearly every platform from the PC and Xbox to the handheld systems like the PSP and Nintendo DS. You won't find another book that crams the length and breadth of our collective obsession into a single volume like this one does.

The Retrospective

The first part of the book is a look back at the some of best games from January through October 2005. We have broken down the games according to the month that they were released. So, in the January 2005 section, we'll discuss the best games released in that month from Resident Evil 4 on the GameCube to Oddworld: Stranger's Wrath on the Xbox and everything else in between. If you missed out on a good game from 2005, chances are it's highlighted in the *2006 Gamer's Tome of Ultimate Wisdom*.

Keep in mind that these entries aren't supposed to be full-length reviews. You can hop online and find dozens of reviews about all of these games. In fact, I encourage logging on to some of the websites and magazines highlighted in this book to read more about a game if one piques your interest. Here you might find a quick tips guide, some reference info on a game's developer, the history of a popular game franchise, or maybe just a quick overview about what a particular game is all about.

Next to the title for each essay you'll find an icon denoting what type of game or topic we're talking about. These icons include

RPG/Adventure

Action

Strategy

Puzzle/Misc.

Sim/Racing

Arcade

Sports

Sprinkled in each month we also have general essays on all sorts of topics, including

 Bargain Bin Specials—These games are still a lot of fun today and cost $20 or less.

 Closet Classics—These essays take a look back at some of the best games from years gone by and why they remain relevant today.

 Grab Bags—Grab Bags are general-topic essays on a wide variety of subjects from the impact of exclusive sports licenses to a list of the most violent games of all time. Think of them as a potluck dinner, only without the food and in word form. Yummy.

 Corporate Graveyards—These essays take a look back at companies in the industry that have closed their doors. We examine their legacies—both the good and the bad.

Finally, each page closes with a Did You Know element. These little morsels of gaming information are there to add a little extra fun and flavor. An example might be, "Did you know that there are two lesser-known Elder Scrolls games, named Dawnstar and Stormhold, that run only on Java-enabled cell phones?"

If so, wow! You know your gaming, my friend. Now go outside and shoot some hoops or something. There is a world out there, you know.

The Holidays

The second part of the book takes a look at some of the high profile games set for release during the 2005 holiday season, as well as some sleepers that might have slipped under your gaming radar due to a lack of press or marketing.

A quick word about the games listed in the Holiday section: Release dates get moved around all the time. It's just part of how the industry works. The games listed in this section are based on what we thought to be true at the time of writing, something that could obviously change by the time you read this. If a game is listed in the Holiday section and then gets pushed back to 2006—sorry. I'm just the messenger here, folks.

THE 360 FACTOR

Many of the games in this section (as well as the 2006 section) are going to be released on the new Xbox 360. Although we obviously discuss several 360 titles in the book (Perfect Dark Zero, Saint's Row, Gears of War, and so on), some games that are due to ship on multiple platforms lack a lot of specific Xbox 360 info at the time of writing. For example, Madden NFL 06's 360 info is scarce at the moment, so the essay on that game relates specifically to the other versions. Such is the way of the print world.

2006 and Beyond

Finally, the *2006 Gamer's Tome of Ultimate Wisdom* takes a look at some of the hottest games that are due out sometime in 2006. As any hardcore gamer will tell you, talking about what games will be on shelves a year in advance is a lot like predicting how ocean currents affect the weather. You can do it, but it requires charts and graphs and a bunch of expensive equipment. And even then there's a distinct probability you'll end up just looking out the window like the rest of us. In other words, don't be shocked if some of the titles in this part of the book are canceled or delayed. (I was going to write an essay on Mythic's MMOG called Imperator, which was canceled a week before the book was finished.) This section is here to give you a good idea of what you can expect to see this year and to make note of which promising titles might be going the way of Duke Nukem Forever.

ABOUT THE PS3 AND REVOLUTION

The 2006 gaming landscape will be changed yet again when Sony and Nintendo release their new next-gen systems in the summer of 2006...or the fall...or winter. Heck, I hear it could be 2007 if the groundhog sees his shadow this year. The point is that while several games have been announced for these platforms, specific game info is limited. I've endeavored to give you some idea what you can expect to see in the 2006 section even though the details are at a minimum at the moment, but nuts and bolts details will have to wait for the next edition.

Once again, thanks for reading the *2006 Gamer's Tome of Ultimate Wisdom*. I hope you find it both informative and, most of all, fun to read.

See you next year!

William Abner

October 2005

January 2005

A Good Start for a New Year

Typically, January is a slow month for game releases. Publishers do whatever they need to, including shipping games that aren't completely finished, in order to meet the "Holiday Rush." If you miss the rush sales, as a rule, aren't as good. Of course there are some companies that have a history of ignoring such unwritten rules and are still selling mountains of units.

Blizzard, for instance, tends to ignore the usual mantra of making an announced ship date and instead releases games when the company feels they're ready. Blizzard has that luxury, though because people know their games and know that they usually deliver the goods.

Still, most gamers are still busy playing their holiday gifts in January. January 2005, however, saw a handful of A-List games. A new Legend of Zelda release on the GBA, Resident Evil 4 on the GameCube, Winning Eleven Soccer 8 (hands down the best arcade soccer game ever made) on the PS2, and the last Oddworld adventure, Stranger's Wrath, on the Xbox. These four games alone made January a stellar month for gamers.

Flops of the Month:

- **Playboy: The Mansion**—How do you create a Heff' sim without sex appeal?
- **The Punisher**—Not technically a "flop" but nowhere near as good as it could have been. In a year of great games based on comics, this was a letdown.

The Legend of Zelda
The Minish Cap

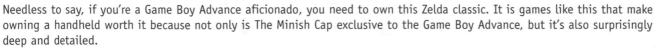

Image courtesy of GameSpy.com.

Don't let its cuteness fool you; The Minish Cap is a highly detailed handheld game.

DOSSIER

Genre: Link and the Magic Hat **Publisher:** Nintendo **Developer:** Flagship
Platform: GBA **Metacritic Metascore:** 89

As GBA games go, it's hard to find too many that are better than The Minish Cap. In fact, in addition to Metacritics's 89 Metascore, Gamerankings.com ranks it as the ninth best GBA game of all time, two-tenths better than Tony Hawk Pro Skater 2. Eat that, Tony!

Needless to say, if you're a Game Boy Advance aficionado, you need to own this Zelda classic. It is games like this that make owning a handheld worth it because not only is The Minish Cap exclusive to the Game Boy Advance, but it's also surprisingly deep and detailed.

The Legend of Zelda: The Minish Cap gets its name from a magical creature called Ezlo, which looks like a green cap. Ezlo teams up with Link and shrinks him to about the size of a human thumb in order to visit the land of the Minish, who are magical tiny gnome-like creatures that Link must enlist to help save Princess Zelda who was turned to stone by the evil sorcerer, Vaati. Does this chick ever stay out of trouble?

The Sword Techniques

There are eight sword techniques in The Minish Cap; they're similar to basic skills in a traditional role-playing game and Link learns these techniques from various people (little thumb-sized people, actually). Here's a quick breakdown of the techniques and what they do, starting with those learned from the character Swiftblade.

Image courtesy of GameSpy.com.

Link lets slip the dogs of war!

- **Spin Attack:** Link charges and then spins around, sword drawn, a full 360 degrees. You need to have completed the Deepwood Shrine before you can learn this move.

- **Rock Breaker:** You need the White Sword before Swiftblade will teach you the Rock Breaker, which is needed in order to defeat the Spiny Beetle creatures. You can also smash pots and vases to get some goodies.

- **Dash Attack:** You need the Pegasus Boots to learn this, but after they're acquired, Swiftblade teaches Link how to charge extra quick with his sword drawn.

- **Down Thrust Attack:** You need Roc's Cape before Link can learn this move, but it allows him to jump and then stab down at his enemies.

- **Great Spin Attack:** The ghost of Swiftblade teaches you this in Castor Wilds. You need all seven Tiger Scrolls before Link can use this, but it allows him to spin several times, taking out multiple enemies in one fell swoop.

- **Roll Attack:** Learned from Grayblade after you have fused Earth and Fire Elements, this attack allows Link to get up with his sword drawn after performing a roll maneuver.

- **Sword Beam:** Learned from Grimblade after acquiring the Flame Lantern, this grants Link the ability to shoot beams of energy at his enemies, but Link must have full health to use it, unless he also has...

- **Peril Beam:** Learned from Waveblade, this allows Link to use Sword Beam when his health is low.

The Secret Blade Brothers

These fellas don't provide new techniques, technically, but they can improve some of Link's current abilities.

- **Scarblade:** Shortens the recharge rate of the Spin Attack.

- **Splitblade:** Shortens the recharge rate of Link's Splitting Meter. (Link can split himself in two.)

- **Greatblade:** This nasty upgrade lets Link use the Great Spin Attack eight times in a row. Ouch.

> **THE MINISH CAP HOME PAGE**
> Not only is The Minish Cap an inventive game, so is its home page at www.zelda.com/minishcap. It's worth checking out even if you don't know Zelda from Zorro.

DID YOU KNOW

The *Legend of Zelda* was converted into a 13-episode cartoon series in 1989 that was part of the live action *Super Mario Bros. Super Show*.

Mercenaries
Pandemic Studios Strikes Gold

Image courtesy of GameSpy.com.

DOSSIER

Genre: Blow 'Em Up **Publisher:** LucasArts **Developer:** Pandemic Studios
Platform: PS2, Xbox **Metacritic Metascore:** 86

Mercenaries is a free-form third-person action game, similar in some ways to, of all games, Grand Theft Auto...aside from the fact that you aren't playing a street thug turned criminal kingpin; instead you're playing a mercenary in the near future. You can hop in and drive any vehicle you find, accept missions, and generally blow the hell out of stuff. See? The two games are almost clones!

If you like to see things blow up, Mercenaries is your game.

Mercenaries is one of the better third-person action games of 2005. You're part of a mercenary team assigned to take out a ruthless Korean general and his cronies, each of whom are listed in a deck of playing cards. (If this at all sounds familiar, well, I guess you can deduce where they got the idea.)

There are a lot of power plays being made in the game because several countries and factions have a stake in what's going on in Korea. As a mercenary, you aren't there to fight for God and country but rather for Benjamin Franklin. Yep, you're after cold hard cash. It's an intensely entertaining action game full of amazing explosions and lots of opportunities to cause a lot of spectacular carnage.

Pandemic Studios Roll Call

Pandemic Studios created Mercenaries for LucasArts. Pandemic is actually a prolific game design studio that has worked for several publishers. I always used to think that you could shop for games solely based on the developer, but too many companies produce hit-and-miss games nowadays and it's just too risky to do that. I remember back when seeing LucasArts on the box meant an automatic purchase; those days have long since past. Pandemic has a similar lineup of hits and misses. Check out some the games in its retinue.

Dark Reign 2 (2000). A ho-hum real-time strategy game. It was polished, but not particularly spectacular.

Army Men (2002). It sold a lot of units and made 3DO a nice profit, but it's no classic.

Star Wars: Clone Wars (2002). Considered to be a very run-of-the-mill action shooter with a *Star Wars* theme.

Triple Play Baseball 2002 (2003). It was so bad that it finally prompted EA Sports to put the franchise out of its misery and create MVP Baseball.

Full Spectrum Warrior (2004). Pandemic started to hit its stride with this classic squad-based tactical shooter. It was the company's best game to date.

Image courtesy of GameSpy.com

Full Spectrum Warrior helped put Pandemic on the map.

Star Wars: Battlefront (2004). The company went back to *Star Wars* and developed this online shooter set in the *Star Wars* universe. It got a bad rap in the press, but I thought it was a very, although not perfect, online shooter. LucasArts was pleased enough to allow Pandemic to create a sequel, which was due in late 2005.

Destroy All Humans (2005). This was released summer of 2005 to wildly mixed reviews. It's the kind of game that is better because of the subject matter and not because of any radical advancements in gameplay. Still, angry Martians are always cool.

THEY SAID IT

"Mercenaries is all about making money, causing mayhem and destruction, playing factions against each other, flying helicopters, hijacking tanks, calling in air strikes, shooting at bad guys, and having as much fun as possible in a video game." —**LucasArts producer, Shara Miller, in an interview with Armchairempire.com**

DID YOU KNOW

A *pandemic* is an epidemic that is geographically widespread; one occurring throughout a region or even throughout the world. Sounds like a great name for a design studio!

Resident Evil 4
The GameCube Exclusive

Image courtesy of GameSpy.com.

Rated M for mature!

DOSSIER

Genre: Scary, Gory, Action Horror **Publisher:** Capcom **Developer:** Capcom Studio 4
Platform: GameCube **Metacritic Metascore:** 96

If you own a GameCube, you've probably already picked up this amazing game, at least according to NPD. Resident Evil 4 (RE4) sold more than 300,000 units in its first full month of U.S. availability and more than 200,000 in Europe. That's a lot of dead bad guys. And if you think the game is scary, imagine what that number might have been if the game weren't exclusive to the GameCube. This from a series that cut its teeth on the PS1?

No offense to GameCube lovers, but...the GameCube? It just seems an odd choice for a first rate gaming franchise to be tied to a third-place game console. Sure, Nintendo games such as Zelda and Mario are going to be GameCube exclusives, but Resident Evil?

If all of this isn't confusing enough, in October of 2004 Capcom announced Resident Evil 4 would in fact make an appearance on the PS2 in time for the holiday rush of 2005. The reason, according to Capcom, was "changing marketing conditions." In other words, money talked and Capcom finally listened. Duh.

Forget What You Know

We shouldn't lose sight of the fact that, exclusivity talk aside, Resident Evil 4 is a wonderful game—we're talking a "game of the year"–quality title. The Resident Evil name doesn't carry the weight that it once did because the franchise has been milked to the point of absurdity, but RE4 is, without question, the best game of the entire series.

There are a lot of changes in both storyline and in gameplay in RE4. Most notably, the humans in the game aren't zombies; they're just crazy humans, which actually make them a lot more dangerous and less "plodding."

The game takes place six years after the events of Resident Evil 3 and the Umbrella Corporation has finally been knocked off. You play the role once again of Leon S. Kennedy who is now a U.S. agent and not a rookie on the Raccoon City Police Department. Leon is sent on a mission to a village in Europe to find the president's lost (kidnapped) daughter. From there, all hell breaks loose.

THEY SAID IT

"It is human nature to want a thrill and being scared is one of the key thrills in a person's emotional range. Roller Coasters, Haunted Houses, American Fast Food...all of it exists because we like to scare ourselves." —**Resident Evil 4 Producer Hiroyuki Kobayashi in an interview with IGN.com**

New and improved storyline aside, what makes RE4 tick is the new camera angles—which are no longer problematic—and an intense and highly believable combat model complete with location-based damage. Great stuff if you don't belong to Moms Who Hate Games. The lack of unlimited in-game saves was a bad move, but thankfully the save checkpoints are liberally spread out.

Image courtesy of GameSpy.com.

Uh, yeah, good luck with that.

Best of all, the game is tense. Really, really tense. Resident Evil 4's atmosphere (as well as its awe-inspiring graphics) of old castles and creepy isolated European villages is spookier than a scene from the Exorcist.

If you're looking for a captivating, gory, scary, and thrilling adventure game it's going to be very difficult to find one better than this. RE4 is the real deal.

BEWARE THE RESIDENT EVIL FAN
At www.residentevilfan.com, you'll find a first rate fan site with tons of info about the entire series of RE games including an active fan forum and detailed descriptions of the games and the movies.

DID YOU KNOW

Resident Evil has been around since 1996. The series is known as Biohazard in Japan and the original is loosely based on a Japanese horror film called *Suito Homu* (*Sweet Home*).

Oddworld: Stranger's Wrath
Because Bounty Hunters Are Cool

Image courtesy of GameSpy.com.

This is not your...older brother's Oddworld game.

DOSSIER

Genre: Bounty Huntin' Bizarro Action **Publisher:** Electronic Arts **Developer:** Oddworld Inhabitants **Platform:** Xbox **Metacritic Metascore:** 88

If you've never played an Oddworld game, shame on you, and you should definitely try to round up some of the older ones, but whether you're a vet or a noob, Stranger's Wrath is an entirely different, but still an odd-but-gorgeous experience.

This is no escape from Alcatraz or a game where you need to set your people free—this time you play a new and mysterious character, Stranger, and you're the one collecting the bounties and kicking the ass.

Mini Boss Bounty Guide

Image courtesy of GameSpy.com.

The battle with Lefty Lugnutz isn't too tough.

Stranger is a crossbow totin' bounty hunter, so you're going to spend a lot of time battling bad guys and collecting bounty. He also catches animals in the wild and uses them as ammo because, well, it's more fun to shoot angry bees than arrows.

You get more cash to spend at the Bounty Store by bringing in your targets alive rather than shot full of holes. Here's a quick guide.

Filthy Hands Floyd. Your first real bounty is a cakewalk. After luring his two "boys" with a chipmunk, just go up to where Floyd is and capture him with the bolamite.

Looten Duke. Focus on his stamina and drain it by first hitting him repeatedly with a thudslug (to knock him down) and then pouring it on with a charged zappfly combo.

Boilz Booty. Shoot the fuel barrel to take out some of the thugs then use the boombat with the zappfly The boombat is a real stamina killer so don't overdo it.

Jo' Mamma. If you don't want to die, *do not* let her minions respawn. Seriously. Not one. To pull off this maneuver, take out the chipmunk and then zappfly the elevator switch to open the doors, run your tail off, and avoid the nailers on your way to the elevator. When you make it to the top, fire as many fuzzles as you can along the ground. When you finally get the chance, boombat her with zappflies.

Meagly McGraw. Meagly has about 20 minions, so you need to deal with them first. To beat McGraw, take out his mount with stingbees. After the pet is out, use the usual boombat or thudslug combos to capture him.

Packrat Palooka. This is the toughest boss to capture alive in the game. Use charged zappflies to hit the switches—only before blasting the last switch, shoot some fuzzles on the

ground along the stage. Then zappfly that last switch to temporarily take his shield down. Immediately hit him with a boombat, taking him off the stage. Then just do the usual boombat or thudslug combo to nab him.

Xplosives McGee. Get McGee down to ground level by taking out the enemies that appear (shoot the barrels). Once he's on the ground level the thudslug/zappfly combo works well, but it will *not* knock him down. Just keep plugging away and avoiding his attacks until he's exhausted.

Lefty Lugnutz. A very easy boss to capture alive, just keep taking out his minions and popping him until he decides to take you on one-on-one. Then use the standard boss capturing techniques.

Elboze Freely. A tricky boss to capture alive, you need to pop him in the back about six times before you can capture him. Use the fans to propel yourself up into the air.

Fatty Mcboomboom. Attacking Fatty early is a mistake. Take out all of his minions. Even though there seems like an infinite number of them—relax, they'll slow down eventually. After they're gone wait for him to do his special "move" and then use the standard thudslug/zappfly combo to wear him down.

Snakes
Free—And Fun—Gaming, N-Gage Style!

Image courtesy of GameSpy.com.

Multiplayer Snakes. It's free!

DOSSIER

Genre: Free Puzzler! **Publisher:** Nokia **Developer:** Iomo **Platform:** N-Gage **Metacritic Metascore:** 85

Free games are awesome, aren't they? Okay, usually free games suck rocks, but Snakes has actually been around a long, long time and the January 2005 release for the N-Gage is a vivid 3D smorgasbord of color. Did I mention it's free?

For the uninitiated, the idea in the original Snake is to stay alive as your ever-growing snake continues to gobble up little blocks. As you capture each block, your snake grows. You move the snake in four basic directions and if you hit the side or the screen or your own body, you lose.

Whither the N-Gage

The N-Gage hasn't proven to be a popular platform for games and a lot of that, I think, is because there aren't enough games like Snakes around that are exclusive to it. Nokia continues to try to take console games and shrink them down into N-Gage form. That doesn't fly. Games like NCAA Football, Call of Duty, MotoGP, Spider-Man 2, and SSX might be great on the Xbox or PS2, but on the N-Gage they're just god-awful.

Image courtesy of GameSpy.com.

Yes, there are exceptions to this. The N-Gage versions of popular games like Splinter Cell: Chaos Theory, Tiger Woods Golf, and X-Men Legends are all pretty darn cool on this smaller stage, but the N-Gage is a platform built for quick, easy to play time-killer puzzle games like Snakes.

The world of Snakes is bright, colorful, and full of flare.

THEY SAID IT

"I think Snakes is a perfect illustration of what we have to focus on strategically. Snakes is unequivocally a mobile game; it fits gamers' expectations of what a mobile game is, and it's already quite popular. We'll absolutely be focusing on mobile-specific content in 2005 and 2006. These games don't necessarily need a cutting-edge presentation to be successful—we can make use of the N-Gage's multiplayer abilities and viral distribution to do things no other console can." — **Gerard Wiener, Director of Nokia's Game Business Program in an interview with GameSpot.com**

FINDING SNAKES IN THE WILD

N-Gage users can snag Snakes free at www.snakesoutbreak.com. A free web version of Snake can be found at www.neave.com/games/snake. It's bland looking, but still addictive.

Snakes: The Next Gen

There are a few differences in the new game from the original. Snakes is now broken down into levels and the goal is not to simply survive but to beat each of the more than 30 levels in the single-player game.

This version of Snakes is loaded with color and power-ups; the snake can now speed up, slow down, absorb damage, put up shields, tunnel warp to other sides of the map, and use other doo-dads that make it more of a game rather than just a time-killing exercise.

You also get a very intricate multiplayer game with various modes and levels of play. Nokia has made it very easy to share the game with other N-Gage users. You can send the game to other users with a click of a button and in a matter of minutes up to four players can battle it out on the Snakes grid.

Hopefully we'll see more games like Snakes appear on the N-Gage. The platform still has a lot of potential for gamers looking for a quick fix or an easy to get into multiplayer game. If you're an N-Gager, you absolutely need to download Snakes to see what all the fuss is about.

DID YOU KNOW

In January 2005, the U.K. sales tracking firm ChartTrack dropped the N-Gage from its regular listing, saying, "The N-Gage chart, though still produced, is of little interest to anyone. Sales of the machine and its software have failed to make any impact on the market at all." Ouch.

Hearts of Iron II
Same Idea, Better Game

Image courtesy of GameSpy.com.

DOSSIER

Genre: Hardcore WWII Strategy **Publisher:** Paradox Interactive **Developer:** Paradox Interactive **Platform:** PC **Metacritic Metascore:** 83

Hearts of Iron II is a grand strategy game from Paradox Interactive, a company known for deep, complex strategy games, including Europa Universalis and Patrician. It

Preparing for war.

encompasses the entire spectrum of World War II from 1936 through 1948, but it's not just about combat. It's also about people, great leaders, technology, trade—the works.

Be warned: There is a very steep learning curve attached to the game, so if you're a novice, you need to go in with the understanding that there is an enormous amount of information to digest. After you get past that learning curve, however, you are left with a truly fascinating game of World War II grand strategy that is a must buy for wargaming die-hards. The amount of stuff in the game borders on the ridiculous, actually.

Bad Memories, New Goodies

The original Hearts of Iron, which followed pretty much the same premise, was a buggy mess on release. The wargaming community, which had been decidedly behind the game, quickly lashed out against it.

Thankfully, the initial release of Hearts of Iron II went much more smoothly and this game is about as bug-free as one can expect from such an enormous project. And for the bugs that did get through, Paradox released a very hefty patch just two weeks after release.

Better still, in the spring of 2005, Paradox released the 1.2 "enhancement" patch, which added all sorts of new stuff, such as a brand new campaign, a new battle scenario (Case Blue), and a much better AI opponent.

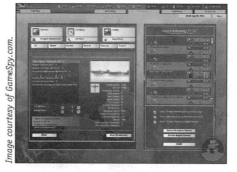
Image courtesy of GameSpy.com.

If you like your strategy games deep and full of info, Hearts of Iron II is for you.

Less Is More

HOI2 is based on the deliberately paced (plodding) Europa Universalis II engine, so if you are familiar with that game, you already know what to expect. For example, the economy model is much less obtuse this time around. Each territory provides a measure of oil, energy, metal, and raw materials. Factories then use these materials (except oil) to build Industrial Points, which can then be spent on supplies, reinforcements, and so on. Anything left over is turned into money, which can then be spent on tech advances and diplomacy. Simple.

Throw in excellent multiplayer support, a clean interface with sharp graphics and you have, without question, the most complete World War II grand strategy game on the planet.

WARGAMER.COM'S HEARTS OF IRON 2 PAYS
Wargamer.com's Hearts of Iron II page at hoi2.wargamer.com is filled with great articles on nearly every aspect of the game.

Master of Magic
Closet Classic (1993)

PC gaming before the days of the screaming video card....

DOSSIER

Genre: Civilization with Spells **Publisher:** MicroProse **Developer:** SimTex
Platform: PC

The year was 1993. I was in college, spending way too much time playing games on my blistering-fast x486 PC. One of the games that ate up hours that should have been devoted to Geology 101 was Master of Magic, a turn-based strategy game from SimTex and MicroProse.

The best way to describe Master of Magic (affectionately known as *MoM*) is Civilization with elves. That's a bit of a simplification, but that really was the general idea. It played a lot like the classic Civilization but instead of the Aztecs battling the Americans, you had master wizards vying for the land of Arcanus.

MoM's tactical combat mode and the vast amount of spells at each wizard's disposal helped make it special. Master of Magic featured more than 210 magic spells divided among six schools: life, death, chaos, nature, sorcery, and arcane. Each school has its own retinue of creatures that you could summon as well as spells that could affect the entire map, a single combat, or a particular city.

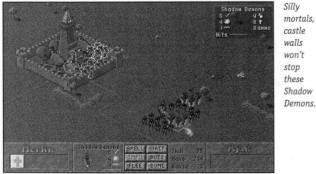

Silly mortals, castle walls won't stop these Shadow Demons.

Combat was revolutionary for its time. When it ensued, you actually controlled each group of units on a tactical map. Nothing was automated. Your choices on the map were critical in determining your success. Do you attack the enemy archers or go for the level 10 hero? When do you use that fireball spell?

Then there's the random factor. So many of today's games miss the boat when it comes to offering a unique experience each time a game is fired up. In MoM, the maps, resources, starting locations, monster locations—everything was generated randomly and consequently, each game was a new experience.

Master of Magic isn't considered as being in quite the same league as other turn-based gems of its day (such as Civilization, Master of Orion, and so on) mainly because the initial release was bug infested to the point of being unplayable. Yep, games were released prematurely even back then. Thankfully, MicroProse issued patches that helped to make MoM the game it should have been out of the box.

MASTER OF MAGIC RESOURCES

Hop over to the Home of the Underdogs at www.the-underdogs.org/game.php?id=687 and download MoM and give it a whirl (you need to run it in DOS). It's still fun today despite the decade old graphics. No 3D card required. Trust me.

The **Master of Magic Heroes Page** at mom.diaspora.ru/txt/heroes.doc is a fantastic website that covers every aspect of the heroes in MoM and how best to use them.

Windows XP users can't play the original MoM without jumping through a lot of hoops. **The Master of Magic Clone Project** at george101.demon.co.uk/mom is attempting to solve that little problem and add a multiplayer mode to boot!

DID YOU KNOW

Sadly, there is no true sequel to Master of Magic. But if you're looking for a spiritual successor, Triumph's Age of Wonders series is the closest thing I've seen to an updated version of this classic game.

Game Review Databases
The Good, The Bad, and The Hideous

The best reviewed game ever? According to GameRankings.com the answer is a definitive... Yep!

There are dozens upon dozens of game review sites on the Internet, from well-established outlets that are read by hundreds of thousands of people a month (such as GameSpy, IGN, and GameSpot) to smaller, one-man operations that are read by three guys in Idaho (and one of them is the guy who created it in the first place).

The problem is that with so many different voices out there commenting on the pros and cons of video games, which should you believe? Thankfully, there are several game review databases that lump most of the reviews together to get an idea of how the critics, as a whole, view a particular game.

There are several databases from which to choose and each offers something a bit different. Here's a look at some of the more popular databases out there.

Game Rankings

Perhaps the most popular database is Game Rankings. Started in 1999 by Scott Bedard, it was later sold to CNET, the company that owns GameSpot.com, among many other websites.

Game Rankings is a highly recognized name with both gamers and industry insiders. In fact, people in public relations constantly refer to how well their game has "scored" on Game Rankings. It's used almost as much as an advertising tool as it is a reference tool for gamers.

The site reviews and previews games just like a regular review site, and also offers user reviews, a message board, and a pay section for industry folk. Still, its meat is the database, which goes back as far as games released in 1998.

MobyGames

Even though MobyGames does offer game review numbers, it's actually best used as a general gaming reference tool. It's a wonderful site to check out because everything is cross-referenced from the developer of a game to its platforms and genre. The database at MobyGames is ridiculously huge and extremely fast and is one of the best gaming resources on the Net.

GameTab

Launched in 2003, this is another review database. GameTab is cool, however, because it also promotes the most popular daily news feeds from around the Internet, which are easily as numerous as the review sites. It's also a great website for price comparisons.

Metacritic

Metacritic has been around since the summer of 1999 and has grown into one of the better resources on the Net, not only for games but for movies, books, and music too. As you've no doubt noticed, I use it in this very book to gauge each game's "Metacritic Metascore." Metacritic is useful because it weighs and balances each review site a bit differently so that an established outlet such as *Computer Gaming World* carries a bit more weight than Joe Schmoe's Game Reviews.

According to Metacritic, NFK2K1 on the Dreamcast is the best reviewed sports game of all time. Yep, better than Madden.

Rotten Tomatoes

Owned by IGN, Rotten Tomatoes is best known as a movie review database, offering up hundreds of reviews from newly released movies. However, it also tracks games. Even though it doesn't use a weighted system like Metacritic, Rotten Tomatoes is simply a hell of a lot of fun to read. It provides quotes from reviews as well as the name of the author rather than just the website. After all, we starving freelancers need all the pub we can get.

Onimusha 3: Demon Siege
Bargain Bin Special

Jean Reno, as Jacques Blanc, getting down and dirty. Image courtesy of GameSpy.com.

DOSSIER

Genre: Japan: Yesterday and Today **Publisher:** Capcom **Developer:** Capcom Production Studio 2 **Platform:** PS2 **Metacritic Metascore:** 85

The Onimusha series from Capcom is a group of third-person action/adventure games available exclusively on the PS2 console.

The trilogy is considered one of the very best on the PS2, which is why it's so surprising that most retail stores carry the latest game in the series, Onimusha 3: Demon Siege, for a mere $15.

For the uninformed, the series is labeled by some as "Resident Evil with swords." That's a pretty generic way of looking at the games because they all offer a lot more than that, but it is survival horror, in a sense, where you slay demons with swords. Still, if you have never played them, you can get all three for less than $40 total, which is an absolute steal.

In Detail: The Onimusha Series

Onimusha Warlords (2001). The original Onimusha drew a lot of comparisons to Resident Evil for its style and survival horror setting. In it, you play Samanosuke Akechi, a master swordsman from Japan around the year 1560.

A year after the battle of Okehazama, where the warlord Nobunaga was slain, strange things begin to happen at the infamous Inabayama Castle. People start disappearing, and word leaks of an evil presence in the castle. The princess seeks the help of Akechi. Meanwhile, Nobunaga, who is apparently now an undead warlord, attacks the castle with a demonic host and it's up to Akechi and his ninja partner Kaede to save the day.

The original game is considered a PS2 classic and can be had in stores or online for as little as $5. This defines the term Bargain Bin Gem.

Onimusha 2: Samurai's Destiny (2002). Back in 2002, Samurai's Destiny was considered to be arguably the best-looking PS2 game of all time. It introduces a new hero, a young warrior named Jubei, and takes place in 1573, 13 years after the events of the original. Nobunaga is back with another demon army bent on taking over Japan and when his village succumbs, Jubei turns vigilante and seeks to destroy the evil warlord.

Onimusha 2 is much more of an adventure game than the original (or volume 3 for that matter). It's more plot driven and has much more dialogue. There is also a fairly cumbersome item-trading system that slowed down the pace of the game a bit (and was removed in Demon Siege).

Onimusha 3: Demon Siege (2004). The latest (and supposedly last) game in the series takes place in Japan in the late 1500s and brings back Samanosuke Akechi, the hero from the original, along with a new character from the present day, Jacques Blanc. Blanc is played by actor Jean Reno (*The Professional; Mission: Impossible*). Sadly, Reno's face is more prominent than his voice work, which is scarce.

Image courtesy of GameSpy.com.

Now that is a flaming sword!

The plot switches from present day back to the 1500s, telling an intricate and intertwining story. It's less action horror and more just straight action with less adventure elements, and it keeps a pretty fast pace throughout its 10–12 hours of gameplay.

There are some significant new features in volume 3. Demon Siege moves to a fully 3D environment and the result is one of the most beautiful PS2 games on the market. Gone is the digital control scheme; you finally get analog control in Onimusha 3 and it's a very welcome addition. Demon Siege is a no-brainer for PS2 action fans and $15 is just an amazing price for such a wonderful and beautifully made game.

DID YOU KNOW

Capcom, a Japanese game developer and publisher founded in 1979, actually stands for "Japan **Cap**sule **Com**puters."

Cavedog Entertainment (1996–2000)
Corporate Graveyard

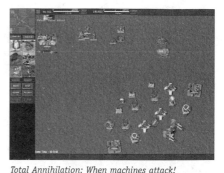

Total Annihilation: When machines attack!

Cavedog Entertainment, founded by legendary developer Ron Gilbert (creator of the classic The Secret of Monkey Island), had a short run from 1996 to early 2000, but they remain relevant today for just their one elite level title: the classic RTS Total Annihilation.

The failure of publisher GT Interactive had a lot to do with Cavedog's demise. GT Interactive lost oodles of money after its bread and butter franchises Deer Hunter and Harley Davidson finally ran dry. I guess even the casual gamer could stomach only so many variations on how to hunt pixilated deer. But Cavedog has to take some of the blame as well. Total Annihilation, although a brilliant game, didn't sell near the number of units as games like StarCraft and Command and Conquer. When you combine that with the fact that the big, highly publicized, follow-up game failed to capture the public's attention, you are looking at problems.

The sad part is that Cavedog had every intention of branching away from the Total Annihilation games and entering the first-person shooter and adventure genres. Four projects—Amen: The Awakening, Elysium, Good and Evil, and Total Annihilation 2—would never see the light of day.

The Cavedog Lineage

Total Annihilation (1997). You'll find an in-depth look at the history of this fantastic game on p. 144 . Briefly, TA was a revolutionary RTS that added 3D landscapes, gobs of 3D units, and an intense gameplay style.

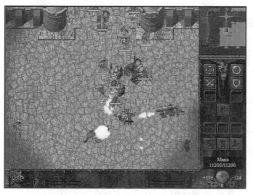

Kingdoms failed to live up to the TA legacy.

Total Annihilation: The Core Contingency (1998). The first TA add-on contained new units and maps, as well a 26-mission campaign with a much-needed map editor.

Total Annihilation: Battle Tactics (1998). This was a fairly uninspired expansion that added 100 new maps, six new skirmish maps, and four new units.

Total Annihilation: Kingdoms (1999). TA: Kingdoms was one of the most anticipated games of 1999 that while fun, failed to live up to its own hype mainly because it wasn't as good as the original Total Annihilation. Kingdoms tried to be more identifiable with gamers, and in so doing also alienated the original TA fan base by changing a lot of what made that game so popular.

Total Annihilation Kingdoms: The Iron Plague (2000). The Kingdoms expansion included the 2.0 game-engine upgrade along with all the new units and maps that Cavedog had released via its website. A fifth race was introduced along with a new 25-mission campaign.

THEY SAID IT

"We would like to thank you for all of your enthusiasm and support over the years; the TA community is certainly still strong, even a few years after the release of the original Total Annihilation. We're proud of the products we've released over the years, and have been very pleased by watching them grow and flourish with third party creativity. You never ceased to amaze us."
—Kevin Brockaway of Cavedog Entertainment

ON THE WEB

RON GILBERT'S WEB BLOG
Found at grumpygamer.com, it's great reading from the founder of Cavedog and creator of some truly classic games, like Maniac Mansion.

DID YOU KNOW

Even though Total Annihilation: Kingdoms was released back in 1999, it runs just fine on a more modern PC running Windows XP. And let's face it, many games from that era won't give XP the time of day.

Online Arcades
The Best of the Best

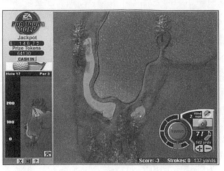

Tiger Woods 2006 this is not, but it's still a fun romp on the links.

What do you do if you're stuck at work with the urge to play a game, with nothing but Minesweeper on your desktop and an IT department that'll have your head if you download anything? Head online, of course!

Obviously, nothing on the Web is going to match Quake 4 or Guild Wars on your home PC, but if you're in a pinch and need some relief, you can access some surprisingly good online arcades that are free, quick to download, and perfect for that 10-minute I-really-need-to-blow-something-up break you so desperately need at around 3 p.m.

The only problem might be getting away with it. If you're in a veal-fattening pen (cubicle) like so many people, you'll have to get creative. Headphones are essential, as is an intelligent monitor arrangement to block any prying eyes. If you really want to get fancy, you can hook up the Spy Tracker Early Warning System ($26.95 at www.3djoe.com) to be alerted when someone steps in or near your cube.

Does anyone else get the feeling the survivors on Lost would find this a welcome sight?

Shockwave.com

One of the oldest online gaming sites, Shockwave.com is loaded with more games than you could ever play in a year of coffee breaks. It has everything from mind-blowing action games (many of which rival their standalone gaming cousins) to mind games, music mixers, sports games, jigsaw puzzles, and loads more. Believe me, I'm not kidding when I say that some of these games are as good as their standalone brethren; many of the 3D action games are as good as some of the crap I've had to review for the PC.

All this goodness doesn't come without a price, though: Some games that truly push the envelope have some hefty system requirements, many are playable only on Windows machines, and all of them have ads you have to sit through before playing. But good things come to those who wait, right? Shockwave.com proves that's true.

Pogo

Probably one of the most recognized online arcades, Pogo is best known for competitive games in which you can win actual cash and prizes. Game categories include casino, card and board games, word games, puzzles, sports contests, and some really cool arcade games. Although the barrage of ads can be annoying, the games are free and some of the highest-quality diversions you'll find anywhere. (Visit www.pogo.com.)

Free Online Games 4U

If you're into classic arcade games, this is another must-visit site (www.free-online-games-4u.com). You'll find clones of everything from Mario to Asteroids to Contra to the original Galaxian. Not all these games are faithful re-creations of the originals, and most are probably copyright or trademark violations of some sort. But if you're in a bind, it probably doesn't matter. Go check 'em out while you still can.

FreeArcade

A little less slick than its more successful commercial brethren, FreeArcade (www.freearcade.com) still packs a lot of fun into its pages. From shooters to sports to puzzles, you'll be sure to find something here that strikes your fancy. Best of all, many of these games are done in Java and play without having to download anything. If you're into classic games, there are some great clones here (including the near-perfect Xevious clone Galaxy and the Tempest play-alike, Web Wars).

Arcade Games Online

Lots and lots of really cool Java games can be played on this site (www.arcadegamesonline.com), many of which are re-creations of old-school arcade games or interesting variations on the theme. The categories cover just about everything from action to sports to text-based fiction. Unlike most other online gaming sites, users can contribute their own games so the database continues to grow at an amazing rate.

DID YOU KNOW

The first coin-operated videogame was the 1971 arcade title, Computer Space, from Nutting Associates. Yep, this was a year before Pong.

Ten Worst PC Games

Games from the Metacritic.com Hall of Shame

Big Rigs take flight... into a sea of grey!

We've all played our share of bad games. But these games, these games transcend badness and move into an entirely new realm of craptitude. You have to wonder how games like this even get published. Who is the executive that looks over a design document for Varmint Hunter and says, "We gotta make this!"

So here they are—the ten PC games that scored the lowest on the Metacritic rating scale dating back to 1999.

10. Mission: Humanity (Score: 27). Everything about this real-time strategy game from 2001 was bad. The graphics, sound, gameplay—even the *name* was bad. Mission: Humanity? Humanity is your mission? What does that even mean?

9. Survivor: The Game (Score: 26). All games based on TV game/reality shows suck. Period.

8. Terminator 3: War of the Machines (Score: 25). I don't like to quote reviews often, but after PCFormat reviewer John Walker's intoned, *"A sim of Arnie's election campaign would be more entertaining,"* there's nothing left to say.

7. Dragon's Lair 3 (Score: 23). How sad is this? To see such a storied name on this list is just depressing. The original Dragon's Lair was an arcade classic from the 1980s. This version from Digital Leisure was a quick buck scam job that tried to cash on the name and nothing more. Everything about it was truly awful.

6. Hooters Road Trip (Score: 22). Yes, the food chain with the well-endowed women serving you chicken wings has its very own computer game. Is it really a shock that it was bad? This is actually some kind of racing game, I think, with Hooters girls thrown in as scenery...or something.

5. Miami Vice (Score: 22). This game was published in 2004. I want to know the guy (and it had to be a guy) that thought a game with Crockett and Tubbs would be cool in the year 2004. GTA: Vice City was cool because it was campy and had great gameplay. Taking this era seriously is a bad, bad idea.

4. Gods and Generals (Score: 19). This is actually a good book that was turned into a bad movie, which was then turned into a really bad game. A first-person Civil War shooter? Huh?

Civil War buffs (like me) will buy damn near anything, but this was like taking $20 and setting it ablaze.

3. Navy SEALs: Weapons of Mass Destruction (Score: 18). I never did understand what the name of this game implied. Do the SEALs find WMD? Are they trying to find them? Do they carry them? What killed this game, though, was its AI or lack thereof. The bad guys would literally stand there and wait for you to shoot them, sometimes without even firing back. Gee, what fun.

A shot from Navy SEALs: WMD. I think this guy is supposed to be holding a weapon of some sort.

2. NRA Varmint Hunter (Score: 16). The name is a dead giveaway, isn't it? When you see or hear the word varmint you're either about to play a horribly bad hunting game or you're watching a *Beverly Hillbillies* rerun, which would be about 1,000 times more enjoyable and entertaining. You're shooting squirrels, people. Squirrels!

1. Big Rigs: Over the Road Racing (Score: 8). It doesn't get much worse than this, folks. Granted, the idea of driving trucks (sorry, *big rigs*) isn't too appealing to me personally, but to each their own. Big Rigs was blatantly broken and unfinished so much that it wasn't even playable. The publisher, GameMill, should be ashamed and embarrassed for releasing this steaming pile to the general public.

DID YOU KNOW

The Top Ten Worst List is actually the Top 12 because Ultimate Demolition Derby, Mission: Humanity, and Druuna: Morbus Gravis scored a 27. I list Mission: Humanity at number 10 because I had the misfortune of actually playing it.

Field Guide to Smacktards
Spotting the Dregs of Online Gaming

If you find yourself up against a spawn camper, it's your duty to make him pay.

If you've spent any time playing multiplayer games, you've run into them. Smacktards (also colloquially known as *asshats*) are those morons whose only mission in life seems to be to ruin the game for everyone else. Typically endowed with the brain of an intestinal virus (and about as pleasant), these folks seem to think that because no one knows who they really are they can get away with behavior that would get them beaten up in real life. There you are, enjoying a nice game and along they come, trash-talkin', spawn camping, crashing trucks full of other players, or otherwise making everyone's life difficult. Sure, you can usually pop a proverbial cap in 'em to shut them up, but it's a big pain.

To help you identify and deal with these folks, here's a handy *Field Guide to Smacktards*. Considering the range of human asshatted-ness, you probably won't find every variety of smacktard in this guide (there's always the rare death fetishist or category-defying demented teenager who's impossible to pigeonhole), but you will find the most common types handily arranged for easy identification. But proceed with caution. They often travel in herds.

The Camper
Often found in games with ranged weapons, the camper loves to hide in a dark hole in an out-of-the-way location so that he can shoot you when you walk by. In some games (sniper duels), this behavior is a virtue. In other, quicker-moving games, the camper can draw the ire of all.

Spawn Camper
Related to the camper is the spawn camper, the dingbat who has spent his time figuring out where the respawn points are. You die, you respawn, and this idiot takes you out. Errghhh!

Exploiter
Exploiters like to think they're clever because they've figured out where bugs in the game allow them to stand so they're invulnerable or invisible to other players. They crawl under a bed, hide behind a corner, or otherwise secret themselves as to pick off any passers-by.

Beggars/Whiners/Complainers
Although each member of this subspecies usually has his own spin on his particularly annoying feature, the basics are still the same: He's never happy, it's always someone else's fault, and he got ripped off.

Team Killers
Too weak and skill-less to win by going after the enemy, team killers like picking off their teammates, preferably with a shot to the back. Luckily, this behavior doesn't go over too well with other team members who will dispatch (and vote for kicking) the offender quickly.

Trash Talkers
Trash talkers clog up the audio channels on Xbox Live or in SOCOM because they'd probably get the floor wiped with their sorry butts if they said half the stuff in real life they say in the game. These socially inept types never learned about that fine line between good-natured taunting and moronic potty-mouth invectives.

Pernicious Soloists
You're playing capture the flag, and they're running your flag to the enemy base. You host a no-rockets game, and they're blasting away like it's the Fourth of July. These folks know what game they're getting into and decide they're the ones who are going to do what they're going to do.

Clan Bangers
Clan bangers are usually mindless herds of asshatters who band together to gang up on nonmembers in team games, talk trash to each other, and otherwise be idiots.

Rookie Driver
There's nothing wrong with being a newbie, just don't take it out on everyone else. If you're new to a game, don't volunteer to drive! If you're in the company of a rookie driver, bail out. Also beware the maniac driver variation, who just crashes into things (and people) for the fun of it.

DID YOU KNOW

The first modern-day MMOG was Meridian 59, published in 1996 by 3DO. Ultima Online, however, is the game that brought the genre into the mainstream (just ahead of EverQuest).

Baldur's Gate
Closet Classic (1998)

Image courtesy of GameSpy.com.

The original Baldur's Gate took the gaming scene by storm in 1998.

DOSSIER

Genre: D&D Brought to Life **Publisher:** Interplay **Developer:** BioWare **Platform:** PC

In the early to mid-1990s, role-playing games on the PC were dead. If the gaming media had cared enough to do so, they'd have buried the genre right next to the plot for parachute pants. But in the late 1990s, RPGs experienced not only a rebirth, but a full-on renaissance. After years of nearly no major releases, games like Fallout and Baldur's Gate literally resurrected a nearly extinct genre.

Baldur's Gate, its expansions, and the heavy duty sequel, were all huge hits—proving that there was still a market, and a big one at that, for well-made role-playing games on the PC.

The Importance of a License

The success of Baldur's Gate can be attributed to several factors: great graphics (for its day), an easy-to-use interface, multiplayer support, detailed character interaction, cool storylines, epic fights, and colorful NPCs. All BG fans have a soft spot for Minsc, the ranger with one too many conks on the noggin and his famous Space Hamster, Boo. How can you not appreciate a character who shouts things like, "Buttkicking for goodness!"

One also cannot underestimate the importance of the Dungeons and Dragons license. The fact that there were literally millions of potential gamers who were already familiar and could identify with the city of Baldur's Gate, the surrounding land of the Sword Coast as well as many of its inhabitants was crucial to the game's financial success. When a skilled developer has the capability to set a role-playing game in the Forgotten Realms world of D&D, it's a potential gold mine.

Baldur's Gate used second edition AD&D rules and allowed you to create any kind of character you wished. It was, for its day, the most faithful rendition of D&D on a computer—ever.

What a Sequel Should Be

After the great success of both the original and the 1999 expansion, Tales of the Sword Coast, Baldur's Gate II: Shadows of Amn hit the scene in September of 2000. Shadows of Amn is arguably the best computer role-playing game ever made. There have been a lot of top-rate RPGs released over the years, but the sequel to Baldur's Gate had everything: a great story, maybe the best villain of all time in Jon Irenicus, intense and entertaining combat, and it was enormous—you could play Shadows of Amn several times through without seeing everything.

If that weren't enough, BioWare released Baldur's Gate II: Throne of Bhaal in 2001, which further added to the Shadows of Amn story. As the game's graphics engine (Infinity) aged, the series was retired after that and BioWare moved on to create Neverwinter Nights.

We'd all love to see a Baldur's Gate 3, but there's no sign of that happening anytime soon. Doesn't it figure? We get 19 versions of Army Men, but we can't get a third game in the Baldur's Gate saga?

Image courtesy of GameSpy.com.

Baldur's Gate II remains to this day arguably the best role-playing game ever created.

BALDUR'S GATE MOD RESOURCES

There's a lot of great user-made content out there for the BG series. Here's some of the more important websites to check out:

Weimer's BG2 Mods: weidu.org/main.html

Pocket Plane Group: www.pocketplane.net/mambo

Baldurdash: www.baldurdash.org

DID YOU KNOW

There are three full-fledged novels about Baldur's Gate, all written by Forgotten Realms trilogy author Philip Athans.

February 2005

A Valentine's Gift for Gamers

February was a great month as several big name games hit the streets. Fight Night Round 2, NBA Street V3, MVP Baseball 05, WarioWare Touched!, Knights of the Old Republic II, and culminating with the release of Gran Turismo 4 on the PS2—there was a little something for everyone.

Flops of the Month:

- **FIFA Street**. NBA Street is great so FIFA Street has to be its equal, right? Um, no.
- **Scrapland**. Another high-profile game from designer American McGee (his claim to fame remains the fact that he did some work on DOOM) which failed to live up to its potential. Not great, not awful, just sort of blah.

Knights of the Old Republic II
The Sith Lords Are in the House

Image courtesy of GameSpy.com.

Dual-wielding lightsabers just looks flat-out cool.

DOSSIER

Genre: Inevitable Sequel **Publisher:** LucasArts **Developer:** Obsidian **Platform:** PC, Xbox **Metacritic Metascore:** 86

The original Star Wars: Knights of the Old Republic is considered one of the best role-playing games ever designed. It was, quite simply, a brilliant game. So, staying true to form, LucasArts said, "Let's do that again!"

KotOR 2 is not radically different from the original in terms of basic design. Although the story is obviously new, the combat and interface is pretty much the same. Developer Obsidian Entertainment took the foundation from the original, created by BioWare, and added some more "stuff" in the form of more Force Powers, feats, skills, companions, and so on.

Unfortunately, an incomplete game was rushed out the door, which is a real shame. The Sith Lords has one of the most incomplete and bizarre endings for any big budget RPG in recent memory. But hey, it's all about the journey, right?

Sith Lords Playing Tips

- If for some bizarre reason you didn't play the original, do that first. It's not technically necessary, but the story will make more sense and you'll have a greater appreciation for what is going on.

- Before doing anything, if you have the PC version, get the patch. The initial release had some serious bugs in it.

Image courtesy of GameSpy.com.

The combat interface is pretty much just like the first game.

- Play on Hard difficulty. The game is just flat-out too easy on Normal.

- Give Atton good equipment. To be more specific would spoil the ride, so just trust me on this.

- Choose a side of the force and stick with it. It's like the quote from *Cannonball Run*, "If you're going to be a bear...be a grizzly!" You'll have access to the more powerful Force Powers if you stick to a certain path instead of bouncing all around. Also, try to avoid mixing Light and Dark Side powers. (They will cost more Force Points.)

- Don't hesitate to mix and match different follower combos. Various story paths open up when different party members are in your group. However, having Kreia in your group gives you an XP bonus, so I advise you to take her along.

- So, you want to be a Light Jedi? Always refuse rewards, try to avoid conflicts, and always save lives when possible. Sith Lords in training should do the opposite, but it's worth noting that one Dark Side act can offset several Light Side acts, which will remove your CON bonus.

THEY SAID IT

"I am Chris Avellone, I am 33, I love girls from Norway, I design computer games, I am one of the founders and co-owners of Obsidian Entertainment, who recently turned out Knights of the Old Republic 2: The Sith Lords in thirteen months, and I have the scars to prove it." —**Chris Avellone in an interview at nma-fallout.com**

THE KOTOR2 RESTORATION PROJECT
Although KotOR2 is fun, it was without a doubt rushed out the door and this huge mod project at magestrix.com/K2End is trying to "finish" the game by adding deleted scenes, and so on.

DID YOU KNOW

Although Knights of the Old Republic (KotOR) 2 was technically Obsidian's first game, the company was founded by industry veterans who worked on such classic titles as Planescape: Torment, Baldur's Gate, Fallout, and Icewind Dale.

Winning Eleven Soccer 8
Mods: Making the Best Even Better

Image courtesy of Gamespy.com.

DOSSIER

Genre: Best Soccer Game Ever **Publisher:** Konami **Developer:** Konami Tokyo
Platform: PC, Xbox, PS2 **Metacritic Metascore:** 89

If you are a serious soccer, football, or futbol fan, chances are pretty good that you have succumbed to the temptress that is Winning Eleven 8 (WE8; also known as *Pro Evolution Soccer 4*, or *PES4*). This is, by far, the best arcade soccer game on the planet.

Not only is WE8 realistic, it looks pretty darn good, too.

If you haven't been exposed to it yet, put down that gamepad, put away that FIFA disc, and start playing the real deal!

Even if you are already a fan that doesn't mean you're getting the full experience. You should be aware that the WE8 community is dedicated to modding this fabulous game to help make it even better. There are mods for both the PC and console versions so no matter what your platform of choice is, there's something out there for you.

This is just a smattering of what you can find on the various fan modding websites. You can find these mods at the various websites listed in the next section.

WE8/PES4 Resources

PES Fan (www.pesfan.com). This is a fantastic WE8/PES resource page with a highly active forum and a great download section. For some mods that were designed using PES4 (the overseas version) you might need to convert the files to WE8 format by using the PESFan editor, which can be downloaded at www.pesfan.com. (You need to register on the site, which is free.) This editor is vital regardless of the platform you are using.

Okay, everybody smile this time!

Image courtesy of Gamespy.com.

Evo-Edit (www.evoedit.com). Another first-rate site dedicated to the editing and modding of WE8.

Soccer Access (www.socceraccess.com/). You have to wade through a lot of pop-up advertisements (unless you have a blocker), but this is a great site for patches and mods, especially if you want Argentinean and Brazilian league files.

WE NATION

WE Nation (www.onlineregister.com/konami/wenation) is not a mod page, per se, but a very good WE8 news and information site nonetheless.

The Files

PESFan The Complete PES 4 Guide (All Platforms). This 82-page PDF file is one of the most comprehensive playing guides ever written for any game. This is a true piece of work and a must for any WE8/PES fan.

British Patch: 92 English Clubs and Champions League (PC). This mod includes all the teams from the British leagues, with updated stadiums and real kits.

92 British Teams Option File (PS2). This file is similar to the PC version, but for the PlayStation 2.

PESFAN V3 Option File (PS2, Xbox). A massive option file that has corrected player names, in-game transfers, new club team kits, sponsors' logos, international kits, and much, much more.

MLS Evolution 2005 Mod (PC, US Version Only). This mod is particularly useful for U.S. soccer fans because it adds the MLS teams and players and is current through March of 2005.

Bebeto's 94 World Cup Patch (Beta; PC). This popular patch adds every 1994 World Cup team with classic kits, players, stadiums, adboards, and so on.

The Wolf Vuelta del Lobo Patch - WE8I (PC). Regarded as the most complete WE8 update available, this is considered a must download for PC users.

DID YOU KNOW

Konami, the publisher of Winning Eleven 8 as well as hundreds of others games, was founded in 1969 as a jukebox rental and repair company in Osaka, Japan.

MVP Baseball 2005
Mods Galore!

Old Yankee Stadium never looked so good! Many classic parks have been totally redone by the mod community.

DOSSIER

Genre: The Best Baseball Game of '05 **Publisher:** EA Sports **Developer:** EA Sports
Platform: PC, Xbox, PS2, GC **Metacritic Metascore:** 87

When publisher Take-Two and Major League Baseball signed an exclusive agreement that shut out third-party game developers from making officially licensed baseball games through the year 2012, fans of EA's MVP Baseball were left with three options:

- Resign to fact that MVP as we all knew it is no more and learn to enjoy other games. (EA plans to instead produce a college baseball game in 2006.)
- Grab some of the better mods off the Internet to help keep the game as fresh as possible.
- Use this opportunity to get outside during the summer to avoid further artery blockage.

Halofan's Angels Stadium mod adds real advertisements, enhanced color, and new dugout suites.

The MVP mod community plans to see what's behind door number two. This thriving community is actually full of castoffs from the High Heat Baseball mod community, which died off when publisher 3DO filed for bankruptcy back in 2003. The High Heat modders were truly amazing in what they were able to accomplish, and they've carried that experience and talent over to their latest obsession: MVP 2005.

This extremely dedicated fan base has turned what is a pretty good, although flawed, game into something very special. Here's a sample of what you can find. The mods listed here are just a small sampling of what can be found at either MVP Mods or Baseball Sim Central.

MVP Baseball 2005 Resources

MVP Mods (www.mvpmods.com/). This should be your first stop. Not only is this a great place to find MVP mods, but there is also a great forum here that has taken on a life of its own. It's a very cool place to simply hang around and talk baseball. To download, you will need to register on the site (it's free).

Baseball Sim Central (baseball.simcentral.net). A huge database of files for nearly every baseball game ever released. Although Sim Central also reviews and previews baseball games, the meat of the site is the fantastic database of downloadable files and its fan forum.

Jim825's Combo Datafile Mods v2.0. An absolute must download for those looking for an added boost of realism. The data file adds better camera views and takes out some of the crazy batter walk-up music. The big change, however, is that it makes it a lot more difficult to throw strikes, which is perhaps the biggest flaw in MVP Baseball.

Spitoon's MVP2k5 MLB Ball. This mod removes the oddly shaped ball in MVP to a pristine white ball that looks just like the umpire took it fresh out of his bag.

Classic Yankee Stadium. There are a lot of stadium mods for MVP 2005, but PaulW's Classic Yankee Stadium is one of the best. It adds amazing new grass textures and accurate stadium advertisements from the 1950s. This is just one example of the many stadium mods that are available. I do so hate the Yankees, though.

Console Mods. Yes, there are some Xbox and PS2 mods for those with an Action Replay or PS2 Maxdrive device. MVP Mods hosts a few of these; they are mainly uniform updates, roster changes, and player portraits, but it's better than nothing. The 1987 Cardinal uniforms are particularly cool. Powder blue, baby!

> ### MVPEDIT
> If you want to do some of your own editing and modding, you absolutely must download MVPEdit (www.glass4.com/mvpedit/), the quintessential MVP modding tool. Additionally, you might need this program to use some of the existing mods.

DID YOU KNOW

EA Sports started its Triple Play Baseball franchise in 1996. It was discontinued due to "declining sales," which led to the creation of MVP Baseball in 2003.

EverQuest Series
A History of Norrath

Image courtesy of GameSpy.com.

DOSSIER

Genre: Sony's MMOG Cash Cow **Publisher:** Sony Online **Developer:** Sony Online/Verant
Platform: PC

EverQuest was not the first ever massively multiplayer online role-playing game. It and Ultima Online were, however, the first ones to really break into the mainstream. EverQuest and its sequel remain immensely popular today despite the fact that the market is getting inundated with new MMOGs every year. EverQuest is the Iron Horse of the genre, the grizzled veteran that shows no sign of slowing down or retiring any time soon. Here's a brief look at the history of this amazing game.

EverQuest's 3D look was a revolutionary step in the evolution of the MMOG genre.

The Lineage

EverQuest (1999). Sony's 500-pound gorilla took the online gaming scene by storm back in 1999 with its 3D graphics and addictive gameplay (it became commonly known as *EverCrack*). While it was a revolutionary step forward in many ways, at its roots EQ is still just a generic MUD (see p.199) with graphics and a monthly fee.

The Ruins of Kunark (2000). The first EQ expansion added a new race (the lizard-like Iksar), a new area to explore in the continent of Kunark, and bumped the level cap from 50 to 60.

The Scars of Velious (2001). This add-on focused primarily on high level characters, giving them more places to explore and better treasure to find. It also added the Coldain Dwarves, and a dragon sect called the Claws of Veeshanm.

The Shadows of Luclin (2001). The cat race called the Vah Shir was introduced in this expansion as a playable race. Shadows of Luclin also introduced much better visuals to the EQ world despite a buggy launch that was eventually patched.

The Planes of Power (2002). An expansion only for characters over the level 50 (it capped at level 60), Planes of Power allowed players to travel quickly to various otherworldly planes in a matter of seconds. To conquer the planes, you needed to work as a team (of at least 40 players).

The Legacy of Ykesha (2003). This was the first EQ digital download add-on. It introduced the Froglok playable race. New mapping tools and guild management were also added and have become staples of the game.

Image courtesy of GameSpy.com.

EverQuest II paints a much prettier picture than the original.

Lost Dungeons of Norrath (2003). Another digital download expansion, this one added the popular augmenting system where players could upgrade their equipment.

EverQuest Online Adventures (2003; PS2). Sony tried to lure console gamers into the world of Norrath with this PS2 MMOG. It didn't take off like Sony thought and the game topped out at about 40,000 subscribers.

Gates of Discord (2004). This add-on introduced Berserkers and Muramites, but is considered the weakest of the EQ expansions because of a buggy launch.

Omens of War (2004). Omens takes place in an alternate plane known as the Plane of Discord. It also bumped the level cap from 65 to 70 and introduced voice commands as well as a lot of new high level content and guild tools.

EverQuest 2 (2004). EverQuest 2 is Sony's answer to World of Warcraft and although it is an amazing graphical package it lacks the charm of Blizzard's classic.

Dragons of Norrath (2005). The latest EQ expansion adds an interactive world map and enhanced guild tools as well as new explorable lands and interface tweaks.

Depths of Darkhollow (2005). Released in the fall of 2005, Sony says, *"For the first time ever, players will have the ability to play as a monster and experience EverQuest lore first hand through the eyes of another character while they do battle against their ancient foes."* Sign me up.

EQ WEBSITES

EQLive.com (eqlive.station.sony.com) is a great place to start for the EQ newbie, the official site is jam packed with EQ information.

GU Comics (www.gucomics.com) is a personal favorite; the EQ-inspired comics here are fantastic.

DID YOU KNOW

Selling EverQuest items and characters on eBay (for real money) became so rampant that in 2001 Sony asked eBay to forbid such auctions. Despite the policing, EQ items are still bought and sold on a daily basis on various auction websites.

NASCAR SimRacing
It's Not Papyrus, but It's Not Bad

Image courtesy of GameSpy.com.

EA's game certainly looks the part.

DOSSIER

Genre: Moderately Realistic NASCAR **Publisher:** EA Sports **Developer:** EA Tiburon
Platform: PC **Metacritic Metascore:** 85

There are racing fans out there who are simply never going to accept the fact that EA Sports has the exclusive NASCAR license through the end of the decade. There are hardcore fans who are devoted to the now defunct Papyrus game studio, the company that formerly developed NASCAR sims for publisher Sierra Sports.

The Papyrus games are classics, no question about it, and it's tough for some people to let go. But this isn't just a case of a bigger company kicking out the little guy because NASCAR SimRacing isn't a bad game. It's not as hardcore as some would like, and it does try to appeal to a wide audience of racing fans, but it clearly lays a foundation that, if built upon, could make this series one of the best NASCAR fans have seen since the glory days of Papyrus. Fact is, some former Papyrus team members worked on the game.

Newbie Guide

So, you're a wet-behind-the-ears PC racing fan and you want to give NASCAR SimRacing a whirl? Before you do, keep these little tidbits in mind:

- **Get a wheel.** This might sound like a no-brainer, but if you want to get the most out of your NASCAR experience you simply have to have a driving wheel; using a gamepad or a keyboard just isn't going to cut it. There's a ton of wheels to choose from like the Thrustmaster NASCAR Pro Force or the Logitech MoMo Force. Although any wheel is usually better than no wheel at all, don't skimp too much.

- **Use the aids.** The game does a fantastic job of getting a newbie's feet wet without making it too hard at the start. There are driving aids for practically everything, so if you are a complete novice you'll have no trouble staying on the track and enjoying yourself.

- **Check your PC at the door.** See those recommended PC specs on the box? Ignore them. If you don't have at least a 2.0GHz PC with a 128MB video card and 512MB of RAM don't even think about playing this game. Seriously, just move along because there's nothing for you to see here.

- **Get the patch!** Another "duh" tip, but the patch at located easports.com is a must because it fixes a ton of glitches; let's just say the initial release was a tad bit rushed.

NASCAR SimRacing does a great job of providing the claustrophobic feeling of being in a stock racer.

Image courtesy of GameSpy.com.

- **Have broadband, will travel.** The game's single-player career mode is cool and all, but the best way to play NASCAR SimRacing is via online with a broadband connection. However, before hopping online to show off your shiny new car, turn down the detail levels (even if you have a screaming fast machine) because if you don't you're going to lag like crazy and wonder why your car is moving in slow motion compared to everyone else on the track.

- **Fear not the poor manual.** The manual that shipped with the game, in a word, reeks. Thankfully, you can download several guides from the EA website. The Paint Guide, Garage 101 Guide, and the Online Guide can all be downloaded or viewed as PDF files at www.easports.com/games/nascarsimracing.

THEY SAID IT

"We developed the game internally at the Tiburon studio in sunny Florida. The team includes veterans from Papyrus, creators of the critically acclaimed NASCAR Racing series, and the critically acclaimed F1 series, as well as experienced staff from the other hit games developed here." **—James Hawkins, producer of NASCAR SimRacing**

DID YOU KNOW

Many real NASCAR drivers use video and computer games as either a way to simply relax or a way to simulate and study a particular racetrack.

Fight Night Round 2
EA Boxing Hits Its Stride

Gatti versus Ward, complete with flying sweat.

DOSSIER

Genre: The First Good Boxing Game **Publisher:** EA Sports **Developer:** EA Chicago
Platform: PS2, Xbox, GameCube **Metacritic Metascore:** 88

EA Sports is best known for its mainstream sports titles such as Madden, NCAA, NBA Live, and FIFA. However, there are many fans who feel that the company's boxing series, Fight Night, just might be the best thing in the vast EA Sports library.

The first two games in the series have set a foundation for great things to come, and with a next-generation console release planned for 2006, it looks like Fight Night is here to stay despite the fact that the sport it simulates is nowhere near as popular as it used to be.

Round 1

Released in early April of 2004, Fight Night 2004 turned a lot of heads for several reasons. First off, very few boxing games were being made. Publishers see a dying sport and run away in terror, fearful of low sales. EA rolled the dice and sank a lot of money into its development as well as the fact that they secured the rights to several real current boxers and those from yesteryear. The chance to control fighters such as Roy Jones Jr. and Roberto Duran was hard for many fight fans to pass up.

Second, EA Sports attempted to incorporate a completely new system in which to fight. This was not a button mashing game where whoever pressed the buttons fastest won, instead EA created the Total Control Punching system. This system makes use of a gamepad's analog control sticks and allows you to execute nearly every offensive and defensive punch that you see in an actual boxing match. It also really helps to capture the flow of a real boxing match because you have so much control over your fighter thanks to the control scheme.

Certainly, the original Fight Night was a revolutionary game but it did suffer from a lack of clinching (a vital part of the sport) and a street theme that didn't fit into the rest of the game. It even had a "bling-bling" ring announcer introducing the fighters in Las Vegas, which was just way out of place.

Round 2

The sequel to Fight Night, Round 2 upped the ante and is considered by many as the best arcade boxing game ever made. In Round 2, EA Chicago continued to perfect the Total Control System and made it even more fluid than before. It also added the much needed element of clinching (holding onto your opponent when you need a breather), and at the same time improved the graphics considerably. It's flat-out gorgeous.

Round 3

Almost no details have been released about Fight Night Round 3 and aside from seeing a running demo for the PS3 unveiling at the E3 trade show in May 2005, no actual details have been released from EA as to its gameplay. One thing is certain: Fight Night Round 3 on the PS3 is going to look disgustingly good and unless EA flat-out drops the ball, it's going to be a heck of a lot of fun, too.

THEY SAID IT

"Our design team, we all go to the boxing gym and take boxing class, but a lot of the boxing class is about tactics and scoring points and not really about trying to knock the living snot out of your opponent. But talking to the boxers and listening to how important it is in real life on varying the power of each punch, we knew it was something we needed to add. It's all about setting up punches." **—Kudo Tsunoda, Producer of Fight Night, in an interview with IGN.com**

Fight Night Round 3 is going to look the part, no doubt about that.

DID YOU KNOW

Prior to Fight Night, EA Sports produced the Knockout Kings boxing series, which was high on flash but about as realistic as Pamela Anderson.

The Sims Universe
A Work of Genius or Just Plain Silly?

The Sims 2: Nightlife is all about getting jiggy with it. In 3D.

Image courtesy of GameSpy.com.

If you play games, you've heard of The Sims. The beauty of Will Wright's creation is that even if you don't play games, you've most likely heard of The Sims. It is, after all, the number one best-selling PC game of all time. (This little essay focuses on the PC version and not the console ports.)

The idea is pretty simple. There is no objective; you don't win a game of The Sims. The goal is really just to try to make your Sims happy and to fulfill their personal goals without letting them fall into depression or worse: dying due to lack of maintenance (food).

Critics argue that The Sims really isn't a game at all but nothing more than a virtual pet or an artificial life simulation. I can't argue about the lack of gameplay. But it is voyeurism at its weirdest and with its considerable sales, there's no denying that it's an addictive "game" that has attracted legions of fans. Certainly, it must be doing something right.

Even cowboys get lucky in The Sims 2.

Image courtesy of GameSpy.com.

The Sims Lineage

The Sims Livin' Large (2000). A "more stuff" expansion with new objects, skills, career paths, and so on.

The Sims House Party (2001). The Sims got their groove on with this expansion that added more party-oriented themes.

The Sims Hot Date (2001). This adds a new city environment and finally allowed the Sims to get a bit, um, flirtatious. This was a highly successful expansion (which is concerning).

The Sims Vacation (2002). Because house parties and sexcapades just aren't enough, this expansion lets you take your Sims on a camping trip or to the beach. Yes, that's it.

The Sims Unleashed (2002). For The Sim addict whose little avatars just have to have a Sim Cat or Sim Dog.

The Sims Superstar (2003). This adds a new studio town and allowed your Sim to become famous.

DELUXE PACKAGING

There are several Deluxe Editions of the Sims games. The first, The Sims Deluxe Edition, includes the original game and the Livin' Large add-on with a game editor.

The Sims Double Deluxe Edition contains the original, Livin' large, House Party, The Sims Creator tool, and some original content.

Finally, and at this point it's getting absurd, there's the Mega Deluxe Edition, which has the original game along with Livin' Large, House Party, and Hot Date. If you bought this, seriously, try to go outside every once and a while.

The Sims Makin' Magic (2003). The final Sims expansion started to get a bit odd. Now you get to cast spells! Perfect for fans of The Sims and the TV show *Charmed*. Both of them.

The Sims Online (2002). Not a bad idea, taking The Sims and shifting it into a full fledged MMOG. The problem is that because there's no game, you're banking on the fact that people will have a lot of interesting things to say. People also used it as a form of, um, shall we say *adult entertainment*. This one totally creeps me out.

The Sims 2 (2004). The Sims sequel is a full 3D game and not a 2D hybrid like the original. It's a much deeper game than the first one, and takes the idea of taking care of your Sim to an entirely new level. You can actually raise your Sim from infancy. Two expansions have also been released: The Sims 2 University and the Sims 2 Nightlife.

DID YOU KNOW

In 2002, The Sims became the top-selling PC game of all time, eclipsing the picturesque adventure game Myst for the top spot.

NBA Street Vol. 3
Get Out the Hot Sauce!

KG throwing it down with mad skillz.

DOSSIER

Genre: NBA Basketball, Sort Of **Publisher:** EA Sports BIG **Developer:** EA Canada
Platform: PS2, Xbox, GameCube **Metacritic Metascore:** 89

Okay, so you like basketball but you're not after an authentic experience. You don't care about fouls, running set plays, or the beauty of a well-executed pick and roll. You could care less if your sixth man is a lockdown defender or if your team lacks the height to battle down low with Shaq. Of course, one could make the argument (and a good one at that) that the games today that *try* to be realistic sims don't capture this stuff all that well, either.

Still, if your hero is Hot Sauce rather than Chauncey Billups, NBA Street is definitely your game. Here's a look at the evolution of NBA Street.

NBA Street (2001)

The original NBA Street was a PS2-only release, which would later be ported to other systems. The idea was to re-create the free-flowing game that is found on the blacktop rather than the more organized NBA game. What was cool about the game was not only the myriad of spectacular moves that the players could make but also the roster of colorful characters that made up the player roster. It was almost like a mini-RPG, with each player having his own specific strengths and weaknesses.

Most games are three-on-three full court playground ball—score to 21 and win by two. You also try to accumulate trick style points by pulling off spectacular moves, good ball handling, high rising blocks, and so on.

NBA Street Vol. 2 (2003)

Volume 2 expanded to the Xbox and GameCube consoles and introduced some NBA Legends into the mix such as Wilt Chamberlain, Dr. J., and Pistol Pete Maravich. In fact, the game sported more than 150 real and fictional characters.

Some new moves were also introduced, such as bouncing the ball off an opponent's head or throwing it off the backboard

THEY SAID IT

"You can jump over tables and dumpsters, all that. I just wish I could do some of those dunks in real life, especially the one where you do a 360 while putting the ball behind your back and dunk. That's the coldest one I saw." —**NBA star Baron Davis in an interview with IGN.com**

DID YOU KNOW

so that you can catch it and slam it. However, the big new feature was the Gamebreaker 2. When you fill the GB2 meter, you're able to pull off moves that are flat-out insane compared to those in Vol. 1.

I wonder why LeBron never does this in a real game.

NBA Street Vol. 3 (2003)

Volume 3 is a significant improvement over the earlier games (which were both very good in their own right). First off, both the PS2 and Xbox versions now support online play, which was long overdue.

There's also a new trick system that follows a pattern with most EA Sports games in that it makes use of the right thumbstick. By flicking the right stick, you can perform ball-handling tricks and other moves (if your player has enough skill). There are so many tricks that you can play the game for weeks and still see new moves.

My personal favorite is the new career mode, which is somewhat like a franchise mode in a regular game. You draft players by spending street points, but they can also be stolen from your team by rivals. You can create your persona from head to toe, decking him out with all sorts of wild gear. In career mode, there is a wide variety of game types, not just the "first to 21" from the other games. You can even spend a week at the NBA Summer (street) League.

The GameCube version of NBA Street V3 allows you to play with popular Nintendo characters such as Mario and Luigi because...well, when you think street hoops, I know you must surely think "Mario and Luigi."

Tekken 5
I'm Not Quite Dead

Image courtesy of GameSpy.com.

Tekken 5 brings the series back where it belongs.

DOSSIER

Genre: Another Sweet Namco Fighter **Publisher:** Namco **Developer:** Namco **Platform:** PS2 **Metacritic Metascore:** 89

I think of Tekken 5 in movie terms: *How Tekken Got Its Groove Back* or *Tekken 5: Return of the Tekken*. You see, Tekken used to be Namco's flagship fighting game back in the day. That is, until Soul Calibur came along and blew everyone's doors off, making Tekken the forgotten sibling.

But although Tekken 5 is clearly a huge leap for the aging series in terms of both graphics and control, I still don't think it's quite as good as Soul Calibur. Still, if you're a Tekken fan or just a fan of fighting games in general, this is a must-have PS2 game. With great graphics, responsive controls, more than 30 unique unlockable characters, and varied fighting backdrops it's really an easy sell.

The Tekken Lineage

- **Tekken (Arcades, PlayStation; 1994).** The original Tekken is an arcade coin-op classic. For younger readers: Yes, there was a time when people actually went to an arcade, fistful of quarters in hand, to play games.

  Tekken was your basic fighting game with eight characters and all sorts of wild animations and moves. The goal was to become King of the Iron Fist. Each character had a backstory (which no one cared about). The game was all about fighting.

- **Tekken 2 (Arcades, PlayStation; 1996).** Tekken 2 was, shockingly, a whole lot like Tekken I, only this time you had to choose among 23 fighters rather than a paltry 8. Although only 10 characters are available initially, there are 13 others that can be unlocked.

- **Tekken 3 (Arcades, PlayStation; 1998).** Even though the roster of fighters shrunk to 18, Tekken 3 is widely

considered the best of the series. Great graphics combined with an amazing arsenal of moves made the third installment a huge, huge hit in both the arcades and on the PSX. This was also the first Tekken game that used fully 3D backgrounds (for the arcade version, anyway).

Image courtesy of GameSpy.com

"Seriously, who fights in that outfit?"

- **Tekken Tag Tournament (Arcades, PS2; 2000).** This is where the series started to lose a bit of its luster. Tag Tournament was by no means a bad game, but for the first time a lot of fans started to vocally express the fact that this was still pretty much the same game, aside from the fact that you fought in teams. Namco did boost the character roster to 33 for this one, though.

- **Tekken Advance (GBA; 2002).** This was a surprisingly good GameBoy Advance version of Tekken. Although not as complete as the standard PSX/PS2 versions, as fighting games on the GBA go, this was pretty impressive stuff.

- **Tekken 4 (Arcades, PS2; 2002).** By now it was clear that Soul Calibur was the new king of the fighting genre, and Tekken was becoming more of an afterthought. Tekken 4 didn't help remove that stigma. The roster dropped back to 19 charters and it was just a rehash of previous games, and on the PS2 actually wasn't all that good of an arcade port.

DID YOU KNOW

There was a 1997 film called *Tekken* based off of the video game. Oddly enough, there was a ton of fighting involved. Go figure.

Gran Turismo 4
Racing on Worn Treads

DOSSIER

Genre: Racing Cash Cow **Publisher:** Sony **Developer:** Polyphony Digital **Platform:** PS2
Metacritic Metascore: 89

No doubt about it, GT4 is a looker.

If you own a PS2, you almost certainly have a copy of Gran Turismo 4 sitting in your game library. It's one of Sony's best-selling and most recognizable brands. Any game that is featured on a national TV show like *The Apprentice* is definitely a mainstream title. (Yes, I like *The Apprentice*, sue me.)

Although there were a few that balked, the game received huge praise from most game review outlets. That said, put me in the group that very much underwhelmed with GT4. There is obviously a lot to like: There's an amazing amount of content and the cars handle beautifully; the physics model is believable and the graphics outstanding, but a racing game with no damage model, no online support (which was promised and then removed), and overly aggressive brain-dead AI just isn't what I'm looking for. For my money, Forza Motorsport (p.88, Chapter 5) is clearly the better game.

Gran Turismo Predecessors

Gran Turismo (PlayStation; 1998). The original Gran Turismo is a legendary console title. It was one of the first console games that proved that a PlayStation game could actually carry with it a lot of depth. The original contained eleven courses, three long endurance courses, and several time trial stages. Gran Turismo is easily one of the most important console releases of all time.

Gran Turismo 2 (PlayStation; 1999). Although the original was a very good introduction to the series, the GT team threw the entire kitchen sink at the design for the sequel. Surprisingly enough, a lot of media outlets were unhappy with GT2, saying it just was a bigger version of the original game and that the graphics were underwhelming. I always thought that this was a very unfair criticism; the simulation mode in GT2 far outshined that from the first title and it added a ton of new cars and tracks.

THEY SAID IT

"Areas such as modifications to cars are areas that I'm always interested in, and I've always wanted to include them, but to include them in GT4, I felt that the overall quality would have been reduced. I'd just like to remind you that there are 700 cars in GT4. To maintain the quality we have achieved in the game would not have been possible if we had allowed users to modify the cars." —**GT top dog Kazunori Yamauchi in an interview with Eurogamer.com**

Gran Turismo 3: A-Spec (PS2; 2001). The first Gran Turismo game on the shiny new PlayStation 2, A-Spec was a gorgeous game, which is really what a lot of people were hoping for with this release. Fact is, people were tired of looking at the PSX and the power of the PS2 took a lot of gamers by surprise. The graphics told only half the story; this was also a much better *game* than the first two editions. It was more focused, realistic, and simply more fun, even though there were fewer cars.

GT4 is still like playing on an island. Can we get online play, please?

GT PLANET

GT Planet (www.gtplanet.net) is a ridiculously informative website dedicated to the GT series. The forum is extremely active as well.

Gran Turismo Pretenders

Gran Turismo Concept 2002: Tokyo-Geneva-Seoul (PS2; 2002). The entire Concept series was pretty underwhelming. Fans wanted another new sequel, but Sony kept releasing these add-ons overseas in Europe, Korea, and Japan. New cars are cool and all, but come on.

Gran Turismo 4: Prologue (PS2; 2004). Selling a highly limited demo of GT4, even at a low price, just sucks. Period.

DID YOU KNOW

As popular as Gran Turismo is, you will not see any Ferraris, Lamborghinis, or Porsches in a Gran Turismo game. Apparently, they are tough licenses to secure.

Racing Gears Advanced
Why Cars and Mindless Violence Rule

The name is Speed. Jack Speed.

DOSSIER

Genre: Tiny Little Racer **Publisher:** GBA **Developer:** Orbital Media **Platform:** Orbital Media **Metacritic Metascore:** 83

This highly addictive game released in February last year is, in my opinion, one of the best GBA games around. A top-down combat racing game full of personality, licensed cars, tracks, and options such as four-player linked multiplayer support, is just a joy to play. You simply cannot top the hilarity that ensues when missiles start firing in this multiplayer racing classic.

Drivers and Cars

There are 12 cars in Racing Gears Advanced and all of them carry the same traits in terms of speed. The only difference, aside from appearance, is in their special abilities. This list of cars and drivers gives you just an inkling of the wide variety of replay value you can get with this little handheld racer.

- **Fat Car.** Fat drives a Dodge Super-8 hemi and has the ability to steal money from other drivers.
- **Gunner.** Gunner drives the Hummer. Fitting his name, he shoots with a much faster rate of fire than other drivers because of his Rapid Deployment ability.
- **Iron Bull.** The aggressive Russian born Bull drives a Chevy SSR, which has the mundane but still important trait of almost never spinning out.
- **Jack Speed.** Jack drives a Lotus Elise that accelerates when hit by an attack from another driver. Attacking Jack is indeed a risky proposition.
- **Spacewave.** Spacewave drives the Lotus Exige, which has infrared vision; smokescreens have no effect on it and it can see cloaked cars.

- **Throttle.** The Aussie called Throttle drives a Corvette Coupe that has Drag Race ability: It can turbo even when sitting idle. Throttle can get out of the blocks like a jackrabbit.

Colorful, detailed and addictive, this is a must buy GBA game.

- **Typhoon.** Another Lotus driver (this time, the 340R), Typhoon packs the Explosive Punch ability, which means his firepower does more damage than anyone else.
- **King Komet.** The King drives the Cadillac Cien and has the mysterious Puppet Master ability, which allows him to take over other cars, for a short time, after he's hit. To unlock him, you have to win the Omega Circuit.
- **Mad Falcon.** The Falcon drives a Lotus Elise V8SE that has the Spin Out ability, which is a very nasty trait that causes other cars that hit him to spin out of control. To unlock it, you have to win the Gamma Circuit.
- **Piranha.** Driving a Mitsubishi 7000, Piranha brings the Light Step ability to the table. She is completely unaffected by oil slicks and land mines. To unlock her, you have to win the Epsilon Circuit.
- **Stingray.** Stingray drives a Dodge M80 and has the Electroshock ability, which stuns enemies on contact, allowing her to zip past them. To unlock her, you have to win the Delta Circuit.
- **Thunderfox.** Finally, Thunderfox drives a Dodge Viper and has the Blaze ability, which allows her weapons to catch other cars on fire after a successful hit. To unlock her, you have to win the Alpha Circuit.

DID YOU KNOW

Nintendo (Ninten) is roughly translated as "leave luck to heaven" or "in heaven's hands." It was founded in 1889 by Fusajiro Yamauchi as a playing-card company. Yes—1889.

The Adventure Construction Set
Closet Classic (1987)

Genre: Roll Your Own RPG **Publisher:** Electronic Arts **Developer:** Electronic Arts
Platform: PCs (DOS, Amiga, Apple II, C64)

People love building their own stuff. Just look around at the fanatical mod communities of some of the games highlighted in this book. Gamers have their own ideas and images of what they want a game to be, and it's not some new phenomena; it's always been this way.

The Adventure Construction Set (ACS) is a prime example of this. Released back in 1985 by Electronic Arts and designer Stuart Smith on the Commodore 64 and Apple II systems, the ACS was all about doing your own thing. The game provided you with some pretty powerful tools (for 1985 and 64KB of memory) to create your own fantasy or science-fiction adventures from scratch.

You had complete control over how you wanted your story to look. You could create your own monsters; you could even hand draw them and if you were good at placing little pixels in the right place, they might actually look like a vampire, or a mummy, or a troll. You could alter the stats of any creature you wanted, place traps, create puzzles, add scenery, and so on. It was a complete adventure designing package.

The ACS also shipped with several mini-adventures and one large, complex adventure called The River of Light, which was like an Arabian Knights kind of deal set near the Tigris River. All the included adventures were built with the same editor that came with the game. It was sort of like BioWare's Neverwinter Nights, except the single player adventure that came with ACS was actually fun.

Watch out for those poisonous snakes in the Garden of Peril!

For those that wanted to build part of an adventure but didn't have the patience (or ability) to create a complete game, you could automate the building process by allowing the program to finish the adventure for you after you set a few basic parameters. It was pretty ground-breaking stuff. Of course, it would take nearly an hour for the game to auto-finish an adventure (something that seemed completely reasonable in 1985).

The interface itself is reminiscent of the early Ultima games. It used a top-down perspective and although the graphics were average at best, even for 1985, they were certainly good enough considering all the other features that came with the package.

Up to four players could play at the same time in a cooperative, turn-based fashion and the adventures that you made were easily transferable so that you could share them with your friends. I clearly remember playing other friends' adventures and thinking how I'd like to add a feature or an idea that they had come up with for my own designs. You could even save your heroes from other adventures and place them in newly made ones, so if your favorite hero completed Rivers of Light he or she could then be used in any other campaign.

Speaking of heroes, in what was a very unique design at the time, your characters improved in the skills that they used. If, for example, you had a small hero that was great at dodging, his dodge skill would improve faster than, say, melee fighting. Twenty years later and we're still adding attribute points for no rhyme or reason in most of our role-playing games (Elder Scrolls excluded).

The ACS wasn't perfect by any means and it's extremely primitive looking by today's standards; even games like Wizardry and The Bard's Tale stand up better than ACS. But there is no denying the impact that Smith's game had on the industry. In 1985, it was the first chance many of us had at making our own games.

THE UNDERDOGS STRIKE AGAIN!

Download the Adventure Construction Set from The Underdogs and remember: It used to take my C-64 45 minutes to auto-finish an adventure. (www.the-underdogs.org/game.php?id=1923)

The construction set craze of the 1980s was actually started by the 1983 hit, The Pinball Construction Set, from Electronic Arts.

Gamer's Guide to Dating
10 Ways to Score Big

If your idea of going out on a date is playing The Singles, you need a therapist, and soon.

It's a common misconception that dating and gaming don't go together. Why? I can't figure it out, but it might have something to do with some negative stereotypes or the perception that gaming is a solo activity. Wrong! If you're inventive enough, gaming can become an essential tool to improving your love life. All it takes is the right technique.

"Technique?" I hear you ask. Yes. Combining two of the most fun parts of your life isn't for the faint of heart. You can't just be a player...you've gotta be a *playah*. Smoove, like buttah. Yeah, yeah, yeah, you might think you've got the moves. Maybe you do. But if you don't (or if you need some pointers to get you started), let me suggest my top 10 tried-and-true techniques to toss into your repertoire.

The ol' controller instruction move. If you have a hottie who's not too familiar with gaming, there's no better way to get close *and* get into the action than a quick controller tutorial. If you've ever seen that famous pottery scene from *Ghost*, you've seen the technique.

Bemani lovin'. There's probably no better way to spice up the evening and get the blood pumping than a friendly, competitive dancing game. Games like Dance Dance Revolution are perfect for showing off your awesome moves and getting to see those of your date.

The Sims. "The Sims," you ask? Yes, playing The Sims together is a great way to get your partner in the right frame of mind. You get everything: fun, frolic, building dream homes, torrid affairs, and shopping—all without leaving the comfort of your couch.

Multiplayer sweet nothings. Here's one for the girls: Use private channels to whisper suggestions to the guys you're pursuing during multiplayer games. Not only do you have their ear during their favorite activity, but it'll probably also make them flustered enough that you'll have no trouble gunning them down.

A weekend at the con. If things begin to get serious, you might want to suggest a weekend at your favorite con. First, the object of your desire might think you're suggesting that you two go to Cannes (as in France). Second, after you get your date there, you'll have a perfect opportunity to introduce her to your world in any one of the many luxurious two-star motels most cons are held in.

Survival horror snuggling. Taking your date to a horror movie in hopes of some hold-me-I'm-scared action is so old school. No, if you really want to show that you're a hip and happenin' playah, turn down the lights, pop in the latest Resident Evil installment, and give your love a little tutorial.

Co-op mode of love. What better way to show your love than playing your favorite game in co-op mode? Not only will you get the chance to get in some gaming action, but there's no way your date can complain that you don't spend any time together.

Shirts and skins. This might require a date with a bit more naiveté than normal, but if you can get her to come over for a night of head-to-head sports gaming, you'll need to be able to tell your teams apart, right?

Strip Mario Party. Who doesn't enjoy a little bit of competitive action? Pull out your favorite version of Mario Party and suggest that the loser of each mini-game must remove an article of clothing.

Come on over and play Duke Nukem Forever. Why whine about the fact that this game will never be released? Use the eternally delayed release schedule to your advantage. Hey, it beats the old "Look at that...we're out of gas" or "Let's go watch the submarine races" lines. The game's not released yet? Would you look at that?! Well, maybe we can find something else to do....

DID YOU KNOW

The show floor at E3 is crawling with attractive women in outfits that would make Andrew Dice Clay blush. Some of them will even talk to you if you let them turn you into a walking billboard of ad stickers.

Disciples II
Bargain Bin Special

DOSSIER

Genre: Digital Crack **Publisher:** Strategy First **Developer:** Strategy First **Platform:** PC
Metacritic Metascore: 84

The artwork in Disciples II is fantastic even three years after the fact.

Disciples is one of the most underappreciated strategy games ever published. It's fun, challenging, well designed, gorgeous, and highly addictive. If you like fantasy-themed, turn-based strategy games, you *simply must* own Disciples II.

This bargain bin special is a bit tricky because Strategy First published several Disciples II editions and expansions after the initial success of the original. I'll cover all the bases below so that you know what you're buying.

The Disciples II Buying Guide

Disciples II: Dark Prophecy. On the surface Disciples II looks like a Heroes of Might and Magic clone, but in reality the only thing the two games have in common is that they are both turn-based and use an overhead map to move your armies. Other than that, the designs are completely different. For one, Disciples II has awe-inspiring artwork combined with amazing unit animation. Even today, the graphics in the game are first rate.

The overhead map was also easy on the eyes.

The combat model is unique and takes getting used to. You may have only six units in your army, including its hero unit (who also fights). These units, after combat ensues, may not move. This isn't a tactical strategy game, but it is highly strategic nonetheless. Placing units in the front ranks makes them susceptible to melee attacks, but units in the back are still vulnerable to arrows and spells. This makes your army makeup *extremely* important. If you can get past the notion that combat involves stationary units, the rest of the game is very easy to get into. Seeing as how turn-based strategy games aren't quite the rage anymore, if you missed out on this when it was released a few years ago you still have a chance at redemption as this can be found in stores or online for as little as $10. It's a *steal*.

Disciples II: Guardians of the Light. This was when it got weird. Strategy First released two standalone expansions: one focused on the light side and the other the dark. The company charged $20 for each add-on even though they added very little new content to the original. Steer clear of both Guardians and Servants of the Dark unless that's your only option.

Disciples II: Servants of the Dark. See Guardians of Light.

Disciples II: Gallean's Return. This simply takes Guardians of the Light and Servants of the Dark and bundles them into one package. This is only available at the StrategyFirst.com website for $20, which isn't a bad deal.

Disciples II: Rise of the Elves. Finally! A truly worthy expansion. Rise of the Elves is a standalone game so you don't technically need the original to play it. Here you finally get to play the elves, including all of their unique units, buildings, and so on. You can find this in stores bundled with other games or at the SF website for $20.

Disciples II: Gold. This is the big daddy. This sucker packs everything above into one convenient box. It breaks our $20 rule for bargain bin listings, but if you want everything that's out there for $30 it's a very good deal.

DID YOU KNOW

Strategy First has announced plans to make a Nintendo DS version of Disciples although no release date has been set.

Metacritic's Top 10 Xbox Games
Also Known As the Halo and Splinter Cell Show

Image courtesy of GameSpy.com.

Splinter Cell is well represented in the Top 10.

Since its release in November of 2001, the Xbox has seen its fair share of fantastic games. The games listed here are the cream of the crop; the games the press drooled over the most according to the review database Metacritic.com.

10. Logjam! (Score: 92). There is literally a logjam for the #10 spot as *nine* games have a 92 Metascore. Those games are (in no particular order): SSX 3, Madden 2003, Madden 2004, NFL 2K3, NFL 2K5, Soul Calibur II, Forza Motorsport, GTA: San Andreas, and Prince of Persia: Sands of Time.

9. Tony Hawk's Pro Skater 3 (Score: 93). Released back in 2002, Tony Hawk's Pro Skater 3 is considered a top-shelf game on other systems but it really shines on the Xbox because of the custom soundtrack feature, improved graphics, multiplayer mode, and a secret level and character exclusive to the Xbox.

8. Splinter Cell (Score: 93). The original Splinter Cell was released in November of 2002 and was lavished with praise. This set the bar for stealth-action games on the consoles and is considered one of the most important and influential console games ever made.

7. Splinter Cell: Pandora Tomorrow (Score: 93). The follow up to Splinter Cell, Pandora Tomorrow improved on the original with stellar multiplayer support via Xbox Live. It also had perhaps the best use of sound ever heard in a videogame on the consoles.

6. Star Wars: Knights of the Old Republic (Score: 93). A summer of 2003 release, not only is KotOR one of the very best *Star Wars* games ever made, but it's one of the best role-playing games of all time. Allowing you to travel down either the light or dark Jedi path, it told the kind of story many *Star Wars* fans were hoping for with the new films, instead we all got Jar-Jarred.

5. Splinter Cell: Chaos Theory (Score: 94). It says a lot about a particular series of games when *three* of them rank among the best Xbox games ever reviewed by the media. Chaos Theory is the latest in the Splinter Cell saga and is arguably the best in the series because it added a wonderfully addictive co-operative mode, which could be played via split screen or on Xbox Live.

4. Burnout 3: Takedown (Score: 94). Considered by many as the best arcade racer ever made, Burnout 3: Takedown is simply a joy to play. It's an over the top arcade racer that is light on realism (although it has a kick-ass physics model) but heavy on graphics, action, and insane crashes.

3. Halo 2 (Score: 95). What's left to say? Halo 2 is, without a doubt, a terrific game and a worthy sequel as well as one of the best Xbox Live games ever made.

2. Grand Theft Auto Double Pack (Score: 95). The double pack included GTA: III and GTA: Vice City in one package. It was the ideal set for those new to the series or for those who don't own a PS2. The Xbox versions of these classics were outstanding. Just keep it away from the kids.

1. Halo (Score: 97). Halo is the most recognized Xbox game of all time, hands down, and end of debate. It showed just how great a first-person shooter could be on a console system. It had a compelling story and a great hero in the Master Chief, great action, and of course, The Flood. If you're an Xbox gamer and you haven't played Halo, drop your Gamer Card off as you exit the building.

Image courtesy of GameSpy.com

Puny Sandpeople, My Jedi has mad skills.

Image courtesy of GameSpy.com

Best. Game. Ever. (On the Xbox, anyway....)

DID YOU KNOW

Halo, Bungie's blockbuster Xbox game, was originally designed as a real-time strategy game that would be available only on Apple computers. Amazing how game designs evolve, eh?

Ion Storm (1996–2005)
Corporate Graveyard

Daikatana and the attack of the robotic frogs.

Ion Storm is the most infamous game developer in the history of the gaming industry. Never has a company received so much attention and produced so little. Ion Storm did develop a few damn fine games, but compared to the level of hype the company has to be considered a big disappointment.

Founded by ex-employees of id Software, many of whom helped create DOOM among other classic games, expectations for Ion Storm were through the roof because the folks there talked a great game and the media ate it up like free chocolate. Ion Storm, in the early years, was quick to tell you how great its games were going to be.

What could possibly go wrong?

Thief: Deadly Shadows wasn't what PC fans had in mind but it was still a fine game.

The Ion Storm Lineage

Dominion: Storm Over Gift 3 (1998). The first Ion Storm game was a run of the mill real-time strategy title that used to be under the 7th Level banner. Dominion was the company's first release, after being in business for two years, and it was a huge, huge disappointment.

Daikatana (2000). John Romero's infamous first-person shooter never lived up to its massive hype. The game went through several team members and years of additional development. It was supposed to be the spiritual successor to Quake, but the end result was a technologically dated game with poor AI and weird monsters. I mean really, robotic frogs?

Deus Ex (2000). The Austin branch of Ion Storm created the company's first hit and Deus Ex would end up being, by far, its best game. Deus Ex was an action/role-playing hybrid set in a futuristic cyberpunk world. It allowed you to approach a problem in multiple ways (stealth, guns blazing, and so on) and had a wonderfully detailed plot.

Anachronox (2001). Anachronox gets a bad rap. Tom Hall's third-person action/RPG is a highly underrated game. The problem is that it took nearly four years to make and by the time it was finally finished, it was a tad dated. This one got panned undeservedly for not being the revolutionary experience that was originally intended. After Anachronox was published, Romero and Hall left the company.

Deus Ex: Invisible War (2003). This was a surprisingly uninspired and oversimplified sequel with a clunky interface. Whereas Deus Ex was a PC game, Invisible War was created with the Xbox in mind and then ported to the PC. That's usually a kiss of death for a PC game and Invisible War proved to be no different.

Thief: Deadly Shadows (2004). The last game published under the Ion Storm banner was the well-made Thief: Deadly Shadows. Like Invisible War, this was developed for the Xbox and the PC simultaneously and while it was certainly fun to play, long time fans of the PC series criticized it for being a dumbed-down version of Thief 1 and 2 (developed by long-departed publisher, Looking Glass Studios).

The End of Ion Storm

In 2001, Eidos closed down the Dallas office. The office in Austin, which developed Deus Ex and Thief: Deadly Shadows, remained open until Warren Spector, the head man in Austin, left the company to pursue other interests. In February 2005, Eidos announced the formal closing of all Ion Storm offices. The company that was founded with the slogan "Design Is Law" was no more.

EVEN MORE ON ION

The Dallas Observer, back in the day, posted an **Ion Storm Expose** at www.dallasobserver.com/issues/1999-01-14/news/feature2.html. This is one of the most fascinating pieces of game journalism ever written.

DID YOU KNOW

After leaving Ion Storm, John Romero and Tom Hall founded Monkeystone Games, a company dedicated to making Pocket PC games. (They have since left Monkeystone, too.)

Text-Based Sports Games

Proving That Pretty Spreadsheets Can Be Fun

Worldwide Soccer Manager is one of the best sports games ever designed.

Although the vast majority of people who play sports videogames do it for the joy of controlling a favorite player, causing a bone-crunching tackle, or playing head-to-head with a buddy, there's another section of the sports gaming population who value one thing above all else: realism. Graphics be damned; if the stats don't look right, it's not worth the effort.

If you want a sports game to reflect the sport it is simulating as close as it possibly can, you really just have one option and that's to play a text-based sports game. No rolling your eyes, folks. Just because a game is text-based doesn't mean it has to look like a glorified spreadsheet. No, you aren't going to get superb 3D graphics with stereo sound, but a lot of the new text games have very clean and approachable interfaces.

If you're a true sports nut, you owe it to yourself to try some of these games because they're amazingly addictive and some make for fantastic multiplayer games.

PureSim—all the news that is fit to print!

Top Text Sims

Out of the Park Baseball (www.ootpdevelopments.com/ootp). Out of the Park (OOTP) is one of the most engrossing baseball sims on the market today. Both pretty to look at and a blast to play, OOTP is working on its seventh edition, which is to be published in 2006 by Sports Interactive. I run an OOTP league myself and this is text gaming at its best.

Worldwide Soccer Manager (www.sigames.com). Worldwide Soccer Manager is the quintessential text based sports game. It's the kind of game that might turn you *into* a soccer fan. It's incredibly deep yet very approachable and is widely considered to be one of the best sports games, text-based or otherwise, on the market today.

Eastside Hockey Manager (www.sigames.com). Take Worldwide Soccer Manager and turn it into hockey. OK, that's a bit of a simplification but it's not all that far off, either. If you love hockey, you owe it to yourself to try EHM.

Front Office Football (www.solecismic.com). Arguably the best text football game around, Front Office Football (FoF) isn't the prettiest girl at the dance but if you want to really get into the nuts and bolts of running an NFL team, this is as good as it gets.

FoF: The College Years (www.solecismic.com). Front Office Football, but instead of running a pro team you get to coach and recruit for your favorite college. Very nice indeed.

Diamond Mind Baseball (www.diamond-mind.com). It's not all that great to look at but if you want absolute statistical authenticity, DMB is the best option. It's a bit pricey and the franchise options aren't as good as OOTP or PureSim but if accuracy is all that matters, this is your best bet.

PureSim Baseball (www.puresim.com). PureSim has come a long, long way since its original release. PureSim has a growing fan base and is definitely worth checking out as an equal competitor to OOTP. It's a true labor of love on the part of the developer and it shows in the finished product.

Total Pro Basketball (www.greydogsoftware.com/tpb). This is a wonderfully designed NBA basketball simulation with a very good franchise mode (far better than anything you'll see in games like NBA Live or NBA2K).

Total Pro Football (www.400softwarestudios.com/tpf). Total Pro Football (TPF) is a better looking game than FoF, but the sim engine is a bit weaker. It does have a much better user interface and the latest update has cleaned up some of its gameplay issues.

ON THE WEB

Most games have forums on their websites, but if you want to talk Front Office Football, **FOF Central** at dynamic.gamespy.com/~fof/forums is the place.

DID YOU KNOW

Worldwide Soccer Manager was formerly known as Championship manager before developer Sports Interactive split with publisher Eidos. Eidos stills owns the name Champsionship Manager but not the game's code.

Syndicate
Closet Classic (1993)

DOSSIER

Genre: Strategy Game Extraordinaire **Publisher:** Electronic Arts **Developer:** Bullfrog Productions **Platform:** DOS PC, Amiga, Genesis, Jaguar, SNES, 3DO

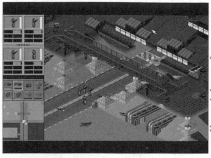

This looked really cool in 1993.

Image courtesy of GameSpy.com.

The word *revolutionary* gets tossed around a lot. Sometimes it's warranted...sometimes it isn't. However, Syndicate, Bullfrog's 1993 classic, truly defines the term.

Through the original, an expansion, and a sequel it spanned several platforms from the PC and 3DO to the Atari Jaguar console; you can literally trace the evolution of the squad-based tactical strategy game from Syndicate to X-COM to Jagged Alliance to Incubation. Even games like Diablo should pay homage to this benchmark action strategy game. If you have ever played a squad-based game where you get to deck out your individual troopers with specific gear and traits, you're playing something that started with Syndicate well over a decade ago.

Being the Bad Guy

Part of the hook of Syndicate was its backstory. In the world of Syndicate, huge corporations have taken over the world, overthrowing governments and brainwashing citizens. You play a marketing exec for one of these mega-companies and it's your job to organize a group of cyborgs to strong-arm your way into certain territories. Marketing at its best, eh?

The game map showed you which province needed cleansed.

Image courtesy of GameSpy.com.

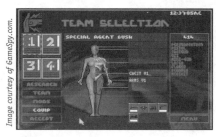

Personalizing your agents was half the fun.

Image courtesy of GameSpy.com.

You lead a four-person team to perform a wide variety of tasks, but most involved laying waste to everything in your path. There were some acquisition missions, but really it was just about cool weapons and outfitting and personalizing your squad.

Syndicate helped to introduce gameplay mechanics such as item research and development, spending your earned money to make your team stronger, and so on. The weapons are stunning for 1993— and the effects no less impressive. To see a flamethrower actually shoot flames in real-time was absolutely amazing.

It wasn't just about guns, though. Your cyborgs could receive implants, as well. Add a better heart for better stamina, add new arms to carry more weight, and add new legs make them move at a faster clip, and so on.

Syndicate was the very first game to allow squad based real-time combat. A simple click of the right mouse button over a target fired your weapon (on the PC) and the left mouse button moved your group. Sounds pretty basic, but in 1993 this was heady stuff.

The biggest problem with the game was that there were no transparency effects at all and the buildings wouldn't peel away when you entered them, so if you went behind a building you played blind—and the same was true if you went inside a building. It could get a bit frustrating, but the rest of the game was so outstanding that the problem didn't prevent gamers from logging dozens of hours completing the more than 50 missions in the game.

Later in 1993 Bullfrog released an expansion pack called Syndicate: American Revolt, which added new weapons and missions. Then in 1996 the odd combo Syndicate Plus was released, which just packaged the original and the add-on together. Later that year, Syndicate Wars was released for the PC and PlayStation. This sequel added a rotating camera, which helped to alleviate the blind building issue. Syndicate Wars was also renowned for the fact that nearly every item on a map could be destroyed.

DID YOU KNOW

Other great Bullfrog games include Dungeon Keeper, PowerMonger, Theme Park, Magic Carpet and, of course, the classic Populous.

The Best D&D Games
Sword-Grabbing Good Times!

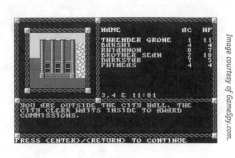

Image courtesy of GameSpy.com.

Pool of Radiance was a huge, huge hit for SSI.

There are a lot of videogames that use licenses from other sources, but no game has been licensed more than Dungeons & Dragons. A lot of *Star Wars* and *Star Trek* games have been released over the years, but their number pales in comparison to how many D&D games have seen the light of day. There have been classics like Baldur's Gate and absolute disasters like Birthright, Descent to Undermountain, and Pool of Radiance: Ruins of Myth Drannor.

Image courtesy of GameSpy.com.

Baldur's Gate II just might be the best game ever.

Pool of Radiance (1988). The original D&D classic and first of the famous Gold Box games, Pool of Radiance is a video gaming classic and really the first time D&D players had a chance to truly see their world on a computer. It's beyond crude by today's standards but it's still one of the most significant releases ever.

Curse of the Azure Bonds (1989). This was the direct sequel to Pool of Radiance and followed the standard sequel shtick of playing pretty much the same, but the design was packed with a lot more stuff. Still, few complained.

War of the Lance (1989). Does this sound like fun? Take the D&D license, specifically the DragonLance universe, and slap it inside a strategy-wargame design where the idea was world domination using the races, heroes, and spells of the genre? It was awesome.

Champions of Krynn (1990). Great story, really bad graphics. That's what I remember the most about Krynn, another game set in the world of DragonLance. It was a return to the roots of the Gold Box games but by now the late '80s graphics had to go. After you got past the looks, though, this was a fun RPG.

Eye of the Beholder Series (1991–1993). This proved to be a staggeringly popular series in the early 1990s, which spanned three games in the Forgotten Realms universe. This was the first D&D game to use a first-person perspective in quasi-3D and used splendid VGA graphics. The first game really was a technological marvel for 1991. Light on story and heavy on the fighting, it was just what the doctor ordered for D&D fans.

Fantasy Empires (1993). Another grand strategy game using the D&D license, Fantasy Empires allowed players to field massive armies, send heroes on quests, etc. Great stuff.

Ravenloft series (1994–1995). Both Ravenloft: Strahd's Possession and Ravenloft II: Stone Prophet were cool because they were the first D&D in series to use free roaming 3D and...they had vampires. As *Buffy* proved, that's always a plus.

Baldur's Gate Series (1998–2001). By now publisher SSI had lost the D&D license and other companies were trying, and failing, to deliver a good D&D game. BioWare's Baldur's Gate showed just how popular this license could be when handled with competence and a passion for the source material. Take great gameplay, a technologically advanced engine, and add the D&D license—then start printing the money.

Planescape: Torment (1999). Baldur's Gate got all the press but many feel than Torment was actually the better game. If you base how good an RPG is on its story, Torment wins hands-down. It wasn't as combat-driven as Baldur's Gate, which turned off some players, but there's no doubt that this is one of the top five RPGs of all time, D&D or otherwise.

Icewind Dale series (2000–2002). Whereas some felt Torment was too wordy, there were just as many who felt Icewind Dale actually had too much combat and too little wordplay. Although not quite the game Baldur's Gate was, Icewind Dale was still a very solid romp that spanned two full games and two expansions.

Neverwinter Nights (2002–2003). Love it or hate it, NWN is a very significant release just because the editing tools alone made it a spiritual successor to the Adventure Construction Set. Although the single player game in the original was underwhelming after the epic Baldur's Gate II, the add-ons provided better solo play but multiplayer is where it's at.

Temple of Elemental Evil (2003). Based off the initial release, this game was a huge disappointment. After the patches, though, ToEE proved to be a fun, albeit story-deprived adventure based off the classic AD&D module.

DID YOU KNOW

Although most fans surely know this, D&D has actually been around since 1974. That, folks, is a lot of dead orcs. There was also a D&D cartoon that ran through 27 episodes in the early 1980s.

March 2005

The Saint Patty's Day Massacre!

God of War thundered onto the scene in March '05, shocking gamers with its ultra-violent and wickedly fun gameplay. God of War was a reason for Xbox fans to dust off that PS2.

Of course, stealth fans sank their collective teeth into another top-shelf Splinter Cell Game as Chaos Theory shipped and lived up to its name, as did the Freedom Force sequel, Freedom Force vs. The 3rd Reich. Shooter fans were plunged, yet again, into World War II in Brothers in Arms: Road to Hill 30 and despite the tired genre, it was so much fun no one seemed to care.

Finally, gamers finally saw the new Sony PSP handheld in action with games such as Ridge Racer, WipEout Pure, and Lumines.

Overall, it wasn't a bad month.

Flop of the Month:

- **PSP Busts**—Although there were some quality PSP launch titles released in March there were an equal number of poor releases for the new platform like Spider-Man 2, World Tour Soccer, Dynasty Warriors, and Gretzky Hockey. Weak games like this put a damper on the PSP's launch.

God of War
System Seller Extraordinaire

Image courtesy of Gamespy.com.

DOSSIER

Genre: Clash of the Titans with Beheadings **Publisher:** Sony **Developer:** Sony Studios Santa Monica **Platform:** PS2 **Metacritic Metascore:** 94

God of War is a visceral, violent, bloody, gore-soaked, no-holds-barred over-the-top fighting feast that has you chopping off limbs and heads on your way to mythological glory. This is the kind of game that has politicians screaming from the rafters, but you just know that half of them are secretly playing during Senate downtime.

Kratos soaked in the blood of the cyclops.

According to the game review database Metacritic.com, God of War is one of the best-reviewed games of all time. In fact, 20 review sources rated God of War at least a 98%. That's some serious praise that justifies the notion that this game is a *system seller*; that is, a game that is so good that it's worth going out and buying a PlayStation 2 just so that you can experience it.

THEY SAID IT

> "The goal of our combat is to make the player feel brutal, letting their inner beast free and just going nuts."
> —**David Jaffe, Game Director of God of War in an interview with IGN.com**

Image courtesy of Gamespy.com.

When minotaurs attack!

God of War Tips

Your journey will take you to classic settings in Greek mythology: The Aegean Sea, the Desert of Lost Souls, Pandora's Temple, and the Temple of the Oracle just to name a few. To progress through what is generally considered a very tough game, you'll have to be quick with the gamepad controls as well as know the ins and outs of the game. Here are some general tips to keep in mind when taking Kratos on his whirlwind tour of death.

- Level up the Blades of Chaos at least twice before you level up anything else. You'll have some effective moves and at level three, you can make a huge dent in bigger enemies and bosses.

- When you're in the middle of an attack and you know you're about to take a savage beating, hold the L1 button down. If you do this correctly, your current movement will stop and you will be in the normal block pose; this prevents you from taking any damage (unless it's an unblockable attack). And don't forget that you can block in mid-air! If you use this strategy, you're going to run into the "counter lag" sequence from the time to time. As soon as the screen does this, release the L1 button and tap the Square button. This causes you to counter the enemies with little recoil time; this is effective on bosses, as well.

- Mini-games are generally used to finish an enemy off. When you see a button appear above an enemy's head, execute the button sequence that normally follows. Following these sequences is critical when fighting bosses.

- Don't waste magic on everything you see because you might need it for bosses or harder groups of enemies. This doesn't mean that you shouldn't use it from time to time, but don't waste it on every undead legionnaire that you see.

- Rage of the Gods is pretty potent when used correctly. Using it for bosses is recommended, but you really don't need to use it (unless you're playing in God Mode). Like magic, pick your spots and use it wisely.

CREDIT WHERE CREDIT IS DUE

The tips in this section are from **Akubarix's God of War Guide** at db.gamefaqs.com/console/ps2/file/god_of_war_boss.txt. Our thanks for letting us print some of the best ones here.

DID YOU KNOW

IGN.com voted God of War the best-looking PS2 game ever made saying, "From the fight at sea in the beginning to the battle of the gods at the end the game simply never lets up with its visceral impact."

Freedom Force vs. The 3rd Reich
Proving Superhero Games Don't Suck

Freedom Force is as much strategy as it is RPG.

Image courtesy of Gamespy.com.

DOSSIER

Genre: Nazis. I Hate These Guys **Publisher:** Irrational Games **Developer:** Irrational Games **Platform:** PC **Metacritic Metascore:** 87

The original Freedom Force, which was released in 2002, came along when comic book fans had pretty much given up all hope of seeing a computer or video game with superheroes in it. Not only are Freedom Force and its sequel, Freedom Force vs. The 3rd Reich, great games, they started the trend of comic book games that shows no signs of stopping.

FFv3R features a lot of the same faces from the original, including Minuteman, El Diablo, Mentor, and The Ant along with some new heroes and villains. This time FF goes back in time from the early 1960s to 1942 to battle the evil Blitzkrieg.

The Third Reich is better than the original in nearly every way; it still keeps its campy Silver Age comic theme, but it sports better graphics, an improved interface, and more destructive environments without sacrificing its classic real-time tactical depth.

THEY SAID IT

"Making games is not like stamping widgets. I like the idea that we know roughly what kind of game we're building, and when it will be done, but it's a giant mystery as to exactly how or when it will stop being a piece of technology and start being a game, or why it will be fun; every day when I walk in the door someone could say "Hey, come look what I did!" and show me something amazing and unexpected." —**Chris Kline, Irrational Lead Programmer in an interview with Freedomfans.com**

Breaking the Curse

The superhero game curse was sort of like the curse of the Red Sox; very few people deep down felt it was actually a *curse*, but it was amazingly frustrating to see so many promising superhero games end up as vaporware.

Games such as Guardians: Agents of Justice, The Indestructibles, and Champions (based on the popular pen and paper RPG), and a few others started out as great ideas and some even made it into the alpha build stage, but all ended up taking the dirt nap before release for one reason or another.

When Freedom Force shipped fans embraced its campy humor and streamlined gameplay that carries the torch for the Silver Age of comic books. What took some a while to warm to it was that it used an entirely new band of heroes and villains. No one had ever heard of Minuteman, El Diablo, Liberty Lad, or The Ant. It's always an easier sell when you can tell fans that they can play as Spider-Man or Batman. Thankfully, the designers at Irrational Games are big comic book fans in their own

DID YOU KNOW

right, so after the initial "Who are these guys?" questions subsided, fans realized that this was a fantastic RPG/Strategy game.

Image courtesy of Gamespy.com.

Wonder Twins powers, activate!

Mod Heaven, Sort Of

The editing tools for Freedom Force vs. The 3rd Reich are available and the modders are hard at work on building complex missions and campaigns, but if you never played the original game, or if you did play it and were not aware of the ridiculously active mod community, you still have some gaming to do! Unfortunately, you won't necessarily be able (legally) to play as your favorite hero: Marvel, showing the worst kind of arrogant, short-sighted thinking in stamping down the creativity of its own fanbase, is extremely quick to threaten legal retribution against any site hosting mods based on their characters. Still, there's a ton of content out there.

FREEDOM ONLINE
Freedom Force Fans (www.freedomfans.com) is the place to go for new mod news.

The Strangers Saga (mike.va.com.au) is a massive, 31-mission mod campaign with a sequel for the original (2002) Freedom Force.

Irrational's Freedom Force should not be confused with the 1988 NES game of the same name by Sunsoft, which involved a counter-terrorist team, AKA the "Freedom Force." The game was one of the few that used the light gun accessory for the NES.

Brothers in Arms: Road to Hill 30
Once More Unto the Breach

Image courtesy of Gamespy.com.

Digital France. I've seen this before....

DOSSIER

Genre: Greatest Generation Shooter **Publisher:** Ubisoft **Developer:** Gearbox Software
Platform: PC, PS2, Xbox **Metacritic Metascore:** 89

How many ways can we fight World War II? I have stormed the digital beaches of Normandy so many times I've lost count and I've killed more virtual Germans than Tom Hanks and Gary Cooper combined. From first-person shooters and real-time strategy games to hardcore wargames, World War II is arguably the most saturated era in all of Game Land. Yet we continue to flock to them whenever the next big thing hits the scene. Brothers in Arms: Road to Hill 30 is no different. On the surface, it's just another squad-based 3D shooter with you as the American Hero doing battle against legions of Germans à la Call of Duty or Medal of Honor. But not only would such a rush to judgment be unfair, you'd also be missing out on one heck of a game.

THEY SAID IT

"I think the Rainbow Six series is really interesting, but I think the squad combat element of Brothers in Arms is a lot more accessible. I also think that the Brothers in Arms squad combat system really gets to the roots of what a real squad leader deals with. It's not about micro management—it's about applying the concepts of fire and maneuver to overcoming real combat challenges." —**Randy Pitchford, President of Gearbox Software in an interview with** *Computer Games* **magazine**

Covering Fire!

Brothers in Arms: Road to Hill 30 is almost as much a strategy game as it is a first-person shooter. As Sgt. Matt Baker of the 101st Airborne, you are in complete control of your squad. You order troops to lay down suppressing fire or to attack an enemy flank, and so on. You simply cannot complete the missions on your own; you must use your fellow soldiers to your advantage. If you ever wanted to play Tom Hanks's role in *Saving Private Ryan* or Captain Winters from the HBO *Band of Brothers* series, this is your game.

Brothers in Arms also shoots for realism. There are no floating armor kits or magic health packs laying around for you to snatch up and instantaneously stitch your wounds in the middle of a firefight. If you take several rounds from a German machine gun, it'll rip you to pieces. Discretion is the better part of valor here.

There are a few hiccups. The missions have a distinct puzzle-like feel to them. You almost get the feeling that the developers have a certain way in which they want you to approach a

mission, so you don't have the complete freedom to get creative that you would in a real battle situation. Still, as World War II shooters go, this is definitely worth the price of admission.

BIA FILEFRONT
Brothersinarms.filefront.com is part of the UGO Filefront network. It's a great place to find BiA mods and files.

Earned in Blood

Released in time for the 2005 holidays, Brothers in Arms: Earned in Blood shows the events from Road to Hill 30 from the perspective of another 101st Airborne soldier, "Red" Hartsock, who was the leader of a fireteam under Sgt. Baker.

Image courtesy of Gamespy.com.

Earned in Blood promises to have more urban landscapes.

It's hard to say whether this is a sequel or more of an expansion pack. Despite Ubisoft's claims that it uses better technology, it still looks a lot like Road to Hill 30. There are new features, to be sure, but perhaps the most anticipated addition is the realized AI that will hopefully make things feel less like a puzzle and more like an unscripted firefight.

Lastly, the game ships with enhanced co-op multiplayer for every platform with maps unique to that mode of play, so you won't be simply rehashing the same maps from the campaign.

DID YOU KNOW

Gearbox Software, developer of Brothers in Arms, also lists the PC version of Halo and the PS1 version of Half-Life on its company résumé.

TimeSplitters: Future Perfect
Where's the Love?

Image courtesy of Gamespy.com.

Future Perfect is an intense action packed thrill ride! How's that for some generic praise?

DOSSIER

Genre: Action/Shooter **Publisher:** Electronic Arts **Developer:** Free Radical **Platform:** PS2, Xbox, GameCube **Metacritic Metascore:** 84

One shooter series that tends to get overlooked is TimeSplitters. The series spans three games going back as far as the year 2000 when the original was released on the PS2. It's an intense action series that takes place in various time periods; an alien race called the TimeSplitters has caused a ripple in the Earth's time stream and basically hijacked periods of history. Future Perfect has been a darling of the press from day one due to its high intensity, fast-paced gameplay, but it has never really garnered the attention from consumers as other games in the genre.

The latest installment of the series takes place immediately after the events of TimeSplitters 2, approximately 400 years into the future. You play Sergeant Cortez, a solider who is charged with going back in time to eradicate the evil TimeSplitters once and for all. Cortez goes back in time as far as 1924, but there are also some missions that take place in the "present day" of 2401.

Quick Boss Guide

To succeed in wiping out the TimeSplitters, you're going to have to face several bosses, some of whom are downright tough to kill. Here's a quick guide to get you through the rough patches:

- **Tank**. Most of your weapons will be totally ineffective in this fight. The key is the TNT scattered about the area, which also respawns so you never run out. Use your K-SMG Grenade Launcher to distract the tank as you strafe around the area. Keep moving. The tank's machine gun fire will nail you if you stay in one place too long. Set a grenade on the tank, which will stall the vehicle long enough for you to plant the TNT behind it. After three or four charges, the tank should say goodnight.

- **Deer Haunter**. There are two ways to handle this. You can keep him at range with a shotgun; just keep moving and plugging him and don't let him corner you. Or you can use the really cheeseball method of going back into the room he came from (through the wall) because he can't go back in there. Just sit down with a sandwich and pop him 'til he falls.

- **Undead Creature**. Another part of the House of Horrors level, this can be a bit tough. Keep circle-strafing and always try to shoot the creature in the face with a shotgun or revolver so that the eyeball on his bellybutton eventually opens up (shoot it when it does).

- **"Princess"**. On the What Lies Below level, this is the "Princess" that Harvey has been on about. She's actually the same "Creature" as before, only a little tougher and this time you have to deal with other bad guys and you need to keep your partner Jo Beth alive. You should use the harpoon gun for this fight. Wait for Princess to open "her" maw and let loose the harpoon to blow up the gas canister in its mouth.

Image courtesy of GameSpy.com.

Don't move; this is only going to hurt a smidgeon.

- **Goliath**. Located on the Something to Crow About level, the Goliath Battle-Mech is big, but not all that tough if. Get close and plant grenades on him. Use everything you've got, and then go get more over on the ramp. If you're really good you can use autofire on him and just strafe him to death.

- **Cyborg Creature**. Also on the Something to Crow About level, this is a tough fight. You should try to use the column as cover, if he doesn't grenade them. You need to blow up all parts of the creature, including the main turret, side turrets, and side grenade launchers. Use the Mini-gun or some grenades to take out the firearms and go for the main turret first because it's the main damage dealer.

- **Crow Creature**. This is it; the final fight. It's actually not all that hard. Use any rapid-fire weapon you want to blow off his legs, and then use a grenade launcher on his exposed backside. Rinse and repeat until he falls. (Note: You can shoot off his hands, but they just regenerate. Don't waste your time or ammo.)

DID YOU KNOW

Nottingham, England–based developer Free Radical was founded by many former Rare employees, many of whom worked on the classic console action game GoldenEye 007.

Devil May Cry 3: Dante's Awakening
Difficult Is an Understatement

DOSSIER

Genre: Sadistically Hard Devil Hunt **Publisher:** Capcom **Developer:** Capcom **Platform:** PS2 **Metacritic Metascore:** 84

The graphics and animations are top notch in this third installment.

Sometimes I don't always agree with the general critic's consensus. Such is the case with Devil May Cry 3: Dante's Awakening. It seems necessary to mention here because many fans and critics regard it as a fantastic game. Personally, I wanted to slice the DVD into bits with a wild stab of my Ginsu knife and bury the remains out in the woods...right next to my copy of Dukes of Hazzard: Racing for Home.

Devil May Cry 3 takes place before you, as the playable character Dante, become aware of his demonic heritage and before the formation of the Devil May Cry devil hunting agency. (Dante is the son of a human mother and a devil prince father named Sparda.) In addition to you, as the hero, the story revolves around Dante's estranged twin brother, Vergil.

A Little DMC History

The original Devil May Cry is considered to be one of the most influential fighting games of all time. It's not a fighting game in the way that Soul Calibur is a fighting game; rather it's a third-person action/adventure in which you do a whole lot of fighting. The original pretty much invented the highly stylized, flashy combat that we see in many action/adventures today. It really was a landmark title back in 2001.

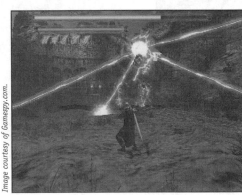

The original Devil May Cry was a landmark action adventure game with great graphics, sound, and a wicked devil-killing hero.

In 2003, Capcom released a sequel, Devil May Cry 2, which stunned the gaming world because it was really, really, bad. Okay, there are fans who think such statements are a bit harsh, but let's be honest. The game was nowhere near as entertaining as the original.

Finally, in March 2005, Capcom went the prequel route in delivering Dante's Awakening in an attempt to bring the game back to its roots.

Where DMC3 Falls Short

Devil May Cry 3 is one of the most beautiful games ever released on the PS2. Packed with oodles of wicked weapons, it is quite possibly the most difficult fighting game I have ever played. Seriously, if you're the kind of gamer who does not like to be frustrated when playing a game, do not, and I repeat, *do not* buy Devil May Cry 3—rent it first to see whether you can handle it and then thank me for saving you $50. Much of the frustration comes from the fact that the combat system is both tricky and yet highly unforgiving.

If, on the other hand, you like a challenge and feel you're up to the task of leading Dante through his rough and tumble journey, by all means have at it. I have never loved and hated a game as much as I did this one. It's one of those games with long breaks between save game points, which tends to want to make me pistol-whip the designers so that they know how it feels.

If you're standing in a game shop, staring at a copy of God of War and Devil May Cry 3, both action/adventure fighting games on the PS2, and you pick up the latter, well, you have been warned.

You can deal out damage with ranged weapons as well.

LEGO Star Wars
Even Jar-Jar Is Cool in Block Form

Image courtesy of Gamespy.com.

DOSSIER

Genre: Parent/Child Bonding with The Force **Publisher:** Eidos/Giant Interactive
Developer: Traveller's Tales **Platform:** PC, Xbox, PS2, GBA **Metacritic Metascore:** 77

Although games like Grand Theft Auto are not ideal for co-op missions with your six-year-old, LEGO Star Wars is the ultimate parent/child gaming experience.

My daughter is four years old, and it should come as no surprise that she likes to play games; after all, dear old dad makes a living playing and writing about these little technological wonders, so it's only natural that she be interested in them, too. I don't just mean stuff like Pooh Bear's Grand Adventure. She absolutely loves to zip through New York in Spider-Man 2, and she even "designed" my hero in City of Heroes (a 7-foot Amazon named Frostmane who looks like Dr. Doom; don't tell Marvel). Unfortunately, it's hard to find games that we can play together and that we can both enjoy at the same time. Enter LEGO Star Wars.

Darth Maul! Isn't he just adorable?

THEY SAID IT

> "We set out from the start to create a game that anyone could play and enjoy. Obviously, that meant that we wanted to have fun with it ourselves but we did also want to make something that we could take home with us, and play with our children; so, yes, the idea of being 'kid friendly' was essential to what we were trying to do." —**Jonathon Smith of Giant Interactive in an interview with *Computer Games* magazine**

Why LEGO and Star Wars Works

LEGO Star Wars was designed with co-operative play in mind, as long as you have multiple controllers. Sure, you can play it solo, but it's much, much better when playing with a friend. Simply press the Start button and the second controller is activated—off you go.

The game starts with *Episode I: The Phantom Menace* and ends with *Episode III: Revenge of the Sith*. The game plays out most of the major scenes from each of the new films. (Let's hope for a sequel based on the classic trilogy!) All the characters are there in cute LEGO format, from Obi-Wan and Yoda to the twin-bladed Darth Maul, and each has unique special powers and are wonderfully animated.

There's no blood (after all, we're talking LEGOs here), it's not terribly difficult, and you never really die when you lose all of your health; instead, you just lose most of your earned token money, making it ideal for a younger gamer. You get to buy special power-ups, unlock special characters (around 50 in all), and relive the best scenes from the movies without the complexity of some of today's more adult-oriented software.

Yep, you can even block blaster fire.

Image courtesy of Gamespy.com.

A quick look at the Metacritic score shows that LEGO Star Wars got some mixed reviews on its release and that's fair. The camera angles can be very frustrating at times, and there are some pretty tough jumping puzzles later in the game (you'll want to help out your youngster with some of these, unless they're especially gifted with a gamepad) and the pod race in Episode I is as excruciating as sitting through the film version. In addition, you need to understand that this is a platform/action game at heart; so, if you despise those kinds of games, the fact that this is *Star Wars* won't matter.

Despite the complaints, parents are always on the lookout for video games to play with their kids, and this is the ideal game to introduce a child to the wonderful world of video games. The best part: You'll have just as much fun.

ON THE WEB

LEGO Star Wars Homepage (www.lego.com/starwars). The game's homepage has a lot of info on the game as well as some great desktop wallpaper. The LEGO X-Wing wallpaper is particularly great.

From Bricks to Bothans (www.fbtb.net). A great website for LEGO Star Wars; not the game, but the actual building blocks.

DID YOU KNOW

Aspyr released a Mac port of LEGO Star Wars in August of 2005. You can buy it at Amazon.com.

The Matrix Online
Too Little, Too Late?

Image courtesy of Gamespy.com

In The Matrix Online, everyone looks cool.

DOSSIER

Genre: It's Not *That* Bad Matrix MMOG **Publisher:** Sega **Developer:** Monolith
Platform: PC **Metacritic Metascore:** 69

I always thought that The Matrix Online, solely from a marketing perspective, was a day late and a dollar short. The reason is because it was released in March 2005, well after the new films were released. The second and third Matrix films were, for a lot of people, letdowns of Jar-Jar Binks–ian proportions, so it took some of the edge off the hype for the Matrix games. Marketing is all about timing, particularly with a licensed product and by the time The Matrix Online shipped, public interest had faded.

It doesn't help that the genre is simply bloated to the point of absurdity right now (with many superior titles). Regardless, if you are a big-time fan of the Matrix, you should note that I think the 69 Metascore is way too low (and why I mention it here at all). The game has improved a lot since its release as patches and upgrades have improved the experience considerably, but I think you still need to be a Matrix-head to get the most out of it, and it's a fair question to ask: How many of them are left?

THEY SAID IT

> "One of the main goals of MxO (Matrix Online) is allowing players an opportunity to participate in the ongoing saga of the Matrix. The creators of the movies, the Wachowski Brothers, have created a story that will unfold in periodic episodes. It is our intent to allow players a chance to interact in a changing world where they can help shape the outcome. To this end, individual players must choose who they wish to support." —
> **Toby Ragaini, Lead Designer of The Matrix Online in an interview with GameFusion.com**

Matrix Online Q&A

Here's a quick (admittedly tongue-in-cheek) FAQ to help get you acquainted with the world of The Matrix Online before diving in.

Q: I want to be Neo! Can I be Neo?

Q: I want to fly like Neo.

Q: I want to be The One, like Neo.

Q: I want to drive a car.

Q: I want to be an Agent like Mr. Smith.

Q: I want to go to Zion and get funky like in the movie.

A: No, No, No,
"see p. 218" (don't make me smack you),
No, No, and No (thank God).

Q: Is there player versus player combat?

A: Sort of, but it is limited to dueling (both must agree to fight) and not outright stalking as in some other games. However, there is also something called *OvO combat*, which stands for organization versus organization. If you log in to a "hostile" server, when you reach level 16, you're officially open to attack by rival organizations.

Image courtesy of Gamespy.com.

Character creation is straightforward, but you can really get creative with your apparel.

Q: Is there a role-playing server like in World of Warcraft?

A: As of this writing, the only "unofficial" role-playing server is Linenoise. If you choose to play on that server, you are expected to play in a very Matrix-y sort of way and always try to stay in character. That means no shouting that you just got back from Ozzfest.

Q: Why should I bother with MxO? I'm not made of loot, ya know.

A: Two things: The combat is pretty darn cool and the world events help to continue the Matrix saga as characters from the movies, as well as new characters, continue the story, with you potentially playing a role.

DID YOU KNOW

Although published by Sega, Warner Brothers and Sony Online Entertainment (SOE) picked up the rights from Monolith to operate The Matrix Online.

Stealth Action Games
The Best Sneaker Series in the Biz

Image courtesy of Gamespy.com.

COOP MODE

Splinter Cell is arguably the cream of the stealth game crop.

3D shooters have come a long way since the days of Wolfenstein 3D and DOOM. Although there are still great games out there—such as Painkiller and Serious Sam—that ask you to simply grab your shotgun and shoot everything that moves in order to survive, there are other games that demand a bit more discretion. Here's a look at some of the most popular games in this competitive genre.

Metal Gear Solid

A landmark game for the original PlayStation console, Konami's Metal Gear Solid (MGS) was one of the games that showcased how console games could be deep and engaging.

The series started way back in 1987 with the release of Metal Gear for MS-DOS and the NES. It wasn't until the PS1 version of Metal Gear Solid that it really took off to become the behemoth that it is today. The name *Metal Gear* comes from the super weapon in the original game; a walking tank that carries nukes. The *Solid* suffix is in reference to the series' hero, Solid Snake, and the fact that the world is in *solid* 3D.

Fans can finally rejoice now that we know that Metal Gear Solid 4 is slated for a 2007 release date. Even though few concrete details are available, seriously, playing an MGS game on a next-generation console? Sign me up.

Splinter Cell

The Splinter Cell games, published by Ubisoft, are part of the amazing Tom Clancy phenomena. It seems as if whenever you slap Clancy's name on a novel or a video game, stores can't keep them in stock. Of course, Clancy deserves a lot of the accolades because his books are riveting suspense thrillers and the video games based on his works are of equally high quality.

There have been three games in the series: Splinter Cell, Splinter Cell: Pandora Tomorrow, and Splinter Cell: Chaos Theory. All the games place you in the role of Sam Fisher, a member of the black-ops NSA organization known as *Third Echelon*.

The term *Splinter Cell* is a reference to a member of Third Echelon who has the use of Fifth Freedom, which is kind of like James Bond's license to kill. Fisher is the first Splinter Cell, meaning he has free reign to do whatever it takes to get the job done.

The Splinter Cell games are a blast to play solo, but they have been a huge success on Xbox Live.

Thief

In 1998, while PlayStation gamers sank their teeth into Medal Gear Solid, PC gamers were introduced to Garrett, the stealthy main character of the classic Thief series from Eidos and Looking Glass Studios.

Thief: The Dark Project, Thief II: The Metal Age, and the 2004 Ion Storm release Thief: Deadly Shadows were all wonderfully made stealth games. Thief has also benefited from its PC roots by allowing gamers to modify the game and release additional missions and other user-made content.

Image courtesy of Gamespy.com.

Thief is a lesson in how not to be seen.

It was a revolutionary game in that it was a first-person shooter, but the idea was to not be seen and to avoid fighting if at all possible. Garrett was not a warrior and he couldn't take heavy punishment as your character can in a typical shooter.

DID YOU KNOW

Paramount Pictures is working on a Splinter Cell movie. Peter Berg (*Friday Night Lights*) will handle the directing duties.

Silent Hunter III
Return of a Classic

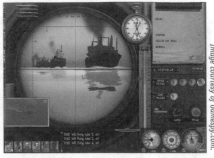

Image courtesy of Gamespy.com.

These convoys are in serious trouble.

DOSSIER

Genre: Hardcore Sub Sim **Publisher:** Ubisoft **Developer:** Ubisoft **Platform:** PC
Metacritic Metascore: 90

Silent Hunter III is the perfect submarine simulation. It's intricately detailed, accurate, and yet very accessible. It's a game for grognards, but it's still something that the masses can enjoy, which is a real trick to pull off.

Set during World War II, you play the role of a German U-boat commander. Usually sub sims are fairly sterile, but there's a definite human element to this game; it's not just a number crunch of data and dials. You're surrounded by real crew members, and not just voices as in most other sub games. They need rest and they need to be at the right place at the right time. Silent Hunter III allows you to feel like you're actually inside a cramped U-boat and not on the submarine version of the Flying Dutchman.

The star of the show is the new dynamic campaign. Your career, if you survive, lasts the entire war and you'll see the waters of the Atlantic change with the times as well. New tech is introduced, and your crew will gain vital experience to deal with the Allied sub killers. The mission layout is also totally open ended; you're given a patrol grid and basic objectives, but who you attack and when is left up to you. As a result, the game's replay value is through the roof.

THEY SAID IT

"Taking damage, having casualties, being under prolonged depth charge attack, reaching the oxygen limit are considered "bad performance" from the player. In this case, expect to see the efficiency of the crew dropping dramatically—you'll need more people to do the same job. You can even reach a moment when everyone is too exhausted to perform anything but minimal U-boat sailing."—**SH3 team development interview with SimHQ.com**

Silent Hunter (1996)

In the late '80s and through the 1990s, SSI was known for its hardline strategy games (as well as being the licensed publisher of D&D games). In 1996, SSI published the Aeon Electronic Entertainment–developed title, Silent Hunter. In the original, you played an U.S. Navy sub commander in the Pacific, battling it out against the Japanese Navy. Even back in '96, the idea of an open-ended mission structure was extremely appealing. You simply went into shipping lanes and tried to take out enemy vessels.

Silent Hunter II (2001)

Five years after the original, Silent Hunter II set sail from Ubisoft. Problems plagued the game's development, so much so that original developer Aeon Electronic Entertainment left the project late in the process and it was finished by a company called Ultimation.

DID YOU KNOW

Image courtesy of Gamespy.com.

For such a hardcore wargame, the graphics are certainly good enough.

The idea is a lot like that of Silent Hunter III: You play a German U-boat commander during World War II. The problem was that the AI was flat-out busted and the single-player campaign was linear and nothing at all like the original's open-ended structure. Toss in unreliable multiplayer gameplay and you had a game that was a huge disappointment for sub fans.

Usually when a game that appeals to a very distinct group of gamers fails as bad as this one the series dies off quickly. Thankfully, Ubisoft stepped back up to the plate and snagged a new internal development team to create Silent Hunter III— the game Silent Hunter II should have been, but with better graphics.

BOOKMARK SUBSIM.COM

The documentation with SH3 is terrible. A great place to talk shop with fellow sub sim fans is SubSim.com. Newbies are welcome.

Grognard is a term that defines a crusty old wargamer who values realism and authenticity over every other game design feature. They tend to be exceptionally difficult to please.

PSP Game Explosion!
Top Shelf PSP Launch Titles

Ridge Racer might still be the best PSP game around, nearly a year after its release.

March marked the U.S. release of the slick Sony PlayStation Portable, AKA the PSP. Any new gaming platform comes with the usual flood of game releases. The problem with the PSP, at least initially, was that there weren't all that many games that were made specifically for it—instead we got a lot of games that were poorly executed PS2 ports.

Regardless, there were some very good launch titles for the PSP to coincide with its release. Here's some that should all be in your PSP library.

Lumines. One of the most popular and critically acclaimed PSP titles, Ubisoft's Lumines (pronounced "luminous") is really the ideal PSP puzzle game. Developed by Q Entertainment, it's yet another grid-based block falling game, but the presentation and execution are nearly flawless. In fact the entire hook in Lumines is the music, visuals, and the way in which they fit snuggly into the gameplay. The goal is to make the falling blocks form a 2×2 square of the same color. If they pile up too high, you lose.

Image courtesy of Gamespy.com.

Lumines in all its colorful glory.

Ridge Racer. Namco's Ridge Racer has been around since 1993. The new edition is available on multiple handheld platforms; however, it's the PSP version that stands out. (Avoid the Nintendo DS version like the plague.) Ridge Racer has arguably the best graphics of any PSP game, so this is the PSP game to get to impress your friends.

The meat of the game is the World Tour Mode in which you enter a series of races using progressively better cars that you unlock along the way. The courses are taken from previous Ridge Racer games, which is something fans of the series are sure to appreciate.

WipEout Pure. Another old racing series, Sony's WipEout has been around since 1995. It's also another gorgeous PSP game but the frame rate suffers a bit; it's not nearly as butter smooth as Ridge Racer. It does pack a very slick Wi-Fi multiplayer mode and it's also the first PSP game to support downloadable content such as tracks, vehicles, and artwork at no charge.

Tony Hawk's Underground 2 Remix. This is basically the same as the other main console versions Activision has released over the years. The only real difference is the addition of four exclusive levels: Kyoto, Las Vegas, Atlanta, and Santa Cruz, each of which has been worked into the game's story mode. Still, it's a slick game with great controls and wild tricks.

Twisted Metal: Head-On. Yet another PSP game from Sony that's based on an old series, Head-On is really a sequel to Twisted Metal 2. This is also the first game in the TM series to ship with full multiplayer support. Basically this is the same gameplay that made the original a classic car combat game. It's one of the few PSP launch games to support both ad hoc Wi-Fi (direct connect) and infrastructure Wi-Fi (wireless).

DID YOU KNOW

Developer Q Entertainment is building quite a rep as a great puzzle developer with both Lumines and Meteos to its credit. The company is currently working on an as of yet unannounced game for the Xbox 360.

Donkey Kong: Jungle Beat
Monkeys and Drums—For Joy, For Joy

This is no dancing game.

DOSSIER

Genre: Expensive Monkey Bongo Game **Publisher:** Nintendo **Developer:** Nintendo
Platform: GameCube **Metacritic Metascore:** 81

It's time for me to 'fess up. This is one of those critically acclaimed games that I just don't get. I'm not saying Jungle Beat is a bad game or a waste of time, but it's going to appeal to a specific kind of gamer and I am not him.

Basically, Donkey Kong: Jungle Beat is a 2D platformer in which you control Kong through a slew of areas in a mad search for bananas. Each area has its own big boss encounter at the end.

That said, the game is really all about rhythm and timing and using the DK Bongos. Whacking the right drum makes Kong run to the right; hit it faster and Kong behaves accordingly. If you hit both drums simultaneously, Kong jumps. Finally, you can "clap" (smack the side of the drum), which is really a catch-all action that makes Kong grab things, swing on vines, and so on.

THEY SAID IT

> "I'd been hearing from many people that recently control [in games] is difficult, and that's when I first had the desire to make a game that was simple and easy to understand. Until now, I've only made games that make use of a standard controller, so I wanted to at last make something that had a different form of input. It was then that I was introduced to the Donkey Konga conga controller." —**Jungle Beat Director Yoshiaki Koizumi in an interview with Famitsu magazine**

The boss battles are by far the best part of the game.

Bongo!

One of the things I couldn't get past with Jungle Beat was using the DK Bongos. First off, they're expensive! If you buy them separately you're looking at spending around $35. For your money, you can use them with games like Jungle Beat, Donkey Konga, Donkey Konga 2, and Donkey Konga 3. (The latter being dance games.) If you're really inventive (and totally insane), you can even play action and fighting games with them. Have you ever seen anyone play Soul Calibur with DK Bongos? Oh, it's a real treat.

Second, it's just kind of goofy. I know a lot of people love their dance pads, Dreamcast maracas, and so forth, but I'm trying to hang on to my last shred of cool and hipness and slapping the side of $35 plastic bongos is just too much for me. It is one thing to have a lot of friends over to play Dance Dance Revolution, but Jungle Beat is a 2D platformer designed to be played solo, for crying out loud!

This is really a lose/lose situation, regardless of age. If you're 12 and your dad catches you playing Jungle Beat, whacking on fake bongos that he and mom most likely paid for, it can be very depressing for a parent. If you're in college, the dancepad party games are actually fantastic ice breakers. Jungle Beat, on the other hand, will usually make people vacate the room and leave you to your toys. Then there's me. I am a 33-year-old who writes about games for a living. I am not hitting plastic bongos unless I get paid.

DID YOU KNOW

Donkey Kong Jungle Beat is the first game to get an ESRB rating of E10+. Yep, it's a trailblazer alright.

MLB 2006 Versus MLB 2K5
Baseball's Best of the Rest

Image courtesy of Gamespy.com.

DOSSIER

Genre: Second-Tier Console Baseball **Publisher:** Sony/2K Games **Developer:** 989 Sports/Kush Games **Platform:** PS2/PS2, Xbox **Metacritic Metascore:** 81/81

The reason I'm lumping these games together is because you should get a really good look at them. They are most likely the only Major League Baseball–licensed games to be available for the 2006 season unless Nintendo actually decides to release its own game this decade or Microsoft decides to dust off the High Heat Baseball franchise it purchased on the cheap and then left to feste. (I'm planning to retrieve this code *Mission: Impossible* style as soon as possible.) MVP Baseball from EA Sports was *clearly* the best baseball game of 2005, and even though it will have a 2006 college game on the horizon, EA is on the outside in terms of Major League Baseball.

Johnny Damon, in MLB 2006, looking like his mountain-man self.

THEY SAID IT

"We actually have an environment team of artists and we send them out to each stadium. They have all access to a place like Comerica, they take photos, go to a night game in order to create a night version of the stadium… It usually takes anywhere from two-to-four weeks to create each stadium's geometry, then they texture it as well." —**MLB 2006 Senior Producer Chris Cutliff in an interview with IGN.com**

MLB 2006—A Step Closer

When I of think 989 Sports, I usually don't think "superb sports simulations." Nothing against the company or Sony for that matter, but the company's track record is that of really bad sports games. That can no longer be said of its baseball franchise, though. MLB 2006 was close—agonizingly close to being an excellent baseball game. It's not as good as MVP 2005, but this is a game worth paying attention to and I can't wait to see what MLB 2007 looks like. That said, there are vital issues that simply must be fixed. MLB 2006's gratuitous anomalies include

- You can force out runners at third base on throws from left field.

- The CPU AI refuses to try a sacrifice bunt.

- The AI lets a pitcher bat in the bottom of the seventh inning and then pulls him at the start of the eighth.

- Too many balls that reach the wall end up as singles.

- As in most baseball games, drawing and issuing a walk is a rare thing. (A major peeve of mine.)

Image courtesy of Gamespy.com.

The pitcher/batter interface in MLB 2K5 was not the problem. It was the bugs.

Major League Baseball 2K5— Call the Orkin Man

Wildly favorable reviews made MLB 2K5 the most overrated sports game of 2005. The game is a bug-riddled mess. Wild pitches and passed balls cause complete havoc, statistical bugs award left-fielders wins rather than pitchers, there are more line drive outs than grounders, and the fielding camera is the worst in the business and cannot be changed. There are bugs in the player creation system, bugs during night games, play-by-play sound bugs, broken pitcher fatigue, and on and on.

I loved the 2K4 version of this series, but anyone who thinks that 2K5 was anything but a major step backward due to the incompleteness of the game is just not paying attention.

THEY SAID IT

"As far as baserunning goes, one of the biggest things you'll see this year is picture-in-picture baserunning. We're all familiar with other sports games where you have a little diamond in the corner of the screen that shows you where your runners are by dots. I've always felt that that's been confusing." —**Chien Yu, Product Manager of MLB 2K5 in an interview with GameZone.com**

DID YOU KNOW

The PSP version of MLB 2006 is one of the best early PSP releases around. It's definitely worth checking out.

Ultra-Violent Games
The Ten Bloodiest Games Ever

Carmageddon was ridiculously violent to the point that it makes Die Hard look like a Disney movie.

Let's get one thing straight: I'm not going to get on a soapbox about violent video games or use this as a pulpit to rage against the machine about censorship. But whenever the news cites DOOM as a violent game, I always think, "DOOM? Guys, have you *seen* Carmageddon?" So seeing as how the mainstream media only wants to talk about games when a tragedy happens, I figured I'd make a quick list of some of the most violent, over-the-top video games ever made, just so the six o'clock news can get their facts straight.

Of course, there are a lot of games that could have made the list, so feel free to make your own choices. In this business, there's enough blood to go around.

One last thing before we begin: Not all of these games are *good games*. Some of them are terrible games that just happen to be violent.

Image courtesy of Gamespy.com.

Leaving brains on the wall in Soldier of Fortune II. Ahh, good times.

Blood (1997–1999). A series of first-person shooters that used the old Build engine (Duke Nukem 3D, Shadow Warrior); they weren't particularly pretty, but boy were they bloody. Any game where you see people dangling and twitching from meat hooks deserves a Violent Video Game Stamp of Approval.

Carmageddon (1997). I never understood why Carmageddon didn't catch more public flak than it did. A game where you earn points by running over and *graphically killing* pedestrians? This game was insane, and I have to admit, a lot of fun.

Grand Theft Auto (1997–2005). Wow, 1997 was a pretty violent year, eh? Anyway, what can I say that hasn't already been said about this series? It's the current poster child for all that is wrong in American society. It's also a kick-ass game.

God of War (2005). With buckets of blood and gore, God of War makes this list because it's such a visceral game. Sure, you're killing mythological creatures, but you're doing it in such a vicious manner that it makes some cringe just to watch.

Kingpin: Life of Crime (1999). Not necessarily any more violent than your run-of-the mill first-person shooter, but I include it here because it was one of the first games to have audio with language right out of a Martin Scorsese movie. "Hey, did you hear that? He said $#@!"

Postal (1997; 2003). This series was all hype built on the back of a couple horrid games. The Postal series garnered a lot of media attention because it was violent just for the sake of being violent. When all you are selling is the fact that you can shoot innocent people, it's not enough to warrant a purchase.

Mortal Kombat (1993–2004). One of the early targets for groups that wanted to ban video games, the classic fighting series just keeps chugging along. Can you say, Fatality!

Resident Evil (1996–2005). I hate to add a game like this because after all, you're killing the zombies! I think it's much more "violent" when you are shooting real people (unless they are Nazis; they don't count). Still, any game that allows zombies to cannibalize you deserves a golf clap.

Soldier of Fortune (2000–2003). Not only do you get to shoot humans, but you get to target specific body parts! Head shot! These were actually really good games that just happened to be extremely violent.

State of Emergency (2002). Another member of the hype machine, it tried to be Grand Theft Auto but instead it was just an over the top violent game that was pretty lousy.

Unreal Tournament 2004
It's All About the Mods

Deathball is just an amazingly fun mod.

DOSSIER

Genre: Mod Lover's Dream Shooter **Publisher:** Atari **Developer:** Epic Games/Digital Extremes **Platform:** PC **Metacritic Metascore:** 93

Unreal Tournament, Epic and Digital Extreme's stellar multiplayer-themed first-person shooter, is arguably the game with the most user-made content, ever. The highly flexible engine simply screams, "Use me baby!" Gamers have done just that, creating wildly inventive and imaginative mods that play nothing like the original game. If you have UT2004 sitting on the shelf, make sure to give these mods a spin; they breathe new life into what is already a fantastic 3D shooter. The mod community behind UT2004 is simply amazing. And although the samples listed here don't even begin to do justice to what is out there, they are a good place to start.

THEY SAID IT

"It's unfortunate that some of these great mods aren't seeing more players. I think part of the problem is that there are so many online multiplayer FPS games out there that it is much harder to gain a critical mass of players for a mod. Today, a new mod typically competes against many other mods and full retail games if it chooses a conventional genre." —**Steve Polge of Epic Games in an interview with Beyondunreal.com**

An airship from the very cool AirBuccanners mod.

MOD SITES GALORE!

ModNMod (www.modnmod.com) and **PlanetUnreal** (www.planetunreal.com) is a great mod site, and it's not just Unreal related.

BeyondUnreal (www.beyondunreal.com) has constant Unreal news updates and loads of downloads.

The Mods

- **AirBuccaneers** (ludocraft.oulu.fi/airbuccaneers). This nifty mod adds new maps and a new game type with air balloons, airships, and other high flying content.
- **Alien Swarm** (www.blackcatgames.com/swarm). The talented folks at Blackcat Games have used the UT2004 mod tools to create a tactical turn-based strategy game!
- **Archasis** (www.planetunreal.com/archasis). A Medieval-themed mod with multiple character classes, several new modes of play, and lots of cool Dark Ages weaponry. There's even an experience point/level up system just like a traditional role-playing game.
- **Carball** (www.carball.net). Think *Rollerball* with cars using the Unreal 2 engine and you get the idea. Carball is hilariously fun.
- **Deathball** (www.deathball.net). A personal favorite, this total conversion of UT2004 combines football, rugby, and a lot of violence. There are even Deathball leagues out there that you can join.

- **Red Orchestra** (www.redorchestra.clanservers.com). This mod rips out the futuristic setting of UT2004 and replaces it with the gritty war torn Eastern Front of World War II. Add tons of authentic weaponry from the period (with tanks!), and amazingly accurate WWII landscapes and you have one of the best mods around.
- **SAS Into the Lion's Den** (www.sas.jolt.co.uk). This is a slick counter terrorism mod involving the three main SAS forces around the world: British, Australian, and New Zealand SAS groups.
- **Troopers** (www.ut2004troopers.com). A UT2004 Star Wars mod! Fight battles on Hoth, the Death Star, Endor, Mos Eisley, Cloud City, and so on. And you get to shoot stormtroopers, which just never gets old.
- **Unwheel** (unwheel.beyondunreal.com). This is a racing mod that allows you to drive pretty much every four-wheel vehicle imaginable, even monster trucks.

DID YOU KNOW

The Unreal 2 engine is extremely popular with other developers. Games like Splinter Cell, Tribes: Vengeance, and Brothers in Arms Road to Hill 30 all use Epic's wonderful game engine.

Whiplash
Closet Classic (1996)

Image courtesy of Gamespy.com.

The Merkur GT was a speedball.

DOSSIER

Genre: Pure Arcade Racing Goodness **Publisher:** Interplay **Developer:** Gremlin
Platform: PC

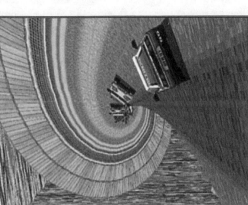

The tracks in Whiplash were flat-out awesome.

Image courtesy of Gamespy.com.

Released in 1996 by publisher Interplay and developer Gremlin Interactive, Whiplash (also known as Fatal Racing in Europe) is one of the best arcade racing games ever made. It wasn't a simulation by any means, but rather an arcade stunt racing game with sim-like elements. You didn't need to be a gear head to enjoy Whiplash; you just needed to like fast cars racing over highly imaginative track designs.

The game sported eight unique cars, each of which had different ratings for speed, braking, handling, and damage (as in how much it could take). The cars added a lot of strategy because you needed to determine whether you wanted a lightning fast car that could handle well but was highly prone to taking damage, or a slower more durable car that was slower on straightaways but maybe handled a bit better on turns. In fact, there were seven car traits in all, which really made the cars stand out from one another.

The cars were only half the fun, though. Whiplash came with 16 over-the-top tracks that really stole the show. Some tracks were fairly basic with only a few sharp turns and maybe a few

jumps. After you played more of the game and unlocked everything, you could race over tracks with full loops, corkscrews, and even extremely long jumps that would make or break a race. The jumps were particularly nasty because if you didn't hit them at the right speed you were toast. Still, this was more about fun racing than sim racing, so it was no big deal that your car could land on its hood and you'd still be able to get back in the race (unless you blew up). Granted, as your car took damage it would lose speed, but pit stop locations on the track could be used to fix your car (costing you precious time).

Although the single player game was a lot of fun, Whiplash was at its best as a multiplayer game, something that was tough to take advantage of in 1996 when multiplayer gaming was in its infancy. I was able to take advantage of the game's awesome multiplayer functionality more than others because at the time I was working in a PC lab at The Ohio State University. At the time, a roomful of blazing fast PCs in a college computer lab was an open invitation for multiplayer gaming (especially with someone like me in charge of the thing). After the lab closed for the day, my friends would show up to play games and Whiplash was a nightly ritual.

The game supported a whopping 16 players and you could even break people into teams of two. You could send messages to teammates via hotkeys and race in a championship mode to see who the better team was over the course of 16 races, using all of the tracks. At the time, it was multiplayer racing at its best. Whiplash is a game that really doesn't get its due as one of the best arcade racers ever mainly because it was a resource hog for its day, which is a fair criticism. If you had the machine to run it, though, it provided hours upon hours of high intensity racing entertainment.

Metacritic's Worst Xbox Games
Ten Titles That Embarrass the Box

Apollo and friends during happier times.

I love my Xbox, I really do, and when developers poison its insides by forcing it to run horribly bad pieces of software, it makes me sad. The Xbox deserves better, no?

From superheroes to games for kids, no publisher is safe from shoving out the door a game that is beyond abysmal, as this list proves.

Batman: Dark Tomorrow might just be the worst superhero game ever, although Aquaman puts up a good fight for that spot, too.

10. Trigger Man (Score: 31). Released in 2004 by Crave Entertainment, Trigger Man is a third-person shooter with you playing a guy in the mob, a "trigger man." The thing is, the game wasn't really broken or terribly buggy—it was just shockingly bad.

9. Robocop (Score: 30). The original *Robocop* is a classic action movie. If you haven't seen the film, go to your local movie rental shop and get a copy. Just avoid this first-person shooter from Titus like you would a swarm of angry bees.

8. Sneakers (Score: 29). No, this wasn't a game based on the Robert Redford movie (another flick you should rent) but rather an action/adventure game from Microsoft about a mouse named Apollo. Here's the problem: Not only was it boring enough to make you want to play Old Maid by yourself, but the controls were too frustrating for kids —its target audience—to use.

7. Dragon's Lair 3 (Score: 26). Okay, how weird is this? Dragon's Lair 3 is, according to Metacritic, the seventh-worst PC game of all time, too (see Page 17, Chapter 2). I guess bad is bad, regardless of the platform.

6. Aquaman: Battle for Atlantis (Score: 26). TDK Mediactive forced this clunker on gamers back in 2003, and I hear Aquaman himself thought it reeked worse than a dead fish. It was dated, stale, repetitive, and all together a waste of money despite the fact that TDK dropped the price to basement levels soon after its release.

5. Stake: Fortune Fighters (Score: 26). This is a fighting game from Metro 3D Inc. You tell me: How would you describe a fighting game if it had bad sound, lackluster graphics, and innumerable camera problems? If you answered, "A lot like Stake: Fortune Fighters," give yourself 10 points.

4. Batman: Dark Tomorrow (Score: 25). Kemco's third-person action/adventure with the Dark Knight was a complete and utter disaster. There literally was nothing redeemable about this game, and even its 25 Metacritic rating is too high. Seriously, it was that bad.

3. Pulse Racer (Score: 24). It's tough to completely mess up an arcade racer. I mean really—just make it pretty and offer responsive controls and you're guaranteed that at least someone will like it. Pulse Racer from Jaleco Entertainment is one of the most boring and frustrating racers around.

2. Drake (Score: 22). Majesco's 2003 money waster was supposed to be a supernatural third-person action/adventure. It ended up being one of the worst games to ever shame the Xbox console thanks to shoddy graphics, a ridiculous aiming model (good luck hitting *anything*), and gameplay that was as entertaining as watching snails race.

1. Nickelodeon Party Blast (Score: 18). I love Nickelodeon. I have watched more Nick Jr. over the past few years than I ever imagined possible thanks to my daughter. And the idea of taking your favorite Nicktoons character in a party game atmosphere sounds like a great game for kids. But it's like IGN said in its 2002 review on this game, "Kids may never want to play games again after playing this, and I'd hate to do that to anyone."

DID YOU KNOW

The waiting truly is the hardest part. The Xbox launched at a retail price of $299 in November of 2001. By March 2004, it sold brand new for $149.

X-COM: UFO Defense
Closet Classic (1994)

Image courtesy of Gamespy.com.

DOSSIER

Genre: Father of Turn-Based Tactics **Publisher:** MicroProse **Developer:** MicroProse/Mythos **Platform:** PC

X-COM: UFO Defense (also known as *UFO: Enemy Unknown* in Europe) is one of the finest strategy games ever designed. Released by MicroProse in 1994 during that company's strategy heyday, it's easily on par with classics such as Master of Orion and Civilization.

I think Otto is in serious trouble here.

X-COM had everything: great graphics for its day, eerie sound, hordes of personality and charm, tactical depth, and lots and lots of options. Industry legend Sid Meier once said, and I'm paraphrasing here, that a great game is all about forcing players to make choices. X-COM was loaded with choices.

"Cool game, but it's no X-COM," was the common lament of strategy gamers in the late 1990s.

Alert! These Aliens Are Ticked Off!

The story behind the action was pretty straightforward, pulp fiction UFO stuff. In 1998, UFOs started appearing in the skies across the globe. Reports of not only sightings and abductions became commonplace and the people were freaking out, demanding that the government take action. So, the most economically dominant countries met in secret to form a covert multinational combat task force to take the aliens head-on. The new organization was known as the Extraterrestrial Combat Unit or X-COM for short.

You were in charge of the X-COM task force from top to bottom. There was a lot more to think about than just sending out your troops to investigate an alien sighting. Nations would actually back out of the X-COM alliance if they felt the service wasn't up to snuff (thus reducing your funding). On top of pleasing countries across the globe, you had to construct buildings at the X-COM base, create new base sites, and hire scientists to study alien technology recovered from crash sites.

Administrative stuff aside, the meat of the game was still hunting down and taking out people-hating aliens of all shapes and sizes. Combat itself was turn-based, with each team member assigned time units that were expended through movement, crouching, firing, lobbing grenades, and so on. Pretty basic stuff, really, but what stood out was the alien weaponry and the fact that your team members were unique.

Each member of your X-COM squad had all sorts of traits that helped them to stand out from one another. I can even recall some of the names of my squad mates. Hersch was green and would freeze almost at the sight of an alien, whereas Sams was a grizzled veteran who could take anything the aliens

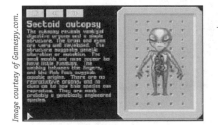

Image courtesy of Gamespy.com.

The alien autopsy...always a fun diversion.

dished out and returned fire with anything in the human arsenal. Consequently, it genuinely hurt your cause if one of your team members was too injured for duty, or worse, gunned down in their prime. For a game to have an effect like that, and that I can remember the names of team members a *decade* after the fact, is a testament to just how amazing and engrossing this game was.

After X-COM

X-COM was extremely popular and was one of the best-selling games of 1994–95 and with any popular game it brought on several sequels, none of which ever quite recaptured the essence of the original.

The series could still be revived though. Atari now owns the rights and with today's graphics and sound technology a 3D turn-based alien-hunting game could be a hit. How about something like the original X-COM using the Half-Life 2 or Unreal engines? Nah...that makes too much sense and would be way too much fun. Forget I brought it up.

X-COM FAN HEAVEN

Xcomufo (www.xcomufo.com) is a still active website dedicated to all things X-COM. It even has a pretty hopping fan forum.

DID YOU KNOW

Another fantastic alien-killing, squad-centered, turn-based game from the 1990s was Blue Byte's Incubation, which many consider the true spiritual successor to X-COM.

The V-Smile
Training the Gamers of Tomorrow

As a parent, I want to introduce my daughter to fun and educational games whenever I can. It's not as easy as it sounds. There are a lot of kids' games available for the PC, but they vary in quality and they still have to be fun for a youngster or boredom sets in.

The V-Smile. Note that it comes with only one controller.

Thankfully, there's the V-Smile from VTech. This wondrous console is designed specifically for kids from 3–7 years old. It hooks up to your TV just like a regular game console. It comes with one enlarged gamepad with a huge button so that little ones have no trouble manipulating it.

Before getting into the games themselves it's important to note that some of them, although they do help in learning numbers and shapes, also help teach gamepad skill. For a gaming parent, it's the best of both worlds.

Games for the V-Smile

By the end of 2005, there should be no fewer than 25 games for the system. I can attest to some of the games personally because my daughter plays the V-Smile at least three times a week and even at $20 a pop, they're well worth it.

The Lion King: Simba's Big Adventure. This game is a platform jumper that also helps kids learn how to count, differentiate shapes, and recognize colors. It even has some basic spelling tools. To play, you guide little Simba through the jungle in a multitude of different mini games.

Care Bears: A Lesson in Caring. This should be the first game your child plays as it's by far the easiest of the games for the 3–5 age groups. You get to control each of the Care Bears as they try to find out the definition of what caring means. It helps with spelling and letter recognition as well as identifying shapes.

Winnie the Pooh: The Honey Hunt. My daughter's favorite game, this colorful platform adventure teaches numbers and shapes, and has memory games and other goodies for those too young to read. If your child is a Pooh fan, he or she will absolutely love this.

Alphabet Park Adventure. This game is pretty tough for youngsters in the 3–5 age range. This is also the game that comes with the V-Smile system, so if you're going to buy the system, I advise picking up one of the previously mentioned games to go along with it.

Winnie the Pooh: The Honey Hunt is a fantastic game for preschoolers.

Games for Older Kids

When your child graduates from the preschool-level games, there are others available that are more advanced that focus on math and reading and problem solving. Children aged 4–6 can play games using Spider-Man, Little Red Riding Hood, and Ariel the Little Mermaid.

The beauty of the V-Smile is that kids love playing the games, but they really do get educational benefits out of it and not just better gamepad reflexes. All the games are nonviolent and kid friendly. For parents who have no idea what "real" games to get a young child, the V-Smile is a great alternative.

THE V-SMILE HOMEPAGE
Find out more about the V-Smile at www.vsmile.co.uk. If you're interested in purchasing one it can also help you locate a retailer.

DID YOU KNOW

Based in Hong Kong, VTech, the company that produces the V-Smile, was founded way back in 1976 and is one of the world's largest cordless telephone companies.

The Hotplate Gourmet
Hey, It's Food!...Sort Of

Who needs to cook when a few coins and the push of a button allows for one stop-snacking?

There are plenty of times when a vending machine might be your only choice for dinner. Maybe you're a college student stuck in your room on an all-nighter who gets the urge to eat after the takeout places are closed. Maybe you're a microserf chained to your cubicle on a big project. Or maybe you're just into the final rounds in your LAN party tournament and you can't get away to grab a bite. Regardless, there are plenty of times when you're going to be feeding money into a machine to feed yourself.

But why suffer? Why make do with a soda and a bag of pretzels when you could use a little creativity and actually create some (marginally) real food with just what's in the vending machine and a microwave—two features of any modern office, dorm lobby, or library (heck, you can make 'em for home LAN parties, too). All you need to eat well are these recipes and a few bucks in loose change. Bon appétit!

Mega Snack Mix 3000 Plus!

- 1 bag Cheetos
- 1 bag mini-pretzels
- 1 bag salted peanuts (without the shell)
- 1 bag Ritz Bitz
- 1 bag M&Ms (peanut or plain)

Directions: Pour into a bowl or bag. Mix well. Eat.

Microwave S'mores

- 1 package Moon Pies
- 1 Hershey bar
- 1 package large cookies or graham crackers

Directions: Cut the Moon Pie in half (through the marshmallow center), sandwich the Hershey bar between the two halves, mush together, and microwave until you see the marshmallow puff up.

SNACK FOOD COOKERY
If you're feeling really ambitious, head over to Planet Twinkie (www.twinkies.com) and check out the recipe section.

Old-Fashion Southern Pick-Me-Up

- 1 bag peanuts (salted, without shells)
- 1 can soda (preferably RC or Pepsi)

Directions: Pour peanuts in soda and drink the whole thing down, being sure to shake the can to get the peanuts to come along with the soda. Yeee-hawww!

DID YOU KNOW

No-Bake Chocolate Vending Machine Cookie Clusters

- 1 Hershey bar
- 1 package Reese Cups
- 1 bag mini-pretzel sticks
- 1 bag M&Ms (optional)

Directions: Break pretzel sticks in half. Put the chocolate and peanut butter cups in a coffee mug and microwave until melted. After everything's melted, dump in your pretzel pieces and mix with a spoon. Drop spoonfuls on a plate and put in the fridge until firm.

Emergency Nachos

- 1 package Doritos
- 4 packages cheese and crackers

Directions: Pile Doritos on a microwavable plate. Dig cheese out of package and place in blobs all over chip pile. Microwave until the cheese melts. If you like it spicy, try finding a left-over packet of hot sauce from Taco Bell.

Fancy Cheese Ball

- 4 packages cheese and crackers
- 1 bag nuts (pistachios work well)

Directions: Using the little red spreader that comes with the cheese and crackers, scoop the cheese out and form into a ball. Crush the nuts and roll the cheese ball in the nuts. Fancy!

SNACKVANA
If you want to know everything—and I mean *everything*—about most every snack food in the world, check out Taquitos.net (www.taquitos.net).

According to the writing of Aaron Sorkin (*Sports Night* and *The West Wing*) more people are killed by vending machines each year than by wolves.

Prince of Persia: Sands of Time
Bargain Bin Special

Image courtesy of Gamespy.com.

From the combat to the somersaults, the animation in Sands of Time is amazing.

DOSSIER

Genre: Jumping with Swords **Publisher:** Ubisoft **Developer:** Ubisoft Montreal
Platform: PC, PS2, Xbox, GameCube, GBA **Metacritic Metascore:** 92

Prince of Persia: Sands of Time is a first-rate action/adventure with great graphics and animation combined with fantastic level design. The follow up, Warrior Within, is also a good game but it lacks the charm that made Sands of Time so compelling. There's another Prince of Persia game in the works, which is tentatively set for a December 2005 release (see the Holiday 2005 section for details) but if you're new to the next-gen versions of this classic series, this is really the best place to start.

The Story

In Sands of Time, the unnamed Prince gets ahold of an ancient dagger that has the capability to slow down and reverse, literally, the sands of time. So, if you screw up a jump or if an evil undead guard slices you in two you can, in a sense, take a do over. It's a great way to avoid having to sit through multiple reloads and although you have only so much "sand in the hourglass," it's usually enough to get you past some of the trickier parts of the game.

The Prince is also able to run along walls for a brief period of time and even leap from wall to wall, performing some truly amazing acrobatic moves in the process. Prince of Persia is the kind of game that elicits ohhs and ahhs from people that are sitting around watching.

Image courtesy of Gamespy.com.

The Prince is like the Energizer Bunny during combat.

The highlight of the game, aside from the acrobatics, is the setting. The "castle" is huge and has some breathtaking levels in it, from outdoor scenes where you are seemingly thousands of feet in the air on a tightrope to multi-colored underground labyrinths. Sands of Time is just as much fun today as it was two years ago, so if you skipped out on this one you can still get it on the cheap for $20 at most retail chains.

More Adventures with the Prince

Prince of Persia (1989). Way back in the age of the dinosaur (1989), Broderbund published the original Jordan Mechner classic on a wide variety of platforms. The original is considered a huge leap in game animation and was one of the first games to use *rotoscoping* (a technology that made the animations look eerily realistic).

Prince of Persia 2: The Shadow and the Flame (1994). Five years later, Broderbund was back with a sequel that had better graphics and larger areas to explore.

Prince of Persia 3D (1999). The Prince's first foray into the world of 3D gaming was not a good one. The game tanked and most people felt the series had run its course... that is, until Sands of Time brought it back.

Prince of Persia: Warrior Within (2004). The follow-up to Sands of Time is a fun romp, but for some reason Ubisoft decided to make the Prince less Ali Baba and more, I dunno, evil-looking-dark-hero guy. Now the Prince chops off the heads of bad guys and can wield two weapons. Thanks, but I'll take Sands of Time for $20.

> ### 4D PRINCE OF PERSIA
> Check out the fan-made sequel to the original by grabbing it from The Underdogs at www.the-underdogs.org/game.php?id=9.

DID YOU KNOW

In 1994, a Prince of Persia fan created 4D Prince of Persia and, in 2003, more Prince fans created a level and sound editor for the 4D game.

April 2005

A Month of Risk Taking

A few companies wandered out on the ledge this month. First, BioWare said, "We don't need no stinking D&D license!" and released its action-packed Xbox RPG Jade Empire, which was a huge hit with both fans and critics alike. Mission accomplished.

NCSoft and ArenaNet said, "We don't need no stinking monthly fee!" and released its MMOG Guild Wars, which critics loved and fans made the number one selling PC game. Mission accomplished.

Majesco and Double Fine Production said, "Let's create a wildly imaginative and hard-to-describe action game and call it Psychonauts!" Critics loved it. Fans had no idea what to make of it. Mission half accomplished. What was it Meat Loaf said? "Two out of three ain't bad?"

Flops of the Month:

- **Stronghold 2**—A lesson in rushed releases, Stronghold 2, a game of castle sieges and town building, could have been a fantastic game but it failed due a staggering number of bugs and gameplay that needed much more polish. For me, this was a huge personal disappointment.

- **Dungeon Lords**—Lesson number two in rushed releases, this hack-and-slash dungeon romp was a travesty of a game that shipped months before it was ready. Dungeon Lords made Stronghold 2 look like a tightly coded masterpiece.

Jade Empire
BioWare's Streak Continues

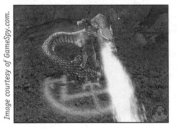
Everybody was kung-fu fighting! With a big axe!

DOSSIER

Genre: Kung Fu Hustle RPG **Publisher:** Microsoft **Developer:** BioWare **Platform:** Xbox
Metacritic Metascore: 91

Jade Empire is BioWare's *Kung Fu Hustle*. The company, best known for classic RPGs such as Baldur's Gate, Neverwinter Nights, and Star Wars: Knights of the Old Republic, shifted gears a bit with this real-time, action-oriented role-playing game set in a brand new world that's not inspired by Dungeons & Dragons or George Lucas.

As if it weren't there already, Jade Empire clearly cements BioWare atop the role-playing development heap. The downside is that there's no PC version and great single-player RPGs on the PC are few and far between these days so, guys—please, throw PC gamers a bone!

THEY SAID IT

> "The things I love about Jade Empire are the action-packed combat system, the cool exploration, and the story and character advancement. Utterly destroying a dozen enemies in a few seconds never gets old." —
> **Kevin Martens, Lead Designer of Jade Empire**

Jade Empire Combat Tips

Jade Empire is an enormous game with a great story, superb visuals, and a lot of fighting. Here are some basic combat tips on how to make the most of your time playing in BioWare's version of Kung Fu Theater.

Harmonic Combos Are Your Friend: You need to learn how to use these because they allow you to wade through lower-level opponents like Bruce Lee on a caffeine buzz. Plus they look really cool. To set up a combo, you need to use a Support or Magic style. For example, Heavenly Wave's Power Attack can begin a combo and after the wave hits, a green circle appears at the opponent's feet, which means you can do a Harmonic Combo. At this point, switch to a Martial Style and land a Power Attack on your foe before the timer runs out. If you do it right, the unfortunate bad guy should explode like a ripe watermelon. Of course, most bosses are immune to these combos, but they're great for killing the basic minions.

Keep Followers in Support Mode: A staple of every BioWare game is that your character will eventually pick up followers along the way and Jade Empire is no different. The difference in Jade Empire is that followers aren't as useful as they are in games like Baldur's Gate or Knights of the Old Republic. It's by far a better strategy to put a follower in support mode so that it makes your fighting prowess a bit better rather than have the follower struggle with one bad guy while you're taking on half a dozen.

Image courtesy of GameSpy.com.

Chinese dragon...he's the one who makes KFC chicken extra crispy!

Evade! Dodge! Duck!: We all like the idea of the tough fighter blocking a punch and shrugging it off like a heavyweight prizefighter, but in Jade Empire it's much better to dodge an attack without taking damage or allowing an opponent to set up a combo move. You also want to roll and flip around a lot during combat by using the B button in conjunction with the left thumbstick; this also helps to prevent an enemy from starting a combo attack.

JADE EMPIRE WALKTHROUGHS
Jade Empire is a game that can be approached from several different angles, and **Gamefaqs** hosts three very thorough walkthroughs at www.gamefaqs.com/console/xbox/game/918890.html. They're perfect for those that are stuck or just want a few basic tips.

DID YOU KNOW

Although best known for classic role-playing titles, BioWare also developed MDK2 and the 1996 action game Shattered Steel. Moving into RPGs seems to have been a smart move.

Psychonauts
How Could Microsoft Pass on This Gem?

Image courtesy of GameSpy.com.

Raz to the rescue!

DOSSIER

Genre: Timothy Leary–Inspired Action **Publisher:** Majesco **Developer:** Double Fine Productions **Platform:** Xbox/PC/PS2 **Metacritic Metascore:** 88

The games industry shares a lot of similarity with the film industry of Hollywood. Publishers, as a rule, hate to take risks. They want sure things and not something that could blow up in their face. There's a reason that most games are either sequels, clones of other successful franchises, or officially licensed titles. This kind of thinking has a tendency to stifle creativity because original ideas are usually pushed aside in favor of the next WarCraft clone.

Psychonauts is a prime example of the kind of game that freaks publishers out; even big money companies like Microsoft. Psychonauts was originally under the MS Games umbrella, but the company pulled out right before it was set to be released and developer Double Fine Productions had to scramble to find the game a new home. It wasn't until Majesco stepped up that Psychonauts was able to see the light of day. A good thing, too, because Tim Schafer's inventive, addictive, and completely bizarre action-platformer is video gaming at its best: creative, ingenious, and yet downright fun.

Just how different is the premise of Psychonauts? You play Raz, a powerful young cadet at psychic summer camp. Raz wants nothing more than to be a full-fledged Psychonaut. These superheroes have the ability to enter the brains of anyone they choose in order to battle that person's mental demons and nightmares. As Raz, you go on a 13-level journey to foil an evil madman's plot to steal the brains of other psychic children.

See? That's not so strange.

THEY SAID IT

"There's no such thing as safe. The bottom of the sales chart is full of derivative games. The only way to mitigate risk is to concentrate on making something great." —**Tim Schafer, founder of Double Fine Productions**

Raz has to travel inside the mind of several bizarre characters and each mind trip is a very different experience for our young hero. Raz learns new psychic powers, such as Telekinesis and Chain Blast, via the use of merit badges that are earned over the course of the game. Psychonauts defines the phrase *surreal gaming experience*. The art, sound, wit, storyline, and gameplay are top-notch and if you're looking for something a bit different, run out and grab a copy of this wonderfully weird game.

Image courtesy of GameSpy.com.

Psychonauts is totally weird, but in a good way....

PSYCHO WEBSITES

Usually listing a game's homepage is a waste of space but in the case of the **Psychonauts Home Page** (www.psychonauts.com) it's required viewing. Go Psychonauts!

Razputin.Net (www.razputin.net) is a great place to go for all things Psychonauts; it includes interviews with Tim Schafer, an audio-ripping program, character profiles, fan forum, and more.

DID YOU KNOW

Tim Schafer, lead designer of Psychonauts and founder of Double Fine Productions, has worked on some of the best games of all time including The Secret of Monkey Island, Maniac Mansion: Day of the Tentacle, and Jedi Knight: Dark Forces II.

Guild Wars

Fee Free and Addictive As All Get Out

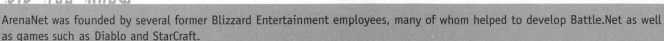

Image courtesy of GameSpy.com.

In the Arena, it's all about teamwork.

DOSSIER

Genre: Feeless MMOG! **Publisher:** NCSoft **Developer:** ArenaNet **Platform:** PC
Metacritic Metascore: 89

Guild Wars has redefined the MMOG genre. In fact, ArenaNet doesn't even like to call it an MMOG because it fails to use many of the usual trappings of online role-playing games. There's no monthly fee, no level grinding, no griefing, and no wandering PK machines ready to kill newbies at a moment's notice. Guild Wars is the evolution of the genre and if you haven't played it by now you are really missing out on one of the best games of 2005, regardless of platform.

THEY SAID IT

"...we want to avoid the possibility of having a 'best' character or strategy, and therefore, we take skill and profession balance very seriously. The skill system in Guild Wars is built on formal mechanics designed by some of the most experienced designers in the industry." —**Guild Wars Producer Jeff Starin in an interview at GameSpot.com**

The Quick Profession Guide

In Guild Wars you pick a primary and a secondary profession. There are six from which to choose and each requires a very different strategy. Your primary profession also brings with it a special *gift skill*, each of which is detailed here.

Elementalist: Energy Storage. When you use this special skill, each experience point invested gives you three bonus energy (mana) points. This allows the Elementalist to keep casting spells without eating up precious spell energy.

Image courtesy of GameSpy.com.

Did I mention that the graphics in Guild Wars are spectacular?

Monk: Divine Favor. For every point invested in Divine Favor, the enemy spells cast on you (or your teammates) heals them for an additional three points of health.

Mesmer: Fast Casting. For each point invested in Fast Casting, spells are cast at an increased rate of speed.

Necromancer: Soul Reaping. For every point invested in Soul Reaping, you gain one energy point when any creature dies.

DID YOU KNOW

Ranger: Expertise. Each point invested in Expertise lowers the energy cost of most Ranger skills by four percent.

Warrior: Strength. With each point invested in Strength, attack skills have an additional 1% armor penetration, which is great when doing battle against other Warrior classes.

Profession Combos

There are 30 profession combinations in Guild Wars. Your primary profession determines armor availability, starting energy, energy regeneration, and the unique gift attribute. The great thing about your secondary profession is that there's no downside to it. So, for example, a Monk/Warrior will have the Monk's armor restrictions, starting energy, and Divine Favor, but all the vicious Warrior skills too.

Warrior/Monk: Probably the most popular choice for new players, the Warrior/Monk can do a whole lot of damage up close and use the armor of the Warrior along with the Monk's ability to heal. Players dub this the *Paladin* profession.

Ranger/Mesmer: This is a really nifty combo that is death incarnate for enemy mages. Sit back with ranged attacks and then let loose with the Mesmer hex spells and watch spellcasters flee in terror. (Or just get really mad.)

Mesmer/Elementalist: Built for ranged killing, you get the fast casting and hexes of the Mesmer and the devastating area of effects spells of the Elementalist. Of course the lack of armor can prove, um, troublesome.

Necromancer/Warrior: This is a tricky combo that can prove deadly with practice. A *NecroWarrior* can be used to hustle to the front of a battle, swinging wildly with a weapon while using skills such as Vampiric Touch to quickly drain the life from more well armored targets.

GUILD WARS FANSITE LISTING

There are dozens of Guild Wars fansites on the Web and www.guildwars.com/community lists many of the better ones.

ArenaNet was founded by several former Blizzard Entertainment employees, many of whom helped to develop Battle.Net as well as games such as Diablo and StarCraft.

SWAT 4

We Promise It's Better Than the Sam Jackson Movie

This is NOT how you want a mission to end.

Image courtesy of GameSpy.com.

DOSSIER

Genre: Cops Storming the Castle **Publisher:** Vivendi Universal **Developer:** Irrational Games **Platform:** PC **Metacritic Metascore:** 85

Tactical shooters are a pretty hot commodity these days thanks to games like Tom Clancy's Rainbow Six series. However, another game in this genre that should not be overlooked is SWAT 4 developed by Irrational Games, the same team that makes the fantastic Freedom Force titles (see p.47).

With top-notch graphics and wonderful atmospheric sound, SWAT 4 captures the real-life tension of being a SWAT officer as well as any game can. And the effectiveness of the game's cooperative multiplayer mode provides unlimited replay value. However, those new to these kinds of games need to keep a few things in mind with regard to the gameplay, which is why I'll run over a few general tips as well as some of the more substantial mods that are available from the SWAT 4 community.

THEY SAID IT

"SWAT 4 uses the Vengeance Engine, Irrational's own version of the Unreal Engine. We've made countless changes to the engine, but one thing that hasn't changed too drastically is the Editor. In short, if you've ever modded any Unreal games before, you should be able to dive right in and mod away." —**Bill Gardner, Irrational Games designer in an interview with** *Computer Games* **magazine**

General SWAT 4 Tips

This Is Not Halo. Sounds obvious, I know, but so many people in multiplayer games want to play SWAT as if they're the Master Chief. In SWAT 4 if you get shot, you're going to get hurt really, really, bad.

Know Your Grenades. Using the proper grenade is vital to succeeding in several of the missions. Aside from knowing what each does, try to use them before you go into a room.

- **Gas Grenades:** A standard grenade that covers a wide area and also affects suspects hiding behind cover. It's worth noting that if a bad guy is wearing a gas mask, this grenade becomes a wee bit less effective.

- **Flashbang Grenades:** These grenades blind/stun nearby enemies. To use them effectively you must make sure that your target can see the grenade when it goes off.

- **Stingers:** These are really just basic grenades that stun nearby enemies. Unlike the gas grenade, if a bad guy is hiding behind hard cover, this grenade is less effective. Stingers will, however, detonate other nearby explosives. (Handle with care!)

Love That Optiwand! The optiwand is a device that allows you to see around corners or underneath certain doors without the enemy's knowledge. This is the most critical tool in the game.

SWAT 4 Mods

Lots of graffiti on the walls...danger! Danger!

Image courtesy of GameSpy.com.

SWAT 4 Mission Editor. The official editing tool released by Sierra and Irrational Games. This tool allows you to create your own content for SWAT 4.

S.S.F. Realism Mod. The S.S.F. mod doesn't drastically change much about how SWAT 4 plays, but rather it tweaks and adjusts certain gameplay elements, weapons, and so forth to make everything a bit more realistic. This is a great mod for multiplayer gaming.

Gear Modification Mod. This mod alters weapons, uniforms, and other gear to be a bit more accurate.

SWAT ON THE WEB

SWAT 4 TOC (swat4.edgegaming.com) is a first-rate fan site that has mods, user-made maps (of which there are many) utilities, and a forum.

DID YOU KNOW

The original SWAT game, released in 1995, was actually a poorly received "interactive movie" and a follow up to the popular Sierra Police Quest graphic adventure games.

Trackmania Sunrise
A Track Designer's Paradise

DOSSIER

Genre: Sleeper PC Racing Hit **Publisher:** Digital Jesters **Developer:** Nadeo **Platform:** PC **Metacritic Metascore:** 81

Trackmania Sunrise is a gorgeous game; the scenery is particularly pretty.

Here's a little gem of a game that fell under many a PC gamer's radar when it was released in May 2005. Trackmania Sunrise is a sequel to the 2002 game, Trackmania, which garnered a respectable 74 rating from Metacritic.com.

Trackmania Sunrise is basically more of the same—it's a better-looking game than the original with more "stuff," so Trackmania vets should have a pretty good idea of what to expect.

This is a pure arcade racing game, so don't expect real-world physics and a detailed garage menu a la Forza Motorsports (see p.88). In Trackmania Sunrise, you're going to go through loops at 600MPH, soar off ramps and take to the air. The sense of speed in Trackmania is as good, if not better, than any other racing game on the market. When you register 600MPH—you know it.

The Gameplay

The star of the show in Trackmania is the tracks more so than it is the cars, which is pretty much the exact opposite from most racing games, even other arcade racers. The tracks are over the top and make the game worth playing because you never really get to race against any AI-controlled cars—just ghost runs. (If this game had a set of AI cars like in, say, Whiplash, ahh...the possibilities.)

Each race lasts roughly a minute, so it's not a big deal to keep trying to beat a set time. The tracks aren't too big and when you're cruising along faster than a speeding bullet, you tend to get through the course at a quick clip.

But there's more to the game than reaching insane speeds and traveling over sadistically designed tracks. The game also allows you to build a better mousetrap via the puzzle mode. Here you get a partly finished track and have to lay down pieces to finish it so that you can complete a race in a certain amount of time. Did you ever own one of those old electric car sets where you clamped the track pieces together to form

whatever monstrosity you could imagine? That's the idea...except that you're really not trying to see what kind of wrecks you can cause.

It also allows more creative juices to flow because as you earn money you can create tracks from scratch as well as use a basic car painting kit.

As a multiplayer game, Trackmania Sunrise disappoints. You get basic hot-seat and network play, but it's a letdown because you never get to race *with* your buddies, just more ghost runs.

Still, if you like racing games with great graphics, and over the top arcade racing with loops and wicked jumps with cars going speeds that would make Evel Knievel tremble, Trackmania Sunrise is worth checking out.

Sunrise Mods

Being a PC game with such rich editing capabilities, Trackmania Sunrise opens itself to being heavily modified. Thankfully, there's a good fan base out there that is cranking out material like Dean Koontz on a caffeine buzz. Here's a few websites worth checking out, as well as some basic mods:

- **The Trackmania Exchange** (sunrise.tm-exchange.com). The best place on the Net to find user-made tracks as well as new tracks from the developer, Nadeo. There's some fantastic track designs ready to download from this site. You can also upload your own creations to the database.
- **Irigy's Trackmania Skins** (tm.njimko.de). Irigy has a great set of custom-made car skins ready for download. His leopard skin car is particularly creepy.

TRACKMANIA IRC

If you have an IRC chat client, you can log on to **www.trackmaniacs.net** to chat live with other Trackmania fans.

DID YOU KNOW

Developer Nadeo has three titles to its credit: two TrackMania games and a soccer management game called Virtual Skipper.

Image courtesy of GameSpy.com.

Midnight Club 3: DUB Edition
Rule #1: Don't Talk About Midnight Club

Midnight Club 3 is about more than cars....

DOSSIER

Genre: Super Fast City Racing **Publisher:** Rockstar Games **Developer:** Rockstar San Diego **Platform:** PS2, Xbox, PSP **Metacritic Metascore:** 84

Midnight Club clearly falls on the arcade side of the racing sim genre with exaggerated physics and insane spins and jumps. One way to describe it is to think of it as The Fast and the Furious: The Video Game (sans Vin Diesel, who might have peaked with *Pitch Black*).

The maturation of this series is an interesting one as Rockstar games continues to tweak the design trying to find the best fit. Without a doubt, the latest version is the best of the series.

THEY SAID IT

"It was important to us to create a game that packs in everything from the console version while not cutting any corners. Other games we've played on the PSP are paired down versions of their respective franchises. Midnight Club 3: DUB Edition is the full version of the game and even adds more." —**Haythem Haddad, Creative Director and Cofounder of *DUB* magazine in an interview with IGN.com**

Check the tires and give her a good once over, k?

The MC Lineage

Midnight Club: Street Racing (2000). The premise of the original, released for the PS2 (a GBA version was released in 2001), is pretty much the same basic idea in all of the Midnight Club games. You played a New York City cabbie, looking for some excitement in your life. What better way to blow off some steam than to join a Midnight Club, a secret club of late-night city street racers? Sort of like the movie Fight Club, and yet totally different.

After joining, you cruise New York looking for "hookmen" (get your mind out of the gutter), who are there to set up races against other clubs. If you win a head-to-head race against a rival, you get to keep his car and add it to your garage. There's definitely honor among midnight street car racers.

Midnight Club 2 (2003). Released for the PS2, Xbox, and PC, the second game was basically the same as the first, but with even better graphics and online support. Although Midnight Club 2 was undoubtedly a good game, it didn't expand much at all on the basic gameplay formula, and consequently, it left some fans wanting a bit more.

Midnight Club 3: DUB Edition (2005). The latest edition of the Midnight Club series is the pinnacle of arcade street racing, in particular because it finally adds licensed cars. There are more than 60 cars in the game from the slick, modern day Lexus to the classic Corvette Stingray. You can even get a Hummer if you can afford to keep the tank full of gas. On top of that, you get the chance to truly customize them in the DUB edition. You can tweak stuff like the suspension systems, brakes, exhaust systems, and so on.

There are also a lot of cars you can win by achieving certain goals. Here's a quick rundown of the highlights.

The Prize	The Requirement
IS300	Win City Tournament in San Diego
Cien	Win City Tournament in Detroit
300C DUB Edition	Win Balboa Park Tournament
'02 Skyline	Beat Unbeatable Street Racers Club
Escalade EXT	Win DUB Tournament in Atlanta DUB Edition
'04 SS1000	Win Hotlanta Tournament in Atlanta
Ninja ZX 12R	Beat Original Riders Club
'69 Corvette	Beat American Royalty Car Club
ME Four-Twelve	Beat By Invitation Only Club
Murcielago	Be crowned U.S. Champion

DID YOU KNOW

Angel Studios, developer of Midnight Club, also developed the popular racer Midtown Madness for Microsoft back in 1999.

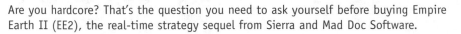

Empire Earth II
The Kitchen Sink of Game Design

Image courtesy of GameSpy.com.

Ready, aim, annihilate!

DOSSIER

Genre: RTS for the Hardcore **Publisher:** Vivendi/Sierra **Developer:** Mad Doc Software
Platform: PC **Metacritic Metascore:** 80

Are you hardcore? That's the question you need to ask yourself before buying Empire Earth II (EE2), the real-time strategy sequel from Sierra and Mad Doc Software.

If you are, if you have the ability to monitor several things at once, have no trouble micromanaging your units, and take it as a personal challenge to learn the intricacies of one of the busiest user-interfaces ever designed—if you feel you're *that* kind of gamer, Empire Earth 2 is for you. This is not, however, a game for the RTS fan that likes a more leisurely paced form of pause-and-play entertainment.

Empire Earth II is a love/hate sort of game. Either the mounds of information will be just what the doctor ordered, or the vast amount of stuff thrown at you will send you running back to Rise of Nations, Age of Empires, or Total War.

THEY SAID IT

"With our eye firmly placed on creating a fun, dynamic and challenging gameplay experience, we put a great deal of work into the creation of the campaigns in Empire Earth 2, as well as the missions. For example, there were massive amounts of historical research, fact checking, timeline creation, battle design, writing, and more behind the campaign development." —**Ian Davis, CEO of Mad Doc Software in an interview with *PC Gamer***

EE2's Tasty Stuffing

Empire Earth II spans 15 time periods (epochs) from basically the dawn of man to the future of fusion power. With so many varied time periods, this game is loaded with literally hundreds of different units spanning 14 unique civilizations from the Aztecs to the Turks, and each has its own trait bonuses and penalties.

Then there's the War Planner. Although the game has several single-player options, EE2 is at its best as a multiplayer game. The War Planner allows you to concoct a battle plan, on the fly, and share it with your online allies. It's an extremely cool tool that allows for true combined arms tactics, surprise flank attacks, and so on. It's basically a less-detailed view of the game map, allowing you to literally draw up your plans on the map. Playing with John Madden as an ally is not recommended.

Empire Earth II Mods

Being a popular PC game, Empire Earth II also has a solid community behind it that likes to crank out new maps,

scenarios, and game mods. Here are a few worth checking out.

Civ Mods. Like I said earlier, Empire Earth II is a huge, epic-scale game. But to be blunt, some civilizations got screwed. Seriously, where are the Russians? Thankfully, a dedicated group of modders have added the French, Dutch, Spanish, and Russians to the mix, all with unique units and traits. The only problem is that by using one of these mods, you take out one of the civs already in the game. The Russians replace the Americans, for example.

Scenarios. Once you get tired of all the maps and battles that come with the game, you can find a ton of original content online. The Western Hemisphere multiplayer map is particularly good, as are the single-player scenarios The Greek City States, The Mongol Expansion, and The Road to Quang Tri.

Image courtesy of GameSpy.com.

Attacking a castle with trebuchets.

EMPIRE EARTH 2 HEAVEN
At **ee.heavengames.com**, you'll find a wonderful fan site dedicated to the Empire Earth series and the place to grab the mod files mentioned here.

DID YOU KNOW

The original Empire Earth was a real-time strategy game that spanned several epochs of human history from prehistoric to the digital and nano ages.

A Brief History of DOOM
Closet Classic (1993)

The graphics in DOOM were revolutionary. No, really!

DOSSIER

Genre: The Most Important Game Ever **Publisher:** id Software **Developer:** id Software
Platform: PC

After 1.5 million copies sold and 20 million downloads, like it or not, DOOM is the most important and significant release in the history of video and computer games. This was the masterpiece that catapulted the industry on a course that would lead it into the mainstream. The idea of playing against a group of buddies in the same office and blowing them to smithereens in real-time was such a radical idea at the time that many people simply didn't believe it until they saw the game in action. Office networks crashed due to too many people playing the game. The administrators at Carnegie Mellon University instituted a "No DOOM" policy during working hours. *TIME* magazine wrote about it; the designers at id Software earned rock star status, and the game went on to be as recognizable as classic coin-op games such as Asteroids and Space Invaders.

When word started to leak around college campuses in December of 1993 that a marvelous game called DOOM was available as shareware, campus servers simply couldn't handle all the download demands. Servers crashed, network techs scrambled to alleviate the stress on their systems...it was a glorious time, indeed.

THEY SAID IT

> "This is the first game to really exploit the power of LANs and modems to their full potential. In 1993, we fully expect to be the number one cause of decreased productivity in businesses around the world." —**Jay Wilbur, id Software, in the official DOOM press release**

What Made It Work

The original shareware version of DOOM is what got gamers hooked. It had nine levels of pure, unadulterated, run-and-gun entertainment and it was totally free.

But DOOM is such an important title not merely because of its popularity but also because of the way it pushed games into the wilds of the Internet. Not only that, but DOOM was one of the first games, if not the first game, to spawn a rabid "mod" scene where gamers took building tools and created their own DOOM levels and models. Who could forget Justin Fisher's classic Aliens DOOM Total Conversion?

Ahh the Imp, now die!!! I remember thee well.

The game engine, dubbed the *DOOM Engine*, stayed in use through 1996 when Final DOOM was released. The main difference between it and id's previous first-person shooter, Wolfenstein 3D, was that the walls in DOOM could be of different heights and shapes and not all rectangles. This free-form design allowed for some highly imaginative levels complete with rising lifts and bridges.

DOOM's lighting and sound were unparalleled and critical to the game's overall success. DOOM was a scary game. Its use of darkness, blatant satanic imagery, and stereo sound marked a new age in gaming. It pushed the envelope so far that it remains, to this day, the poster child for politicians that go after the gaming industry's use of violence and blood.

DOOM ONLINE

Everything related to DOOM, from the classic to the new version, can be found at **Doomworld** (www.doomworld.com).

Download what is considered the best ever DOOM and DOOM II Total Conversion, the **Aliens TC** (www.doomwadstation.com/main/aliens.html).

PSP owners can even get some good old-fashioned DOOM nostalgia right on their handheld. Just visit **PSP Emulation News** at psp-news.dcemu.co.uk/doompsp.shtml.

DID YOU KNOW

In the early stages of DOOM's development, id Software planned to offer different playable characters with various strengths and weaknesses before opting for the simpler Marine hero.

Unreal Championship 2
The Liandri Conflict

The graphics in UC2 were simply amazing.

DOSSIER

Genre: Super Fun Online Mayhem **Publisher:** Midway Games **Developer:** Epic
Platform: Xbox **Metacritic Metascore:** 85

Unreal Tournament, released for the PC back in 1999, set the gaming world ablaze with its multiplayer-oriented design. It even proved be to more popular than the multiplayer shooter from id Software, Quake 3: Arena. But it wasn't until 2002 that the series morphed its way to consoles when Atari released an Xbox-only version called Unreal Championship. Although it didn't make quite the same splash as it did with PC gamers, it was still a big hit with console fans.

The sequel on the Xbox, Unreal Championship 2: The Liandri Conflict (UC2), not only has an extremely long name but is also one of the best shooters on the market for Xbox gamers.

Basic Hand-to-Hand Tips

Although UC2 has a single-player mode, the meat of the game is on Xbox Live, where it can prove to be a tad tricky for new players because of its combination of shooter and fighting game mechanics.

The game offers both first-person and third-person views. UC2 is kind of like Unreal meets Mortal Kombat. You can get into some wicked hand-to-hand fights in the game, but it takes learning some of the moves necessary to bash your opponent during close quarter fighting.

LightAttack: A very weak attack that does little damage but is so fast it's difficult to defend. It can really annoy the pants off other players.

Strong Attack: A slow attack that is a bit risky but delivers a lot of damage if it connects. A good time to perform this attack is if your opponent tries it first and misses because it will leave him open for a counterattack.

Jump Attack: This is a great counter-move for nimble opponents who like to dance around a lot. Leaping on these annoying jitterbug fighters is a great way to shut them up. However, a Strong Attack will stop (bloodily) a Jump Attacker in his tracks.

Some of the new melee weapons look like lightsabers.

Deflect: It takes a lot of practice, but if you perfect this move you will not only be able to deflect melee attacks but also missile attacks like an Unreal version of a Jedi.

Shield: Your shield is best used to defend against a series of light attacks, and then to counterattack while your opponent charges up a heavier assault.

Lock On: It is adviable, especially when first learning the ropes, to use the camera lock-on feature when in hand-to-hand combat; it's an easy way to keep your opponent in your crosshairs, so to speak.

Coup de Grace Moves

The Coup de Grace is like a finishing move in a fighting game. Each character has a different combo that you need to know before you can use it. Here's a quick guide.

Character	Controller Moves
Anubis	⚔⚔, ↑, ⚔ Ⓡ Trigger
Arclite	⚔⚔, →⚔ ⚔ ⚔ Left
Brock	⚔⚔,→, ←, ⚔ ⚔
Devastation	⚔⚔, ↑, ←, ↓, →, Ⓛ Trigger
Gorge	⚔⚔, →, ⚔ Ⓛ Trigger + Ⓡ Trigger, ⚔
Lauren	⚔⚔, ←, →, Ⓡ Trigger
Malcolm	⚔⚔, ↓, ↑, ⚔ Ⓛ Trigger
Raiden	⚔⚔, ↑, ↓, ↓, ↓, ⚔
Raptor	⚔⚔, ↓, ←, ↑, →, Ⓡ Trigger
Saphire	⚔⚔, ↑, ↓, Ⓛ Trigger, ↑, ⚔
Selket	⚔⚔, ↓, ⚔ ⚔ Ⓛ Trigger, Ⓡ Trigger
Sobek	⚔⚔, Ⓡ Trigger, ↓, ↑, ↑
Szalor	⚔⚔, Ⓛ Trigger + Ⓡ Trigger ↓, ↓, Up
Torgr	⚔⚔, Ⓛ Trigger, Ⓡ Trigger, Ⓛ Trigger, ↑, ↑, ↓

DID YOU KNOW

Although developer Epic is most known for the Unreal series, the company was founded way back in 1991 with the release of the ANSI-based game ZZT.

Donkey Kong
Closet Classic (1981)

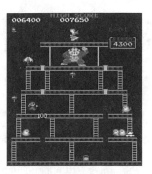

This is one of the early levels in the original Donkey Kong.

DOSSIER

Genre: Coin-Op Classic **Publisher:** Nintendo **Developer:** Nintendo **Platform:** Arcade

It might be hard for younger readers to comprehend this, but there was a time when going to the local arcade was not only kind of hip, but it was also the place to go if you wanted to play the best games. It was a heck of a lot more fun to play Space Invaders, Track and Field, and Frogger than it was to play Atari Basketball. Even the ports of the classic arcade games were a lot more fun in the arcade than they were on the Intellivision or the Commodore 64.

On top of that, going to the arcade wasn't all that expensive. You could go to a mall arcade with five bucks and play *20 games*. Try going to an arcade today with five bucks and you'll last about 15 minutes.

Donkey Kong was part of the golden age of coin-op arcade games, along with other classics like Pac-Man and Tempest, that helped to usher in a new wave of platform games that would later be seen on home consoles.

THEY SAID IT

"Donkey Kong wasn't directly influenced by Beauty and the Beast. I mean it's true I've been influenced by art at times, but not so much by story. With Donkey Kong, we began development on that game originally with the idea of using Popeye in it. So it wasn't so much that I was influenced by the story of those movies." —**Shigeru Miyamoto in an interview with G4Tv.com**

Good luck deciphering this one, folks!

The DK Experience

Donkey Kong first hit the scene in 1981 and introduced two characters who would end up being video game staples in Mario and Donkey Kong himself. Actually, Mario was initially known only as the nondescript "Jumpman," but Nintendo would later rename him Mario. Mario was trying to rescue "Pauline" from the clutches of the evil King Kong clone that held her hostage at the top of each level. Mario had to scale each stage (there were 21 in all in the original game), dodging barrels, little fireballs, and other traps along the way. Hammers were also available, allowing Mario to go on the offensive to smash barrels rather than having to avoid them. The hammer was the Donkey Kong version of the magic spheres in Pac-Man.

This is such a significant game because it helped to establish Nintendo in the United States with its first huge stateside hit. After Nintendo released its NES console, the company would be here to stay—Donkey Kong paved the way for all of that to happen.

Do the Donkey Kong! Go barrel smashing!

In true video game fashion, the Donkey Kong and Mario franchises have been milked to the point of absurdity. Donkey Kong himself has been in no fewer than 25 Nintendo games over the years from classics like Donkey Kong Jr. to more obscure games like Donkey Kong Country Barrel Maze. An entire Donkey Kong family tree has sprung up from Funky Kong and Swanky Kong to Candy Kong. It's mildly insane, actually. Kong has danced in Jungle Beat and battled Kremlins in Donkey Kong 64. He's no longer the big mean kidnapper, but rather a cute monkey with a heart. How sickly sweet.

Nintendo has steadily used the big ape successfully over the years and he remains one of the most recognizable figures in gaming history.

DONKEY KONG FLASH GAME
Play the original Donkey Kong on **The Magic Box** website at www.the-magicbox.com/flash-donkeykong.shtml.

DID YOU KNOW

The popularity of Donkey Kong spawned a song called *Do the Donkey Kong* by Buckner & Garcia on the *Pac-Man Fever* album. Ahhh. the early 1980s...innocence mixed with ridiculous taste.

Best of PC Gamepads

Getting Your Game On, Sans a Mouse or Keyboard

Logitech's cordless Rumblepad 2 is a big step up from the first version.

Console games are usually wedded to the controller that came with their box, but hardcore PC games often employ a plethora of controllers to match the games they're playing. The mouse and keyboard combo is probably the most popular (and probably the best) for FPS games (try playing Halo on your Xbox and then your PC if you don't believe me). However, different situations often call for moving beyond the mouse.

Wired Gamepads

Gamers making the transition from console to PC often want controllers like the one they're used to. Whether your other box is an Xbox, a GameCube, or a PS2, there are controllers out there that match the form and functionality of what you're used to.

Logitech Dual Action Gamepad ($19.95). PS2 gamers will feel right at home with this controller (if they don't miss the rumble feature). The familiar dual analog sticks, D-pad, and button layout make the transition from PS to PC an easy one. Logitech also has a slightly more expensive ($29.95) rumblepad that will be of interest to those who like that extra kick.

Gravis Eliminator GamePad Pro ($29.99). Another PC controller with a D-pad and no sticks, the Eliminator GamePad Pro sticks out because of its unique Precision button that allows pinpoint control over the D-pad instead of the usual 10 positions most controllers allow. Oh, and don't forget: It's "ribbed." Ahhh....

NYKO Air Flo PC ($24.99). Speaking of "ahhh," the NYKO Air Flo PC game controller is probably the biggest breakthrough in gaming comfort since the catheter. It looks a lot like an Xbox controller with the analog stick and D-pad swapped on the left side. What really sets the Air Flo apart, though, is the built-in fan that directs nifty jets of cool air over your palms as you play.

Wireless Gamepads

Cords are, like, sooooo twentieth century. When you're in the midst of an online firefight, who the heck wants to get tangled up in a cable or, worse yet, yank the dang thing out of the back of your PC? Wireless controllers set you free to fire at will...and not get hung up on retro cords.

Logitech Cordless Rumblepad 2 ($39.99). Like its wired brother (refer to the previous section), the Rumblepad 2 is one of the best PC gamepads around. Take away the wires and it's pure gaming goodness. Like most wireless controllers, this pad uses RF technology that maintains an excellent connection with your PC, so you have no line-of-sight issues!

NYKO Air Flo Wireless ($30). The same hand-cooling technology found in the NYKO Air Flo PC now comes to you in a wireless package (actually, this one has a variable speed fan, to boot). Using RF transmissions, this pad offers excellent response without having to maintain a line of sight with your PC. You'll also like the fact that this gamepad has a sleep mode to help conserve battery life.

Thrustmaster FireStorm Wireless ($39.95). Long heralded for its high-performance joysticks, Thrustmaster makes controllers that are ergonomically designed and, above all, endure. The Firestorm is an Xbox-like pad and sports a D-pad, dual analog sticks, triggers, and five buttons on the top of the unit. No drivers or special hardware are needed: just plug and play.

Nyko's AirFlo PC controller keeps you cool when the game gets hot.

Thrustmaster has been making quality controllers forever. This foray into the gamepad market is tops.

DID YOU KNOW

On the Japanese markets, hardware manufacturer Logitech uses the brand name Logicool. Nope, I'm not sure why either.

The Elder Scrolls Series
Closet Classics (1993–Present)

The Elder Scrolls saga from Bethesda Softworks is one of the most successful PC role-playing franchises in industry history. It belongs on the shelf next to such heralded classics like Ultimate, The Bard's Tale, Wizardry, and Fallout. And with the next chapter, The Elder Scrolls: Oblivion having been released in time for the 2005 holidays, now is a good time to reflect back on the history of this storied franchise.

Bloodmoon allows you to get in touch with your inner werewolf.

The Elder Scrolls Lineage

The Elder Scrolls: Arena (1993). The series started off with the 1993 release of Arena, which introduced gamers to the land of Tamriel. This game came off the heels of the ground-breaking Ultima Underworld series. Arena kicked it up a notch, however, not only by using a "3D" camera but also with an enormous world with the completely open-ended style of gameplay for which the series would later be famous. Arena sported 400 cities. *400*! Unfortunately it was a tad bit buggy, which would become another running theme with the series.

The Elder Scrolls II: Daggerfall (1996). At the time, Daggerfall was the most ambitious RPG ever designed. It took the basic idea of Arena and juiced it to the point of absurdity. "See Daggerfall" now appears next to the word *huge* in the dictionary. It was one of the first games to try the living world approach by not only letting you do what you wanted (you could even create a custom character class), but the world would react a certain way toward your character depending on your rank, class, and affiliations. Sounds great, and it was...after the patches. The game received no fewer than 10 significant updates before it was deemed playable. Once it was fixed, it was a fantastic RPG.

The Elder Scrolls Legends: Battlespire (1997). The series shifted gears with Battlespire, which was a more linear adventure than the previous games. It was really more action game than RPG, and fans were unclear how to react to it. It never had the following of the first two games, and rightfully so given some insanely difficult gameplay and long loading times after your character went tits up.

Daggerfall set the bar for both enormous game worlds and number of crash bugs.

> ### TAMRIEL REBUILT
> As if Morrowind wasn't big enough, there is an ongoing mod project at **www.tamriel-rebuilt.org** to create the entire world of Tamriel using the Morrowind editing tools.

The Elder Scrolls Adventures: Redguard (1998). While fans were starving for another Daggerfall, they instead got another curveball in Redguard. This was a third-person action/adventure where you played a Redguard "pirate" in search of your lost sister. This wasn't a bad game (it was much better than Battlespire), but it didn't stop fans from jonesing for another deep role-playing game.

The Elder Scrolls III: Morrowind (2002). In 2002, Bethesda finally got it. Morrowind still stands today as one of the greatest achievements in role-playing game design. Not only was it the biggest single-player RPG ever designed, but it also was arguably the prettiest. This came as something of a surprise given that the previous Elder Scrolls games weren't exactly lookers, even in their heyday. Morrowind was so huge that it was possible to get utterly lost inside its world, not touching the main plot lines for weeks at a time—something that some gamers think of as a fault, whereas others extol as a virtue. This game reaffirmed Bethesda's role in the future of the genre.

The Elder Scrolls III: Tribunal (2002). The first expansion for Morrowind added a new main storyline along with nice enhancements such as a journal organizer.

The Elder Scrolls III: Bloodmoon (2003). The second and last expansion for Morrowind sent you to an isolated island where you had to deal with werewolves...or join them. All told, Morrowind and its expansions provided literally hundreds of hours of gameplay.

The Elder Scrolls: Oblivion. Oblivion is set to take the series to the next level. It's big and disgustingly pretty, and should be available in time for the 2005 holiday season.

DID YOU KNOW

There are two other lesser-known Elder Scrolls games named Dawnstar and Stormhold that run only on Java-enabled cell phones.

Indie Games
Mount and Blade and Other Killer Titles

Mount and Blade looks as good as a lot of big commercial releases.

The gaming industry is still pretty young. We're talking about something that has been around as a viable retail market only since the late 1970s. So, for an industry that is really only about 30 years old, things sure have dramatically changed since the "good old days."

I'm not one of those people that feel that the games from yesteryear were all better than the games we play today. Fact is, today's games are pretty darn cool. Still, the industry is merging into a small group of big multinational publishing companies like Sony, Microsoft, Nintendo, and Electronic Arts.

These companies are also after the same thing: money. That is, after all, the nature of the biz. The problem is that creativity too often gets lost in the shuffle because creativity means risk and risk is not something that most companies like.

Independent games, or *indie* games, on the other hand, are usually all about creativity. And while it's true an indie game's usually small budget means a weaker AI and less-than-cutting-edge graphics, many of these games are so creative that any flaws are easy to overlook. There are a lot of good indie games out there for the PC; you just need to know where to find them.

Mount and Blade

Mount and Blade is primarily the amazing work of two people: a husband and wife team with no prior professional game design experience. But make no mistake, Mount and Blade is an absolute blast. As of this writing the game isn't even finished yet; it's currently in Beta, but you can download a shareware/trial version from www.taleworlds.com to get your feet wet.

Basically, Mount and Blade is a medieval role-playing game in which you create a character and wander the 3D countryside, entering towns, forming alliances with NPCs, and making enemies. Although there's no magic in the game, the combat model, which includes horse combat and basic swordplay, is extremely cool.

You can buy the game right now in its unfinished state for $15 and it comes highly recommended. (You'll get the complete game free if you buy it now.) Oh, and best of all, there is already a dedicated mod community hard at work coming up with all kinds of cool ideas.

Other Indie Games

There are a *lot* of indie games out there, and you can get a feel for some of them at various websites, but here are two others that are worth checking out.

Big Box of Blox (www.jollygoodgames.com/blox). A puzzle game with amazingly weird graphics, Big Box of Blox is definitely worth checking out if you like falling-block puzzle games.

Lux (sillysoft.net). Inspired by the classic board game Risk, Lux is a colorful strategy game of world domination with surprisingly good AI (there are 11 CPU opponents in all) as well as basic network support. Sillysoft also has a space conquest game called Pax Galaxia that is worth checking out.

Lux combines colorful maps with very solid computer AI.

DID YOU KNOW

Every spring, Oakland, California hosts the Indie Game Jam, an event "designed to encourage experimentation and innovation in the game industry." Check it out at www.indiegamejam.com.

GameCube Bargain Hunting
Bargain Bin Specials

I'm telling you, The Simpsons: Hit & Run is a great, great game!

Finding a bargain on older GameCube games is a shade tougher than games on other platforms. First off, it can be a bit more difficult to find some of these at game stores. And second, some of the top-shelf GameCube games from a year or so ago often still sell at full price. As of this writing, if you want to buy a new copy of Metroid Prime 2: Echoes, you're going to pony up 50 bones. Pikmin 2 is still going strong at full price as well, despite it being over a year old. It's the same with Paper Mario: The Thousand-Year Door.

There are deals to be had, however. Although you can always find deals on used games at places like eBay, you can also find a handful of great GameCube games for $20 at big name retail stores or by shopping online via Pricegrabber.com.

If you skipped these GameCube games when they were released, now is a great time to pick them up.

F-Zero GX (2003). If you like racing games with blistering speeds and highly creative track designs, the F-Zero series is a great choice. You're driving an intergalactic hover vehicle...that just screams speed, doesn't it? With more than 30 unique cars and various tracks this is a must-own racing game for the GameCube, even a couple of years after its release.

Gladius (2003). Gladius got a bad rap. Yeah, it has some issues; the gameplay isn't as thrilling as it could have been but come on...a role-playing game about gladiators? That right there is enough to warrant a rental. It's slower paced with a turn-based combat system, but if you like the genre, this is a highly underrated game.

Gladius in action.

Legend of Zelda: The Wind Waker (2003). The first Zelda game on the GameCube, the Wind Waker is also one of the best. The Wind Waker is the Zelda game known for its cel-shaded graphics, so if you're one of those gamers who hates this technique (it makes everything look sort of cartoony) or refuses to accept Link as anything other than an anime character, maybe $20 is too much. Graphics aside, The Wind Waker is a Zelda classic and if you're new to the series this is a good place to start.

Metal Gear Solid: The Twin Snakes (2004). Have you ever played a Metal Gear Solid game? No? You like stealth-based action? You also own a GameCube? Please, do me a favor and go buy this game. At $20 for a newcomer to the series, it's almost like stealing

Metal Gear Solid is still a fantastic game.

Tales of Symphonia (2004). The fourth game in the Tales series, Tales of Symphonia is a classic Japanese RPG. If you like that style of game then this is a no-brainer. Great characters, a cool story, and a unique sense of style thanks to the art direction by Kosuke Fujishima, it's a complete shock that this is selling for $20.

The Simpsons: Hit & Run (2003). Yep, The Simpsons: Hit & Run. If you love the show, you absolutely need to own this game. It's not exclusive to the GameCube, but it's far and away the best *Simpsons* game ever made. It's funny, witty, and a great satire of Grand Theft Auto.

DID YOU KNOW

When the Nintendo Revolution is released, it will mark the eleventh game system from Nintendo, going back to the 1985 NES.

Ten Worst PS2 Games

Grab Bag

Metacritic Reveals the Dregs of the PS2 World

Image courtesy of GameSpy.com.

No game console is without its share of dogs and the ones listed in Metacritic.com's worst ten are deserving of induction into the hallowed Pantheon of "Stuff That Sucks." The titles listed here are the kind of games that you hide when your friends come over to play games, lest they find out that you actually laid down money to play MTV's Celebrity Deathmatch.

Knight Rider 2 ranks as one of the worst game ideas of all time.

The Ten Worst-Reviewed PS2 Games

10. Frogger: The Great Quest (Score: 32). Oh, how you have sunk dear, sweet Frogger. How I used to love standing in the arcade, dodging cars and leaping from lily pad to lily pad. You sold me out, my little green friend. May you get hit by a Pontiac and end up as roadkill.

9. MTV's Celebrity Deathmatch (Score: 32). Does it *really* surprise you that a game called MTV's Celebrity Deathmatch is on this list? The funny thing is that someone at Take 2 thought this was a great idea.

8. Transformers Tataki (Score: 31). I freely admit that I never played this game; I had never even heard of it before researching this hilarious and entertaining essay. It was a Japanese import that was never available in the States and reviewed by only a handful of websites. Still, a 31 score...ugh.

7. Antz Extreme Racing (Score: 31). This incredibly bad kart-racing game had absolutely nothing to do with the movie or its characters other than the graphics. Add in bad controls and boring gameplay and you have a recipe for a Worst Ten finalist.

Antz Extreme Racing...shudder.

Image courtesy of GameSpy.com.

6. Shrek Super Party (Score: 30). This game came and went without any real fanfare, and was reviewed by only four sources. *GameNow* magazine did give it a 0, though. Think about it: This game didn't score any more points than the games I've designed and I've never designed any.

5. Dragon's Lair III (Score: 28). Okay, by now you really should get the point that this was a bad, bad game. It made every Worst Ten list for every platform that it was on, including the PC, Xbox, and PS2.

4. GoDai: Elemental Force (Score: 27). 3DO released this incredibly dated action game back in 2002. It had a pitiful frame rate, poor graphics, and frustrating controls. Other than that this was an A-list game....

3. Miami Vice (Score: 27). I already discussed this travesty on the Xbox Worst Ten list, but *Miami Vice* circa 2004 was just a terribly bad idea in the first place. The fact that it sucked should shock no one.

2. Knight Rider 2 (Score: 26). I realize that Hasselhoff is some sort of cult hero today, and he was indeed great in the *SpongeBob* movie, but is there really a need for a 2004 version of Knight Rider? What was worse, ol' Dave wasn't even voiced in the game. How in the world do you make a Knight Rider game without the voice of David Hasselhoff?

1. Gravity Games Bike: Street. Vert. Dirt. (Score: 24). Games that receive reviews that are beyond bad usually have technical problems aside from design issues. This "extreme" BMX game was so buggy that it was almost unplayable. GameSpot said it best: "In short, the game plays like an unfinished product rushed out the door and has absolutely no redeeming qualities whatsoever." That's a bad review, folks.

Shine on you crazy diamond...shine on.

Image courtesy of GameSpy.com.

DID YOU KNOW

It appears that the Miami Vice franchise isn't done wreaking havoc on the world of pop culture. As if the game weren't enough of a travesty for one lifetime, look for a *Miami Vice* movie in 2006 at a theater near you.

Oddworld Inhabitants (1994-?)
Corporate Graveyard

Abe's Exoddus is a platforming classic.

You can't truthfully say that Oddworld Inhabitants is dead. The company still exists, but in April 2005 it shifted its focus away from games to movies and TV. Nevertheless, the gaming industry lost out big time when Oddworld Inhabitants left the biz.

Founded in 1994 by computer animation veterans Sherry McKenna and Lorne Lanning, the company went on to create some of the most imaginative games in the history of the hobby (and also sell more than four million games to date). Games such as Oddworld: Munch's Oddysee and Oddworld: Abe's Exoddus are staples of the console platformer genre.

Despite the success of each of its games, Oddworld co-founder Lorne Lanning told the Hollywood Reporter in April 2005 that the company was shifting gears as well as location. Lanning said he doesn't like the way in which the industry is heading, with less creativity and too little control given to developers. Lanning had simply had enough. His comments echo those of a lot of people inside and outside the industry. The corporate hunger for easy cash cows to milk dry is a huge reason why we see so few brand new intellectual properties. Instead we get bombarded with sequels, games based on movies and other licensed properties, and, of course, sports games.

THEY SAID IT

"If you speak to any developer and they don't tell you they have the same frustrations that I had, they're lying. We closed the studio because of what the realities of the marketplace are. There is currently only one financing model in the games industry, and that is that the publisher pays for the entire game; it handles the manufacturing, the marketing, the distribution, the advertising, practically everything, much the way it used to be in Hollywood pre–United Artists. But, as the film industry matured, it took on a more sophisticated financing structure. But not in the games industry." —**Lorne Lanning in an interview with The Hollywood Reporter.com**

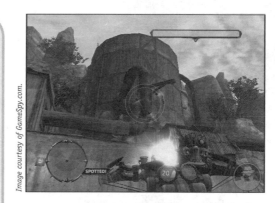
Image courtesy of GameSpy.com.

Oddworld went out with a bang; Stranger's Wrath is arguably the company's best game.

The Oddworld Lineage

Oddworld: Abe's Oddysee (1997). A classic PlayStation platformer that was also released on the PC, Abe's Oddysee introduced gamers to Abe, a lovable Mudokon who works at RuptureFarms, who tries to save his fellow Mudokons from the evil boss Molluck the Glukkon. If you never played the original game, it's perfectly acceptable if that last sentence made absolutely no sense to you. Trust me, it was great.

Oddworld: Abe's Exoddus (1998). This was a pretty straightforward PS1-based sequel, albeit with even stranger creatures and sharper visuals, Abe's Exoddus removed the now famous Abe from retirement on yet another 2D platforming adventure.

Oddworld: Munch's Oddysee (2001). Solely an Xbox release, this was a truly fabulous game that teamed Abe up with Munch (the last of the Gabbits), in a game combining puzzles, platforming, and adventure themes. With even more bizarre creatures and wildly imaginative gameplay, this is one of the most creative and unique games ever made, but it was also extremely playable and an absolute blast.

Oddworld: Stranger's Wrath (2005). The most recent game (also Xbox only), Stranger's Wrath, introduces the hero known as the Stranger, a rough-and-tumble bounty hunter who really is a big shift away from Abe and Munch. Here you can switch to a third-person viewpoint for the first time in an Oddworld game. This was also a lot more action oriented than previous games. (For more detailed information about Stranger's Wrath, refer to the January entry.)

DID YOU KNOW

There's a book about Oddworld called *The Art of Oddworld Inhabitants: The First Ten Years*. It was published by Ballistic Publishing in November 2003.

Larry Bird and Dr. J: One-on-One
Closet Classic (1983)

Crude early '80s graphics aside, this was one great basketball game.

DOSSIER

Genre: The First Great Hoops Game **Publisher:** Electronic Arts **Developer:** Electronic Arts **Platform:** Commodore 64, Apple II, IBM PC

Of all the sports genres, basketball has been the slowest to develop. In fact, there was a long stretch before we even had the chance to play a true five-on-five basketball game. I remember going to software shops in the early 1990s, looking for a new hoops game, and only seeing games like Michael Jordan in Flight (a three-on-three game) on the shelf.

You have to remember, it wasn't until 1995 when EA Sports released the first NBA Live game and took the sports gaming world by storm. Before that the classic 1989 release, Lakers Vs. Celtics, was a five-on-five game, as was the brilliant TV Sports Basketball released in 1990; but by the mid 1990s, both were a tad dated and people wanted something more.

All these games, however, even going back to the classic SportTime Basketball (the first game to have a franchise mode, by the way) and the Fast Break series from Accolade, need to pay homage to one game in particular: Larry Bird and Dr. J: One-on-One.

The game actually had foul shots!

The History

Released in 1983 on a wide variety of platforms from the C-64 to the Apple II, this game really marked the beginning of EA Sports. Even with its crude sprite graphics, which looked marvelous at the time, it set several benchmarks for the genre. First off, you could actually play *against* the computer. This was amazing stuff for 1983. This was right around the time of the Intellivision console system, which had absolutely no AI at all in its sports games. The Intellivision basketball game was released a mere two years earlier, so being able to play alone was utterly amazing. Sure, the AI was simple, but for an 11-year old it was the most fascinating experience you could imagine.

The game modeled fatigue, pump-fakes, blocked shots, and there were several shot types from fade away jumpers to tomahawk dunks (usually performed by Dr. J) that could even shatter the backboard.

Playing the game against another person, however, took things to an all new high in sports gaming. It was the classic match-up: Bird's three-point shot against the Doc's high-flying antics. Even though the game is extremely simple by today's standards, it marked a major transition in sports games. It's the gold standard of early basketball games.

In 1988, Electronic Arts tried its hand at a sequel called One-on-One: Jordan vs. Bird that was released on the PC (DOS) and the C-64/128.

The sequel, which obviously had better graphics, was nowhere near as fun. By 1988, the landscape had shifted a bit. Games were starting to get a bit more sophisticated both in gameplay and graphics, and Electronic Arts added new features but also removed nearly everything that made the original the game that it was.

There was an ill-conceived slam-dunk contest which was nothing more than a timing drill, a three-point shootout (another timing drill) and the one-on-one game itself, which was hampered by clunky controls and sluggish animations.

It was also the first time I remember seeing the invisible barrier in EA basketball games. If you played against the AI, as it were, driving past either Jordan or Bird was extremely tough to do because an invisible force field around each player. This "feature" would end up as a staple of EA basketball games throughout the 1990s and into the new millennium.

By the late 1980s, legendary games like TV Sports Basketball, SportTime Basketball, and the aforementioned Lakers Vs. Celtics were on the stage and they completely obliterated Jordan Vs. Bird. That shouldn't overshadow the fact that in 1983 Electronic Arts created one of the most influential sports games of all time. Larry Bird and Dr. J: One-on-One is as important to the evolution of basketball games as Wolfenstein 3D is to the evolution of the first-person shooter.

DID YOU KNOW

This month in 1983, David Plummer, age 14, scores 7,119,700 points on Tempest after playing the game for more than six hours at Midtown Amusements in Canada. That, folks, is a lot of Tempest.

May 2005

The Summer Doldrums

For me, May means The Kentucky Derby and the Electronic Entertainment Expo (E3). They have nothing in common other than the Derby is the first Saturday in May and E3 takes place the same month. The industry unveils a lot of its new toys at E3 and the press reports back on how great they all look.

Actually, E3 and the Derby have another thing in common: I end up losing money attending both of them.

Aside from the big trade show party, there were a few notable releases this month. Forza Motorsport for the Xbox was released and hardcore drivers everywhere were smiling ear to ear as a result. WarioWare Twisted! for the GBA once again proved that Nintendo can make an addictive handheld game using the most bizarre premises. PSP fans finally got to see Hot Shots Golf: Open Tee, which might be the best handheld golf game ever made. Finally, a little known Diablo clone called Fate was quietly released by WildTangent and ended up being one of the most pleasant surprises of the year.

Flops of the Month:

- **Imperial Glory**—This was supposed to be Napoleon: Total War but ended up being a muddled mess with a lack of realism and hectic battles. The graphics were cool, though.
- **Star Wars: Episode III Revenge of the Sith**—When you saw the "Lava" scene at the end of *Episode III*, did you say to yourself, "Whoa, this looks like a videogame"? Yeah, me too. This was a terrible *Star Wars* game. Not only was the gameplay repetitive, but it only lasted maybe six hours. Shameful.
- **MVP Baseball 05 PSP**—Another attempt by EA Sports to cash in on the new PSP and yet again the company failed miserably.

Star Wars Galaxies
The Rage of the Wookiees Expansion

A common sight in SWG: Players hanging around waiting to get healed.

Image courtesy of GameSpy.com.

DOSSIER

Genre: Online Role-Playing with Wookiees **Publisher:** LucasArts **Developer:** Sony Online Entertainment **Platform:** PC **Metacritic Metascore:** 73

Never has a game shown more promise only to end up as surprisingly mediocre as is the case with Star Wars Galaxies (SWG). The idea sounds like a no-brainer. Take the immensely rich and diverse setting of *Star Wars*, throw in thousands of players, and let the fun begin! It didn't quite work out like that, though.

What fans got was a shockingly bland game that didn't seem to have a whole lot to do with a galaxy far, far away. Fortunately, the game's expansions, including the May 2005 release of Rage of the Wookiees helped smooth things over a bit. Here's a look at the evolution of Galaxies.

THEY SAID IT

"Star Wars Galaxies is set just about 20 years *after* the *Revenge of the Sith* movie. For instance, with Rage of the Wookiees, we are adding a number of series of quests that take you to the relics of the Clone Wars. You'll learn what happened in the time between the end of the Clone Wars through the time of *A New Hope* and you'll loot some very cool artifacts from those times as well." —**Julio Torres, Producer of Rage of the Wookiees in an interview with PCGamezone.com**

actually turned into a pretty cool *Star Wars* flight sim because of this expansion and the patches that followed.

Image courtesy of GameSpy.com.

Rage on, Wookiee. Rage on.

The Galaxies Universe

An Empire Divided (2003). I think the best way to summarize this initial release of Galaxies is from my own personal experience. I created a character with the hopes of becoming a bounty hunter. I couldn't just start as one, though. I had to start out with a lower profession and work my way up to the advanced career of bounty hunter. Fair enough.

So, I head out to Tatooine and find a mission kiosk where I accept a mission to clear out a bug-infested nest for some farmers. I walk for an eternity and come across the area that needs cleared. There are no farmers, just critters. I shoot them, netting me some experience points and some skill improvements. That's it. Level 1 character or no, it's not much fun feeling like you're just the Orkin Man.

Jump to Lightspeed (2004). By the time this first expansion, Jump to Lightspeed, had arrived, patches and updates had started to improve the game. This add-on focused mainly on starships, which is to say it added them. The game has

Rage of the Wookiees (2005). The latest expansion includes a new storyline, a completely overhauled combat system (for better or for worse) and includes the Wookiee planet of Kashyyyk.

To be fair, the game is almost nothing like it was when it was first released. The team at SOE has added a slew of content since then, including personal mounts, speed bikes, land speeders, starships, user-made cities, Jedi training, and so on. Just don't expect too much from it until your character reaches the higher levels.

The Trials of Obi-Wan (2005). The folks at SOE weren't done with expansions last year, however. In November, for the rather steep price of $29.99, SOE debuted a downloadable expansion called "The Trials of Obi-Wan." In this expansion, Obi-Wan himself sends players on various high-level quests on the planet Mustafar (where he chopped up Mr. Fussy Pants...er...Anakin). Among the rewards is a "lava-like" lightsaber. Yes, you read that right: *lava*. I don't get the appeal either.

DID YOU KNOW

Originally, Sony and LucasArts had planned on Xbox and PS2 ports of Star Wars Galaxies. As the development continued and delays popped up, those plans were axed.

E3
The Evil That Men Do

Enter this building at your own risk....

For years, E3 has been the gaming Mecca for every geek with a tacit professional connection to the industry. Over the course of three days, the floors of the L.A. Convention Center are flooded with industry pros looking to do business, gamers looking to catch a glimpse of the next generation of video gaming, models in shameless outfits, and enough PR and marketing people to handle spin for seventeen presidential administrations.

For a gamer, it's like an amusement park. You go there and it's loud, games are literally everywhere, and it's like one big gaming party. But when you're there to work, a big gaming party makes for a lousy work environment.

THE E3 HOME PAGE

Read up on E3 or register for the show at **www.e3expo.com**. Because it's only open to industry professionals (this includes part-time sales clerks at the local EB World), you need to know someone that can get you in or be able to forge press credentials.

The Games

There are a lot of games on display at E3. How many? Imagine a GameStop exploded onto 770,000 square feet of floor space, but with huge blaring speakers and enormous displays at every turn showing every major game likely to see shelves over the following year or two...or three or more. (Paging Duke Nukem Forever.)

You really can see the current trends in the industry by simply walking the floors of E3. E3 2005 was littered with console platformers, sports games, and games that are trying to rip off Grand Theft Auto. PC gamers were inundated with MMOGs and little else. Rare is the turn-based strategy game, the flight sim, the graphic adventure, or the PC sports game—a stark change from the late 1990s, when PC games played a much more prominent role.

Yep, the gaming industry sure has matured. Yes, siree.

The Media

E3 isn't about the media. We're there, running and working our little tails off, making appointments and seeing game presentations for three straight days. But we are secondary figures; the show is really for industry big wigs and behind-closed-doors deal making. Some companies try to court retailers to get them to carry their game. A merger deal might take place. You just never know.

The Booth Babes

Finally, E3 is also known for the booth babes, half-naked women in bizarre garb who wouldn't know Mario from Sonic who are basically there so people can stand in line to get a picture taken with them.

This isn't just about being sexist (even though it is), it's about hypocrisy. When you have the executives from every big-name publisher giving speeches about how the gaming industry has "grown up" what does this really say about the maturity of the industry?

Perhaps if some of these companies would spend less money on elaborate E3 displays and paying women to flaunt their assets and instead spend more time making better games, we'd all be a lot better for it. (That said, my editor says he'd like to give a shout out to "Tiffany," who modeled for the ill-fated Space Bunnies Must Die in 1998.)

The Reality

If you ever get the chance to go to the show, do it. The first time you go to E3, you'll have a blast. Just remember that it is one big dog and pony show, don't take it too seriously, and bring a set of ear plugs. You also have my condolences if you have to go in a vain attempt to conduct business on the show floor.

DID YOU KNOW

E3 2006 will once again take place in May at the L.A. Convention Center. This time the doors open (technically only to industry insiders) on May 10th through the 12th.

Forza Motorsport
Racing Sims Don't Get Any Better

Image courtesy of GameSpy.com.

DOSSIER

Genre: Xbox Turismo **Publisher:** Microsoft **Developer:** Microsoft **Platform:** Xbox
Metacritic Metascore: 92

Forza Motorsport is Microsoft's Gran Turismo killer. If you love racing simulations, Forza is a system seller; a game that you simply *need* to own. It sports more than 230 unique cars, in excess of 30 tracks, and the ability to customize your car like no other racing game before it. Throw in great online play via XBL, and you have a certified winner of a racing game.

There are a lot of cars in Forza from which to choose.

There are several modes of play in Forza, but the meat of the offline game is the career mode. It's here where you earn cash by winning races so that you can buy and trick out more cars.

My favorite part of career mode is the ability to upgrade your cars in a ridiculous number of ways. You can buy a ton of different parts, add spoilers, body kits, and so on. The feeling that you are driving *your car* makes for a very gratifying experience.

Also noteworthy is that in Time Trial and Free Run modes you can run on *any* track you like. It uploads your best time to the XBL servers and you can download and race against any ghost run available so that you can, technically, race against a buddy who uploaded his race last week.

THEY SAID IT

"There are three key differences between Forza Motorsport and Gran Turismo: vehicle modding, vehicle damage, and physics. Our modding engine uses real aftermarket parts, which means you'll be buying parts that you can actually find in car shops. There won't be generic "Wing - Composite - Type 1" in Forza. Speaking of damage...we've got a full damage model. Slam into another car or a wall, and you're not just going to wreck your paintjob, but you'll trash parts." —**Dan Greenawalt, lead designer for Forza in an interview with webquad.com/forza**

Intangibles

The driving model is simply outstanding. All the cars are unique and for hardcore sim drivers there is enough realism to keep you satisfied.

The CPU AI is top notch, which is one of GT4's biggest problem areas.

The damage model. It and the general collision detection, are superb. The damage looks great but also has a huge effect on the effectiveness of your car.

The game has a lot of driving assists, but you earn more cash and are generally rewarded more for learning how *not* to use them.

Good luck handling this sucker....

Image courtesy of GameSpy.com.

Online

Forza is regularly one of the top-ranked Xbox Live games. It should also send a message to Sony that Gran Turismo desperately needs online play. So many people are playing Forza on XBL that it's clear that Sony has missed the online boat.

As you play the game online, you can buy and sell or trade cars with other gamers. This is a huge selling point to the game because it allows for interaction with other players outside of the actual racing. In addition to the trading, you can join or form car clubs (sort of like a clan in a first-person shooter), upload ghost runs, and so on. It's a fascinating online experience. The fact that it runs at a butter-smooth 30 frames per second doesn't hurt, either.

TABWIN'S FORZA FORUM
At tabwin.9.foumer.com, you'll find a fantastic forum for Forza dissuasion including tutorials and customization tips. The site also has a handy car trading forum.

DID YOU KNOW

Forza includes a feature called Drivatar, which allows you to train the game's AI to copy your driving skills, methods, and preferences and then let the AI race for you.

Fate
Addiction, Thy Name Is Fate

DOSSIER

Genre: Diablo with Personality **Publisher:** Wild Tangent **Developer:** Wild Tangent
Platform: PC **Metacritic Metascore:** 85

We can forgive you if you've never heard of Fate. After all, you aren't going to find it sitting on the shelf at your local game shop. You can only buy Wild Tangent's independently developed game online at www.wildgames.com. With Fate, Travis Baldree—who serves as the game's producer, designer, and programmer—has created the best $20 bargain of 2005.

If you're into action-oriented role-playing games, you simply owe it to yourself to go to the game's home page at www.fatethegame.com and take a look for yourself. It looks good, plays even better, and is hopelessly addictive.

Fate is all about combat. If you need a detailed storyline, look elsewhere.

THEY SAID IT

> "Once you've completed the randomly generated uber-quest for your game, you have the option to retire—at which point you can pass down one of your treasured pieces of armor or weaponry as a family heirloom. Then, you can start a new game as your own descendant, with a better starting Fame rank and your family heirloom." —**Travis Baldree in an interview with IGN's RPG Vault**

The Game

The Basics. At its core, Fate is a single-player dungeon crawl RPG that uses a three-quarter perspective (sort of like Diablo, a game with which it shares many basic traits). You start off at your home base in the town of Grove. It's here where you pick up quests from local villagers and then venture off into the Dungeon Gate. Completing quests earns you experience points and Fame. The designers described the game as a lot like Sid Meier's Pirates! (see p.121) in that your real goal is to become a famous adventurer. This might sound bland, but Fate trumps its predecessors with its finely honed sense of style.

The Stuff! People like a lot of "stuff" in their role-playing games. A dungeon crawl, in particular, just wouldn't be the same without a lot of magic weapons and armor for the adventurer to find. Fate has inordinate amount of goodies. Axes, clubs, maces, polearms, crossbows, swords, and staffs—and inside of those basic weapon classes are literally hundreds of unique weapons, each with varying statistics, names, and unique looks. It's just remarkable how much stuff there is in this game and it's the same way with both armor and spells.

Replay Value. Fate's replay value is off the charts because the quests are randomly generated, as are the dungeons (which use more than a dozen different graphic tile sets). If you play though the game and then I play through it, we're going to have two vastly different experiences. In fact, Fate encourages you to finish the game more than once through the game's retirement function, which then allows you to pass on a family heirloom to your next character.

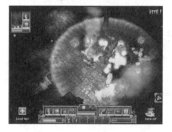

Does this look like a $20 budget game developed by a small indie company? I don't think so, either.

Style. Sometimes when you play a game you can really get a sense that the developers had a lot of fun creating it and this really rings true with Fate. Take the pet feature, for example. At the start of the game, you choose a dog or cat as your loyal companion. It barks (or meows), it wanders off checking out the scenery—in short, it acts like a pet. However, it's not a cute little guy that simply gets in the way. The pet is a crucial part of the design.

Feed your pet a fish and it transforms into one of any of the 12 animal types in the game, such a lizard or wolf. It all depends on the kind of fish. When transformed, your pet becomes a major ally when fighting some of the tougher monsters. This does not look or play like an indie budget game and it's one of the best games of 2005, regardless of platform.

> **FATE ONLINE**
> If you want to mod Fate, be sure to grab the **Mod Kit** at download.wildgames.com/wildgames/fate-modkit.zip.

DID YOU KNOW

The Fate PC game should not be confused with the FATE pen-and-paper RPG, which stands for Fantastic Adventurers in Tabletop Entertainment and won third place at the 2003 Indie RPG Awards for Best Free Game of the Year.

Yohoho! Puzzle Pirates
No Pillaging, Just Acronyms

A meeting of pirates. The interface is very clean and efficient.

DOSSIER

Genre: Online Puzzles with Pirates **Publisher:** Ubisoft **Developer:** Three Rings Design
Platform: PC **Metacritic Metascore:** 79

Yohoho! Puzzle Pirates (www.puzzlepirates.com)has actually been around for a few years now, but I'm slapping it here in the May section because after years of being an indie project, Ubisoft hopped on board to properly publish the game, releasing it to stores in May of 2005 for $20 (plus $10 a month). If you are a puzzle fan and enjoy MMOGs, you owe it to yourself to give this whimsical game a try. It also helps if you like pirates.

The idea is simple enough: You're a pirate sailing the seas and to do piratey-type things, by completing Tetris-like puzzles. The puzzles vary from swordfighting to ship sailing. This is not an action game where you conk players over the head with a sword. Another cool aspect to the game is that the economy is totally self-sufficient and community-driven because shops are managed by the players and not NPCs (like in other MMOGs), so the economy fluctuates based on supply and demand (sort of like the World of Warcraft auction house). You can even join and form crews to team up with other pirates, take temporary jobs, and so on. There's a surprising amount of depth here aside from the puzzles themselves.

THEY SAID IT

> "I've wanted to make a pirate game for years, and it began to really press upon my mind around February, 2000. The name Yohoho! dates from then. The idea of a puzzle-based online world came around a year later, my notebook dates it at March 11th, 2001. Around this time my girlfriend and I were afflicted by Bejeweled addiction. By the 24th of March, I'd scribbled down the broad strokes of the game, including the Puzzle Pirates name. My 2001 GDC notes are overrun by little pirates." —**Designer Daniel James in an interview with IGN.com**

Swordfighting, Puzzle Pirates–style!

The Puzzles

There are approximately 15 different tasks (puzzles) in Puzzle Pirates. The games range from original designs to spin offs of classic puzzles like Tetris, Alchemy, Puyo Puyo, Dr. Mario, and even chess.

The tasks that you perform by solving these puzzles (either by yourself or in duels with other pirates) include drinking, sword fighting, sailing, gunnery, navigation, alchemy, distilling, shipwrighting, treasure drops, bilge pumping, carpentry, and battle navigation. New puzzles are also being created on a steady basis.

The People

There are a lot of people wandering around inside the world of Puzzle Pirates, each of whom can be identified by the color of their name. Here's a quick guide so you know who is who.

OceanMasters: Basically these are the moderators of the game. Like a dungeon master, they're there to answer questions, enforce rules, and so on. Their names appear in blue.

Greeters: Greeters are experienced players chosen by the OceanMasters to help out new players. Their names appear in pink—but only to Greenies; to everyone else, they're yellow.

Pirates!: Your run-of-the-mill player. Their names appear in yellow. Arrrrgh!

Greenies: A greenie is a new player and usually has no idea what he's doing.

Swabbies: The swabby is an NPC. Actually, make that NPP (non-player pirate). They're in the game to fill the roles of absent players and you can also challenge them to drinking contests and sword fights. Their names are white and have a piratey adjective prior to their first name.

DID YOU KNOW

In late 2005, developer Three Rings Design announced its second game called Bang! Howdy (www.banghowdy.com), a multiplayer tactical strategy Western!

Hot Shots Golf: Open Tee
Fun over Realism

Image courtesy of GameSpy.com.

DOSSIER

Genre: Handheld Anime Golf **Publisher:** Sony **Developer:** Clap Hanz **Platform:** PSP
Metacritic Metascore: 80

Hot Shots Golf has been around for quite a while now—going all the way back to the *Nice drive!* original PlayStation. If you've played one of the older games in the series, you already have a pretty good idea of what to expect in the PSP version: cartoony characters and a ton of unlockable content, all wrapped up in a nice and cheery atmosphere.

The graphics and sound are a shade underwhelming, but it plays seamlessly over an ad hoc wireless network for up to eight players. (Oddly enough there is no hot seat option or online Internet play, though.)

The PSP version of Hot Shots Golf is pretty much exactly what the doctor ordered for fans of the series who are looking to take their game to the PSP. You can't ask for much more than that.

THEY SAID IT

> "HSG: Open Tee definitely includes some new features for the portable gamer in mind—the first being the structure of gameplay. In the main single-player mode, Challenge Mode, most of your matches can be finished in 10–30 min; this is due to the events being nine holes or being able to end Match Play events early. This is perfect for the 'twitch-gaming' that players-on-the-go can appreciate." —**Product Manager Mark Valledor in an interview with GameBizdaily.com**

The Characters of Open Tee

There are 10 characters in Open Tee, 8 of which need to be unlocked. They all carry with them individual stats and traits that help them stand out from one another. Here's a quick rundown of six golfers, including a basic stat sheet (using basic clubs and balls).

Mika. Mika is a control player who doesn't hit for much power but has no significant disadvantages. (Power Shots: 7)

Power: 254	Impact: 21
Control: 18	Sidespin: 12
Spin: 16	

Rio. Similar to Mika, Rio has the advantage of being able to play even better out of the rough. (Power Shots: 8)

Power: 258	Impact: 20
Control: 17	Sidespin: 16
Spin: 18	

Alia. Alia packs slightly more power along with added control...just don't ask her to put a lot of sidespin on the ball. (Power Shots: 6)

Power: 262	Impact: 18
Control: 20	Sidespin: 9
Spin: 19	

Image courtesy of GameSpy.com.

He definitely got all of that one.

Shu. Shu is the sandman. If you're in a bunker, he's the man for the job. He also comes with nice base stats. (Power Shots: 7)

Power: 270	Impact: 17
Control: 16	Sidespin: 21
Spin: 21	

Julie. A low-ball hitter who is dynamite out of the rough, Julie's a tough opponent. (Power Shots: 7)

Power: 274	Impact: 16
Control: 19	Sidespin: 14
Spin: 14	

CJ. CJ is straight as an arrow, but suffers big time if he manages to hit in the rough, which doesn't happen very often. (Power Shots: 6)

Power: 282	Impact: 15
Control: 24	Sidespin: 5
Spin: 13	

DID YOU KNOW

Released in December 2004, Open Tee was the #1 selling PSP game in Japan through the first half of 2005, outselling both Lumines and Ridge Racer.

Fire Emblem: The Sacred Stones
Rock, Paper, Scissors on the GBA

DOSSIER

Genre: Top Shelf GBA Game **Publisher:** Nintendo **Developer:** Intelligent Systems
Platform: GBA **Metacritic Metascore:** 85

The kingdom of Renais, ruled by Fado, the peerless Warrior King. ▼

Image courtesy of GameSpy.com.

This is not just a straight-up fighting game, there's a lot of detail and character development.

Fire Emblem, a deep game of tactical-strategy and role-playing, is a pretty amazing series but in North America it's something of a well-kept secret. Sacred Stones is the eighth game in the franchise's history, but only the second to reach North American stores, so stateside we've only tasted a few bits and pieces of this series.

Sacred Stones is the third portable Fire Emblem game and is one of the most fascinating GBA games available today. Seriously, if you own just *one* GBA game, I think it should be Sacred Stones. If you want to play a game that shows off just how compelling and detailed a GBA game can be, this is it. There's more back-story here than you'll see in most big budget PC and console RPGs—and the tactical strategy combat model is superbly done. There's even first-rate multiplayer support so that you can take your trained troops online to battle other players.

THEY SAID IT

"Nintendo's campaign for Fire Emblem: The Sacred Stones was most likely the last big push any game will receive on the Game Boy Advance. It's true that third parties are going to continue supporting the GBA in full force, and Nintendo still has a few titles coming as well (DK: King of Swing and Mario Tennis Advance, most notably), but no GBA games on the horizon seem to have the potential to match the unique, multi-faceted marketing push NOA gave The Sacred Stones."
—**GameBizDaily.com**

Troop Classes

There are several troop classes in Fire Emblem, such as Pirate, Wyvern Lord, Cleric, and Falconknight, and each has its own strengths and weaknesses. The combat system works great, but also takes some time to get used to in that the rock/paper/scissors feel to fighting makes it seem a little too simplistic at first. Thankfully, the use of magic levels adds another layer of depth to the combat and in reality it's not a simple affair at all. Troops have all kinds of stats, such as speed, luck, resistance, movement, constitution, defense, and so forth. When you toss in all the individual skills, you can see how things can get hairy *really* fast.

Image courtesy of GameSpy.com.

Time to get it on: I like Syrene in this match up....

Basic Strategy

Here are some basic strategy tips to help newbies get started:

- Axe beats spear, spear beats sword, sword beats axe. Light (magic) beats dark, dark beats anima, anima beats light. Bows deliver auto criticals to flying units.
- Avoid using your super buff characters early on because they'll eat up all the experience that your green troops need.
- Terrain is crucial in providing advantages during combat, particularly to defense and dodge.
- Mixing armies is absolutely crucial because if you load up one of a particular type, you will eventually find an army that you cannot beat.
- Even great characters need support from healers.
- Keep in mind that death is *permanent* in Fire Emblem games after you save your progress. Tough game, eh?

FIRE EMBLEM FAN FORUM
At **s7.invisionfree.com/FESS**, you'll find a highly active fan forum for the series; if you have a question then this is the place to ask.

DID YOU KNOW

Intelligent Systems, designer of the entire Fire Emblem series, also co-developed WarioWare: Touched! (as well as several other Nintendo games such as the 1985 game, Duck Hunt).

The Best of *Star Wars* Games

The Force Is Strong with These Games

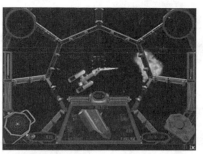

TIE Fighter is considered the cream of the Star Wars crop.

With any highly popular license, you can bet your bottom dollar that the gaming industry is going to jump all over it. This isn't just true today; it's pretty much always been the case. Take *Star Wars,* for example. Games using the license have been cranked out on a fairly steady basis since the early 1980s. There have been literally dozens of *Star Wars* games published over the years from coin-op arcade games to revolutionary classics like X-Wing to complete disasters like Force Commander and Yoda Stories. Here's a look at the very best games from a galaxy far, far away. (Queue the Imperial March theme music!)

Super Star Wars Series (1992–1994). Considered by many to be the first great *Star Wars* series, these SNES platform classics were loosely based on the original trilogy. You could choose a character before each level and even take part in ship combat.

X-Wing and TIE Fighter (1993–1994; 1999). These games set the bar. X-Wing allowed you total freedom inside the cockpit of an X-Wing fighter, which was something every kid who saw *Star Wars* dreamed of doing. Several expansions were spawned from these games such as B-Wing and Imperial Pursuit, all of which were a joy to play. TIE Fighter, however, was the best of the lot and is considered to be one of the best games of all time. The series took a break and returned with the 1999 release, X-Wing Alliance. With a great storyline, modernized graphics and the same thrill-ride flight action sequences this was a fabulous continuation.

Dark Forces/Jedi Knight Series (1995–2003). Dark Forces was the first attempt by LucasArts to make a first-person shooter. The first game hit the shelves during the height of the DOOM craze, and it is rumored that LucasArts started the series due to all the popular fan-made *Star Wars* DOOM mods. Regardless, LucasArts delivered a fantastic game with an engine that let you crouch and look up and down (hey, for 1995, this was *big deal*). It was also much more story driven than DOOM and there is the bonus factor that you got to kill stormtroopers, which was just *trés* cool.

Dark Forces was a revolutionary shooter, back when shooters were still evolving.

Super Star Wars. Where's Ben Kenobi when you need him?

Dark Forces II: Jedi Knight introduced light sabers and Force Powers, but it wasn't quite as groundbreaking as the original. However, mod tools were made available that spawned a highly active JK modding community that is still strong today. The expansion to Jedi Knight, Mysteries of the Sith, was actually better than the original game. The series stayed with the Jedi theme with the next two popular releases, Jedi Outcast and Jedi Academy.

Star Wars: Knights of the Old Republic Series (2003–2004). I already discussed KotOR 2 back on page 22, but it never hurts to give another ringing endorsement for two of the best role-playing games ever designed. It is a testament to these great games that many *Star Wars* fans feel that the writing and the plots are better than those of the new movie trilogy; this is PC storytelling at its very best. It's also worth noting that the URL www.kotor3.com has been reserved, so hope springs eternal that the series will continue.

ON THE WEB

Chips & Bits (www.chipsbits.com) currently stocks some of the old classics like TIE Fighter, Dark Forces, and Jedi Knight for around $10 each.

The Massassi Temple (www.massassi.net) is the number one site for Jedi Knight modding and level editing, complete with tips, tools, and a forum.

DID YOU KNOW

The first official *Star Wars* video game was 1982's The Empire Strikes Back on the Atari 2600, in which you defended some blocks that were supposed to be the Rebel base on Hoth.

The Bard's Tale
Closet Classic (1985)

Genre: Hall of Fame RPG **Publisher:** Electronic Arts **Developer:** Interplay **Platform:** Amiga, Apple II, Atari ST, Commodore 64

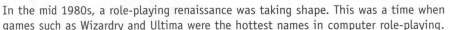

The Bard's Tale was a revolutionary RPG.

In the mid 1980s, a role-playing renaissance was taking shape. This was a time when games such as Wizardry and Ultima were the hottest names in computer role-playing. Then, in 1985, Interplay and Electronic Arts released Tales of the Unknown Volume I: The Bard's Tale and the landscape would never quite be the same again.

The Bard's Tale was not the first game that slapped a party of adventurers together in an attempt to beat an evil bad guy. But the story, although certainly entertaining, was not the driving force behind the game. The Bard's Tale floored players with its colorful pseudo-3D graphics and animation. Gamers were transported to the city of Skara Brae, which came alive as you actually "walked" through the town in a first person view.

The game wasn't all about a fancy game engine; it was a very solid role-playing game with multiple character classes, some tricky puzzles, and tons of personality. The Bard's Tale was truly ahead of its time and is still considered one of the pioneers of the role-playing genre.

Image courtesy of GameSpy.com.

Shifting Suns Studios's the Devil Whiskey is the spiritual successor to The Bard's Tale.

The Bard's Tale Lineage

Tales of the Unknown Volume I: The Bard's Tale (1985). Written by Michael Cranford, the original Bard's Tale was initially released for the Apple II, but ended up being ported to MS-DOS, Commodore 64, Atari ST, and Amiga, among others. The game was even ported over to the NES. The plot involved your six-character party taking to the streets of Skara Brae in an attempt to defeat the evil wizard Mangar. The game sported a whopping 10 character classes and more than 70 spells.

The Bard's Tale II: The Destiny Knight (1986). The second game of the series used pretty much the same engine, but was a lot bigger in terms of locations and overall scope. Instead of just one city, you could travel to up to six inside the game's vast Wilderness area. A new character class was introduced (the Archmage) and enemy distance was now a factor during combat.

The Bard's Tale III: The Thief of Fate (1988). The Thief of Fate was the first game not written by Michael Cranford. The setting was once again Skara Brae, although this time it was in ruins as a mad god had taken residence. You had to travel to several different dimensions to defeat him. The last game was by far the biggest of the three and included such features as an automap and two new character classes (the Geomancer and Chronomancer).

The Bard's Tale Construction Set (1991). In 1991, Interplay released this set of editing tools so fans could create their own game using the Bard's Tale III engine. You could create your own story, import graphics, and so on.

The Bard's Tale (2004). In 2004, InXile Entertainment released a 3D adventure game using the Bard's Tale name on the Xbox and the PS2, with a Windows version planned for fall of 2005. This new game was nothing whatsoever like the classics, and the reception to it was decidedly mixed.

EVEN MORE BARD'S TALE GOODNESS

Shifting Suns Studio recently released **The Devil Whiskey** (www.devilwhiskey.com/main.html), a spiritual successor to the original Bard's Tale, which stays very true to the original game's style.

For those that just cannot get enough Bard's Tale, check out the series of **Bard's Tale Novels** based on the games at www.geocities.com/thebardstale/novels.html.

Interplay published Dragon Wars in 1989 using a "clone" of the Bard's Tale engine. It's commonly referred to as the fourth game of the series, despite the lack of the Bard's Tale name.

Looking Glass Studios
Corporate Graveyard

SHODAN is quite possibly the best villain ever.

Last month we discussed the fall of Troika Games and how the ambitious role-playing designer released fantastic but unpolished games that ended up ruining the company. With a company like Looking Glass Studios, it's much more difficult to pinpoint how such a great developer could possibly sink into financial debt and close its doors.

Did its publisher, Eidos, kill Looking Glass by sinking untold millions into games like Ion Storm's Daikatana? That didn't help. Was the fact that Looking Glass was up to its ears in debt the reason? That definitely didn't help. What about retail busts like Terra Nova? That certainly contributed. There is no single reason why Looking Glass eventually folded. It was a culmination of many internal and external problems that eventually killed the company.

The Looking Glass Lineage

Ultima Underworld I and II (1992; 1993). These games helped revolutionize not only the RPG genre but games in general. Although many point to Wolfenstein 3D as the original 3D shooter, Ultima Underworld was actually the original first-person game, with a full 360° movement. It, as well as the 1993 sequel, plopped gamers inside the wonderful world of Ultima like no other games before it.

Madden Football '93 (1992). Yep, Looking Glass made the Sega Genesis version of EA Sports' Madden Football. Oddly enough, despite all the groundbreaking games on this list, Madden '93 was the company's best seller.

System Shock I & II (1994; 1999). It doesn't get any better than this, folks. The original System Shock was released during the first-person shooter explosion when games like DOOM ruled the roost, but System Shock was not like DOOM; it was better. It's still hard to classify the game because it was really a blending of FPS, adventure, and RPG traits. To this day, there is no better computer game villain than the ruthless AI known as SHODAN. If you stumble across either of these games, buy them on sight.

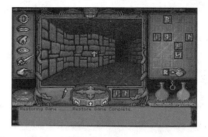

Ultima Underworld was way ahead of its time.

Terra Nova: Strike Force Centauri (1996). This was one of Looking Glass's financial missteps. Terra Nova was a squad-based action/strategy game that placed you in the role of a member of a futuristic strike team who wore custom-sized powered battle armor. The game itself was fantastic, but it flopped at the cash register.

Flight Unlimited I, II, and III (1995; 1997; 1999). Flight Unlimited tried to do battle with Microsoft Flight Simulator and ultimately lost.

British Open Championship Golf (1997). This golf game was actually a lot of fun but it was no Front Page Sports: Golf or Links series.

Thief I and II (1998; 2000). This is another groundbreaking series that went against the grain of other games in the first-person shooter genre. Instead of grabbing your gun and blasting everything to bits, the idea behind the Thief games was not to be seen. With fabulous level design and intense stealth gameplay, the Thief games were a critical and commercial success.

DID YOU KNOW

The classic System Shock AI villain known as SHODAN actually stands for Sentient Hyper-Optimized Data Access Network and was voiced by former Looking Glass employee Terri Brosius, who also voiced Viktoria in Thief I and II.

Grab Bag

Xbox Hacking
Learning the Dark Arts

Gaze upon the innards of your Xbox and despair. Isn't it pretty?

Ahh, the urge to explore! Over the centuries, the drive to go where no one has gone before has driven humans to climb treacherous mountains, fly deep into space, and even place various foreign objects into their noses, all in the endless quest to push the envelope just a little bit further. But what should the intrepid adventurer do today when it seems like there's nothing left to explore?

Tear into your Xbox, of course!

Perhaps because of Microsoft's reputation for being a bit, shall we say, *resistant* to anyone reverse-engineering its products, the Xbox hacking scene operated on the down low in the early days, with hackers swapping stories and discoveries on hastily constructed websites, on obscure IRC channels, and through emails. Today, however, the scene has come out into the open and anyone with a yen to explore, a modicum of electronics skill, a handy soldering iron, and a web browser can access a wide range of online resources dedicated to hacking the Xbox.

If you have the urge to rip into your Xbox to see how it ticks, know this: Opening the case *will* void your warranty. Second, the Xbox isn't designed to be opened and isn't inviting to electronics neophytes; you'd better know your way around a soldering iron before you even think of taking things apart. If you want to get into Xbox hacking, your best bet is to find a cheap unit on eBay that you haven't formed an emotional attachment to and save your main machine to play all those games you've acquired. Then look over the following resources, see what people are doing, ask questions, and work through some of the projects in your head before you take that first step.

Happy hacking!

TOP 5 XBOX HACKING SITES

Xboxhacker (www.xboxhacker.net). The granddaddy of Xbox hacking sites, Xboxhacker.net isn't pretty, but it does a great job of keeping up on the latest news, software, and hardware hacks from brave Xbox explorers around the Net.

Xbox-hacker.com (www.xbox-hacker.com). Well-designed and comprehensive, Xbox-hacker.com is a great source for new Xbox software such as the XboxMediaPlayer.

Xbox-news (www.xbox-news.co.uk). A labor of love from one Xbox hacker to the world, this site provides some great information for the beginning Xbox hacker.

Xbox Developer (www.xboxdeveloper.net). The source for...umm...unofficial Xbox software. You'll find Bochs (an x86 emulator to play old DOS games), utilities for hacking into Xbox games, and even home-brewed Xbox games.

The Beginner's Guide to Xbox Modification (www.xbox-scene.com/articles/beginnersguide.php). Although the main Xbox Scene site is active and chock-full of resources, all beginning Xbox hackers should read this Beginner's Guide first.

Death by DMCA?

Hacking the Xbox: An Introduction to Reverse Engineering (www.hackingthexbox.com; $24.99) was written by Andrew "Huang" Bunnie, the guy who invented Xbox hacking back in 2002. *Hacking the Xbox* is a fascinating combination of a DIY hacking guide, treatise on reverse-engineering, and a cautionary tale on the perils of running afoul of the Digital Millennium Copyright Act (DMCA). Originally slated to be published by Wiley, Huang ended up publishing the book himself after Microsoft's legal beagles harassed the publisher into not releasing it.

Although *Hacking the Xbox* probably isn't for the casual script kiddie who just wants to play pirated games, it is an amazing look inside the process of exploring the new (and heavily guarded) territory inside a new piece of hardware. Through dozens of pictures, circuit diagrams, and pinout descriptions, Huang walks you through everything from opening your Xbox to installing new LEDs, fixing broken power supplies, building new USB adapters, and cracking the Xbox's built-in security protocols.

If you're interested in really learning what's under the hood of your game machine, this book is the definitive guide.

DID YOU KNOW

The term *hack* has several meanings from one who writes program source code (a hacker), someone who works hard at boring tasks, a cab driver, or a mediocre and disdained writer. Um, yeah, let's move on.

Crimson Skies: High Road to Revenge
Bargain Bin Special

It's been a tough day at the office for this pirate.

Image courtesy of GameSpy.com.

DOSSIER

Genre: The Real "Led" Zeppelin **Publisher:** Microsoft **Developer:** Microsoft **Platform:** Xbox **Metacritic Metascore:** 88

Time for me to wax nostalgic. A couple of years ago, I tore the ligaments in my ankle playing basketball and my doctor instructed me to stay off it for the first four weeks of rehab. It was painful and it was frustrating, but it was during this month of being locked to the couch that I decided to pop in Crimson Skies: High Road to Revenge. It's a testament to the game's greatness that it was able to take my mind off of my grapefruit-sized ankle; the game sucked me in whole and didn't let go until I was able to walk again.

Xbox vets are sure to know all about Crimson Skies: High Road to Revenge but if you're a newbie, you need pick this one up. You can snag a copy brand new for $14.99, which is a fantastic price for such an addictive game. Even two years after its release, it still plays great, looks great, and is one of the best Xbox Live games on the planet. Some versions of the Xbox Live Starter Kit ($70) actually come with the game included.

THEY SAID IT

"The first thing we did was make Crimson Skies an action game, not a simulation. This is not a game about the physics of flying an airplane. We spent a lot of time perfecting the flight model and making it easy to pick up and use. Instead of something to learn and master, it's about getting right into the action. Then we added special moves and a camera look to make it hard to master. These have very real benefits when playing competitively over Xbox *Live*." —**Jim Deal, Project Lead on Xbox.com**

Crimson Skies is still one of the best games available for the Xbox.

Image courtesy of GameSpy.com.

It's set in an alternative history—it's the United States of the late 1930s, but the Great Depression has divided the nation into several warring factions. With the railroads and highways pretty much extinct because they run through hostile territory, all commerce, travel, and thievery have shifted to the skies.

In the single-player game, you play air pirate Nathan Zachary, a sort of Indiana Jones–type character who is swindled out of his airship and zeppelin at the start of the game. From this rather clichéd beginning the story takes you to several locations such as the desert to deal with the Native American pilots and Chicago to battle ruthless air-mobsters. The story itself is shown through very well done cut scenes combined with impressive voice acting.

Even though it's technically a flight sim, you should go into it with the understanding that this is an arcade game first and a flight sim second. It's designed to be approachable for a mainstream audience, so you shouldn't expect anything too hardcore here—it's a popcorn action game that is sure to leave you with sore thumbs and a huge grin on your face.

After you're done having Nathan save the day in the solo campaign, you need to take this puppy online. There's still a very active online community for Crimson Skies despite its age, and Microsoft has released new planes and maps that are not available in the solo game.

CRIMSON SKIES UNIVERSE

You can learn all about the CS universe at www.crimsonskiesuniverse.com from the Xbox games to the board game. The world behind the game is truly fascinating and its depth is barely scratched in the Xbox game.

DID YOU KNOW

Crimson Skies was a cool game universe well before the Xbox version. Originally it was a board game from FASA that made its first electronic appearance on the PC, courtesy of Microsoft. They're all great.

Top 10 GBA Games
Metacritic Rates the Best of the Best

Image courtesy of GameSpy.com.

Castlevania. Spooky.

No system has quite the eclectic choice of games as the GBA. You have to hand it to Nintendo—the company is one of the biggest risk takers in the industry and those risks have resulted in some of the most inventive products around. Based on the Metacritic Top Ten list, the GBA's heyday was between 2000 and 2002, when most of the Top Ten games were released, but people are still getting plenty of mileage out of their "old" handheld. Here's the list:

10. Castlevania: Aria of Sorrow (Score: 91). There's just something compelling about a good vampire game. The Castlevania series has proven immensely popular on the GBA. Aria of Sorrow is a fantastic game and one that I personally feel is underrated—for my money, it's better than Circle of the Moon.

9. Golden Sun (Score: 91). Golden Sun (and its sequel, for that matter) proves just how deep a GBA can be. An RPG in nearly every sense of the word, it's GBA RPGing at its best. Full of mythology, character depth, and charm, it's still a blast today.

8. Advance Wars (Score: 92). It shouldn't come as a surprise that the classic GBA strategy game is on this list. Again, this is the kind of game that not only shows the diversity of the GBA but also that the "old generation" handheld could deliver a strategy game with surprising depth but with the usual Nintendo charm.

7. Metroid Fusion (Score: 92). Fusion just edged out Zero Mission for a spot in the top ten. Not particularly revolutionary, but as side-scrolling action games go, it's tough to find a better GBA game than Fusion.

6. Castlevania: Circle of the Moon (Score: 92). Although I do prefer Aria of Sorrow, this is a fine game, no doubt about it. The graphics are a bit underwhelming, but the 1800s setting is ideal for a Castlevania game.

5. Super Mario World: Super Mario Advance 2 (Score: 92). On its face this should not be a classic game. Seriously, how many times can Mario and Luigi save Princess Peach? How many times is this woman going to get kidnapped? Regardless, the game itself is a must-own for GBA gamers.

4. Mario Kart Super Circuit (Score: 93). It's hard to find too many faults here—great graphics and tight racing controls in a game that just oozes charm.

3. Super Mario Bros. 3: Super Mario Advance 4 (Score: 94). Voted as the 2003 GBA Game of the Year by Metacritic, Super Mario Advance 4 is the quintessential side-scrolling platform game. I always thought that this game showed some the GBA's limitations rather than playing fully to its strengths. Quibbles aside, there's no denying its place in GBA history.

2. Tony Hawk's Pro Skater 2 (Score: 95). You know, it's weird. When I was growing up and skateboarding was just starting to take off, Tony Hawk was known only in skater circles, and usually only by those that were really into it. I recall a friend getting a Tony Hawk brand skateboard and I had no clue what a Tony Hawk was. Now the guy is considered pure Americana.

1. Legend of Zelda: A Link to the Past (Score: 95). You had to guess that Link would show up on this list at some point. With The Minish Cap just missing the list, it's fitting that A Link to the Past cruises in at number one.

Image courtesy of GameSpy.com.

Racing the Mario way.

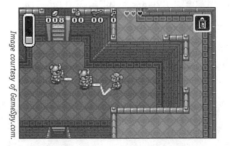

Image courtesy of GameSpy.com.

That crazy kid Link is always stirring up trouble.

DID YOU KNOW

In May 1999, *Next Gen* magazine listed its top 50 video games of all time. Ms. Pac Man was #41, which clearly shows that *Next Gen* was completely insane. Need more proof? Defender was #25 and DOOM was #28. Uh, okay.

Little Big Adventure
Closet Classic (1994/1996)

Twinsen chilling out before he starts his hunt for FunFrock.

DOSSIER

Genre: Do Not Taunt Happy Fun Ball **Publisher:** Activision **Developer:** Adeline
Software Platform: PC

This is a series that doesn't get near the recognition that it should. You rarely hear the LBA games mentioned in the same breath as other adventure games. That's a shame, because they are, without a doubt, some of the most original, charming, and inventive games ever made. The games were released in 1994 and 1996, respectively, and together they remain one of the most underrated series of all time.

The Journey of Twinsen

The Journey of Twinsen took place on the planet Twinsun. In the first game, the evil Dr. FunFrock has made the planet his own police state, dealing in clones, oppressing the people, and kidnapping Zoe, the girlfriend of the game's hero, a Quetch named Twinsen. Twinsen was a unique hero with a unique weapon—a little magic red ball that he used to knock people out, activate switches, and so on. It was like Thor's hammer, in small red ball form.

The game was blazingly nonviolent; it wasn't that Twinsen was above hurting people (that ball could leave a mark) but there was no bloodshed of any kind. It's also worth noting that most of the characters in the game are based on toys or animals. You won't find a gun-toting human anywhere in an LBA game. You will, however, find Quetches (humanoids), Rabbibunnies (walking rabbits), Grobos (bipedal elephants), and Spheros (cute, round bio-androids), all of which make up the four main races on Twinsun.

You could walk around the enormous world and never sit through a loading screen, which was almost unheard of back in the mid 1990s. It was a perfect blend of puzzle solving, action, and creativity that sold more than 400,000 copies worldwide, a nice chunk of sales back in the day.

LBA2: Twinsen's Odyssey

In 1996 a sequel was released called Little Adventure 2 (also known as Twinsen's Odyssey). The story picked up where LBA left off. With FunFrock out of the way, everything was hunky dory on Twinsun until a violent storm, which was then strangely followed by alien visitors called Esmers, who turned out to be anything but friendly.

The style and atmosphere was the same for the sequel, only this time Twinsen explored not only Twinsun but also other planets known as Zeelich and the Emerald Moon. Twinsen's Odyssey proved even more popular than the original, selling more than 550,000 copies worldwide. It used even more cut scenes and added additional music and dialogue.

Looking back on it, it's hard to really classify the Little Big Adventure games into one genre. I suppose technically they're adventure games because there's a huge world to explore and interact with, but there were also RPG aspects, such as different levels of magic and personal inventory housing the 28 unique items found in the game. I guess the best way to describe it is to call it an action/adventure/puzzle/RPG set inside an original and highly creative world where your hero carried a magic red ball. Yeah. That sums it up perfectly.

The LBA games were full of charm and also full of interactive environments and objects, like this telescope.

GETTING BIG ONLINE

The **Encyclopedia Twinsunica** (www.cs.vu.nl/~bkarel/lba) has an amazingly detailed look at the world of the Little Big Adventure.

At **The Underdogs** you can get a taste of the old days by playing the original game. Point your browsers to www.the-underdogs.org/game.php?id=645.

DID YOU KNOW

The team behind the development of Little Big Adventure also headed up work on the original Alone in the Dark.

June 2005

Hot Coffee, Anyone?

Sure, June saw some solid game released like Nintendo DS hits Meteos and Kirby Canvas Curse, as well as the popular online PC shooter Battlefield 2, but the number one title on nearly every gamer's mind was Grand Theft Auto: San Andreas.

The latest game in the storied franchise for the most part lived up to its heritage, but with nearly every GTA release there was a bit of controversy. The "Hot Coffee" debate pulled the gaming industry into mainstream news yet again when it was discovered that there was a locked section inside GTA: San Andreas that allowed users to view explicit sex scenes utilizing a simple tweak to the PC game files.

Although technically this was the work of a third-party modification, it was so easy to mod that it's hard to leave Rockstar Games blameless. As a result, several retail chains initially pulled all copies of San Andreas from store shelves, the ESRB changed the game's rating to AO (Adults Only), and even politicians chimed in as to how sick and perverted the game was. I guess carjacking and indiscriminately killing people was just fine for "mature" gamers, but a modded sex scene was just too much!

Anyway, a lot of hot air was spewed back and forth between lawyers and board directors and eventually Take 2 released 2nd Edition versions of the game with the Hot Coffee part removed from the game. All is well and you are free to buy the game at local retailers today. There's no unedited sex, but there's still a lot of gunfire. God Bless America.

Flops of the Month:

- **Batman Begins**—Great movie, bad game.
- **Fantastic Four**—Bad movie, bad game.
- **Splinter Cell Chaos Theory Nintendo DS**—Another handheld port of a classic console game bites the dust. A poor frame rate (it ran way too slow and choppy) and weird controls pretty much killed the game.

The Grand Theft Auto Series
A Brief History

Getting some "tats" in GTA: San Andreas.

One of the most popular and controversial game franchises of all time, Grand Theft Auto wasn't always the cutting-edge game and political tool that it is today. In fact, the original top-down 2D versions weren't even considered particularly great games. (Metacritic's Metascore for GTA2 is a mere 70.) The series has come a very long way since its late 1990s roots. Let's take a look, shall we?

THEY SAID IT

> "The distortion of the game's content has reached epic proportions, but it's important to remember that fans of Grand Theft Auto greatly outnumber the critics. We tend to find that our critics fall solely into the category of those who don't play the game." —**Rockstar Games CEO Terry Donovan in an interview with** *Computer Games* **magazine**

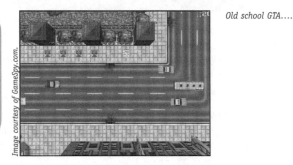

Old school GTA....

The Grand Theft Auto Lineage

Grand Theft Auto (1997). Released on the PS1 and PC, Grand Theft Auto (GTA) was a fairy primitive-looking, top-down 2D action game that had you, as a criminal, driving around cities in various cars earning points by doing dastardly deeds such as stealing cars and smashing up other vehicles. Many of the later game's features, such as the ability to freely go where you wanted, were in the original design. It was violent, but in a campy, 2D, not very threatening sort of way.

Grand Theft Auto: London 1969 (1999). Take the original Grand Theft Auto, move it to London, where you drive on the other side of the road, and you pretty much have an idea of what this "sequel" offered. It was roundly panned by critics.

Grand Theft Auto: London 1961 (1999). This is a fairly obscure free download expansion for GTA: London 1969. It was released only for the PC and you must have both GTA and the London 1969 expansion to play it.

Grand Theft Auto 2 (1999). The true sequel to the original, GTA 2 kept the top-down 2D perspective but it added seven rival gangs to the mix. Now not only would the police chase you around the city, but the city SWAT team or even the *army* would try to run you down. The series was starting to go completely over the top and the groundwork was being laid for something truly special.

Grand Theft Auto 3 (2001). This is where the series began attracting legions of fans; it also started to catch flak from gaming outsiders who saw it as a trainer for would-be criminals. This is where the series went 3D, while at the same time maintaining its completely open-ended gameplay. Not enough credit is given to the people at Rockstar Games because the GTA series is so much more than a satirical look at thug life. It's just flat-out fun to play, and that fun really all started with this version.

Grand Theft Auto: Vice City (2002). Vice City's selling point was the *Miami Vice*–like setting combined with the campy take on 1980s music and culture. Underneath the humor was the same old GTA design: open-ended missions with highly adult content such as murder, drug trafficking, counterfeiting and protection rackets. Gamers loved it, politicians...not so much.

Grand Theft Auto: San Andreas (2004). The latest installment is as popular as ever. It's also the biggest GTA game ever made because it spans an entire state, including three whole cities. It takes place in the early 1990s, so instead of the bright lights and sailboats of *Miami Vice*, San Andreas takes its queue from films like *Boyz n the Hood*. The good news is that although it adds a lot of new game elements, it's still the same old GTA at heart and despite the criticisms, that's a very good thing indeed.

DID YOU KNOW

Actor/director Ron Howard made his directorial debut with the 1977 movie, *Grand Theft Auto*. No hookers were killed in his version.

Meteos
A Puzzler for the DS

Image courtesy of GameSpy.com.

DOSSIER

Genre: Fun with Blocks **Publisher:** Bandai **Developer:** Q Entertainment
Platform: Nintendo DS **Metacritic Metascore:** 89

The Nintendo DS is the ideal platform for puzzle games and Meteos is without a doubt one of the best puzzle games on the market today. If you're a DS owner, this game simply has to be in your gaming library.

Like a lot of puzzle games, Meteos has multicolored blocks falling from the top of the screen. It's your job to manipulate the blocks in a certain way to win. (There's actually a storyline in Meteos, but I'll spare you the details.) However, unlike games like Tetris, you don't flip the blocks around and you can't even move them while they're falling. It's a bit simpler than that but no less addictive.

Blast off!

THEY SAID IT

"It's kind of hard to explain, but I'm heavily inspired by the hardware I'm working on. When I first saw the Nintendo DS hardware design, it really gave me a lot of inspiration. The two screens and touch panel really change the game—I wouldn't do a game like Lumines on the DS." —**Tetsuya Mizuguchi, designer of Meteos in an interview with 1up.com**

Playing Meteos

The object is to get three of the same colored blocks in a row, either vertically or horizontally. You can move the blocks vertically, after they have landed, keeping them in their original column. When you get three in a row, they blast off like a rocket and are sent back up into the sky. You move the blocks with the DS stylus, a great way to use the device.

One of the twists is that each "planet" (level) is different. There are 32 planets in all and each has a different gravitational pull, for example. It might take more than three blocks in a row to blast off a big chunk on some of the planets, which makes it very difficult in the later stages of the single player game.

It's important to note that Meteos is not an easy game. The blocks start falling at a rapid clip and it can be a tad bit overwhelming at first; it takes patience and practice to get the hang of it. Each planet takes less than five minutes before you win or are inundated with blocks.

Other Nintendo DS Puzzlers

Polarium. Rated a 74 on Metacritic, Polarium really is a love-it-or-hate-it kind of game. It's low on glitz but is extremely challenging. It's another falling block game, but this time you flip them to form all-white or all-black rows. You can also create your own puzzles and send them to friends, if you're into that sort of thing.

Electroplankton. Easily one of the coolest names for a game, Electroplankton is less of a puzzle game than it is a music game. Actually, you can make the argument that it's not really a *game* at all. You manage your little planktons...and that's it. There's no objective, you just simply create and manipulate your electroplankton to make cool sounds and visuals. The game even comes with headphones, so you know how much the audio plays a role in its design; this is not a game to play on an airplane without the headset. Oh yeah, and it's more addictive than a triple espresso.

METEOS ONLINE

At netfiles.freespaces.com/bestgames/play/meteos/meteos.html you'll find a very bland **Flash version of Meteos**, but it does do a good job of giving you an idea of what it's like.

Once again, our friends at **Gamefaqs.com** come through with some extremely detailed hints and tips on how best to play the game (www.gamefaqs.com/portable/ds/game/922233.html). If you're stuck, check 'em out.

DID YOU KNOW

Developer Q Entertainment is also the creator of the ridiculously addictive PSP game Lumines.

Kirby Canvas Curse
Just What the Heck Is Kirby?

The world of Kirby is always bright and cheery...and admittedly kind of weird.

DOSSIER

Genre: Kirby in Pink Ball Form **Publisher:** Nintendo **Developer:** HAL Laboratory
Platform: Nintendo DS **Metacritic Metascore:** 87

Kirby is one weird little hero. Nintendo fans have been adventuring with this pink little glob for more than a decade now. His latest escapade, Kirby Canvas Curse, on the Nintendo DS system is arguably the best Kirby game to date.

The story, as it is, goes like this: An evil witch has transformed our little pink poof monster into a little pink ball. Kirby has to travel through seven worlds to defeat the witch. That's pretty much it. In many ways it's a typical Kirby game: bright, cheery colors complimented by very happy, upbeat music. However, the star of the show is actually the DS itself.

Kirby is controlled using the DS stylus and not a D-pad or button control. You draw lines or platforms that propel Kirby through the level. He isn't walking around on his own, it's up to you to guide him in the right path by creating these rainbow pathways. In addition to using the stylus, you can also tap Kirby to give him a speed boost, and when he's speed bursting he can stun enemies.

It's an amazingly addictive game that takes you on a tour of several different (and all very colorful) environments such as a machine world, an underwater world, an ice world, and so on. Canvas Curse really is the DS at its very best and is a definite must buy if you're a fan of the system.

Go, Kirby go!

Kirby in the Machine World—the game has a lot of unique environments like this.

The Faces of Kirby

Kirby has appeared in no fewer than 20 games from 1992 through 2005. Here are a few of the more notable ones.

Kirby Dream Land (1992). This is the original Kirby adventure on the Game Boy. Kirby didn't have any of his special powers, but he did eat the bad guys, showing us early on that Kirby was one...odd protagonist.

Kirby's Dream Course (1995). Kirby made many appearances on the SNES system. This was an isometric view "golf" game...with Kirby as the ball. In "Kirby circles"—and don't you just want to be in one of those—this is regarded as the hardest of the Kirby games.

Kirby Air Ride (2003). Kirby finally made his way to the GameCube in this racing game where Kirby and the computer-controlled drivers raced on top of stars rather than in traditional cars.

Kirby and the Amazing Mirror (2004). This little gem on the Game Boy Advance was multiplayer friendly and was also more open ended than your standard Kirby game. There are also several "Kirbies" running around—each a different color. You have to say this about Nintendo: It's not afraid of innovating...or at least trying to.

> ### KIRBY'S RAINBOW RESORT
> Get in touch with your inner Kirby at the popular fan site www.classicgaming.com/kirby.

DID YOU KNOW

Kirby is one popular little pink...thing. So popular, in fact, that he has his own anime called *Hoshi no Kaabii* (Kirby of the Stars) that appears on 4KidsTV as *Kirby Right Back at Ya!*.

The Medal of Honor Series
A Brief History

Image courtesy of GameSpy.com

You can't walk four feet into a game store today without tripping over a Medal of Honor game. Starting in the late 1990s on the original PlayStation, it has proven to be one of the most successful shooter franchises in history and shows no real sign of slowing down. Not every game in this storied series is a classic. In fact, some are just downright bad, but you can't deny that it has legions of fans and keeps earning its way at the cash register. Here's a look at the games that make up the Medal of Honor series.

The D-Day invasion in Allied Assault was an amazing gaming experience.

Rising Sun failed to deliver on almost every level. What was up with the elephant?

Image courtesy of GameSpy.com.

Roll Call

Medal of Honor (1999). A huge success on the original PlayStation, Medal of Honor (MoH) was compared to the classic PS1 games such as GoldenEye and was considered a must have for action fans as well as WWII buffs.

Medal of Honor: Underground (2000). This was a refreshing change of pace because you played Manon Batiste, a woman enlisted in the French Resistance. Also a PS1 exclusive, the missions were just as exciting as the original, but critics started to point out how predictably the AI behaved.

Medal of Honor: Allied Assault (2002). PC gamers got their first taste of the MoH franchise with this blockbuster release. Allied Assault was a great game from start to finish, but what the vast majority of gamers remember about it was the amazing D-Day mission. Never before had gamers stormed the beaches of Normandy in a first-person view; it was pure chaos and one of the most memorable moments in gaming history. There was also a pair of decent, but overpriced ($30) add-ons: Spearhead and Breakthrough.

Medal of Honor: Underground (2002). This GBA game was not published by Electronic Arts and was universally panned by critics. It was so bad that GamesDomain said, "It's more like somebody's high-school programming project than an actual commercial game." Ouch.

Medal of Honor: Frontline (2002). The series moved to all three next-gen consoles with Frontline, and although it was well received by fans and critics, frame rate issues took its toll (particularly on the Xbox). Overall, though, it was a nice debut on the new high powered systems.

Medal of Honor: Infiltrator (2003). This was a wonderful (but short) GBA version of MoH that all but erased the bad memories left by Underground.

Medal of Honor: Rising Sun (2003). The first real stumbling block for the series, Rising Sun was criticized across the major consoles for its sloppy controls, nonexistent AI, and a graphics engine that was starting to get a bit long in the tooth.

Medal of Honor: Pacific Assault (2004). The series came back to the PC with mixed results. It lacked the polish of Allied Assault, and the linear missions were starting to wear a bit thin in an era in which open-ended gameplay ruled the day.

Medal of Honor: European Assault (2005). European Assault is by no means a bad game, but it also shows how slow the series is to progress from its late 1990s roots. Weak multiplayer, weak AI, and even more linear gameplay are causing the series to stagnate.

Medal of Honor: Airborne (2006?). Set to be a potential PS3 launch title, details on Airborne Assault are scarce, but it's safe to say that the series will continue as long as gamers line up to buy them. Hopefully Airborne Assault will allow gamers a bit more freedom.

> ### PLANET MEDAL OF HONOR
> From daily news to all the best MoH PC mods, **www.planetmedalofhonor.com** is the place for fans of the series.

DID YOU KNOW

The original Medal of Honor on the PlayStation sparked a controversy in Germany because the infamous Nazi swastika symbol appeared throughout the game. The game was put on the index of youth endangering media in Germany in 2000.

Battlefield 2
The Multiplayer Mayhem Continues

DOSSIER

Genre: World War II: Again **Publisher:** Electronic Arts **Developer:** Digital Illusions
Platform: PC **Metacritic Metascore:** 91

The BF2 Experience mod is all about realism.

When the original Battlefield 1942 was released back in 2002, it was an immediate hit with fans of first-person shooters who loved to play online. In fact the entire game centered around hopping onto servers, jumping into authentic World War II–era tanks and planes, and blowing each other to bits. As an offline game, BF1942 was pretty dull and was really useful only as a training ground for online play.

Battlefield 1942 proved so popular that several sequels were released for it, including the popular Battlefield Vietnam, complete with its classic rock music tracks.

Battlefield 2 (BF2) is the natural progression of the series as it moved things into modern times. Its setting is a hypothetical war between the United States, China, and the Middle Eastern Coalition (MEC). It uses modern weaponry and vehicles and has proven to be enormously popular with action fans since its release in June 2005.

Like BF1, this game is all about playing online. However, Battlefield 2 is a significant upgrade from previous games in the series both graphically and from a design standpoint. Chances are if you're into playing shooters via your broadband connection, you already own the game. (If you don't, you should—it's great.)

> ### MODS GALORE!
> There are a lot of mods being worked on using the Battlefield 2 engine, so to keep up to date on the BF2 news and mod scene check out any of the following websites: www.totalbf2.com, battlefield2.filefront.com, www.planetbattlefield.com, and www.bf2.org.

BFPirates is definitely worth keeping an eye on. Avast!

Battlefield 2 Mods

One thing you might not know about BF2 is that there is a very dedicated mod community for the game, and those groups are cranking out all sorts of great user-made content. Here are just a few examples of what's out there:

BF2 Co-Op Mod (users.on.net/~codebasher). This is a very popular mod for solo gamers as well as those who like to play co-operatively.

BF2 Battlefield Experience (battlefield2.filefront.com; do a search). This mod is a realism mini-mod that attempts to make every weapon and vehicle as accurate as possible. To play this mod online, you need to find a server that supports it.

BF2 Autoloader (battlefield2.filefront.com; do a search). This nifty little mod doesn't modify the game, but it acts as a great server browser to allow you manage things a bit easier and find friends to play.

Mods in Progress

BF2 is still a fairly new game, so you need to give the modders time to get their stuff out to the public. These mods are, as of this writing, still being worked on; hopefully by the time you read this, they'll be ready to go.

Battlehammer 40K (www.battlehammer40k.com). Battlefield 2 with Warhammer 40K units? Oh yeah, sign me up. Right now it's going to pit the Space Marines against Chaos and a third race that is yet to be determined.

BFPirates (www.bfpirates.com). It's Battlefield 2 but with swashbuckling pirates and Spanish galleons! This one is close to being ready, so be sure to check it out; the screenshots are fantastic. Yarrgh.

Red Alert: A Path Beyond (dynamic.gamespy.com/~renalert). A BF2 mod that converts everything into the world of Command and Conquer: Red Alert.

1944: D-Day (www.1944online.com). This is pretty self-explanatory, but it's a total conversion mod that tries to simulate the entire 1944 invasion of France.

Rise of Kobol (www.bsgmod.com). A total conversion based on the TV show *Battlestar Galactica* (the new version). Incidentally, if you don't watch the new *BG* series yet, you should start.

DID YOU KNOW

Developer Digital Illusions has a lot of games to its credit, including several educational games such as JumpStart Wildlife Safari and Dino Adventures.

RollerCoaster Tycoon 3: Soaked!
Getting Wet and Wild in Your Theme Park

Image courtesy of GameSpy.com.

Who doesn't like chillin' in a public pool? (Don't drink the water.)

DOSSIER

Genre: Watery Coaster Add-on **Publisher:** Atari **Developer:** Frontier Developments
Platform: PC **Metacritic Metascore:** 79

I was upset at the initial release of RollerCoaster Tycoon 3. It wasn't a problem with the design, graphics, or gameplay: It was the bugs. The game was simply rushed out of the door before it was ready and it suffered as a result. Since then, it's been patched up and is much more stable and playable, which made it so much easier to look forward to playing the Soaked! expansion.

Basically, there are two parts to Soaked!: First there is the obligatory "more stuff" philosophy used in every expansion. You get new rides, coasters, shops, laser light and water park shows, and pathways (you can even build paths underwater and into mountains).

The other portion of the game refers to its title. In Soaked!, you get to add a water park extension to your main theme park. It's a no-brainer of an idea, really, because almost every major amusement park nowadays has a water park sitting next to it. You can build all sorts of wet and wild rides for your peeps to play in, such as swimming pools and all sorts of water slides. Just make sure to bring a fairly beefy PC because the game is still a resource hog.

THEY SAID IT

> "I guess it wouldn't be a real water park without that, would it? They will and we're also adding a fun element there so you'll know what they've done." —
> **Producer Ken Allen, answering a question on IGN.com as to whether little peeps will pee in the pools**

Image courtesy of GameSpy.com.

The Coaster Cam is just awesome.

The RollerCoaster Tycoon Lineage

RollerCoaster Tycoon (1999). RollerCoaster Tycoon took almost everyone by surprise when it was released in 1999. It wasn't the first ever theme park game, but it captured the public's imagination like few games before or since. Who knew that managing and constructing a 2D amusement park, complete with goofy music and little people that vomited after riding a loopy coaster could be so much fun? Not only could you build your park how you wanted it, but you could even create your own mega-coasters from scratch and share them with your friends online.

RollerCoaster Tycoon: Corkscrew Follies (2000). Basically this added more rides and themes to the original game without changing all that much.

RollerCoaster Tycoon: Loopy Landscapes (2000). Ditto for this release. Both add-ons were well received because people just could not get enough RollerCoaster Tycoon.

RollerCoaster Tycoon II (2002). The "sequel" upset a lot of people because it used pretty much the same engine as the original yet still carried a premium price tag ($40); this was not the kind of sequel fans wanted because it looked almost exactly like the old game. Was it fun? Technically, yeah, it was. Was it worthy of being called a sequel? Not really.

RollerCoaster Tycoon III (2004). Finally, the third installment added a 3D view and a lot of new goodies, including the totally wild Coaster Cam. If not for the bugs in the initial release, I'd call it a classic, but the number of bugs that got in the way was beyond the pale.

RollerCoaster Tycoon III: Wild! (2005). As of this writing, Wild! is still in development but should be available by the time you read this. This expansion turns your park into the wild kingdom by adding all sorts of animals in the form of a small zoo.

> **RCTCOMPETITION**
> My favorite hangout for all things RCT from downloads to news updates can be found at **www. rctcompetition.com**.

DID YOU KNOW

The original RollerCoaster Tycoon was later ported over to the Xbox back in 2003, but unlike the PC version, it received a lukewarm reception from gamers and critics alike.

Conker: Live and Reloaded
Don't Taunt This Squirrel

He might look cute on the surface, but this squirrel is dynamite!

Image courtesy of GameSpy.com.

DOSSIER

Genre: Foul-Mouthed Squirrel Action **Publisher:** Microsoft **Developer:** Rare LTD.
Platform: Xbox **Metacritic Metascore:** 78

Squirrels are cute. They're literally everywhere in our neighborhood, so when there's nothing better to do (power outages, Saturday nights, that sort of thing), we watch them gather nuts, scurry along power lines, and chase each other playfully around trees. Our dog loves to chase them, although if he actually caught one I'm not sure he'd have a clue what to do with it. Technically, they're rodents but they possess a cuteness that rats will never achieve.

I bring this all up as a point of reference because Conker is nothing like the squirrels in my neighborhood. He drinks beer. He pees on stuff. He talks like a drunken sailor and he's armed to the teeth.

Conker: Live and Reloaded is really a game in two distinct parts. The solo game is primarily an Xbox rehash of the N64 version of Conker's Bad Fur Day. It's not identical but it's the same premise, with the cussing and sexual innuendo intact. The second part takes place online via Xbox Live. The multiplayer portion of the game is where it shines: It's a 16-man class-based Team Fortress–type system, only with squirrels. How can you not love that?

THEY SAID IT

> "Conker: Live and Reloaded probably wouldn't have happened if it weren't for a console like the Xbox because of the whole Xbox Live aspect of it. That is what we are really proud of. To create the game that we wanted, we simply couldn't have done it on any other console." —**Louise Ridgeway, Lead Animator for Live and Reloaded in an interview with TeamXbox.com**

Multiplayer Character Classes

When battling it out online, you need to understand the different classes that are available. This isn't just a run-and-gun multiplayer game; there's a bit more to it than that. Here's a quick rundown of the classes that are available and some of what makes them tick.

Demolisher. The Demolisher is terribly slow but packs a serious wallop with his bazooka. A Demolisher can kill a target with one direct hit, but the long reload times are a big problem in the thick of a firefight. Demolishers also have the capability to go berserk for a short time, which boosts speed.

    Speed: Poor   Power: Scary
    Armor: Excellent

Grunt. When you think grunts, you think common soldiers. That's basically the Grunt's role here, as well. The capability to self-heal goes a long way in making the Grunt a powerful unit.

    Speed: Average   Power: Average
    Armor: Average

Long Ranger. This is the game's annoying sniper class. Using a Long Ranger is fun, but you're probably going to die a lot because the opposition will hunt this class constantly. Their Infravision skill helps Long Rangers target the entire field.

    Speed: Good   Power: Good
    Armor: Poor

Sky Jockey. The Sky Jockey might be weak on the ground, but in the air (in a vehicle like Steed or Mule-52) it's a whole new ballgame. They are big time targets of Long Rangers, though.

    Ratings are vehicle dependent

Sneeker. Lightning fast, the Sneeker is great at quick, close-quarter fighting and hit-and-run tactics. They can cloak and use a Feign Death ability that makes them even…"sneekier."

    Speed: Flash-Like   Power: Good
    Armor: Paper Thin

Thermophile. A crazy walking squirrel that shoots fire. He's as tough as he sounds.

    Speed: Below Average   Power: Very Good (fire tends to
    Armor: Very Good   burn stuff)

DID YOU KNOW

Squirrels are found on every continent in the world except Australia and Antarctica.

Destroy All Humans!

It's Like *Mars Attacks*, but Better

Image courtesy of GameSpy.com.

DOSSIER

Genre: Anal Probe Simulation **Publisher:** THQ **Developer:** Pandemic Studios **Platform:** Xbox, PS2 **Metacritic Metascore:** 76

Silly monkey! You are no match for Crypto!

Destroy All Humans! is not a great game, but it's also not a *bad* game. What separates Destroy All Humans! from the pack, however, is the fact that it's loaded with personality and is, at times, pretty damn funny. I really have to give credit to developer Pandemic for trying something a bit different. Any game that lets you play a classic movie alien hellbent on taking out mankind gets bonus points from me. Long live Ed Wood.

You play the role of an alien called Crypto Sporidium 137. You're from an alien race full of clones (hence your number). You're sent to Earth on a sort of recon mission but when you learn of a secret agency's dastardly plot, you go on a monkey- (your pet name for humans) killing rampage. The gameplay itself can be a bit mundane and repetitive, but the world around the game is wonderfully done from the sound and graphics to the numerous references to 1950s pop culture.

I can't fully recommend Destroy All Humans! at a full retail price, but it's certainly worth tooling around with as a rental or at a discount price, particularly if you love classic sci-fi B-movies.

THEY SAID IT

"...the biggest pitfall is not properly planning the music's implementation. Videogames require careful thought or the music just won't work well with the game. In the same vein each piece of music should avoid being repetitive. If it is, it will get old real fast and the player will mute it. In a film score repetitive music can be an attribute as the score will likely only be heard once. But with videogames the score is heard over and over." —**Garry Schyman, composer and music director for Destroy All Humans! in an interview with Teamxbox.com**

Image courtesy of GameSpy.com.

Crypto takes to the air to blow more stuff up.

Crypto's Arsenal

There's a wide variety of classic sci-fi gadgets that Crypto uses in his attempt to, well, destroy all the humans. Here's a taste of the base weapons, each of which can be upgraded during the course of the game:

Zap-O-Matic. Your basic lightning handgun weapon; you start the game with it and it never runs out of ammo. It also doesn't pack a lot of punch, initially, until you turn it into a chain lightning weapon.

Disintegrator Ray. A cool weapon, visually. But one of your goals is to collect human DNA and using this tends to evaporate the target, making it a tad hard to collect a sample.

Ion Detonator. This is another weapon that makes it impossible to collect DNA; it's like a grenade launcher. It also can hurt Crypto because of its the blast radius, so beware.

Anal Probe. This is the classic alien "weapon." You'll have to see it in action to believe it, but it's the ideal DNA collector. Ugh.

Death Ray. This is the basic flying saucer weapon, and not a handgun like the others. It tends to leave a mark.

Sonic Boom. This is another saucer weapon, which is ideal for blowing up buildings. It also throws monkeys around like rag dolls and is pretty hilarious to watch in action.

Quantum Deconstructor. A mini-tactical nuke; use it only when Crypto is downright mad.

In addition to the weapons, Crypto can use mental powers to do all sorts of nasty things to us monkeys. Powers such as brain scanning, hypnosis, and brain extraction (ouch) are at his disposal. If aliens ever do visit Earth, let's hope Crypto137 was left back at the ranch.

DID YOU KNOW

Destroy All Humans! is available for wireless phones (Cingular, T-Mobile, Nextel, and Sprint). U.S. customers should text CRYPTO137 to 69847. Check the fees; the game isn't free.

Out of the Park Baseball 6.5
Who Needs Pretty Pictures?

Out of the Park 2005 looks like it will be the Cadillac of baseball sims.

DOSSIER

Genre: Baseball Without Polygons **Publisher:** Sports Interactive
Developer: Markus Heinsohn **Platform:** PC **Metacritic Metascore:** 89

Out of the Park (OOTP) is a rarity. It's a text-based game with no 3D graphics, no advanced surround sound, and no signature batting stances. It's also the most addictive baseball game around. In fact, I have been running an online OOTP league (with 30 other players) since 2002. We're talking more than four years of consistent play. Only the most die-hard fans play the arcade baseball games for more than a few months at a time.

One of the main reasons OOTP is such an addicting sim is that baseball is really all about stats; more than any other sport, stats drive baseball. OOTP tracks a ton of stats and keeps them for your entire league's history. Players come up through the minors, and retire, and can even make the Hall of Fame. You make all the calls from setting lineups and pitching rotations, drafting rookies, working trades, setting ticket prices, signing free agents, and so on.

THEY SAID IT

"The biggest reason for joining SI was that we still have the same OOTP development team, and we have absolutely no restriction from SI in terms of game design. We benefit greatly from their experience and superior technology, while they may learn a little bit from us as well." —**Markus Heinsohn, designer of OOTP on publishing the next OOTP through Sports Interactive**

Image courtesy of GameSpy.com.

The OOTP News page details the top stories from around the league.

The Future

As a general rule, if a series reaches five versions, you know it at least has a dedicated fan base. OOTP is working on version seven, dubbed Out of the Park Baseball 2006. The new version, which should be available in April of 2006, promises to be bigger and better than ever now that popular European publisher Sports Interactive (publishers of the ultra popular Championship Manager series) has jumped onboard with additional funding and marketing power.

Sports Interactive is going to give the game a fresh coat of interface polish. You'll now be able to manage and use one of 300 teams with more than 7,500 players in 26 leagues worldwide. You also get all minor league teams as well, so if you want to simply manage the Toledo Mud Hens and leave the Detroit Tigers to their fate (usually a very, very sad fate) that option is available to you. Additionally, a new pitch-by-pitch mode should please the real hardcore fan who wants to control and see every minute of a game.

OOTP RESOURCES

The Lahman Database (www.baseball1.com/statistics). OOTP is compatible with this huge database that compiles information on nearly every player ever to suit up for the big leagues. When used with Out of the Park Baseball you can, for example, go back and play the 1927 season and manage the New York Yankees and Babe Ruth. The database imports all the players and teams from that year and off you go. Even more amazing is that in the subsequent rookie drafts, real rookies will be made available each year, all the way through modern times.

OOTP Forum (www.ootpdevelopments.com/board). The official game forum is packed with information as well as a forum for those seeking to join an online league.

The OOTP Download Center (www.ootpdownloadcenter.com). OOTP has a dedicated mod community and this site hosts most of the best ones, including draft utilities, stat trackers, face packs and interface skins and a whole lot more.

DID YOU KNOW

Did you know that Out of the Park Baseball is made by a German baseball fan that has never actually been to a real major league game?

Xbox Cheat Tools
Those Who Can't, Cheat

The Mega X-Key looks like a pen drive.

With its 733MHz custom Pentium 3, 64MB Micron DDR SDRAM, 250MHz NV2X graphics board, 8GB hard drive, and 5x DVD-ROM, the Xbox is more like a desktop PC than any other console on the market. However, to keep the Xbox from becoming a cheap subsidized PC, Microsoft went to great lengths to lock down the console from those who install alternative operating systems (such as Linux), run nonstandard software, or otherwise monkey around in its guts.

The security features built in to the Xbox have made developing cheating hardware a bit more of a challenge than other consoles and has actually led to a dizzying array of cheating options. Cheating on the Xbox can take many forms, from software-based solutions (like the Action Replay), to USB-based hardware keys that plug in to the controller ports (like the Mega X-Key), all the way to rip-your-box-apart mod chips where cheating is just the beginning.

For the truly hardcore hobbyist, Xbox modding and hardware hacking are covered elsewhere in this book. But if you just want to get more out of the games you're playing (okay, if you want to be a dirty cheater), here's a selection of hardware- and software-based cheating options that go beyond the ones built in to your games.

Action Replay
$29.99, available from www.codejunkies.com

If you're familiar with other game consoles, you're probably familiar with the Action Replay (AR), a software-based system that uses preinstalled and user-enterable codes to unlock goodies such as extra ammo, weapons, lives, and other god-like powers in your games. Many games also feature secret hidden levels, characters, skins, and even mini-games. The Action Replay lets you access all of them.

AR for the Xbox is a software/hardware combo that comes with a disc to install cheats and an 8MB memory card for storing Action Replay powersaves and even uploading new ones from your USB-enabled PC using the AR docking station (included).

Mega X-Key
$34.95, available from www.lik-sang.com

A slightly more controversial cheating tool is the Mega X-Key. Basically a 32MB memory chip with cheating software, the Mega X-Key has earned the ire of many online gamers because it gives users access to Xbox Live data when editing games on their PCs after plugging in the Mega X-Key. Offline, the Mega X-Key lets you download saves that unlock all the typical cheat booty, including extra lives, weapons, unlocked levels, special powers, and all that other stuff that helps you crush through levels like a gaming god. You just plug it in to your Xbox (using the USB/Xbox cable) to load and unload your saves and plug it in to your Windows PC to edit saves, share them with friends, or hack the data files.

X Mod Chips
Various prices, available from www.modchipsource.com

Commercially available mod chips let you do all sorts of things with your Xbox that Microsoft never intended, but why use them to cheat? Because just like the other products mentioned here, mod chips can give you the ability to transfer files to your PC so that you can modify them. How to do so is worth a little bit more detail than we have space for here, but if you want to download some prehacked files, go to trainers.maxconsole.com.

If you want the freedom of a modded Xbox but don't want to hack into your own baby (or don't have the skills to jam extra chips into your Xbox), check out the premodded boxes at www.modchipsource.com.

DID YOU KNOW

The Action Replay actually got its start way back in the late 1980s with the Commodore 64 as a "Turbo Module" that allowed for faster disk access and disk copying abilities.

3DO (1991–2003)
Corporate Graveyard

Image courtesy of GameSpy.com.

Heroes of Might and Magic was the only game that my wife played as much as I did.

In 1991, Trip Hawkins, co-founder of mega publisher Electronic Arts, left to form SMSG Inc. (which would later be known as The 3DO Company) with the help of seven other partner companies, including AT&T, Time Warner, and oddly enough, Electronic Arts.

The company was founded on the idea that it would create a game system that used a CD rather than a cartridge, a radical concept in the pre-PS1 days. The media coverage, for the early 1990s, was extensive and in October 1993, the 3DO Console was released to the public...at $700 a pop. The price was bad enough, but the games available for the 3DO were hardly system sellers, setting the stage for Sony's PlayStation to run the table. This is when 3DO turned away from console manufacturing and into game publishing.

Opinions on 3DO (the company) run the gamut from love to hatred. On the one hand, 3DO released some high quality games such as Heroes of Might and Magic and High Heat Baseball. On the other hand, it released something like 20 versions of Army Men. In May 2003, the company finally filed for bankruptcy and sold off its most popular licenses to various publishers.

THEY SAID IT

"This filing gives us more time to complete transactions in the interest of our stakeholders. While we hope that this news will generate additional new opportunities, at this point we are focused on pursuing either the sale of the entire company or the sale of its assets." —**Trip Hawkins, Chairman and CEO of The 3DO Company**

The 3DO Lineage

Might and Magic (1987–2002). The best thing to happen to 3DO was developer New World Computing, which created the Might and Magic (M&M) line of games as well as Heroes of Might and Magic. Might and Magic was a traditional RPG, first created for the Apple II and C-64 systems back in 1987. This popular series spanned nine versions and several technological makeovers. Although considered one of the early benchmarks of the RPG genre, 3DO milked the M&M line for more than it was worth, ultimately killing the franchise.

Heroes of Might and Magic (1995–2002). One of the best, if not *the* best, series of games that 3DO published, Heroes of Might and Magic took creatures from the M&M world and plopped them into a wonderful turn-based strategy game design. Ubisoft bought the rights in the 3DO fire sale and are working on a fifth installment (see p.254 xxx.)

High Heat Baseball (1998–2003). Now owned by Microsoft, High Heat Baseball (see p.131) was the gold standard of arcade baseball games from 1999 to 2001 before the series

started to fall apart. The early games in the series were a revolutionary blend of arcade action with baseball realism.

Image courtesy of GameSpy.com.

High Heat Baseball was the king of arcade baseball before 3DO's collapse.

Uprising (1997, 1998). Uprising is important because, well, it was a lot of fun; it was also one of the very first games to blend 3D shooter action with real-time strategy gameplay.

Army Men (1998–2004). Now owned by Crave, this series was 3DO's biggest-selling franchise. It also upset a lot of gamers because the company released no fewer than 18 Army Men games in seven years, while ignoring its other games that had a considerably more loyal following.

Meridian 59 (1996–2005). This is another game that deserves mentioning because it was a pioneer of the MMOG genre. Meridian 59 is still active today, actually, under the Near Death Studios label, which bought the rights in 2001.

MERIDIAN 59 LIVES
Still alive and kicking after ten years, Meridian 59 is one of the oldest MMOGs around and you can check it out at the official website (meridian59. neardeathstudios.com).

DID YOU KNOW

After leaving 3DO, Trip Hawkins founded Digital Chocolate, a company that focuses on mobile phone gaming. There's nothing like setting the bar high.

The Front Page Sports Series
Closet Classics

FPS: Football had fantastic graphics for its day.

Today's big budget sports games all have a lot in common. Gamers simply demand certain features to be present. However, back in 1993, things were a whole lot different. When Sierra and Dynamix came on the scene with the release of Front Page Sports: Football, the sports game industry would have to adopt a new set of standards.

It was no longer acceptable to release a PC sports game without reams of stats, custom options, career mode, and detailed player ratings. It was football for the true football geek. It was also one of the games that helped fuel the PC/console sports wars of the mid to late 1990s. While PlayStation fans had action games like Madden, PC users were pouring over rookies for their FPS: Football rookie draft. To the most die-hard sports gamers, it was a no-brainer as to which was better and it would take EA Sports to adopt many of the features found in Dynamix's masterpiece.

THEY SAID IT

"I want to apologize to all our loyal customers for releasing a product before it was ready. We knew the potential for this product but we let the impending end of the football season influence our decision process. We dropped the ball." —**Sierra President David Grenewetzki on the Football Pro '99 recall**

FPS: Baseball Pro had a unique camera perspective, but was much better as a pure sim game.

The Front Page Sports Lineage

The Front Page Sports: Football Series. When the original Front Page Sports Football (FPS) was released in 1992 it was, quite simply, the most ambitious computer football game ever made. At the time, the ideas of playing a career mode and drafting rookies through continuous seasons were simply unheard of. In fact, it took EA's Madden franchise several years before EA Sports even attempted to add a bare-bones franchise mode. All was perfect, for a while, but in the late 1990s, the series began to stagnate, finally falling to pieces with the release of a buggy, unfinished FPS: Football Pro '99. The result was the biggest game recall in industry history. Sierra recalled the entire batch, all 50,000 copies, and sent out a letter of apology to its fans. While the series never recovered, it should be remembered as a true innovator.

The Front Page Sports: Baseball Series. The baseball series wasn't quite as polished as the football franchise, although it, too, was way ahead of its time. The game's "real life" physics was something no other baseball game could hold a candle to at the time, and its career mode was second to none. It was perhaps the first baseball game to even attempt a real simulation and still have arcade gameplay.

The Front Page Sports: Golf Series. There are a lot of fans of the critically acclaimed Tiger Woods Golf series from EA Sports. However, anyone who loves those games should pay homage to the 1997 release from Sierra and Headgate Studios, Front Page Sports: Golf. This was the very first game to use the TrueSwing interface, in which you moved your mouse back and forth to swing the club. Before this, all golf games, such as the popular Links franchise from Access Software, used the double- or triple-click method. After FPS: Golf shipped, golf games were never the same again.

FRONT PAGE SPORTS LIVES ON

Not quite gone, not quite forgotten, past owners of the originally FPS games can head over to The Underdogs and download both **FPS: Football Pro '95** (www.the-underdogs.org/game.php?id=3937) and **FPS: Baseball '94** (www.the-underdogs.org/game.php?gameid=1615).

At **ONAFA League** (www.fbpro.net/onafa) is one of the best FPS league sites around, and it's still banging around like an Energizer bunny.

DID YOU KNOW

Sierra and Dynamix initially had plans to create Front Page Sports: Basketball and Hockey franchises but the idea died when Sierra shut down its sports division.

Neverwinter Nights
Closet Classic (2002)

For a three-year-old game, NWN still looks pretty good.

Image courtesy of GameSpy.com.

Released in the summer of 2002, Neverwinter Nights (NWN) proved to be yet another hugely successful role-playing game for developer BioWare, the developer of the classic Baldur's Gate series.

Fans and critics alike have debated the merits of the game ever since its release, but I have always been of the opinion that NWN was more about potential than payoff. Take away the robust editing tools and multiplayer component, and you are left with a very mediocre single-player RPG.

However, by including the Aurora Toolset, the developers allowed gamers (with some basic scripting programming experience) to create their own modules or even their own full-length campaigns using the same tools the developers did when creating NWN. The result is an astounding amount of original content available for download. If you walked away from the game a while ago, now is a good time to check out the community that sprung up in its wake because Neverwinter Nights 2 is tentatively set for a 2006 release.

Free Fan Mods

I cannot stress enough the fact that this list is not a complete catch-all of the great mods out there; these are just some examples of the good stuff. If you haven't checked these out, it's time to prepare yourself for dozens of hours of (free) gameplay.

New tilesets have added many more outdoor environments for modders to play with.

Image courtesy of GameSpy.com.

Penultima ReRolled by Stefan Gagne. This five-part series is a classic example of the creativity that the NWN mod community possesses. With module titles such as Below the R0Ot, Pastor of Muppets, and Homeland Security, you can see that this is more tongue-in-cheek than most but don't let that fool you. This is an excellent series full of witty dialogue and fun encounters. It's about as good as it gets.

Shadowlords by Adam Miller. This is another whopping five-part series for 1–4 players; each mod lasts anywhere from 2–5 hours, so you're getting a lot of gameplay when you combine them all. This series is loaded with detail and has a very intricately told story that presents the heroes with several choices in which they can go down the light or dark path. (Miller's Dreamcatcher series, as well as the follow-up named Demon, also come highly recommended.)

Tales of Arterra by Kevin Chan. There are two modules in this series (The Lost and The Awakening); both are single-player only adventures that require NWN and both expansion packs (Shadows of Undrentide and Hordes of the Underdark). This is a "find your true identity" story that—although not all that original—is done extremely well. This is a heavy dialogue mod that is light on fighting.

Foreboding in Sylvani by Tseramed. It's worth noting for fans of the Ultima series that "Tseramed" is supposedly Ken Demarest, the lead programmer of the legendary Ultima VII. Regardless, this is an enormous 30-hour behemoth that is an absolute blast. Make sure that you get the latest version (earlier versions were a bit buggy). This mod is so detailed it even has *cut scenes*. You need the Hordes of the Underdark expansion as well as a "Hakpak" with content custom made for use with this mod to play.

Harper's Tale by Dave Mason. This four-part series, designed for single-player use only, requires both NWN expansions to play. Light on the dialogue and heavy on the fighting, this is a great module for those who like the rough stuff. This requires downloading the Harper hakpak.

NWN VAULT

At nwvault.ign.com you'll find an active NWN site that also hosts every mod and hakpak file listed here as well as a ton of other mods that I didn't have room to mention. Also check out the NWN Mod Hall of Fame on this site.

DID YOU KNOW

Neverwinter Nights is actually named after an old online game available on the AOL network. It was online from 1991 to 1997.

Game Rental Services
Why Pay $50 a Pop?

Image courtesy of GameSpy.com.

This is Max, Blockbuster's new late fee collections representative. I suggest you pay the man.

Games are expensive. I know you don't need me to tell you that, but man...$50 a pop can put a serious dent in your wallet. Thankfully, you have options outside of going down to your local game shop and buying the latest and greatest at full price.

Video game rental services have become enormously popular over the past few years and for good reason: They provide a much cheaper way to get your gaming fix. Renting and returning is a fantastic way to try before you buy or just to play around with a game for a couple of weeks without shelling out 50 bucks. Here are some of the more popular services for you to try.

Top 5 Services

GameLender. If you're looking for console game variety, GameLender (www.gamelender.com) is a fantastic choice. Offering rentals for older game systems such as the N64, the Dreamcast, and even the Sega Genesis, GameLender offers more games than any other service with more than 7,000 games in stock (most other services provide approximately half that number). Service options include

- Bronze Package: $19.99 monthly for two games simultaneously
- Silver Package: $24.99 monthly for three games simultaneously
- Gold Package: $34.99 monthly for five games simultaneously

Gamefly. One of the most popular and best priced rental services, Gamefly (www.gamefly.com) is very reliable and usually fairly fast in delivering your games. You can also buy the game you rent if you choose to do so. It doesn't have as many games as GameLender, particularly older games, but it carries most new releases. Service options include

- $13.95 monthly for one video game
- $21.95 monthly for two video games simultaneously
- $29.95 monthly for three video games simultaneously

Gamerang. Gamerang (www.gamerang.com) is a very popular and fast service; you usually get your games within one to three days after placing an order. Service options include

- $14.95 monthly for one video game
- $19.95 monthly for two video games simultaneously
- $27.90 monthly for three video games simultaneously
- $35.85 monthly for four video games simultaneously

GPlay. GPlay (www.gplay.com) offers nearly 3,000 games, along with user reviews on video games. It's notoriously quick in delivering games—usually in just one or two days. Service options include

- $13.95 monthly for one video game
- $21.95 monthly for two video games simultaneously
- $29.95 monthly for three video games simultaneously

International Online Gamers Club. A little slower than the other services, the IOGC (www.iogc.net) is the only service to offer PC game rentals, so that helps the company stand out a bit, if you don't mind the extra wait. Service options include

- $15.99 monthly for one video game
- $24.99 monthly for two video games simultaneously
- $34.99 monthly for three video games simultaneously
- $39.99 monthly for four video games simultaneously

BUT WAIT, THERE'S MORE...

There are many other services out there, such as GamesNFlix, Numbthumb, RentZero, and so on. If you ask 10 people about these services, you're most likely going to get 10 different responses. Everyone that uses these services will eventually have a bad experience, usually with delivery times. Things happen, ya know? I've just given you a basic outline of the features of each of the most popular services. Do a little more research at their web pages to find the service that best fits your needs.

DID YOU KNOW

The Nintendo GameCube was originally codenamed "Dolphin." The Nintendo Dolphin. Sounds like a mascot.

Top Ten PC Games
Metacritic's List of Top-Shelf Titles

Image courtesy of GameSpy.com.

When viewing the Metacritic Top Ten PC game list, you should keep in mind that the database only goes back about nine or ten years, so early classics, such as DOOM, don't qualify. (Although DOOM II is listed with an 83 score.) Still, this list is filled to the brim with A-list titles. If games like System Shock 2, GTA: San Andreas, WarCraft 3, and Rome: Total War, can't crack the list, you know it's an exclusive club.

There's always room for Star Wars. *It's sort of like Jell-O that way.*

Image courtesy of GameSpy.com.

Half-Life 2—it's really good. How shocking!

10. Logjam! (Score: 93). It would be unfair to list one game here when in fact five games earned a 93 Metacritic score. Grand Theft Auto 3, Homeworld, Maniac Mansion: Day of the Tentacle, Unreal Tournament 4, and Star Wars: Knights of the Old Republic are all top-shelf PC games and deserve to make this list. It's cool to see Maniac Mansion: Day of the Tentacle, an old school LucasArts adventure game, get the respect it deserves. That game was released in 1993 and there were enough reviews in the database to qualify.

9. Civilization 2 (Score: 94). This is arguably the best turn-based strategy game of all time. The classic game from Sid Meier and Brian Reynolds is just as compelling today as it was back in the mid 1990s.

8. Diablo (Score: 94). The ultimate role-playing hack-and-slash action game, Diablo took the world by storm when it was released back in 1996. It also caused the breakdown of many a left mouse button.

7. Command & Conquer (Score: 94). C&C is one of the most important releases in the history of our hobby. This game, along with Warcraft, helped to usher in the genre of real-time strategy games.

6. Grim Fandango (Score: 94). Grim Fandango is a simply marvelous graphic adventure from LucasArts. It's a real shame that the company doesn't try to make games like this anymore. Who knew the Land of the Dead could be so much fun?

5. Quake (Score: 94). Wow—Civ II, Diablo, and Quake all came out in '96. Not a bad year, eh?

4. Grand Theft Auto: Vice City (Score: 94). Grand Theft Auto 3 was a great game but Vice City had a cool Miami flavor that was hard to beat. Plus there's that Flock of Seagulls song.

3. Baldur's Gate II: Shadows of Amn (Score: 95). Baldur's Gate II might be the best role-playing game ever made, regardless of platform. I have played this game through five or six times, which is a testament to how great it is and to how sad I am.

2. Half-Life (Score: 96). A masterpiece. The saga of Gordon Freeman is the best first-person shooter ever made, in my opinion. Smart, tense, and technologically brilliant, it's just a joy to play. In fact, I played the 1998 original start-to-finish about a year ago, and it was *still* a great game. What could possibly be better than Half-Life?

1. Half-Life 2 (Score: 96). Oh, well, okay. Half-Life 2 is definitely a worthy choice for the #1 game even though technically it scored the same as the original. I'll give the new game the nod just because of how amazing it looks and how realized the world is. I should dock points and place it at number two because of the Steam distribution/authentication mechanism, but it's not the game's fault that Steam is pure evil.

DID YOU KNOW

Because early PCs didn't use a mouse, adventure games like the Quest games from Sierra On-line required you to type in instructions like "Get bread" and "Open door" to perform actions on screen.

Interstate '76
Closet Classic (1997)

Image courtesy of GameSpy.com.

The racing area was enormous with its desert landscapes.

DOSSIER

Genre: Funkafied Combat Driving **Publisher:** Activision **Developer:** Activision
Platform: PC

Not all driving games are about racing. There have been a lot of vehicle/combat games released over the years—Auto Assault is even taking the idea online, MMOG style. One of the best games in the genre, though, was the 1997 release from Activision called Interstate '76.

This was one of the very first "retro" games to have been released long before Rockstar Games made Grand Theft Auto: Vice City, which plunged gamers into the mid 1980s *Miami Vice* scene.

Interstate '76 was all about 1970s funk and style. It was *Starsky and Hutch* but with fully loaded muscle cars with guns. Lots of guns. In fact, the game sported about 25 different weapons that you could install on your rod. Flamethrowers, mortars, machine guns, you name it.

Best of all, it was funky.

Image courtesy of GameSpy.com.

Taurus (left) was so cool they should name a car after him.

I kid you not, a bad-ass driver named Groove Champion who drove a Picard Pirannah. His "mentor" of sorts is a hip, afro-sporting driver named Taurus. The characters themselves were a huge part of the campaign. This was a game that fed off its personality and its music.

The soundtrack for Interstate '76 remains of the best in gaming history. (You could even buy it separately.) It fit perfectly with the setting: 100% '70s funk intermingled with takes on classic 1970s action shows like *Charlie's Angels* and the aforementioned *Starsky and Hutch*. The campaign did a wonderful job of making you feel like you were part of a 1970s TV show or low-budget movie.

Get That Funk

Interstate '76 was about more than just the setting, though. It had great graphics and a surprisingly tight physics engine and driving model that let you take the wheel of all sorts of 1970s vehicles from muscle cars to vans. I recall driving my Dover Lightning and hand braking to do a 180° spin and blast enemy cars that were tailing me—it was exhilarating.

Set during a fuel shortage in an alternate history version of the southwest United States, the main campaign (dubbed "The Trip") was 17 missions in length. The scenarios varied from straight-up "kill 'em all" tasks to actually racing other combat drivers (and usually killing 'em all after the race).

In was what sort of a funkadelic version of *The Road Warrior*, vigilantes cruised the desert, protecting the last gas stations from power hungry oil merchants. You played the role of, and

THE 1980S WERE NOT COOL

A year later, Activision released Interstate '76 Nitro Riders, which was a standalone add-on for the original game; it added new weapons, as well as force feedback and improved 3D chipset support, but it wasn't as flavorful as the first game and the lack of a new storyline hurt.

In 1999 Activision tried milking the series with a sequel, this time set in 1982. Interstate '82 was a mess of a game, and not just for trying to make the 1980s look cool, which is simply impossible. I'82 should serve as a lesson to publishers who try messing with a good thing.

DID YOU KNOW

The cars in Interstate '76 were all fictional because Activision didn't have the licensing to add real ones. Instead Activision created "real" cars but named them with fictional tags, like the Dover Lightning and the Moth Truck.

Spider-Man 2
Bargain Bin Special

Image courtesy of GameSpy.com.

DOSSIER

Genre: Web Travel Simulation **Publisher:** Activision **Developer:** Treyarch **Platform:** Xbox, PS2, GameCube

Zipping through Manhattan is actually half the fun.

Spider-Man 2 was a big hit for Activision in 2004 and not just because of the impact of the movie; this is a great, great game. It was released on several platforms, but I need to make it very clear that the PC version is pure garbage pressed onto a CD. It might have the same title, but it's not the same game that was released on the consoles so avoid it at all costs.

In Spider-Man 2 you play the famous web-slinger as he tries to stop Dr. Octopus from blowing up the city. The main storyline is pretty much ripped right out of the movie with some extra villains thrown in for good measure.

The game received widespread praise from gamers and critics alike for its Grand Theft Auto–style open ended gameplay (sans the blood and hookers). What is especially cool about the game, though, is that you can swing through Manhattan at breakneck speeds, doing flips and tricks along the way. After you complete missions and earn points you can spend them at the Spidey Store to buy upgrades such as new attacks, increased swing speeds, and so on.

THEY SAID IT

"At any company, the producer is generally responsible for the game being great, getting completed on time, and coming in within the budget. If any of this goes wrong, then the producer gets yelled at, because he was supposed to foresee the difficulties and fix it before it became a critical problem." —**Bill Dugan, Executive Producer of Spider-Man 2 in an interview with CurmudgeonGamer.com**

there as fast as you can (just make sure you find the entrance to the hospital; dropping them on the roof isn't good enough).

Spidey and Black Cat take on Shocker.

Image courtesy of GameSpy.com.

Nonplot Missions

You're going to be doing a lot of side missions to earn enough Hero Points to advance the chapters. Some of these get kind of boring, but what's a superhero to do? Here are some of the missions Spidey can undertake.

The Ambush. If you swing over to help someone in distress and they apologize to you, that's a bad sign. Be ready for a bunch of thugs to jump out of the shadows.

Armored Car Robbery. The cops are here, but tied up by the bad guys. Stopping the robbery is important, but you get more points if you free the police, so don't forget.

Car Jacking. Some fools take a stolen car for a joyride and you need to swing quickly to catch up with the car, smash it until it stops, and then clean up the bad guys. Make sure to dodge the bullets when riding on the car's hood.

Save the Injured. At times you'll stumble across people that need to be rushed to the hospital. Check the city map and get

The Hanging Man. How these guys get stuck on a ledge I have no idea; (just crawl up the building and save them.

Jewel Thieves. Robbers love to break into local stores. Find the entrance, go in, and take care of them. Battling it out indoors does make it more difficult to make use of your webs.

Drowning Crew. This one is tough. Spidey hates the water in this game so swimming is not an option. You need to get onboard a ship and save the crew before it sinks. You need to Super-jump to get on the boat.

Lost Balloons. A little girl has lost her balloons. I never could save those damn things.

SPIDER-MAN: THE PERIL OF DOC OCK

At www.spiteyourface.com/spidey.html you'll find a hilarious little movie of Spider-Man battling Doc Ock in LEGO form from the people at Spite Your Face Productions.

DID YOU KNOW

Spider-Man first appeared in 1962 in the Marvel comic *Amazing Fantasy #15*. His own series appeared the following year. You can actually purchase a CD-ROM, called *40 Years of The Amazing Spider-Man*, which contains scans of the first 500 issues.

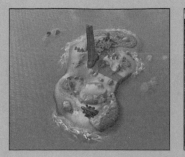

July 2005

Football in July

Nothing says football like the middle of summer, right? This was a very slow month for big releases, which was highlighted by EA Sports's NCAA Football 06. Personally, I thought this game really underachieved, but it's still an extremely popular football series (which just goes to show that people don't listen to me). I'm talking to some lawyers next week about rectifying that.... They know people who know people.

Beyond that July wasn't exactly the busiest of months. Sid Meier's Pirates! turned a few heads, but with games like Codename Panzers: Phase Two and Space Rangers 2, this month was more about hidden gems than about jaw-dropping blockbusters.

Flop of the Month:

- **Killer7**—A fair shooter with really cool art style, Killer7 is a classic example of a game that had too much style and too little substance.

Halo 2
Multiplayer Maps Galore

Image courtesy of GameSpy.com.

An overhead view of the huge Containment map.

DOSSIER

Genre: Adding Life to a Classic **Publisher:** Microsoft **Developer:** Bungie **Platform:** Xbox **Metacritic Metascore:** 95

If you have an Xbox, chances are good that you have played, and thoroughly enjoyed, Halo 2. (If you haven't bought the game and have an Xbox, I have to assume you bought the console for its fabulous décor and don't actually *play* games.)

The Halo 2 Multiplayer Map Pack is a pseudo expansion for the award-winning sequel. Microsoft calls it an expansion pack, but in reality it's a $20 map pack with some bonus features thrown in for good measure. As someone who loves PC games as much as console games, charging 20 bones for nine new maps is more than a little gauche, but Halo 2 fans have very little choice if they want to play with some freshly made maps in their multiplayer sessions.

The good news for those who have waited this long is that by the time this book is published, all nine maps will be free to download via Xbox Live. So, if you're reading this and don't have the maps—get cracking!

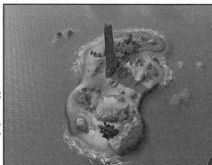

Image courtesy of GameSpy.com.

The Relic map is just a small island in the middle of an ocean. Close quarters fighting is unavoidable.

The Maps

Containment. Ideal for games like Capture the Flag and Assault, this huge, snow-covered map features two open-air bases that face each other with a large no man's land battlefield in the middle that's littered with land mines.

Warlock. A small map reminiscent of the old teleportation Wizard map in the original Halo, Warlock is great for close firefights in team games.

Turf. Turf is a pretty large map that is set on Old Mombasa and is full of narrow corridors and blind corners.

Sanctuary. Sanctuary looks a lot like the single player Halo 2 map, but it's still pretty to look at, complete with stone outcroppings and waterfalls.

Gemini. A smaller map with interior and exterior sections and a lot of teleporters, it was designed for no more than six players (Slayer games in particular).

Relic. A medium-sized Assault or Capture the Flag map, Relic is set on a desert island in the middle of an ocean. Relic's landscape is the remnants of a large battle, complete with a downed Pelican Dropship.

Elongation. This is based on the Longset map from the original Halo. Elongation, which takes place on a floating space station, has two long hallways separated by a wall with a high platform on both sides. Two conveyer belts—each running in a different direction—line the two hallway sections, which causes total chaos during team matches.

Terminal. This is a large map designed for Capture the Flag and Assault games, but it also works with larger team games as well. Terminal is a large outdoor mall that was supposedly a peaceful hangout before the Covenant caused all hell to break loose. There are also two train tracks that run down the middle of the map. Don't get hit.

Backwash. If you ever wanted to play Halo 2 in a swamp, this is the map for you. Inspired by the swamp level in the original, Backwash is a small Slayer map. What makes this map so special is the thick layer of fog that limits visibility to the point that it makes the game extremely intense.

DID YOU KNOW

Bungie Studios has been around since 1990, developing classics like Halo, Marathon, and Myth. Its first game was a Pong clone called Gnop, which is actually Pong spelled backward.

Sid Meier's Pirates!
Capt'n Jack Sparrow Would Be Proud

Image courtesy of GameSpy.com.

Avast! Arrhhh and Yo Ho Ho!

DOSSIER

Genre: Sid Meier Goodness **Publisher:** Atari **Developer:** Firaxis **Platform:** PC/Xbox
Metacritic Metascore: 87

Sid Meier is arguably the greatest game designer of all time. He has either designed or co-designed such classics as Civilization, Colonization, Alpha Centauri, Gettysburg!, and the original Railroad Tycoon, among many others. Perhaps the most beloved Meier games are the 1987 hit Pirates! and the 1993 follow-up, Pirates! Gold. The games' open-ended style of play, which we've come to expect in today's games, was both unique and revolutionary for its day.

The original Pirates! had it all: multiple ship combat, sword-fighting, raids on cities, and rescuing lost damsels in distress. If you made enough money and fame, you could even retire to a tropical island.

As Meier continued to crank out great games in the late '90s, fans continued to beg, plead, and whine about an updated version of the classic swashbuckling adventure game. PC fans got their wish with the November 2004 release of the appropriately named Sid Meier's Pirates!, whereas Xbox gamers would have to wait until July 2005 to get their hands on it.

THEY SAID IT

> "When deciding what concepts to leave in and what to leave out, we asked two important questions: 1. Is it any fun? 2. Does it fit in our heroic world? If the answer was "no" to either question, we discarded it."
> **—Jeff Briggs, Firaxis CEO and President**

The Xbox version adds multiplayer support (on the same machine) as well as the ability to hop on Xbox Live. Slugging it out against another pirate, or pirates, is a lot of fun. That said, the relatively slow pace of the game lends itself better to the PC than a console. If multiplayer isn't an issue, go with the PC version. It looks a bit better and the controls are more intuitive.

Ya'argh!

The new version of Pirates! shows why Meier and the rest of the team at Firaxis are The Mensa Institute of game design. They didn't try to reinvent the wheel with the new edition; it kept almost all of the great stuff from the 1987 game, but added some new wrinkles and wrapped it all up in a beautiful 3D graphics package. The game is totally open-ended, so you're free to do whatever you want, whenever you want. In fact, the game "ends" only when you decide to hang up your sword and call it a career.

Image courtesy of GameSpy.com.

The Xbox version is pretty good, but to get the full effect, you need to play the PC version.

PIRATES! ONLINE

Before Firaxis released the new version, fans had to get their Pirates! fix by playing the old game, **Pirates! Gold for Windows**. You can get it from www.theunderdogs.org/game.php?id=2346.

A great fan site dedicated to all things Pirates! is **Addicted to Pirates** (www.addictedtopirates.com). The site has a highly active fan forum and downloads such as mods that offer cool new flags, sails, and clothes for your scurvy dog pirate.

Eagle Games is working on **The Pirates! The Board Game** (www.eaglegames.com). These are the same blokes that published a board game version of Sid Meier's Civilization.

DID YOU KNOW

A pirate's life for you? Most seventeenth-century pirates were nothing more than toothless murderers on the run. The vast majority died before their thirtieth birthday. What fun!

NCAA Football 06
It's Football-esque

Image courtesy of GameSpy.com.

DOSSIER

Genre: Arcade Football **Publisher:** EA Sports **Developer:** EA Tiburon **Platform:** PS2, Xbox **Metacritic Metascore:** 87

There's no doubt that NCAA Football 06 is infinitely better than the 2005 version. That said we'd like to set the bar a bit higher given that the 2005 version was the worst edition of NCAA football since the series launched, circa 1642...BC.

The graphics are better, but very similar to the 2005 version.

The latest version, despite the 86 Metacritic score, is both hit and miss. The new Impact Players feature is a cool idea, but it makes specific players so good that it unbalances the gameplay. However, there are still too many dropped passes to wide open receivers, throwing a deep pass works too often, and somehow EA Sports broke the sim engine so that it's almost impossible for anyone but a QB to win the Heisman Trophy.

Still, it's a fun college game even with its flaws. It's particularly fun playing in a multiplayer dynasty with a group of buddies because you remove the AI from the equation.

Image courtesy of GameSpy.com.

Impact players are a bit too much of an impact in NCAA 2006.

Discipline Doldrums

One of my biggest beefs with NCAA Football 2006 (and with 2005) is the off-the-field Discipline system. In NCAA Football 06, teams can get in trouble with the NCAA, just as they do in real life. Putting aside just how much "real life" gamers want to see in a football, the feature is still flat-out broken.

The real NCAA does not care, at all, if a player breaks team rules. It is beyond silly for the game's NCAA violation interest meter to rise because my kicker missed a team meeting. Along these same lines, there are times that the game advises you as coach to bench a player for the first half of a game because he's "not making grades." Again, this makes no sense: Either a player is eligible or he isn't. There is no in between.

An easy fix for stuff like this is to use two separate violation meters: one for the NCAA (if a player does something *really* bad or does something minor that the NCAA polices) and an Athletic Director meter for when a player breaks team rules. The coach could get fired by the A.D. for running an "outlaw" program where players never get punished for anything. That would make a lot more sense than the NCAA giving your team

the Death Penalty and taking away tons of scholarships just because your backup linebacker failed Linguistics.

Understanding Sliders

The gameplay sliders are a huge part of NCAA 06. Playing on All-American level with default sliders is a surefire way to get a highly unrealistic game against the AI. Here are a few pointers to help you make it a more authentic game:

- The Human Run Ability slider can be no lower than 40% for fast players to still outrun slower ones.

- If you find the running game too easy, lower Human Run Blocking but also consider raising the CPU Defensive Awareness. This slider is just as important for run defense as it is pass defense.

- Raise the Human and CPU catching sliders. If you don't, you're going to see anywhere from 10 to 15 dropped passes per game, which is absurd.

- Completing the deep pass is too easy in NCAA 06. One way to help fix this is to increase (drastically) the Human and CPU defensive Knockdown sliders.

ROSTERS WITH NAMES!
If you have an Action Replay, Max Drive, GameShark, or similar hardware, you can download real NCAA rosters for the Xbox and PS2 from **FKRosters** at fkrosters.com. (It's free, although donations are welcome—that's a lot of work!)

DID YOU KNOW

Michigan's Desmond Howard is the 2006 NCAA cover boy. Howard last played college ball back in 1991. This marks the first time that a retired NFL player had made the cover of a current EA Sports videogame.

Codename: Panzers, Phase Two
Because Tanks Are Cool

Image courtesy of GameSpy.com.

Tanks are the key in most Codename: Panzers battles.

DOSSIER

Genre: Underrated WWII RTS **Publisher:** CDV **Developer:** Stormregion **Platform:** PC
Metacritic Metascore: 80

If every great game sold a lot of copies, it would make the world a much better place. Unfortunately, that's not reality. Reality is that a lot of A-list games slide under the radar due to a lack of press, poor marketing, limited shelf space at retail stores, and so forth. That's where a book like this can shine some light on games that didn't get the attention they deserved.

In 2004, Codename: Panzers, Phase One was one of the best games you didn't play. In fact, you can consider this little essay two for the price of one because although Phase Two is also a damn fine game, Phase One is still selling at $20 a pop at most retail stores, making it an unofficial Bargain Bin Special.

THEY SAID IT

> "With these tools everything will be possible: You can make your own maps for single and multiplayer, extensive missions with scripted results and design various mission goals, change units, etc." —**Achim Heidelauf, Producer of Codename: Panzers, Phase Two, in an interview with PC Games**

Get More Pub!

Panzers Phase Two, just like Phase One, is a tactical RTS without the usual trappings such as base building, resource management, and shuffling villagers. In a Codename: Panzers scenario, you usually have a core group of units and what you see is what you get. If you lose three crucial tanks, well, nicely done, General Patton! In subsequent missions, you'll have to make do without them.

Units earn experience and improve as the campaigns progress, meaning you start to get attached to your troops, particularly your tanks and their crew members. It's also a cool game mechanic because elite units dominate green ones. Phase Two provides those classic gaming moments in a strategy game when you see your elite tank crew get obliterated and you know deep down you have just lost the battle even though it's not over yet.

Although there are other realistic units in the game, tanks rule the day. This is not an overly complex wargame, nor is it a twitch fest-RTS. It's somewhere in the middle. Take armor, for example. It's easier to blast a tank from the rear rather than from the front because the armor is thinner in the rear. It's

also impossible to destroy a tank with a group of infantry shooting their rifles. You need another tank, a bazooka, flamethrower, or a mine to defeat a tank. This is not Command & Conquer, but exact realistic accuracy is not the goal; it's a great mix of fun and realism.

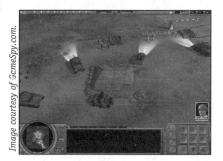

Image courtesy of GameSpy.com.

Night missions are particularly fun.

A Few Missteps

It's not all wine and roses. The pathfinding AI in Panzers is hit and miss. The storyline, although well written, is wildly hokey in parts through the liberal use of cheesy cut scenes. The fog of war also takes some getting used to because you have an unusually limited line of sight and units, even tanks, can get right up on you before you know it—you can hear them, but it's often hard to get a good view until it's too late. Finally, there's a lot of sand. And when there's no beach to go with it, let's face it, sand is boring.

Still, with good multiplayer support, sharp graphics, great sound, and a mission editor, Phase Two has legs. If you like this genre of gaming, by all means pick it up. CDV could use the sale.

DID YOU KNOW

The third game in the series dubbed, obviously, Phase Three, is set for a 2006 release. If you're a fan of the genre, you simply must not overlook the release of this game.

Talking Games in Public
The Do's and Don'ts of Game Discussion

You are only making it more difficult for every Star Wars *fan when you do this sort of thing.*

You know the situation all too well. You're at a dinner, a wedding reception, or any kind of social event with some friends. Among those friends are people that you either play games with on a regular basis or those that you know play games or are interested in the same kinds of movies as you; inevitably the subject comes up, either by choice or because of your insane friend with the social tact of a diseased rhino. What to do?

As much as we like to admit otherwise, games are still a fairly niche (geeky) hobby. Yes, the industry likes to tell everyone that it's as popular as the movie industry, but debating the social commentary of *To Kill a Mockingbird* is much more acceptable in society than discussing the best way to mod your superheroes in Freedom Force vs. The 3rd Reich (p.47). Here's a quick guide to talking about games for the next time the subject comes up.

The Party Scene

If women are around, particularly women that you do not know, keep the gaming discussion off the table. You might try stuff like The Sims (they might have heard of it), Madden Football (it's manly), or Grand Theft Auto (they'll think you're a bad boy), but it's still risky. Sometimes you can also get away with stuff like Dance Dance Revolution or other party games. Yes, some women like games too, but don't blame me if you drone on about your Halo kill stats and end up driving home alone.

Never, under any circumstances, allow your gaming friend to bring up last night's LAN party or role-playing session. This is social suicide. Sure, someone might know what you are talking about but using the words *Wood Elf*, *+5 Sword of Might*, or *Master Wizard* will cause people to leave skid marks on their way out the door. (Refer to www.flashplayer.com/animation/8bitdnd.html.) Just imagine the result of a conversation such as

You: So, did you see the latest Adam Sandler movie?

Female Friend: Yeah. He's hilarious.

Your Gaming Friend: Dude, the LAN party was awesome. Thanks for hosting it. But you are so wrong. No way does Han Solo beat Captain Kirk in a fistfight.

Don't let this happen to you.

Image courtesy of GameSpy.com.

Dance Dance Revolution is often a safe topic when talking about games with strangers.

Adult Dinner Party

These can get a bit tricky because it depends on the guests. After all, you can't escape them like you can a large party. If it's a formal get-together, it is best to avoid the subject of games altogether unless someone else brings it up first.

However, if the subject of games or movies is broached, it's best to keep a few things in mind. First off, *Star Wars* is cool, *Star Trek* is not. I like *Star Trek* as much as the next guy, but trust me on this. Second, graphics matter more than gameplay in universal discussion with nongamers. Saying how lifelike a game looks makes more sense than saying how great a game's AI is. Finally, it's best to admit to playing games as a way to relax. Admitting to staying up until dawn in order to finish Half-Life 2 is likely to leave you off future invite lists. Unless that's the goal of the dinner, avoid such admissions.

If You're Married...

Talk about what you want. We've earned the right to be as strange as we like. Besides, the cat is most likely way out of the bag at this point anyway, so go nuts.

DID YOU KNOW

Alex Kidd, a bizarre monkey-like boy hero, was Sega's official mascot before the company switched over to the popular Sonic the Hedgehog figure in 1990.

Wing Commander: Privateer
Closet Classic (1993)

DOSSIER

Genre: Han Solo Simulator **Publisher:** Electronic Arts **Developer:** Origin
Platform: PC (DOS)

Not a bad-looking explosion for 1993!

Origin's Wing Commander series, which started back in 1990, set the gaming world ablaze with its story-driven gameplay and exciting space battles. Before classics like X-Wing and TIE Fighter, there was Wing Commander, forging its own legacy as one of the most influential titles of all time.

Wing Commander: Privateer, released back in 1993, was different than the other games in the series in that you didn't play the role of a good guy fighting the evil, alien Kilrathi. In Privateer, you played a Han Solo–like smuggler for hire who did what was needed to survive. The game was open-ended, and you didn't have to follow the main plot threads if you didn't want to.

Privateer is actually the big brother (some would argue the smaller cousin) to a game called Elite, which was released in the mid 1980s and used similar game mechanics. Elite was an innovative game, but Privateer had the advantage of being a bit more modern as well as having the important Wing Commander license.

Let's buy some new guns...big guns!

The Gameplay
You started the game with a small scout-class ship and you earned money by doing missions in order to upgrade your ship with new weapons and armor, eventually buying better ships all together (there were four in the game). You could earn this loot by doing basic merchant missions, taking some spice from one planet to another, or by doing more dirty work such as bounty hunting.

During your smuggling/merchant missions, you would run into members of the key factions in the game. There was The Confederation, Militia, Bounty Hunters, Merchant Guild, Kilrathi Empire, Retros (religious fanatics), and Pirates. At the start of the game each faction had a set attitude toward your character, which would change over time depending on what you did during the course of the game. Fly a mission for The Confederation, for example, and the Pirates will want nothing to do with you (and vice versa).

The Privateer Lineage
Privateer: Righteous Fire. The official expansion for Privateer added new weapons, armor, droids, ship upgrades and a new main plot thread.

Privateer: Speech Pack. Back in the early 1990s games didn't have a lot of pre-recorded speech. This was before the days of CD-ROM/DVD games when slapping voice work on the disk was as easy pressing a button. Us old folks installed games using several (and sometimes I mean *several*) 3.5" floppy disks. The Privateer Speech Pack added voice work for the in flight taunts and other communication orders.

Privateer II: The Darkening. The only reason I mention this was because it's officially a Privateer game although it had very little to do with the first game or Wing Commander in general. Privateer II had real actors in full motion video sequences doing all sorts of silly stuff. This was back when game companies really tried to push the whole "we're interactive movies" crap. Games are not interactive movies; they're games. All we wanted was another Privateer and we got a bad movie of the week instead.

PRIVATEER REMAKE
Now this is cool. A group of hardcore Privateer fans at priv.solsector.net are creating a "remake" that will run on modern day machines complete with modern graphics. (Well, better than the old game, anyway.) Version 1.0 is done and is a 189MB download file. Enjoy!

DID YOU KNOW

In 1996, the USA channel ran a short-lived Wing Commander animated series, which was set before the events of the first game. It included the voices of Mark Hamill (Luke Skywalker!!!) and Tom Wilson (Biff from the *Back to the Future* movies).

Console Racing Sims
Grease Monkey Heaven

Image courtesy of GameSpy.com.

There are quite a few top-shelf racing sims available and in the pipeline for today's console racing enthusiast. I'll keep the list limited to more "realistic" racers rather than over-the-top arcade crash fests. If you're serious about racing, these are some of the games to check out.

Forza is one of the best-looking racing games ever created.

Image courtesy of GameSpy.com.

Hugging the turn in MotoGP 3.

Forza Motorsport (Xbox). Developed and published by Microsoft, Forza has proven to be a huge hit with Xbox gamers, in particular on Xbox Live. It's also a very serious racing game with high-end physics; this is not an arcade game. Oh, and it's also drop-dead gorgeous. The game's difficulty is masked by driving aids so that newbies can get up to speed without the frustration of crashing at every turn. Forza is arguably the best Xbox game of the first half of 2005. It's that good.

Gran Turismo 4 (PS2). One of the most popular PS2 franchises of all time, GT4 adds everything but the kitchen sink (except online play). With more cars and tracks and an amazing graphics engine, this is the definitive racing game on the PlayStation 2. If you're a racing fan, you almost certainly already have this, but keep an eye out for the PSP version later this year.

MotoGP 3 (PS2, Xbox, PC). THQ's MotoGP 3 adds street bike racing with a new Extreme Mode where you'll get to zip through the urban streets of Japan, and the countryside of France, all with unique weather patterns. Toss in 16 new Extreme Mode tracks and 16 new bikes and MotoGP 3 is one hell of a bike sim.

Project Gotham Racing 3 (Xbox 360). Project Gotham Racing has been popular on the Xbox ever since the console first launched. The third version of the high performance car sim is focused on providing a true sense of speed unlike past versions of the game; add in more tracks, cars, and goodies on top of the fact that it's most likely going to be an Xbox 360 launch title and there's a lot to get excited about.

ToCA Race Driver 2006 (PS2, Xbox, PC). ToCA Race Driver 2 was a big hit with racing fans and the 2006 edition is shaping up to be a huge upgrade with more than 30 racing styles and a new focus on online play. Every car in ToCA 2006 is a licensed auto; there are no concept cars in this year's game, but several "classics" will make an appearance.

DID YOU KNOW

Gran Turismo 5, which will be available on the PlayStation 3, will be the first GT game to model car damage.

Freelancer
Bargain Bin Special

Even a few years after release, Freelancer still looks good.

DOSSIER

Genre: Han Solo Simulator **Publisher:** Microsoft **Developer:** Digital Anvil
Platform: PC **Released:** 2003

Freelancer, a free-form PC space combat sim, was a long time in the making. Chris Roberts, the founder of developer Digital Anvil and also the creator of the classic Wing Commander space sims, promised gamers the moon when the game was first announced.

Through several delays and four years of development, Freelancer was finally released in March of 2003 (and Chris Roberts was no longer with the company). Usually when a game goes through such a long development process, it ends up a mess with missing features and dated technology. Freelancer bucked the trend: It's one of the best space combat sims on the planet and its mouse-driven control scheme makes it easy to play without a flightstick-style controller. It's also the ideal Bargain Bin game because you can grab the game brand new from retail chains for no more than $19.99. If you haven't played this wonderful game, you really should give it a look.

THEY SAID IT

"One of the beautiful aspects of Freelancer is that you can go anywhere and do anything ... whenever you want to. That is one of our core design philosophies, and it also applies to the story. We obviously think we have a great storyline that is both exciting and involving, but we don't want to force anyone into it. Freelancer has been specifically structured in a way that allows players to join or exit the story whenever they want." —Phil Wattenbarger, Producer of Freelancer in an interview with GameSpy.com

The Solo Game

In the single-player portion of Freelancer you play Edison Trent, a survivor of an attack on your space station by unidentified spacecraft. You have a small bankroll of money and no ship. It's no shock that you soon do grab a ship and start to do missions that unravel a plot full of political intrigue and war on an interplanetary scale.

The storyline is extremely involved and the world of Freelancer is realized in amazing detail. But what's especially cool is that you can opt out of the story and just explore the world of Freelancer at your leisure. Winning the game opens up even more areas for you to explore. Freelancer is a huge game and you can play it for a long time, well after the actual story is over. It's Grand Theft Auto in space without the drugs and hookers.

The game's world is bustling with activity as police ships patrol local areas, trade ships stick to shipping lanes, and so on. You are part of a living world and not just a solo pilot in a vacuum.

Ugh...asteroid fields.

Multiplayer and Mods

Freelancer thrives in multiplayer mode because there is a highly active game community and it's always easy to find a game. Players have formed squadrons, set up web pages, and so on. At its core, the multiplayer game is just like the solo game but without the storyline.

Along these same lines, the Freelancer mod community is extremely active, pumping out content on a regular basis. There are small mods that add ships and weapons to full-blown total conversions that create an entirely new game. There's even a wonderfully made *Star Wars* mod called Free Worlds.

Freelancer offers a lot, both online and off, and for $20 is an absolute steal, even nearly three years after release. If you like space combat sims—you simply need to own this one.

LANCERS REACTOR
At **www.lancersreactor.comt/t** is a very active fan site for Freelancer with a forum as well as a ton of detailed game mods ready for download.

DID YOU KNOW

After leaving Digital Anvil, Chris Roberts founded Point of No Return Entertainment (www.pnrfilms.com), which is a studio that plans on making movies, TV shows, and games.

Home Networking
Sharing Your High-Speed Connection

Linksys routers are among the popular and reliable on the market in their price range.

Ahh! There's nothing like spending a quiet Sunday at home fragging your friends in an online game. Sure, they might talk a little trash, but that's just part of the fun. Besides, I've found that a rocket or two right between the eyes quickly resolves most disagreements.

But if you're going to play online, you're going to have to get on the Internet, preferably with a broadband connection. For most of us that means DSL or cable—both work equally well. But unless your game box is the only one in the house, you're probably going to want to share that high-speed connection with the other humans in your domicile. People tend to get testy after you've hogged the connection for the fourteenth hour or so.

To share your high-speed connection, you need a router, like the Linksys model pictured here. With a router, all you have to do is plug the incoming broadband connection into the incoming port (sometimes labeled the uplink or WAN port) and plug all the other machines that need to share the connection into the remaining network ports. Voilà! Home network. Shared connection. Broadband multiplayer bliss.

Router Configuration Tips

Read the directions. I know, real men (or women) don't read manuals. Baloney. Read it. Unless you set up LANs for a living, you're going to need to know how your router works before you configure it.

Learn to use your router's firewall—period. There's a lot of nasty stuff out there on the Net, and most of it wants to take over your computer and use it as a spam relay or porno server.

Don't panic. If things don't work correctly, start from scratch. Turn everything off, read the directions again, and configure everything in order.

Networking settings are a little like exotic, shiny weapons. If you don't know what one does, don't touch it!

Tech support is (usually) your friend. If your setup doesn't work, call your ISP first and if its support team can't resolve the problem, call the manufacturer.

Wired or Wireless?

When you start looking at routers, you're immediately going to realize you have to make the choice between wired and wireless routers. They both have their pros and cons, and the choice depends on what kinds of computers you have, your budget, and what you're trying to accomplish.

Wired routers are fine if you have a couple of computers to share in a relatively small space or are good at running cables through your walls. Your boxes have to be physically connected with cables (usually a nice, decor-friendly bright blue) to your router.

Wireless routers usually include both wired ports and wireless antennas. Wireless (also known as *Wi-Fi*) networking is fast (enough), it doesn't require cables, and one wireless access point can cover a large house. The downside is that all your devices need Wi-Fi capability to get on your net.

> ### WHO'S WHO IN ROUTERS
> There are plenty of good router brands out there, and a trip to your local electronics retailer should bag you any number of choices to fit your budget. Here are three of the best:
>
> **Linksys** (www.linksys.com). One of the most popular brands, it's cheap, easy to set up, reliable, and chock-full of home networking goodness.
>
> **NETGEAR** (www.netgear.com). Inexpensive, reliable, and nearly as ubiquitous as Linksys. If you want an alternative to wireless, check out its Wall-Plugged Ethernet Bridge that lets you use the power lines in your home as network cables. Cool!
>
> **D-Link** (www.dlink.com). Another popular quality router manufacturer. D-Link makes some other nifty home networking products, too, including the iEye wireless videophone that turns your TV into a *Jetsons*-like videophone.

DID YOU KNOW

Wi-Fi actually means *Wireless Fidelity* and is a trademark of the Wi-Fi Alliance, a trade organization that tests and certifies equipment compliance with the 802.11x standards.

Space Rangers 2
The Game You Don't Know, but Must Play

Image courtesy of GameSpy.com.

Flying the galaxy in Space Rangers 2.

DOSSIER

Genre: Multi-Genred Masterpiece **Publisher:** 1C Company **Developer:** Elemental Games
Platform: PC **Metacritic Metascore:** 81

There are games that slip under the radar, and then there are games like Space Rangers 2 that are so far off the radar that they're only sold in stores overseas. This doesn't classify as an indie game because 1C Company is a large Russian publisher. It's a shame that, as of this writing, few North American websites or magazines have reviewed Space Rangers 2 because it's a fabulous game.

Fortunately, gamers on this side of the pond can order Space Rangers 2 online. Websites like gogamer.com carry it and will deliver it stateside and to Canada. So, given all that, what exactly *is* Space Rangers?

THEY SAID IT

> "A unique feature of the game is that the world around the player is not static, it is a living world. There are not so many RPGs where there is a living game world and it develops all by its own. The game can even come to an end without players taking active part in the events that happen in this world. AI-controlled rangers do the same as the player—buy and sell, collect different items, decide what path to choose." —**Ilya Plyusnin, Creative Director of Elemental Games (the developer of Space Rangers) in an interview with IGN.com**

Image courtesy of GameSpy.com.

The real-time battles are just one small portion of the game.

You'll meet several races and NPCs with their own goals and ambitions, which might or might not cross with yours. You can be an aggressive ranger or a sneaky merchant/thief.

You can do battle during planetary missions via the game's real-time battle mode and during the fights you can even switch to a first-person view of the carnage.

The shocking part is that it all works and comes together in such an amazing way that after playing it to the point of exhaustion, I sat back, and actually felt sorry for the vast number of gamers who surely had no idea of its existence.

If you like the classic 4X space strategy games, you need to own this one. It's one of the most intriguing and brilliantly designed games to come along in a while. Find a copy by any legal means necessary. You'll thank me for it.

Meet Space Rangers 2

Space Rangers 2 is a tough game to classify. It has elements of role-playing, real-time strategy, turn-based strategy, open-ended space exploration, and more—much more. When a game tries to blend so many genres into one big smorgasbord, it usually ends up a muddy mess, but this game is the proverbial exception that proves the rule.

You start off as a novice pilot exploring space and looking for a better ship. You can do this by taking on missions, raiding other merchants, or scrounging around for minerals to sell. How you go about your business in the game is entirely up to you. The free will provided in Space Rangers makes Grand Theft Auto feel scripted.

This is an entirely open-ended game set inside the most truly alive galaxy created in any game, ever. There are more than 60 star systems and hundreds of individual planets. There's a major plot thread, which you can ignore or take part in at your leisure.

ON THE WEB

I, and many others, would never have heard of the game if not for my friend Bill Harris, who runs the popular **Dubious Quality Blog** at dubious quality.blogspot.com. This blog is a must-read.

Find out more about the game at the **Excalibur Publishing Limited** home page (www. excalibur-publishing.com).

DID YOU KNOW

The original Space Rangers was also sold only overseas back in 2002 and is included in the packaging of Space Rangers 2.

Papyrus (1987-2003)
Corporate Graveyard

Papyrus was the first company to capture the colors of NASCAR.

Most developers have a niche. Even though they might branch off into different genres, many of them have a bread-and-butter area of expertise. Papyrus (Papy) dealt exclusively with auto simulations; not necessarily racing games, but hardcore driving sims. In fact, this was by far the most respected driving sim company on the planet until Vivendi Universal (the pillager of Sierra Online) pulled its plug in the summer of 2004 after EA Sports obtained exclusive use of the NASCAR license.

Vivendi felt that highly accurate driving sims on the PC were too "nichey" to market to the masses and not worth spending a lot of development cash on. Papyrus was another casualty of a poorly run publishing house that, at least in my view, lacked the vision to keep one of the best PC game developers afloat. There is just no excuse for a company like Papyrus to get dismantled.

The good news is that many former Papyrus members, including its founder, Dave Kaemmer, now have a new company called iRacing.com Motorsports Simulations. So, maybe the era of the PC racing sim isn't over just yet.

The Papy Lineage

Papyrus cranked out over 15 titles in its history; all of which were racing sims. Here's a look at the company's most prominent releases.

Indianapolis 500: The Simulation (1989). Back in 1989, racing games were considered "light" fair. Indy 500 is considered by many to be the first true North American racing simulation. It had crude graphics and sound, but it captured the attention of gearheads everywhere. It showed racing junkies just what you could do with these home computer things.

IndyCar Racing (1993–1995). Although the NASCAR and GPL games get most of the attention, I absolutely loved the IndyCar series. The original IndyCar Racing was the first time I had ever experienced racing against a buddy over a phone modem, and I was blown away. For 1993 the graphics were outstanding, the racing fairly realistic, and the ability to

custom paint your car added more flavor to what is one of the best racing sims of all time.

The original IndyCar Racing. Hey, for the early '90s this looked hot.

NASCAR Racing (1994–2003). This was Papy's bread-and-butter series. I recall when the original NASCAR Racing was in development the word out of Papyrus was that controlling one of these things was like trying to control a beast (but in a good way). This was not going to be a remake of IndyCar using only closed-wheel cars. This was a whole new ballgame. The company also tapped into a huge fan base that was waiting for a game to call its own. NASCAR fans ate up this series with a spoon.

Grand Prix Legends (1998). Grand Prix Legends, a game based on the 1967 GPL season, is considered (and rightfully so) to be the most realistic racing sim ever designed. Not for the casual fan, it made the hardcore racing fans absolutely giddy due to its unheralded realism. The problem? It didn't sell like the NASCAR games because of the subject matter and its extreme difficulty.

DID YOU KNOW

Although Papyrus is known for its sims, it is also credited with co-developing a 1993 space strategy/adventure game called Nomad.

The High Heat Baseball Series
Closet Classics (1998–1991)

High Heat captures the battle between pitcher and hitter perfectly.

DOSSIER

Genre: Best Baseball Game Ever **Publisher:** 3DO **Developer:** Team .366 **Platform:** PC

This classic series really isn't all that old. In fact, it met its demise only a few years ago after publisher 3DO went belly up (see p.112) and sold the rights to Microsoft who has, as of yet, done nothing whatsoever with it.

I also should point out that this Closet Classic entry is specific to the PC versions of High Heat Baseball from '99 through the 2002 versions of the game. It was all downhill after that. Here's a quick look back at why this is still considered by many to be the best PC baseball franchise of all time.

Never the best-looking game, High Heat had it where it counted. The gameplay was brilliant.

A Brief History of High Heat Baseball

High Heat Baseball '99. The original High Heat Baseball, released by 3DO and developed by Team .366, received very little fanfare. But PC baseball fans, at the time, were starving, absolutely starving, for a moderately realistic arcade baseball experience. The game wasn't licensed by MLB, so it didn't have real players and teams, had limited statistical tracking capabilities, and lacked a franchise mode, but the gameplay was addictive and had enough realism in it that hardcore baseball fans were both surprised and intrigued.

High Heat Baseball 2000. Despite a buggy release, High Heat Baseball 2000 was very *important* in that it truly advanced the genre. It wasn't until after the patches that the game reached its potential. The number of new features from High Heat '99 to 2000 remains one of the most amazing one-year advancements in sports gaming history. From a basic arcade game to a full-fledged career simulation with amazing statistical tracking and the best pitcher/batter interface ever designed (yes, better than MVP Baseball), this is the game that started it all.

Sammy Sosa High Heat Baseball 2001. Name oddity aside, High Heat 2001 was another big step up for the series. It added the All-Star game, night games, rookie drafts, Internet play, several old-time parks such as Shibe and the Baker Bowl, and a refined pitching model.

High Heat Baseball 2002. This was the pinnacle. High Heat Baseball 2002 on the PC is, in this sports nut's opinion, the best baseball game of all time. The basic gameplay from 2001 was intact but this version added better graphics and sound, September roster expansions, third strike drops, rain delays, improved cut-off system, catcher snap-throws, check swing appeals, base coaches, on-deck batters, player suspensions, and complete HTML support for online leagues. This game was so good that I would still play it if I could get it to work under Windows XP.

High Heat Baseball 2003. High Heat 2003 wasn't a *terrible* game, but it marked the first time that the series had taken a step back. It was too easy to make contact with the ball in this version and there were very few new features aside from the graphics update.

High Heat Baseball 2004. The last High Heat release was also the worst because it was a total console port. High Heat 2004 didn't even have mouse support on the PC. I'm serious. A PC game released without support for the *mouse*. Gone was the spreadsheet-like interface and easy navigation, and in its place was a complete monstrosity of a design. I'd rather play High Heat '99 than this one.

> ### TUNE ME BABY
> An innocuous text file named tune.txt in High Heat's PC version was the primary reason it was so much better than the console editions. The Tune file allowed you to edit literally everything in the game from the friction between the ball and the grass to the speed of a fastball. It was way, *way* better than the sliders of today's sports games.

Ten Worst GameCube Games
Metacritic's Worst Reviewed GC Games

Image courtesy of GameSpy.com.

Charlie's Angels the game was worse than the movies. That, my friends, is saying something.

There is a running theme with the games on the Metacritic "Worst" Ten GameCube list. None of the games, not one of them, come from Nintendo. These are all third-party pieces of garbage that should be forgotten—lost in the annals of videogame lore forever.

From Disney and Shrek to digitized versions of Will Smith and Drew Barrymore, no one is spared!

10. Disney Sports: Basketball (Score: 37). This was a three-on-three basketball game with Disney characters such as Mickey Mouse, Goofy, and Donald Duck as the stars. This idea on its face isn't all that bad: What kid doesn't like Mickey? The problem was that even kids thought this was boring with a poor control system.

9. Disney Sports: Skateboarding (Score: 36). Did you read the description of the Disney basketball game? Tony Hawk for kids, this was not.

8. Jeremy McGrath Supercross World (Score: 36). There was a time when Acclaim's Jeremy McGrath games weren't too bad. When this mess of a game was released, that time had passed.

7. The Sum of All Fears (Score: 36). A lot of PC gamers cannot stand console ports—games that were designed for the consoles but then transmogrified into PC games. The Sum of All Fears returned the favor; this was a PC port for the GameCube and ranking it only at #7 is being kind.

6. Shrek Extra Large (Score: 36). Fun with press releases: Brand new and exclusive for the GameCube, Shrek Extra Large is stacked with 10 levels, twisted fairy tale characters, awesome cut-scenes, and action-packed gameplay! A total of 10 warped fairy tale levels, brand new twisted fairy tale characters, and great power moves such as punch, kick, grab, super-flatulence, and belch! Those PR folks could sell water to a drowning man, couldn't they?

Image courtesy of GameSpy.com.

The Sum of All Fears. The fear is actually paying money for this thing.

5. Bad Boys II: Miami Takedown (Score: 35). You know, this game deserved to be atrocious. The *Bad Boys* movies are two of the worst films ever made and I'm sort of happy the video game stunk, too. Bad movies should never make good games.

4. BeyBlade: Super Tournament Battle (Score: 33). Bad graphics, weak controls, and amazingly simple gameplay spells doom for this edition of BeyBlade.

3. Batman: Dark Tomorrow (Score: 29). Oh, it's dark alright.

2. Aquaman: Battle for Atlantis (Score: 27). I think Aquaman is due for a major comeback. Have you seen the HBO series *Entourage*? James Cameron is making an Aquaman movie! Woo hoo!

1. Charlie's Angels (Score: 23). This is another example (one of many) of a publisher trying to cash in on a license using babes as a selling point. This also tries to break my rule from the Bad Boys game—bad movies should never make good games, and Charlie doesn't disappoint. I think Riddick comes close to breaking that rule. Riddick was a great game but a pretty average movie. Average is not abysmal, though. *Charlie's Angels* (as well as *Bad Boys*) are the epitome of Hollywood schlock and a score of 23 is actually too high for this game.

Image courtesy of GameSpy.com.

Mickey fouls out in Disney Basketball.

DID YOU KNOW

Aquaman is actually a very old comic book hero, first appearing in *More Fun Comics #73* back in 1941. He's only two years younger than Batman, although not nearly as cool.

PC Case Modding
Because Normal Is Boring

The perfect case mod for all you Wasteland and Fallout fans.

Why do people rip apart perfectly good PCs and install neon lights, windows, glow cables, and water-filled cooling systems? Why do people spend thousands to trick out Dodge Neons? Why do people make (and buy) any of the Aquaman games? Because people are weird, that's why.

Okay. That's not entirely fair. Weirdness has something to do with it, but individuality is a much better answer. People mod their PCs because they want to be different, want to have a cool box that makes their friends' eyes pop out, and want to have one of those machines that makes everyone else at the LAN party drool with envy. Sometimes modifications like an overclocked PC with an exotic cooling systems give their computers a performance boost, but the real reason people mod their PCs is because it's cool.

In the early days of case modding (and in the more exotic forms today), most mods were constructed by do-it-yourselfers with a lot of electrical/mechanical skill who could roll their own components. Just take a look at these two *Maximum PC* Rig of the Month award winners (courtesy of *Maximum PC* magazine) for the lengths modders can go to.

Today, though, the case modding scene has gotten pretty lively and plenty of exotic mods can be had via mail order from a variety of sites. If you're ready to get down to modding, here are some sources for the coolest gear.

If you have a soft, furry cat, this airy design might not be for you.

ThinkGeek (www.thinkgeek.com). Overall, this is probably one of the coolest geek culture sites on the Web. Besides the nifty clothing, cool toys, whacked-out gadgets, caffeinated beverages, and books, ThinkGeek carries a huge line of case modding supplies for the discriminating mod freak. From wacky cases and power supplies (including the MSI Mega PC Barebones Kit that also includes a built-in stereo) to hard-to-find glow wires, CPU water-cooling systems, and even audio cassette decks for your tower, ThinkGeek is truly a one-stop shop for you techno-cool folks.

Case-Mod.com (www.case-mod.com). Case-Mod.com is a superstore for modders, stocking dozens of cases, drives, lighting supplies, fans, cool lighting, power supplies, and cooling gear. If all you want to do is remake your home PC in a cool acrylic case or want to indulge your deepest desires to overclock your CPU into meltdown stage (but avoid the meltdown), start searching here. One of the nicest features of Case-Mod.com is its online customer support: During normal business hours, you can chat live one-on-one with its customer service reps to deal with any issues you might be having. They won't tell you which multiplier to apply to your CPU or how to hack your BIOS, but they will help you pick the mods right for you.

ATACOM (www.atacom.com). These guys carry a huge selection of products for both the home-brew PC builder and hardcore case modder. From every accessory you can possibly think of (including cool stuff for PDAs and laptops) to mega-cool light-up speakers (check out the Sicuro units), if you can think of it, they probably have it. For those who really want to blow away the n00bs at the next con or LAN party, check out the modular Aerocool case systems that lets you create fully functional PCs that look like cars, trucks, airplanes, or even animals. Ooohhhh, animals.

GideonTech.com (www.gideontech.com). Not really a store, GideonTech.com is a hub, resource, and idea bank for modders with links to just about every major mod source and manufacturer online. True to the geek roots of site members, GideonTech.com has scads of articles and how-to pieces on modding esoterica that go far beyond just snarfing in a nifty light-up fan. Learn how to build a remote for your PC, turn it into a wet bar (really!), cool down your video card, or even dye your own plastics for some truly mind-blowing effects. Even if you have no desire to hack into your plastic, the VP Gallery of user-provided mod pictures will be sure to have you oohing and ahhing for hours.

DID YOU KNOW

This month in 2001: The film *Final Fantasy: The Spirits Within* was released nationwide. Considered a technological wonder, the movie flopped at the box office.

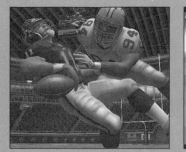

August 2005

Puppies and Football

Madden NFL 06 hit the scene in August to both thunderous applause and a whole lot of whining. Although I'm not drinking the NCAA Football 06 Kool-Aid, I've got a full pitcher of it to share when it comes to the controversial Madden NFL 06 "vision cone." I think the idea of throwing to a location is pretty darn cool, and that Madden NFL 06 is arguably the best game in the series' long history. Surprisingly, a lot of Madden fans hated the new cone. I just don't get it; people want EA Sports to try new stuff and when they do people complain because it's something they aren't familiar with. What gives, guys?

Another high-profile game released in August was on the Nintendo DS as gamers took their little Nintendogs for a spin. This is the kind of game that gamers turn their noses up at until they try it and it attracts nongamers in hordes. What better way to reach the latter audience than with puppies that you can talk to via the DS microphone?

Finally, the Year of the Comic Game continues as The Hulk: Ultimate Destruction showed gamers that the Hulk could be cool and, after that weird Hulk movie, that was a bit of a challenge.

Flop of the Month:

- **Lizzie McGuire 3: Homecoming Havoc**—I had such high hopes for Lizzie. Sadly, she disappointed me. Curse you, Lizzie! Hey, give a poor author a break; it's not like I had much to choose from when it comes to high profile games that flopped this month. Some would argue that Darkwatch wasn't as good as we'd hoped, but I dug that game, so those people are just wrong.

Madden NFL 06
Madden: Part 18 (It's True)

Madden is now the only NFL game in town.

DOSSIER

Genre: Greybeard of Football Games **Publisher:** EA Sports **Developer:** EA Sports Tiburon **Platform:** PS2, Xbox, PC, PSP, Nintendo DS, GameCube, Xbox 360
Metacritic Metascore: 88

Pressure. That's pretty much the word of the day when it comes to EA Sports flagship title, Madden NFL. EA Sports ticked off a lot of hardcore gamers when the company and the NFL collaborated to sign an exclusive licensing deal, cutting off Madden's competitors (namely the NFL 2K series) at the knees.

Regardless, Madden's sales have been extremely strong, which goes to show you that deep down the masses don't care about any of this licensing stuff (see p.143). They just want to play games.

Ouch.

Not So Super

Let's get this out of the way. Madden's new Superstar mode is the dumbest thing to hit video game football since the invention of the Mascot game. The idea is to take a rookie into the league, hire an agent, and live the life of an NFL star. Not a bad idea, but the problem is that it's a horribly underdeveloped feature (just like NCAA Football 06's Race for the Heisman mode). Do you like getting 40 fake cell phone messages from Terrell Davis and Rich Eisen, all saying basically the same thing? Do you think it's cool to go to a barber to pick out your haircut? Do you want your draft status dictated by a phony IQ test instead of running drills at the NFL Combine? What a waste.

Vision and Precision

Now we're talking! Although the new Superstar mode is sure to leave a bitter taste in your mouth, the new passing model is one of the coolest new features to grace a football game in years. For the first time ever in a football game, a quarterback's field awareness is directly tied to how he plays when being controlled by a human. When he drops back to pass, a bright cone that simulates his vision appears on the screen.

If you try to throw outside that vision cone, his accuracy plummets. The cool part is that a QB like Tom Brady has a cone that is almost the size of the entire field, whereas Kyle Boller has a much smaller window. It's a fantastic way to simulate field vision, and for this EA Sports deserves huge credit. It doesn't take away the evil that is Superstar mode, but it helps.

Franchise Tips

Control all 32 teams. That's right. Set all 32 teams to human. Then go into each coach profile and put every CPU assist feature on so that the CPU runs each team. However, leave the Draft option set to human. The draft AI in Madden is horrid. Unless you don't care that CPU teams will draft kickers in the second round, you should pick for them.

The injury bar. Inside the settings menu is an injury bar for both played and simmed games. If you want added realism, raise the played game bar and lower the sim game bar. If you don't, you're going to see a crazy number of season-ending injuries during the year.

Online franchise. A slightly hidden feature is the fact that you can run an online franchise with your friends by using the new EA Sports Locker feature. It's time-consuming because each team has to play one at a time, but if you have a few buddies, it is a great way to play.

> ### MADDEN MANIA
> **Madden Mania** (www.maddenmania.com) is an immensely popular fan site dedicated to all things Madden.

DID YOU KNOW

Deactivated and buried inside the audio options underneath all the rock/rap stuff (and nothing says NFL like the Foo Fighters) are 10 authentic NFL Films soundtracks. Turn on and enjoy.

♟Chaos League: Sudden Death
Football with Orcs and a Body Count

Hey buddy, nice tattoos....

DOSSIER

Genre: Blood Bowl Clone **Publisher:** Digital Jesters **Developer:** Cyanide **Platform:** PC
Metacritic Metascore: 72 (this score is insane)

Although the original game, Chaos League, didn't catch on in the United States (mainly because it was never available from the major retail chains), it was popular enough across the pond to warrant an expansion pack, dubbed Sudden Death. Given that, a little background is in order.

While fans waited ever so patiently for Games Workshop to release an official computer version of its popular fantasy football tabletop game, Blood Bowl, publisher Digital Jesters and developer Cyanide Studios decided enough was enough! Spawned from the depths of their offices came Chaos League, an obvious homage to Blood Bowl that fans have devoured whole.

The idea is simple: Take several fantasy races, such as dwarves, orcs, and elves, mix in American football, blend it with rugby, add in the fact players can get killed while on the pitch and you have a recipe for a great game.

Sudden Death was released in early August in Europe, but still has yet to make an appearance stateside. It's a fantastic upgrade to what is already an addictive strategy/sports game. Let's dig into some specifics....

There are several new pitches in the add-on, and they look really slick.

What's New in Sudden Death

New races. Sudden Death includes three new races that can take the field and wreak havoc. They are

- **The Gnomes:** Short, slow, and yet highly resourceful, the gnomes field all manner of mechanical contraptions on the pitch.

- **The Cicutas:** Lizard-like creatures who are fast but not particularly strong. They can poison their opponents, however, which makes them extremely dangerous.

- **The Damned:** Not quite undead, all we know is that they're "evil and very strong," which should make owners of elf teams a bit fearful to say the least (elves being the pansies that they are).

New stadiums. Four new stadiums are included in the expansion, each with its very own weather patterns that affect gameplay.

DID YOU KNOW

THEY SAID IT

"We doubled the number of skills. Of course, older racers will have access to some new skills with certain restrictions. For example, you will have 'Rain of Turkeys,' 'Hypnotism,' 'Immolation'...plenty of new toys to 'share' with your opponent." —**Patrick Pligersdorffer of Cyanide Studios in an interview with Chaos League Players**

Captains. Teams can now hire a player captain, who will grant significant moral support for teammates if he's on the pitch. Of course, being a captain also makes him a target for enemy ogres. It's a rather tough job.

Player view. You'll be able to see replays from a first-person viewpoint of any player you choose. So, now you can get a hands-on view of just how you smacked that dark elf around on the way to the end zone.

Other stuff. Digital Jesters enhanced the AI with more race-specific team logic, a true turn-based mode rather than the stop-and-start mode from the original (although real-time is still an option as well), player contracts, the ability to attack the ref, and additional multiplayer features.

MUST VISIT CHAOS LEAGUE WEBSITES
The **Bloodweiser Challenge League** (www.jubaal.co.uk/bcl) is a highly popular online league that shows you just how fanatical fans are about the game.

Chaos League: Sudden Death is bundled with the original game. So even though it's an expansion, you get the whole package for around $30 by ordering it online. That, my friends, is a bargain.

Ghost Recon 2: Summit Strike
More Add-On Goodness

Gritty, realistic, and intense, Summit Strike might be the best game of the series to date.

DOSSIER

Genre: Tom Clancy Is LOADED! **Publisher:** Ubisoft **Developer:** Red Storm Entertainment **Platform:** Xbox **Metacritic Metascore:** 84

When you see a Tom Clancy game on the store shelf, it's usually a safe bet that it's pretty good. Between the Rainbow Six and Splinter Cell series, we're talking about a lot of A-list games. The Ghost Recon series, on the other hand, has been hit and miss: Some of the games are top-of-the-line military shooters whereas other versions, usually the ones on the PS2, are surprisingly bad.

Fortunately, Ghost Recon 2: Summit Strike, a $30 standalone expansion of sorts to Ghost Recon 2, is one of the good ones. Aside from the fact that the game packs in a *lot* of new content, for $30 it's really a great deal because it's so big you could classify this as a true sequel.

THEY SAID IT

"Along with all the available downloadable content weapons, we have kept the weapons from Ghost Recon 2 in Summit Strike. Several of the weapons were renamed to match their updated versions or regional specific variants, but players will have no problems finding their old favorites." —**Jeff McGann, Lead Designer, Ghost Recon 2: Summit Strike**

What's New in Sudden Strike

Sudden Strike offers a massive graphics overhaul, including new weather effects such falling snow and sandstorms as well as other visual enhancements.

There's a brand new 11-mission campaign that starts out in Kazakhstan. The Ghosts are brought in to "neutralize" a Pakistani warlord named Rahil, who is trying to take over the country by force after the death of the president and his cabinet. You know—your usual Ghost Recon–type stuff.

The new campaign is very well done, all except for the teammate AI which is really the weakest part of the game. Sometimes it seems as if they *try* to get shot; they're like Vin Diesel in *Saving Private Ryan*.

Still, if the AI drives you too batty, you can hop on Xbox Live and try some of the new multiplayer games. Summit Strike is a very safe buy for fans of the series or for fans of military shooters in general. At $30...it's quite the expansion.

The Recon Lineage

Ghost Recon (2001). A fantastic tactical team shooter, the original Ghost Recon for the PC kicked all sorts of ass. It was named IGN and *PC Gamer*'s Best PC Game of 2001. Conversely,

the PS2 version, released in 2002, was universally panned for being a dumbed-down console version of the PC game. Fortunately, the Xbox version (2002) was on par with the PC edition.

Something going boom during a Summit Strike mission.

Ghost Recon: Desert Siege (2002). This took place in the year 2009 in East Africa. It was a $20 expansion for the PC that was pretty well received by fans of the original.

Ghost Recon: Island Thunder (2001). The first expansion for the PC and Xbox (2003), Island Thunder was yet another fine addition to the series. This time the mission was Cuba in 2009 after the death of Castro. Yes, a fantasy, I know.

Ghost Recon: Jungle Storm (2004). Ghost Recon's second attempt to convert PS2 gamers failed miserably. And I never did get the whole Ghost Recon N-Gage thing. Ick.

Ghost Recon 2 (2005). Cancelled on the PC (Arghh!), the console sequel was yet again great on the Xbox, and a disaster on the PS2 and the GameCube.

GHOST RECON RETREAT

A very good fan site for the series, **GRR** (ghostrecon.3dretreat.com) is a good place to find PC mods for earlier Recon games.

DID YOU KNOW

There's a lot of hype surrounding the Xbox 360 version of Ghost Recon: Advanced War Fighter (AKA Ghost Recon 3). For details on that game, flip to p.220.

Nintendogs
Because Real Dogs Make a Mess

Image courtesy of GameSpy.com.

This cuteness of this game makes manly men quite ill.

DOSSIER

Genre: Digital Pooch Sim **Publisher:** Nintendo **Developer:** Nintendo **Platform:** Nintendo DS **Metacritic Metascore:** 83

Do you love dogs? Do you own a Nintendo DS? If so, please run out and get this game. I don't know if Nintendogs is good enough to warrant buying a DS; this isn't *quite* system-seller material, but it's without a doubt one of the most charming little games available on this or any other system. That is, if you have the patience to simulate the training of your virtual puppy. (Sorry, kitty fans. Cats made their own bed by being individualistic snobs, so no game for them!)

Nintendogs is a simulation that allows you to pick (buy) a cute little puppy of a particular breed, name it, and train it to do tricks, enter dog shows, and generally just be a cute little digital companion. Using the DS voice technology, you teach your pet to do stuff by actually talking into the DS microphone. As with a lot of DS games, you may get a few weird looks if you play this one in public. How many games ask you to talk at your handheld with words like, "Sit, Captain Hobbes! Sit!"

Unlike many DS games (like, say, WarioWare) if you show the game to a stranger you are more likely to get an "oohhh, how cute" response rather than just a blank stare.

THEY SAID IT

"We narrowed down the candidates into dogs and cats—after all, they are the two main types of companion animals loved by people all around the world. Why dogs instead of cats? Well, one of the things we really wanted to do was to let players teach tricks by utilizing their own voices. Cats are at a disadvantage when it comes to learning tricks, and also we wanted to have animals with much more fun-loving natures—we wanted the animals to be able to take part in contests, such as agility competitions, and we wanted people to be able to take their pets for a walk." —**Hideki Konno, designer of Nintendogs in an interview with Eurogamer.net**

Different Breeds, Different Versions

There are three different editions of the game and the main difference between them is related to the different breeds available in each version. You also get a different set of toys (rubber bones, flying disks, and so on) with each version.

I should point out that you need not worry if you want to play with breeds that are listed in different versions. You can unlock any of the 18 breeds with one version; it's just that you get to start out with the six breeds that come with each particular edition. Oh, and your puppy never dies, which would be incredibly unnerving, to say the least.

DID YOU KNOW

Chihuahua & Friends. This version of the game includes the Chihuahua, German Shepherd, Boxer, Cavalier King Charles Spaniel, Yorkshire Terrier, and Shetland Sheepdog.

Image courtesy of GameSpy.com.

Training your puppy is half the fun. The other half is watching them act like puppies.

Dachshund & Friends. In this version you have access to the Miniature Dachshund, Golden Retriever, Beagle, Pug, Siberian Husky, and Shih Tzu.

Labrador & Friends. Finally, the Lab version gives you the Labrador Retriever, Miniature Schnauzer, Toy Poodle, Pembroke Welsh Corgi, Miniature Pinscher, and the Shiba Inu.

I have to admit, the lack of a Wired-Haired Terrier and the Rottweiler (these guys get a bad rap) is a bit upsetting but hey, that's still a lot of breeds. There are also two hidden breeds that can be unlocked in every version: the Jack Russell Terrier (Eddie from *Frasier*) and the childhood favorite, the Dalmatian.

According to the American Kennel Association, the Labrador Retriever is the most popular breed in the United States, followed by the Golden Retriever.

Advance Wars: Dual Strike
Three Strikes and You're Out

Image courtesy of GameSpy.com.

Missiles away!

DOSSIER

Genre: Handheld Turn-Based Strategy **Publisher:** Nintendo **Developer:** Intelligent Systems **Platform:** Nintendo DS **Metacritic Metascore:** 90

Turn-based strategy games are ideal for a handheld like the Nintendo DS. Real-time combat can get a bit hectic on the small platform, but a game that allows you to sit back and strategize, like Advance Wars: Dual Strike, fits the system like a tailored glove. Dual Strike's campaign is story-based, introducing you to a lot of colorful commander characters, but the gameplay is pure turn-based tactical strategy as you move military units across a map, taking out enemy units and capturing headquarters in the process. The new version has every unit from previous games as well as new units like the Megatank, aircraft carriers, and stealth fighters. It uses nearly everything the Nintendo DS has to offer and it does it well.

The only thing missing is a way to scream into the mic to issue commands. That would be cool...hey, if I can tell my digital dog to roll over and fetch a rubber bone, why can't I tell my tanks to open fire? It is my goal to be inadvertently detained for questioning while sitting at an airport. Columbus, Ohio residents should look for me on the local news. It will be tagged with the lead, "Local man arrested after telling his video game toy to, 'attack the Black Hole's units.'"

Image courtesy of GameSpy.com.

The graphics are bright and colorful and look great on the DS.

The Advance Wars Lineage

The Advance Wars series has proven to be popular here in the United States, but its history goes back a lot further than what some American gamers may realize. The 2001 release, Advance Wars, was the first game released in North America and in Europe, but the series has been around in Japan since the late 1980s.

Famicom Wars (1988). The original game, released in Japan, was available for the NES (the Famicom in Japan). As you'd expect from a game released back in the late '80s, it wasn't quite as deep as later releases. It only had two armies (Red Star and Blue Moon) and a smaller selection of maps.

Game Boy Wars (1991). Game Boy Wars was released in the early days of the GB franchise and because Game Boy Color wouldn't come out for a few years later, it was relegated to

black-and-white, which I think pretty much destroys the entire charming atmosphere of the game.

Game Boy Wars Turbo (1997). Hudson Soft developed Turbo, which marked the first time Intelligent Systems was not at the helm. Still in black-and-white, it was a pretty straightforward sequel only with a few more maps.

Game Boy Wars 2 (1998). Another Hudson Soft release, it was in color! Yeah! That only took 10 years.

Super Famicom Wars (1998). Intelligent Systems was back at the controls in SFW. The series did allow four armies but still lacked a true campaign.

Game Boy Wars 3 (2001). Hudson Soft returns to continue the series on the Game Boy. As a sequel, it wasn't all that different from earlier releases; but it did have better graphics, so it had that going for it.

Advance Wars (2001). Finally, North American and European gamers could get their hands on a game in the series. Intelligent Systems was back in the driver's seat for good with this GBA release. It added a campaign and started to build more depth around the world. Oddly enough, the game wouldn't reach Japan until 2004.

Advance Wars 2: Black Hole Rising (2003). This game continued the plot from Advance Wars as Sturm and his Black Hole army continued its fight against the Allies. The game added new CO Powers and a lot of new units and also included a map editor and multiplayer support.

DID YOU KNOW

Because Advance Wars was released on September 11, 2001, it was almost pulled off the shelves because of the terrorist attacks.

Dungeon Siege II
More Fun with Monsters and Swords

Image courtesy of GameSpy.com.

The colors fly as all hell breaks loose.

DOSSIER

Genre: 3D Hack and Slash, The Sequel **Publisher:** Microsoft **Developer:** Gas Powered Games **Platform:** PC **Metacritic Metascore:** 80

Just like the original, Dungeon Siege II is a hack-and-slash action-based RPG. You fight masses of enemy units, obtain cool items, grow in power, and so on. It's pretty much your basic dungeon crawl–type game but with very nice graphics, sound, and atmosphere. There are also none of those evil load times! This is an extremely long game; we're talking anywhere from 40 to 60 hours of gameplay, which is a huge plus if you enjoy this style of hack-and-slash RPG. Granted, the story is pretty basic. There's some cool backstory, but you're out to kill the Foozle, the big bad guy at the end of the game who threatens mankind, yadda, yadda, yadda.

And although it might not be game of the year material, it's impossible to deny that it has an addictive quality and a very good deal of polish to it. I think the 80 score fits here pretty well; it's good, and fans of this kind of game will come away happy, but at some point this series has to try to branch out a bit. I always get the feeling that these games could be so much better.

Dungeon Siege II Mods

The original Dungeon Siege developed a large fan base and an active mod community and the sequel is no different. After just a month, there are already some handy mods available with a lot more on the way:

Super Shops. Looking for a great item to buy? Then the Super Shops mod is the perfect add-on. This shop makes the Black Market look like Wal-Mart.

Guru's Rare Everywhere. If you're looking for some "phat loot" every time you kill a bad guy, Guru's mod is for you. When you kill an enemy an item based on your level (+5 to +100) is dropped from a rare/unique item set. Is this blatantly cheating? Of course it is, but you paid $40...do what you want.

No Movie Intro Mod. Mods do not get much simpler than this, but few are as handy to have on your system. The intro movies (both the Microsoft and Gas Powered Games) take too damn long to load. This removes them and allows you to get right to the action.

2x4x XP Mod. The leveling in Dungeon Siege II can be a bit slow at times. This mod allows you to make the experience point bonus for killing monsters twice or even four times the amount, making leveling up a bit easier.

Mega-Set Modpack. This mod actually contains 23 separate small mods. The pack changes the Dungeon Siege II loot tables for common monsters.

Pet Inventory Mod. This handy mod allows every pet in the game to carry four pages of inventory.

THEY SAID IT

"In general, Gas Powered Games likes to give players a lot of freedom about how to play the game. Some people really enjoy playing maps and mods they made with indestructible characters, and that's still possible in network or anonymous Internet games. But most people like to play the game fairly, so we created the GameSpy vault. When you play on GameSpy, you use characters that are stored on GameSpy servers. There are no mods or custom maps allowed in GameSpy games, so it's much safer." —**Daniel Achterman, co-designer of Dungeon Siege II in an interview with DSHeaven**

Guru's Mega Info Pack. This impressive data list contains the hard numbers on practically everything in the game from potions and items to monsters and spells.

8-Player MP Mod. This mod allows you to play with up to eight players in a multiplayer game.

Project Britannia. Not a Dungeon Siege mod per se, but this project looks amazing nevertheless. This group of modders is trying to re-create the Ultima games using the Dungeon Siege engine. (www.projectbritannia.com)

WHERE TO GET THE MODS
You can find the mods listed here from various Dungeon Siege fan sites, including **Siege-Mods** (siege-mods.com), **Planet Dungeon Siege** (www.planetdungeonsiege.com), and **Gametoast** (gametoast.com/ds2) .

DID YOU KNOW

The original Dungeon Siege received a T for Teen rating from the ESRB. Dungeon Siege II received an M for Mature, despite not being much more violent or graphic in nature.

Darkwatch
Finally, an Undead Western

Even your horse is undead.

DOSSIER

Genre: Vampire Hunting Wild West Shooter **Publisher:** Capcom **Developer:** High Moon Studios **Platform:** Xbox, PS2 **Metacritic Metascore:** 75

Darkwatch had a bumpy ride as it meandered into stores in August 2005. Internal strife, the loss of a publisher, company buyouts, numerous delays...it was a bad scene. Usually when games goes through so much turmoil, they end up being a complete and utter disaster. Surprisingly, Darkwatch came out pretty clean. It's not revolutionary (even though the setting is awesome), but it is a lot of fun while it lasts.

In the game, you play an old west outlaw named Jericho Cross. Cross is also a train robber who decides to ambush a treasure train. This ends up being a bad move because the train is under the protection of The Darkwatch, an ancient and secret outfit dedicated to the destruction of supernatural evil. As luck would have it, you find a vault, open it up only to realize that instead of bags of gold, it contains a vampire lord (and you thought Geraldo was unlucky when he opened *his* famous vault).

The vampire bites you, cursing you forever as a member of the undead. The rest of the game is your hunt, with the help of some Darkwatch allies, to track down the vampire named Lazarus to remove the curse and win back your soul.

THEY SAID IT

> "Several of the team members have a real passion for history so that was the first avenue we explored. Clearly, the World War II category is well-represented so we looked a little further back in history. Figuring that ancient Rome might not make the best setting for an FPS, we looked in a more recent time frame and settled on the old West—an under-represented area in gaming until recently. And giving the player vampiric powers really tied the knot, giving us a cool set of alternative abilities that are not commonly seen in the FPS genre." —**Brent Disbrow, Senior Designer of Darkwatch in an interview with TeamXbox.com**

Basic Powers

As a vampire, you have access to several powers. Some powers you can use at any time, but others require the use of blood energy. Here are some of the basic ones:

Blood Shield. The shield prevents you from taking damage, but has only so much life in it; as you take hits, the shield weakens.

Blood Vision. This is Cross's ability to locate enemies and weapons through vampiric sight.

Vampire Jump. Your basic super jump. A quick double tap of the jump button sends you flying through the air like the guy in *The Lost Boys*. You can also change directions while in mid-air using this power.

DID YOU KNOW

Advanced Powers

As the game progresses you'll find "victims of Lazarus." It's up to you whether to free these souls or feed on them. If you free them, you get a boost to your good power bar; if you feed on them, your evil bar increases. When these bars max out, you earn a new power.

Fear. Makes enemies flee from your sight. (Good)

Mystic Armor. Provides a boost to your defense (what did you expect?). (Good)

Silver Bullet. Increases shooting attacks with holy fire. (Good)

Vindication. Casts a chain-lighting like spell to fry the bad guys. (Good)

Black Shroud. Acts as both added armor and also deals damage to those that attack you. (Evil)

Blood Frenzy. Makes Cross a truly devastating hand-to-hand fighter. (Evil)

Soul Steal. A ranged attack that drains a victim's soul. Ouch. (Evil)

Turn. Makes your enemies turn to attack one another for a short time. (Evil)

Targeting different undead body parts is always fun.

The PS2 version of Darkwatch has co-op mode so that you can blast bad guys with your buddy, whereas the Xbox version contains XBL support.

Battle of the Sports Licenses
Better Sales Through Bribes

Madden NFL 06 will be the only licensed football game in town.

The sports gaming market is big business. Professional sports leagues are also big business. So what better way to celebrate their bigness by joining together to fight the forces of evil! It's unfortunate that in this case the forces of evil appear to be gamers.

If squashing and removing the competition is the American way, EA Sports and Take 2 Interactive are doing everything that they can to be as patriotic as possible.

Football

The most widely talked about license agreement is the one between the NFL and EA Sports that effectively eliminated the popular NFL2K series from the marketplace. The deal states that only EA Sports can create NFL games through the year 2015. Other companies can make football games but if you want real players, teams, logos, and stadiums, you'll have to buy Madden or whatever else EA Sports wants to make. EA followed this up by inking another deal with the NCAA so that only EA Sports is allowed to make college football games with real teams and logos (basketball is still open).

Baseball

Take 2 (2K Games) got in on the act by first condemning EA's NFL agreement and then inking a deal with Major League Baseball and its Players Association. This deal was a bit different in that it states that manufacturers of a hardware unit may still make a Major League Baseball game, but third-party companies couldn't. In other words, Take 2, Microsoft, Nintendo, and Sony can make a baseball game, but EA Sports (or anyone else) can't. This deal is pretty much an "Anti-EA Sports" agreement because it smacks EA's MVP Baseball series right out of the park, so to speak. EA Sports responded to this by shifting its baseball series to the college ranks. It is yet to be determined whether people actually want to play a college baseball game, but we'll soon find out.

The Rest

The common misconception is that these are the only exclusive deals currently in place. They're the most high profile, but they are not where this story ends. EA Sports also has the licenses for the PGA, NASCAR, FIFA, UEFA Champions League, and the AFL (the Arena Football League). It also has a new 15-year agreement with ESPN so that all EA Sports games will have some ESPN flavor, for better or for worse.

It's easy to get mad at the companies involved, but a finger of shame has to be directed at the leagues themselves. No one forced the NFL or MLB to sign these exclusive agreements. This is all about cash, plain and simple.

The fear, of course, is that sports gamers will be the ones who are punished because of all this. When you take away the threat of competition, it's easy to understand why many people feel that this will stifle creativity, quality and innovation. With only one choice for football, baseball, and so forth, will EA Sports and Take 2 continue to make good games? It's a fair question, and one that we won't know the answer to until the sports games of 2006 and beyond.

Take 2 was upset with the EA/NFL deal, but not enough to stop it from signing a similar deal with MLB.

Total Annihilation
Closet Classic (1997)

Total Annihilation used 3D units, which was a huge deal in 1997.

DOSSIER

Genre: Revolutionary RTS **Publisher:** GT Interactive **Developer:** Cavedog Entertainment **Platform:** PC **Metacritic Metascore:** 86

In 1997, real-time strategy (RTS) games were staggeringly popular. Even though the genre is anything but dead today, in the late '90s it was populated by some of the most well-known and recognized franchises in history. Games like Command and Conquer, WarCraft, Age of Empires, and StarCraft exploded onto the scene and dominated PC gaming sales charts for years at a time.

One such game that also belongs on this list is Cavedog's revolutionary RTS, Total Annihilation (TA). Released that same year, it directly competed with Command and Conquer and Age of Empires and although it didn't sell as well as those money-making machines, it was a truly groundbreaking title.

THEY SAID IT

> "Total Annihilation was my first nonsports title. I was totally inspired by Command and Conquer. After playing it, there were a few things I wanted to do. I wanted to have the tanks be able to fire when they were retreating. It was so horrible to have your tanks get their butts kicked, and then while you're retreating, get finished off. There was no retreat." —**Chris Taylor, creator of Total Annihilation in an interview with PCGameworld.com**

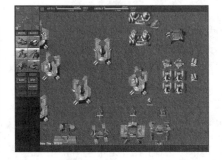

TA had a lot of units, but lacked the personality of other RTS games.

What Made TA Great

First off, Total Annihilation was the first real-time strategy game to use 3D units and terrain. While other games still used flat 2D landscapes, TA had rolling hills, mountains, and so on. And, most importantly, you could actually use the terrain to your advantage.

Then there are the units. Although the factions in the game were rather obtuse, the unit makeup for each was astounding. The original game shipped with 150 units, which by itself is quite a bit, but when you toss in the Core Contingency and Battle Tactics expansion packs, the total number leaps to a staggering 500 units with 175 missions.

Another advancement was the introduction of physics-based gameplay. This was pretty much unheard of in an RTS before Total Annihilation. The developers claimed that it used true Newtonian physics. Now I wouldn't know Newtonian physics from a Fig Newton, but TA did play differently than your standard 2D game. Things like momentum, inertia, and missile trajectories all played a crucial role during a battle.

What Held TA Back

Even though TA had a devout following, there were reasons why it didn't sell as well as some other RTS games. The big reason was that it was hard to really identify with the factions. Whereas in Age of Empires you controlled classic civilizations from the past, in TA you recruited emotionless machines. Additionally, the single-player AI was fairly weak. It was in multiplayer that the game truly excelled and retained its fan base.

Looking back at TA today, it's easy to see why it was regarded so highly by its legions of devoted fans. However, it's also a great example of the "twitch gamer" label that many of the earlier RTS games carried. It was a very fast-paced game with a slew of super high-powered weapons and unless you were really handy with zipping around the map, controlling units at breakneck speed, you were doomed.

Still, it is impossible to deny Total Annihilation's place in gaming history. It introduced so many important features that it's arguably the most influential RTS game of the late '90s and it is still being played today, eight years after its release.

DID YOU KNOW

Chris Taylor, creator of Total Annihilation and Dungeon Siege and founder of Gas Powered Games, got his start in the 1980s as the designer of Hardball II.

PlayStation 2 Cheat Hardware
When Skill Simply Isn't Enough

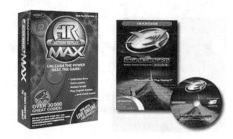

The Action Replay and Game Shark are ideal PS2 add-ons for taking control of your gaming experience.

There are two schools of thought when it comes to cheating in games. One school says that anyone who uses cheats is a loser wimp smacktard who doesn't have the skills to play games the way they should be played. Those who think this way are a very vocal school, and spend inordinate amounts of time flaming newbies who ask questions about cheating on discussion boards. The other side (the one, not coincidentally, promoted by the cheating hardware industry) says that cheats are okay because you bought the game, dammit, and you want to finish it and should be allowed to use whatever means are at your disposal to achieve those ends. At least these folks have goals in life.

Cheating on a PlayStation 2 (and by *cheating*, we mean going beyond using FAQs, controller-enterable codes, or exploiting bugs) requires two things: a piece of hardware that plugs into your console and special codes (affectionately known as *codes*) specific for each game. With these codes, you can achieve godlike gaming powers getting access to goodies like infinite ammo, infinite health, all weapons, all vehicles, hidden characters, and inaccessible levels.

But the fun doesn't stop there. Although your PlayStation 2 can play DVDs, it's limited to playing only DVDs designed for your region. For most folks who want to watch Hollywood movies, this doesn't matter, but for those with more esoteric tastes who want to play imports, the region system usually prevents it. Cheating hardware often includes hacks that let your PlayStation play out-of-region DVDs, literally opening up your machine to the world.

Action Replay Max

www.codejunkies.com; $29.99

Gone are the days when entering codes required a steady hand on the controller, an onscreen keyboard, and lots of patience. The Action Replay Max autodetects your games and presents an onscreen menu that gives you access to all the...er...tweaks available. Just navigate through, pick your cheats (more than 30,000 are available!), and play. For PS2 users with a network adapter and broadband, the Max also allows you to download codes directly from the manufacturer. If you're a sports game fan, the new Action Replay Max even lets you download roster updates from the CodeJunkies.com website or from fan sites—essential if you want your games to be as up-to-date as possible.

The Max also lets you finally gain control over your memory cards. Not only can you pack more than 10 times the data on a single card using Action Replay Max, but you can also download saves from the Internet.

GameShark 2 with Media Player

www.gameshark.com; $39.99

The first, and probably the most popular, cheater on the market, GameShark created the whole code phenomenon. One of the best things about the GameShark 2 is that it has a huge online community base with dedicated hackers releasing codes all the time. It comes preloaded with codes for more than 55,000 games and can be updated via the optional SharkPort right from your PC. The SharkPort also allows you to upload game saves and memory card files to the Net, giving you the ability to share with your friends.

The Media Player addition to the GameShark comes with the Media Player software, an MP3 player, MPEG Movie Player Technology, and photo image viewer software for the PlayStation 2.

ESPN 2K5 Video Games
Bargain Bin Specials

NBA 2K5 is a great bargain at $10.

Okay, so I'm cheating a bit on this Bargain Bin entry. After all, Take 2 Interactive released all of these games in 2004 with a $19.99 price tag, so they already qualify as bargain games.

However, as sports licenses continue to get snatched up, prices for the 2006 class of sports games have gone back to the regular $40–$50 range, so bargain hunters could do a lot worse than picking these games up for $20 (or better yet, go shopping online where they can be had for as little as $5 at auction houses such as eBay).

NFL2K, oh how I will miss thee.

MLB 2K5 was a major disappointment, so bargain buyer beware.

The ESPN 2K5 Game Roster

ESPN College Hoops 2K5. Arguably the best basketball game ever made, college or pro, this is an absolute steal at $20. With a deep recruiting model in dynasty mode combined with excellent gameplay, College Hoops 2K5 is simply a must-own for basketball fans. It's also extremely addictive on Xbox Live. There is nothing more fun than playing in a custom College Hoops tourney online if you can find enough dedicated people to play. This is Xbox sports gaming at its very best.

ESPN NHL 2K5. This game flew under the radar because of the state of the National Hockey League. With no real NHL regular season, NHL 2K5 was brushed aside. I have seen this for sale online for $5, which is an astounding price considering that this was the best arcade hockey game ever made until 2K Games released the 2K6 version last fall. Seriously folks, if you're still playing EA Sports hockey, run to your local game shop and get NHL 2K5 on the cheap and you'll never play an EA Sports hockey game ever again. It's *that* good.

ESPN NFL 2K5. The first game in years to seriously challenge Madden at the cash register, NFL 2K5 is a marvelous football game. Is it better than Madden? Well, that's a debate that continues to rage between fans of the two games. You may want to hold on to this game because it may very well be the final Take 2–published football game for some time. Rumors keep flying around about Take 2 publishing an unlicensed football game, but don't hold your breath.

ESPN NBA 2K5. Another top-shelf game, NBA 2K5 continues to go head to head with NBA Live. (Many fans still insist that NBA Inside Drive is the better game, but that franchise is apparently dead.) Regardless of which is the better, this is a great bargain at $10.

Major League Baseball 2K5. I mention this game as a warning, not as a recommendation. MLB 2K5 was a major disappointment. In fact, MLB 2K4 is the better game in this writer's opinion, but if you're looking for a baseball fix, MVP Baseball from EA Sports is the way to go. Of course, Take 2 has the official baseball license now, so MVP is dead. It figures that Take 2's worst game from its 2004 lineup is the one that gets the exclusive license.

Sometimes life just isn't fair.

ROSTERS AT OPERATION SPORTS
Hop on over to the OS forums (www.operationsports.com) to get up-to-date rosters for these year-old games.

DID YOU KNOW

ESPN, the sports news network, has been around since 1979. ESPN originally stood for *Entertainment and Sports Programming Network*, but in 1985, its official name was shortened to ESPN, Inc.

Gamers As Athletes
Don't Kid Yourselves

Image courtesy of GameSpy.com.

Just because you're good at Counter-Strike does not mean you can call yourself an athlete.

Let me just get this out of the way right now: Gamers are *not athletes*. In no way, shape, or form is a guy that kicks ass in Halo an athlete, even if you want to stretch the meaning of the word to Clintonesque proportions.

I defer to Mr. Webster: An athlete is defined as *A person possessing the natural or acquired traits, such as strength, agility, and endurance that are necessary for physical exercise or sports, especially those performed in competitive contexts.*

Image courtesy of GameSpy.com.

Being good at Madden does not make you any more of an athlete than the next guy.

Defining Sports

To break this definition down, I guess we should try to define *sport*, which is something sports fans have been trying to do for decades. Is golf a sport? Is auto racing? Sailing? Bass fishing? That's a slippery slope. Let's put gamers into a better context. Is *chess* a sport? Of course it isn't.

Again, Mr. Webster, help us out here. *Sport* is defined as

Physical activity that is governed by a set of rules or customs and often engaged in competitively.

An activity involving physical exertion and skill that is governed by a set of rules or customs and often undertaken competitively.

Well, games can certainly be competitive. No doubt about it. I've broken enough controllers in my life to know that. But physical activity? Unless moving your mouse or holding your gamepad while slurping down soda and cramming handfuls of greasy chips down your throat qualifies, we have a problem.

And the second part is really just another way of saying the first part. But this is why golf is a sport and gaming isn't. It's a *physical activity*. Sitting in your butt-grooved chair and

winning a best-of-seven Capture the Flag Quake match doesn't make you Michael Jordan; it makes you a gamer.

The Verdict

Now I realize that in Korea gaming is pretty much considered a sport. You can literally tune in and watch people play StarCraft on television there. Just because people are loopy enough to want to sit and watch people play a real-time strategy game doesn't make the game a sport.

And don't even call gamers *Cyberathletes*. Athletics just flat-out don't enter into it. Why is there the need for the sport label? Is there anything really wrong with gaming not being called a sport? Are the professional gamers out there that get paid to compete in tournaments somehow shamed if their talent for sniping people in Counter-Strike isn't considered physical activity?

What got me all stirred up over this is when I read a column in a gaming magazine that claimed that gamers are, "*a highly evolved breed of extreme athlete.*" I really wasn't sure whether this was satire, sarcasm, or some form of mental cross-wiring that affected the writer. (Hey, it happens.) Gamers are extreme athletes like Carrot Top is a fine stage actor.

The article continued, "The top players form teams, compete in leagues, hire full-time coaches, and adopt strict training regimens. They sweat. They earn six-figure salaries and scoop up endorsement deals."

They sweat *because* they're not athletes, not the other way around.

You should know by now that I love games. I play some kind of computer or console video game nearly every single day. I'm not an athlete because I do it. Nor am I taking part in an athletic event when I fire up a game of Sid Meier's Pirates!. Folks, they're games. We're gamers. We need to accept that.

DID YOU KNOW

The CPL, Cyberathlete Professional League, was founded in 1997 and is still active today. Find out more at www.thecpl.com/league/. (It's still not a sport.)

MotoGP 3
Because Two Wheels Are As Fun As Four

This is one great-looking bike sim.

Image courtesy of GameSpy.com.

DOSSIER

Genre: Extreme Motorcycle Sim **Publisher:** THQ **Developer:** Climax Studios
Platform: Xbox **Metacritic Metascore:** 85

MotoGP 3 is a serious bike sim the same way that Winning Eleven is a serious soccer sim. This is not an arcade racer for the Xbox. Although you can tone down the difficulty, this is meant to be played by gearheads first and foremost. It's tough. No doubt about it. It's also a lot more challenging, particularly in the area of braking, than its predecessors. If you hear anyone say that this is the same game as GP2 but with new tracks—they lie.

THEY SAID IT

"Extreme Mode will provide the player with Grand Turismo-style gameplay. The player will be able to build up a library of Motorcycles; ranging from 600cc sports bikes to 1200cc monsters. Each bike will be finely tuned to provide players true simulation feeling with out the frustration of other titles. We feel MOTOGP's handling on tight backstreets will be enough to draw in the masses." —**Greg Bryant, Lead Designer MotoGP 3 in an interview with Xbox World Australia**

I think you need at least one screw loose to do this for a living.

Image courtesy of GameSpy.com.

The Gameplay

MotoGP 3's career mode spans a 16-race season, complete with the real professionals from the GP circuit. You create a custom rider, slap a custom logo on your bike, choose your gear, and off you go.

The courses are almost carbon copies of the real thing and you have to go through the rigorous tests of practicing, qualifying, and the prerace setup if you want to compete against a very aggressive AI on the higher levels of difficulty. MotoGP 3 is great in that on the easy settings it's very forgiving and the AI bikes leave you plenty of room to play catch-up, but if you play it as a true sim on the hard settings, be prepared for a very challenging series of races. You can also opt to play against real players offline via the ghost riders by downloading other player's profiles, sort of like Forza Motorsport or using the VIP Profiles in ESPN NFL 2K5.

Between races, you can spend earned attribute points to increase the skill of your rider, making it easier to brake, turn, and so on as you gain experience.

As sim-heavy as the game is, there is a new Extreme Mode that adds some fictional courses to the mix, which diehards will either accept with open arms or shun without batting an eye. You can still just stick to the real tracks if you prefer, but the Extreme Mode is actually pretty cool in that it presents you with 16 well-designed fictional courses (in real locales) and a myriad of riders.

For many fans, though, the best way to enjoy the game is online via Xbox Live. Up to 16 players can take part and the online community is both active and for the most part courteous. Most people online are just after a realistic fun time. You won't find too many people trying to play Rock 'em Sock 'em Robots on two wheels. In fact, you can find a lot of people who are after a full hour-long race.

OFFICIAL MOTOGP
www.motogp.com is the official website for the real MotoGP. If you want to learn more about the sport, this is the place.

DID YOU KNOW

GP racing involves prototype machines that are not available to the public. Unlike other forms of bike racing, such as Superbikes, which are highly modified versions of retail street bikes.

Tomb Raider Games
They Didn't Always Suck

Image courtesy of GameSpy.com.

Can Tomb Raider: Legend bring the series back to its glory days?

I'm sure that there are a lot of young readers out there that really have no idea that once upon a time Tomb Raider was a truly fascinating game. Before the rehashed sequels, the continually increasing bra size and shrinking pants line of Lara Croft, and the predictable and tired *Tomb Raider* movies starring Angelina Jolie. Before all of that, Tomb Raider *did not suck*.

In fact, the reason that the Tomb Raider franchise exploded like it did in the late '90s was because of how good the original game actually was. If it wasn't for the fact that Tomb Raider was a revolutionary action/adventure, none of the other stuff would have mattered.

Image courtesy of GameSpy.com.

Angel of Darkness had nothing to do with tombs or raiders.

When Lara Was a Heroine

To date, there have been no fewer than 13 Tomb Raider releases—none of which comes close to being as original or as fun as the first game, which as developed by Cored design and released for the PC, PS1, and Sega Saturn by Eidos on Halloween of 1996. That was the same year that id Software released its classic shooter, Quake.

Unlike the classic shooters of the era, Tomb Raider was a third-person adventure, where you got to see Lara in full, and not just through her viewpoint (which was admittedly part of the game's appeal).

What also made the game stand out were the amazing environments and the animation that allowed Lara to do all sorts of tricky moves. Tomb Raider was about trying to find ancient artifacts, not killing bad guys. In fact, most of the enemies in the first game were animals and other creatures, not people.

It was an amazing experience for its day. Sort of like Prince of Persia, but in pseudo-3D with great graphics and tricky puzzles. It gave gamers a chance to play an Indiana Jones–type character—the fact that Lara was a digital hottie wasn't the point; the game itself was remarkable.

The Other Stuff

The series started to decline rather rapidly. You can make the argument that the games continued to sell (and sell rather well), which is true, but Lara started to lose some of her Indiana Jones luster right off the bat with the 1997 sequel, Tomb Raider II: The Dagger of Xian, which had Lara leave the ancient jungle ruins and instead head to China to look for a lost dagger. A lot of people complained that it was just a knock-off sequel rather than something truly "new," which would be a running theme of the series' criticism through the years.

The biggest problem with the Tomb Raider sequels is that Eidos started cranking them out at an amazing pace. From 1996 through 2003, Eidos released several sequels, gold editions, and sequels of sequels. ABC didn't ape *Who Wants to Be a Millionaire* as much as Eidos did Tomb Raider. By the 2003 release, Lara Croft Tomb Raider: The Angel of Darkness, Lara had almost completely been removed from her archeological roots; she was a stealth-action hero, killing bad guys like she was in Splinter Cell. Sporting unresponsive controls and a lot of bugs—it carries a 50 Metascore over at Metacritic.com. It was that bad.

Eidos isn't giving up, though. There are still people out there, apparently, that want to play more Tomb Raider games. Tomb Raider: Legend is slated to be released late 2005 on the PS2, PC, PSP, and the Xbox 360. Go with God.

THE LEGEND HOME PAGE

Visit the **Tomb Raider: Legend** home page at www.tombraider.com and decide for yourself whether Legend can resurrect the franchise. Don't blame me for being skeptical. Fool me once, shame on you. Fool me 12 times, shame on me.

DID YOU KNOW

There are several Tomb Raider novels: *The Amulet of Power* by Mike Resnick, *The Lost Cult* by E. E. Knight, and *The Man of Bronze* by James Alan Gardner. All are published by Ballentine Books.

Acclaim Entertainment (1987-2004)
Corporate Graveyard

All-Star Baseball deserved a better fate.

There are a lot of game companies that, when they fail or have to file bankruptcy, send a shockwave through the industry. It's common to hear questions such as, "How could Looking Glass close?" or "Cavedog made Total Annihilation. How did that company fade so quickly?"

With Acclaim, well, it sort of all makes sense. The company started 1987, and made most of its cash in the arcade circuit. Actually, it ported a lot of arcade games into home-based formats, such as the classic Mortal Kombat series. Acclaim was also the first company allowed to create third-party software for the Nintendo 64. In fact, in the mid 1990s, one could argue that Acclaim was doing pretty darn well for itself.

Ultimately, however, the company was best known, however, for releasing bad games...excruciatingly bad games. When you keep doing that, the cash flow is eventually going to stop and you're going to have to get a new job. Acclaim tried the sports market, the shooter market, the platformer market, and so on. None of its games were as good as those of its competitors.

Acclaim filing for Chapter 7 bankruptcy in 2004 was a shock only in that it took so long.

The Acclaim Lineage

Acclaim released a lot of games over its 13-year run. Most of those games were pretty poor, but the company did manage to release a few gems during that span.

All-Star Baseball (1999–2004). All-Star Baseball (ASB) is actually one of Acclaim's best series. Although the game struggled in its early years, by the time the baseball wars were in full swing with MVP and MLB2K, the All-Star Baseball series was holding its own, at least in the eyes of the critics. I liked the concept of the later ASB games, but the cursor-based hitting model remained a sticking point. This series deserved a lot better than it got from its publisher.

Burnout (2001–2003). This was another good series from Acclaim that was later picked up by Electronic Arts. The early Burnout games were developed by Criterion and were high energy racing games with very sharp visuals. If Acclaim had focused on making more games like Burnout rather than stuff like BMX XXX maybe it would still be around.

Crazy Taxi (2001). This was a port of the classic hit-and-run taxi game on the Dreamcast. Acclaim was merely the publisher; it was a Sega game through and through. Still, Acclaim's name is on the box, so it gets points for its release.

Turok (1997–2002). The original Turok: Dinosaur Hunter was a pretty cool game. Not great by any means, but a fun shooter nevertheless, and it also made Acclaim a nice little profit. Even the sequel, Seeds of Evil did pretty well. It was the later games, particularly Turok: Evolution, that drained the coffers.

Burnout was another popular game from Acclaim. If it had published more games like this...

Archon
Closet Classic (1983)

DOSSIER

Genre: Battle Chess Predecessor **Publisher:** Electronic Arts
Developer: Free Fall Associates **Platform:** Atari, C-64, Apple II, Amiga

Archon circa 1983. This looked great back then.

Remember the scene in *Star Wars* where R2-D2 is playing Chewbacca in a game of virtual space chess? As a kid, that scene fascinated me. I remember thinking how cool it would be to be able to actually play a game like that. In 1983, Free Fall Associates and Electronic Arts teamed up to deliver a game called Archon, which was close to capturing the feel of the *Star Wars* game that gave birth to the classic line, "Let the wookiee win."

Archon is yet another example of a Closet Classic game that by all rights should be an ideal fit for a modern remake. Seriously, Archon, using 2006 technology and multiplayer support? I am *so* all over that.

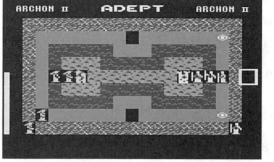

Adept used the same battle engine, but the board design was totally unique.

Light Versus Dark

It's easy to mistake Archon for an elaborate chess game, given that it's played on a chessboard. In this game, however, each piece represented a classic creature from mythology or fantasy, such as the dragon, basilisk, unicorn, golem, and shapeshifter. When they met, it was a battle between light and dark for control of the square, with each piece having its own unique power.

The fights were in real-time and supported the joystick (a big draw in 1983), but it was the difference in the units that really made the game work. The pawn units (knights and goblins) packed very little punch but were fast. Golems, on the other hand, were slow, methodical units but could do great damage by hurling boulders across the arena. I especially loved the phoenix, which could transform, for a few seconds, into a ball of fire that damaged anything near it.

The board itself also played a role. The Light units had more health when fighting on light squares, and vice versa. On top of that, many of the board colors changed each turn, which could turn the tide of a game in the blink of an eye. This made for some very tough decisions during the course of the game, particularly in how you used your strong pieces.

The end game occurred when all of your opponent's pieces were taken or when a player controlled the five "power points" on the board.

Archon: Adept

A year later, the same team released Archon II: Adept, which was another wonderfully designed game and also the kind of sequel that publishers rarely release today.

Adept abandoned the entire chess motif and instead went for a more original design involving earth, wind, fire, and water. The monsters in the game were now summoned by one of your four "adepts" and most were bound to a particular region (the kraken was in the water realm area, the salamander in the fire zones, and so forth). You could also cast spells like Banish (removes a piece from the board), Imprison (prevents a piece from moving until the light cycles had shifted), and so on. It was a much more eclectic design than the original, but no less fun.

> ### ARCHON EVOLUTION
> Curve Software is in the middle of creating an updated version of the game, called Archon Evolution (www.archonevolution.com). Check it out and pray that it does justice to the original!

DID YOU KNOW

In 1994, Archon Ultra was released. A remake of the original, with modem support and updated graphics, it didn't play all that well and the controls were sluggish. It tanked at retail.

Top Ten GameCube Games

Metacritic's Best of the Best for the GameCube

Image courtesy of GameSpy.com.

Good day, sunshine.

The GameCube is the little engine that could. I still find it amazing that Nintendo's console is now considered the underdog of the big three. But in North America at least, that's the reality. Still, the platform is home for some of the most creative games in the industry, including the 10 gems listed here.

10. NFL 2K3 (Score: 92). If you're a diehard sports gamer, you own more than just a GameCube. I don't even think that's a generalization; I don't know one person who plays a lot of sports games who is also exclusively a GameCube player. The games just don't sell all that well on this system. In fact, NFL 2K3 was the last of the series to even be available on the platform; both 2K4 and ESPN 2K5 were Xbox/PS2 games.

9. Super Smash Bros. Melee (Score: 92). Released back in 2001, Super Smash Bros. Melee is a fantastic game based on the N64 original. A fighting game with all the classic Nintendo characters with great four-player fighting? That's an easy sell.

8. Prince of Persia: The Sands of Time (Score: 92). He jumps, he leaps, he climbs, and he carries a dagger that can halt and even reverse the sands of time! The never named Prince is one bad dude and The Sands of Time is one of the best action adventures ever made.

7. Super Mario Sunshine (Score: 92). The 2002 classic is maybe a tad bit overrated, but is still a very well-made Mario platform adventure. It also has the distinction of being the happiest game title ever.

6. Viewtiful Joe (Score: 93). Viewtiful Joe is the simple story of an average fella named Joe, who is watching a movie with his girlfriend Silvia. A villain emerges from the screen to steal his girl and Joe must then enter the movie and save the day, hero style.

5. Soul Calibur II (Score: 93). Namco's 500-pound gorilla, it remains one of the best fighting games ever made, if not the best. The GameCube version includes Link from the Zelda series.

4. Madden NFL 2004 (Score: 94). I know Madden is ultra popular but a 94 score for Madden 2004 is just too darn high, particularly on the GameCube.

3. Resident Evil 4 (Score: 96). I spoke at length about this wonder game back in the January section. Go read that and then you'll understand why this game deserves to be on this list.

Image courtesy of GameSpy.com.

Metroid Prime still kicks all sorts of ass.

2. Legend of Zelda: The Wind Waker (Score: 96). The most controversial Zelda game due to the cel-shading cartoon graphics, it still is a wonderful title despite the different look.

1. Metroid Prime (Score: 97). I think this is a no-brainer. Metroid Prime, even three years after its release, is still a fantastic game and the number one reason to own a GameCube. Retro's classic first person action/adventure is one of the best games ever published, not just on the Cube but on any platform. It was, and still is, that good.

Image courtesy of GameSpy.com.

Viewtiful Joe is one slick looking game.

DID YOU KNOW

In August of 1995, *Mortal Kombat* the movie is released by New Line Cinema. As the top-grossing picture in the country, it nets $23 million within the first weekend, which just goes to show you that people will pay to watch anything.

The Incredible Hulk: Ultimate Destruction

Don't Make Me Angry

Image courtesy of GameSpy.com.

DOSSIER

Genre: Green Monosyllabic Monster Smash **Publisher:** Vivendi Universal **Developer:** Radical Entertainment **Platform:** Xbox, PS2, GameCube **Metacritic Metascore:** 84

It's about time the big green fella got his due in a videogame. After the dismal 2003 release of The Hulk by the same publisher/developer team, Radical is back with Ultimate Destruction. In what has to be the best year ever for videogames based on comic book superheroes, The Incredible Hulk: Ultimate Destruction is near the top of the heap.

The Hulk takes on flying HulkBusters.

If you take the fun parts from Spider-Man 2—the open-ended environments, combo-filled combat, fun upgradeable powers, and smooth animation—and replace the web-slinger with the towering Incredible Hulk, you have a good idea of what to expect with this one.

THEY SAID IT

> "Marvel has been extremely supportive of our 'reinvention' of the Hulk.... It's all in the spirit of the overpowered anti-hero. The Hulk you see in our game is in no way dumb, he's savage and primal—a cunning and inventive fighter." —**Eric Holmes, Lead Game Designer in an interview with Planetgamecube.com**

The Hulk's Adversaries

Although the goal of Ultimate Destruction is for mild-mannered Bruce Banner (the Hulk in human form) to find a cure for his "illness," he also has to survive in a world where everybody is out to get him—from super villains to the United States military, there's a good variety of enemies that you have to deal with.

General Ross. He's in charge of capturing or killing the Hulk. Ross is not technically a bad guy; after all, if the Hulk were really running around a city and scaring the hell out of people, I'd want him subdued ASAP. However, Banner is also in love with Ross's daughter...so this time, it's personal!

Devil Hulk. The Devil Hulk is a weird creature that is trying to take over the mind of Dr. Banner. Finding a way to rid yourself of this parasite is a huge part of the game's storyline.

The Abomination. Voiced by Ron Perlman (*Hellboy*), The Abomination is government insider Emil Blonsky, who has an obsession with the Hulk's abilities.

Mercy. A member of Blonsky's staff (a bodyguard, actually), she's a mutant as well with powers such as telekinesis and mind-blast.

HulkBusters: A U.S. military unit, these 'mechs are designed to be able to take the Hulk one-on-one or in groups. There are Infantry Busters, Combat Wardens, Capture Wardens, Destroyers (huge three-story high 'mechs), and HulkBuster Titans (who double as Boss Units that can really hurt the Hulk).

Infantry. Usually just a nuisance, the military grunts pack machine guns (which do little damage) and rocket/missile launchers (which do a bit more).

Cops. When you take a bus and throw it at a helicopter, it will usually attract the police unless there is an *extremely good* custard-filled involved...or a warm bear claw. (I kid, I kid.)

Military tanks. Even though a beat cop with a six-shooter isn't a threat, an Abrams Tank with exploding shells really hurts! Actually, there are four different tanks after you during the course of the game, from Bradley Fighting Vehicles to Multiple Rocket Tanks that fire guided missiles.

Military aircraft. Fast and hard to hit, they definitely pose a threat to the Hulk, particularly in swarms. Huey attack choppers, Comanches, and Falcon Fighters all come after you during certain missions.

Image courtesy of GameSpy.com.

Vent your frustrations on the city's slow cab service.

DID YOU KNOW

The Incredible Hulk goes back to well before the campy TV series starring body-builder Lou Ferrigno. He was created by Stan Lee and Jack Kirby for Marvel Comics way back in 1962.

September 2005

Superheroes and Ninjas!

September 2005 was a great month for gamers.

More top-shelf games based on comics hit the street with the release of both Ultimate Spider-Man and X-Men Legends II: Rise of Apocalypse. Namco followed up the superhero bunch with Ninja Gaiden Black, which is arguably the coolest action-fighter ever. Indigo Prophecy proved that there's nothing like a cool story and that videogames had the power to tell one, and Relic Entertainment once again brought us back into the grim world of Warhammer 40K with a fabulous Dawn of War expansion called Winter Assault. Toss in more Tiger Woods, another Burnout game, the final chapter of Myst, maybe the best NBA hoops game ever made in NBA 2K6, and Namco made us still love Katamari. All in all, not a bad month.

Flops of the Month:

- **Top Spin**—A lesson that choppy gameplay and long load times can ruin an otherwise good game.
- **Marvel Nemesis: Rise of the Imperfects**—I saw a TV commercial for this a few days before it shipped and it looked really cool. Then I played it. The advertising people are slick; the game is not.
- **Frogger: Ancient Shadow**—George Costanza has forever ruined Frogger for me.
- **NHL 06**—EA Sports just flat-out does not get hockey. Do yourself a favor and pick up NHL 2K6 instead.

Warhammer 40K Dawn of War: Winter Assault

Because a Summer Assault Makes Too Much Sense

DOSSIER

Genre: 40K Is Awesome **Publisher:** THQ **Developer:** Relic **Platform:** PC
Metacritic Metascore: 84

Image courtesy of GameSpy.com.

The Imperial Guard will bring BIG guns to the party.

The Warhammer universe has seen its fair share of computer game interpretations (see page 171). Dawn of War, a gorgeous, action-packed, real-time strategy game, is arguably the best. The hit from Relic and developer THQ was heralded by critics and fans as one of the best games of 2004. And like any popular game with the backing of a solid license, the inevitable expansion pack was sure to follow!

Bring on the Imperial Guard

Dawn of War: Winter Assault adds two new campaigns, more units, and the Imperial Guard as the new playable faction. Fans of 40K know what that means: Big, big tanks and a whole slew of cheap infantry. Many Warhammer fans scoffed when it was made public that the Guard was to be the new faction because there are certainly more appealing choices in the 40K universe, such as the *Alien*-inspired Tyranid race, but the Imperial Guard does require gamers to employ different strategies.

Although Dawn of War is all about attacking and pressing forward, the Guard is a choice for defenders. Using their heavy armor and vicious ranged attacks, they like to sit back in heavily fortified bunkers and blast the enemy with impunity. This is a radically different strategy from the Orks, Space Marine, and even the Eldar, and it should make for a more interesting and varied game.

In addition to the new Guard units, the game's original races are getting some new toys with which to play. The enigmatic Eldar get fusion gun–wielding infantry called Fire Dragons that love to target vehicles; Chaos gets Khorne Berserkers, vicious melee units who lack subtlety but make up for it in strength; Orks get Mega Armored Nobz, infantry who can take an amazing amount of punishment before falling; the Space Marines get Chaplains, which are hero units specifically designed to boost the effectiveness of ranged troops.

THEY SAID IT

"We're trying to make sure that this is an experience that players of Dawn of War can't turn back from and after they play the Winter Assault expansion they won't want to go back to the original." —**Jonathon Dowdeswell, Producer, Relic Entertainment in an interview with Gamespot.com**

DID YOU KNOW

Image courtesy of GameSpy.com.

When Bloodthirsters attack....

Dawn of War Mods

For those of you who want to get all you can out of the original before grabbing the expansion (which renders these mods inoperable), there are a lot of great Dawn of War mods out there that you should definitely check out.

Demon and Witch Hunters (www.innocence-proves-nothing.com). This is a very cool mod that lets you play Inquisitor forces.

Thousand Sons (www.joust3d.com/forums). A mod still in progress that lets you use the Thousand Sons Chaos legion.

Tyranid MOD (forums.relicnews.com). A mod still being worked on that adds the vicious Tyranid. The screenshots of this mod are fantastic.

Cadian Gate (cadinq.dowfiles.com). A well put-together mod that uses Imperial Guard forces; see how the modders did compared to the developers of the expansion!

DoWpro:WA (dow.lerp.com/mods/DoWpro_WA_1.43.rar). This mod can be used in conjunction with Winter Assault. It really digs into the nuts and bolts of the design and tries to add more balance (and a bit more 40K accuracy) to skirmish games. It heavily alters the game, so read the docs that come with it before installing.

DOW FILES

DoW Files (dawnofwar.filefront.com) is one of the best places to download and read about DoW mods.

Warhammer 40K, the tabletop game, has a long history dating back to 1987. It has spanned four editions, each continuing to streamline the rules for better gameplay.

The Total War Series
Tweaking It to Perfection

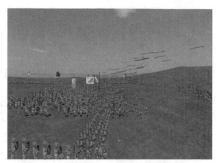

The Hellenic conversion for Medieval: Total War is an amazing piece of mod work.

DOSSIER

Genre: Fun with Barbarians **Publisher:** Activision **Developer:** The Creative Assembly
Platform: PC

The Total War series from The Creative Assembly is one of the most popular and critically acclaimed strategy series of all time. It all started with the 2001 release of Shogun and the Mongol Invasion expansion, and then the games got better and better with Medieval: Total War and the Viking Invasion add-on. It was the 2004 release of Rome: Total War and the subsequent release of the Barbarian Invasion expansion in September 2005, however, that really helped the series take off with mainstream audiences. Not only was it still a deep game that blended real-time battles with turn-based global strategy, but it looked like a million bucks.

The games are also highly "moddable" and the Total War community is extremely active by adding new units, campaigns, and even creating practically brand new games in the process. It is literally impossible to list all the mods on one page. There are lots of high quality mods out there, so don't limit your searching to the ones listed here. Do your own hunting to find exactly what you like. One thing is certain: There is enough content out there that you could spend all day just downloading it.

The Knight's Panther cavalry charge into battle in the upcoming Warhammer mod.

Total War Mods and Resources

The Lordz Modding Collective (www.thelordz.co.uk). This is a total conversion mod for Medieval: Total War that uses Napoleonic era troops rather than swords and knights. These guys are working on a second Napoleonic total conversion using the Rome: Total War game as a base. Check out the screenshots; these guys are serious!

Hellenic Total War (www.hellenictotalwar.com). This 97MB total conversion uses the Medieval: Total War Viking Invasion expansion as its base. The mod goes from 750 B.C. until the rule of Alexander the Great. This is another first-class total conversion that is well worth your time.

China: Total War Tsin Empire Invasion (www.stratcommand-center.com/chinamod). This Rome: Total War total conversion, formerly known as the Three Kingdoms Mod, adds more than 20 new units, along with new maps and sounds.

Historic Battles Mod (www.stratcommandcenter.com/ninja-cool/battles.php). This is a nifty Rome: Total War mod that adds several historical battles such as Guagemela, Cannae, and Pharsalus.

Mods in the Pipeline

There are a ton of potentially great mods in the works for Rome: Total War. Here's a few that might pique your interest.

Warhammer (www.zodiak-productions.com). Being a certified Warhammer nut myself, I cannot wait to get my hands on this total conversion and send my Ork army into battle.

The First Age (www.firstagemods.com). This is a Middle Earth mod that takes place well before the *Lord of the Rings*.

Middle Earth: TW (www.metw.net). Another Middle Earth mod, this time based on the books. It's currently in beta and is partly playable. Expect a more complete version to be available by the time you read this.

Rome: Total Realism (rometotalrealism.com). This is currently available as a beta, but according to the developers it's not quite ready yet. The idea isn't to totally redo Rome: Total War but to make it extremely realistic and not quite as generic.

THE TOTAL WAR CENTER FORUMS

There are lots of very good Total War websites out there, but the **Total War Center Forums** at www.twcenter.net/forums is a great forum for general discussion as well as for its fabulous mod section that discusses several upcoming projects for all the Total War games.

DID YOU KNOW

Although best known for the Total War series, The Creative Assembly has also worked on several titles for EA Sports such as Rugby, Cricket, and FIFA International Soccer.

Fable: The Lost Chapters
Carrying the Torch for Soloplay RPGs

Image courtesy of GameSpy.com.

Take that! You evil...scorpion thing.

DOSSIER

Genre: Charming and Easy RPG **Publisher:** Microsoft **Developer:** Lionhead Studios
Platform: PC **Metacritic Metascore:** 84

To be a PC gamer today, you need to have a modicum of patience. Eventually most of the top-shelf console games get ported to the PC. It's not a certainty, but a lot of good games make their way to the PC eventually, including Halo, Star Wars: Knights of the Old Republic, Grand Theft Auto, and so on.

Fable: The Lost Chapters, however, is a bit different from your run-of-the-mill console port because developer Lionhead Studios added new content specifically for the PC version. Granted, this is still the same game that was released on the Xbox back in September of 2004, so if you played the game on the console, it's a tough sell to buy it again just for the new stuff. But for those PC gamers who skipped the Xbox version, this is a great time to give the game a look.

THEY SAID IT

"The PC control setup is very different—in a good way. The mouse is a wonderful little device; the freedom and accuracy it gives to camera control is quite refreshing. First-person archery feels like it has 'come home' to the PC. In addition, the inclusion of a shortcut bar is a very 'PC' thing to do. With so much choice, if you don't like our controls ... you can just reconfigure them!" **—Dene Carter, Lionhead Studios Creative Director in an interview with Computer and Video games.com**

Image courtesy of GameSpy.com.

Dodging would be a good idea in this situation.

It's About the Choices, Stoopid

Fable is a highly story-driven RPG that forces the player to make moral choices throughout the course of the game. The choices you make have a huge impact on the way your character is treated and how NPCs react to your presence. It also uses the morphing technology from Lionhead's Black and White game, so your character's appearance changes as moral choices are made, as time passes (your character ages), and when your character increases a basic attribute.

The fine details are what make Fable easily one of the most charming RPGs ever made. For example, you are never given a real name, you can't even choose one at the start, but you do earn (or buy) titles like "Assassin" and "Chicken Chaser." As a result, the townsfolk can be heard mentioning you by your title as you walk by. "He doesn't look like no Chicken Chaser to me."

The New Stuff

The new content in the PC version is literally a "lost chapter" from the Xbox version that was cut out. Given that the Xbox version of Fable was rather short, extending the game a bit with this extra chapter is just gravy.

This lost chapter includes nine new regions, 16 new quests, new monsters, spells, weapons, armor, and player accessories such as several new hats (some of which look wildly funny). You can even import your own player tattoos. More importantly, The Lost Chapters should help flesh out the original story.

If there's one problem with the game, it's that it's a bit too easy. I played through it start to finish without dying *once*. Still, the journey itself was a blast, which is really the most important thing.

ALTER EGO

Alter Ego is a regularly updated Fable fan site at alterego.lionhead.net/wordpress with all kinds of info about the Xbox and PC versions.

DID YOU KNOW

Lionhead Studios, with veteran designer Peter Molyneux leading the way, was founded as a spin-off company from Bullfrog, the company best known for the classic Populous and Dungeon Keeper games.

Tiger Woods PGA Tour 06
The Best Gets Better

Tiger goes old school in Rivals Mode.

DOSSIER

Genre: Reigning King of Golf Games **Publisher:** EA Sports **Developer:** Headgate
Platform: Xbox, PS2, 360, GameCube, PSP, PC **Metacritic Metascore:** 86

The Tiger Woods series, formerly known as EA's PGA Tour before EA signed Tiger Woods to be the namesake of its golf franchise, has had a checkered past to say the least. Back when it was called PGA Tour, it was a decent golf game with the standard triple-click swing method and sharp graphics. As the series continued, things started to fall apart; the Tiger Woods games from the late 1990s and early 2000s were absolutely rotten.

Then EA Sports made one of the smartest moves in the history of the company: It signed Headgate Studios to develop its Tiger Woods golf line. After a year of getting settled in, Headgate took the series from the bottom rung to the upper echelon.

THEY SAID IT

"Real golf is not a point and shoot game. By using the new mechanics, we've added much more control to each swing, so users can add touch and finesse to their shots. Reading the course, understanding what shot you need, and now having the ability to control that is what the Dual Analog System allows for." —**Producer Sherief Fattouh in an interview with Teamxbox.com**

TrueSwing

Headgate Studios cut its teeth working for Sierra (swallowed whole by Vivendi Universal) back when Sierra actually published sports games. The Front Page Sports: Golf line helped revolutionize the genre on the PC platform mainly because it shunned the old click-click-click swing method used in every other game and instead used a method called "TrueSwing."

TrueSwing required you to move your mouse back, simulating the swing of the golf club, and then forward, accelerating through the ball, just like a real golf shot. When TrueSwing first appeared in the original FPS: Golf, die-hard cyber duffers were slow to embrace it. Slowly but surely however, the golf community accepted TrueSwing as the wave of the future. The sequels to FPS: Golf, PGA Championship Golf '99 and PGA 2000, remain two of the best PC golf games ever made and they were both developed by the folks at Headgate Studios.

Evolution of a Tiger

It was a real bummer to see the PGA/FPS: Golf series go the way of the dodo, and there were lots of rumblings when EA Sports signed Headgate to take over the Tiger Woods line. But to their credit, EA has allowed Headgate to develop the PC version of Tiger Woods into a fantastic golf franchise. Each year it gets better and better and the mod community goes out of its way to create fantastic courses for use on the PC, allowing you to play the entire PGA season if you so desire.

As for Tiger 06, the important thing to know is that it's a vastly superior effort on the PC to the 2005 version. Finally, playing on higher difficulty levels introduces a significant challenge in staying on fairways, hitting from the rough or off a slope, and putting over long distances. It's a must-buy game for any fan of the sport.

TIGER ON THE WEB

Although Tiger 06 comes with plenty of built-in courses, PC users can also make their own using the **Course Design Tool**, which is available at ftp://ftp.ea.com/pub/easports/misc/TigerWoodsPGATour06.

If you lack the skills (or time) to design your own courses and would rather marvel at the work of others be sure to check out **Course Downloads** at www.coursedownloads.com.

The create-a-golfer feature on the PC is insanely detailed.

DID YOU KNOW

Tiger Woods 06 on the Xbox 360 promises to have amazing visuals, but at the expense of fewer courses (only six) from which to choose.

Burnout Revenge

High-Octane Racing Without the Pesky Realism

Image courtesy of GameSpy.com.

Some of the crashes in Revenge are hilariously vicious.

DOSSIER

Genre: Road Rage Sim **Publisher:** Electronic Arts **Developer:** Criterion **Platform:** Xbox, PS2 **Metacritic Metascore:** 91

The Burnout series is made up of racing games for people that don't like racing games. If you're looking for licensed cars, real world tracks, gear ratios, and tire pressure—hoo boy, are you playing the wrong game!

Burnout is about mayhem behind the wheel of a car. You earn points for causing others to crash, catching big air, turning into oncoming traffic and generally driving like a Corey in *License to Drive*. This is not a racing sim; it's a guilty pleasure. It's the German chocolate cake of racing games.

If you're a fan of this series by all means—rush our and grab a copy of Revenge. You won't be disappointed despite the fact that it's more along the lines of Burnout 3.5 rather than Burnout 4. Revenge isn't a huge leap from Burnout 3: Takedown. It's technically a better game, but you shouldn't go into it expecting anything revolutionary. Here's a quick hit list of what's improved.

Demolition Derby at 150MPH

You can now use traffic as a weapon. No longer do you cause basic accidents; rather you can smash into a car ahead of you, which could then take out another racer that is close by. It's kind of like playing pool with cars.

Checking traffic, as it's called, looks downright cool, too. There are some massive wrecks that take place when you start slamming into others' cars at warp speed. Burnout Revenge's graphics are amazing and it's the wrecks that help make the visuals stand out. Try to check a bus— try it one time, that's all I ask.

The downside to checking is that the AI has a heck of a time taking you down, which gives the human player a *huge* advantage. This doesn't make it any less fun, but still, some sort of challenge from the AI would go a long way.

It's not just bumper to bumper—you need to watch out for flying cars.

Image courtesy of GameSpy.com.

THEY SAID IT

"Well, as they say, revenge is sweet. And the new Burnout is definitely sweet. They also say revenge is a dish best served cold. I'm not sure about that part, but it's fun when it's served up at 150mph with full boost firing as I slam you into the wall or into the path of a semi heading down the other side of the road!" **—Alex Ward, Creative Director of Burnout Revenge in an interview with GameSpot.com**

Crosstown Traffic

That was my one and only Jimi Hendrix reference in this book, so savor it. The highly touted new mode called Traffic Attack, I have to admit, isn't all that special. I like crashing into things as much as the next guy, but when the entire point of a mode is to crash into as many cars as you can for as long as you can—well, that gets old, and quickly. The salvation is that throughout the entire single player experience, you'll only have to spend about 20–30 minutes playing Traffic Attack games.

Kill the AI

So, the AI is rather inept. So what? Burnout Revenge is at its best when playing with a buddy on a split screen or online. Racing against another human in a traditional racing game is great, but racing against another player when they are rifling cars at your head is a whole new ballgame. If you want to get the most out of Revenge—go online.

DID YOU KNOW

The original Burnout was a 2001 PS2 release by the now-defunct publisher/developer Acclaim Entertainment (see p.150). It was ported to the Xbox and GameCube in the spring of 2002.

Myst V: End of Ages
The Final Journey Begins

Image courtesy of GameSpy.com.

Myst V keeps up the tradition of gorgeous scenes with tough, tough puzzles.

DOSSIER

Genre: I Need Blue Pages!! **Publisher:** Ubisoft **Developer:** Cyan Worlds **Platform:** PC
Metacritic Metascore: 80

"I hate this game!"

That was me back in 1993 when I sat down with a group of friends in an attempt to figure out the secrets of Robyn and Rand Miller's classic adventure game, Myst. I loathed the game at first, but not because it was poorly designed or lacked creativity; I hated it because it highlighted the fact that I had the logical thinking capacity of a turnip.

Twelve years after the release of the original and three follow-ups later, Cyan is back at the controls for the last installment of this famed series. While it's not a requirement to have played the other games, I'm not going to lie—it helps. Without wanting to spoil anything, I will say that End of Ages is a very satisfying conclusion to the series. Loose ends are tied and decisions are made that provide a firm sense of finality.

THEY SAID IT

"We don't have any plans to make any further Myst games, although I don't know what the future holds. The story is tied up in a way that is satisfying from our point of view. It's not about the fireworks and fanfare; it's about the way we do things with Myst. Telling a great story in a subtle, quiet way and having substantial repercussions at the end to tie it all up, and this was a good time to wrap things up." **—Rand Miller in an interview with Adventure Gamers.com**

Breaking New Ground

Myst was groundbreaking for several reasons. Aside from being the flagship title of the first-person graphic adventure genre, it was a CD-only game. This was a *big deal* back in 1993 when most games were still ushered out on 3.5" disks. As a result, the graphics in Myst, particularly on the Mac, were beautiful. The scenery and the sounds were the game's main attractions.

Myst also has the distinction of being one of those games that "hardcore" gamers hated. Me? I hated it because it made me feel like a dope. Others hated it because there wasn't a lot of "game" to it. It was a bunch of pretty pictures with interactive puzzles, which I guess just wasn't enough like DOOM to please fans getting their first taste of first-person shooters. It was hip to hate Myst.

The hipsters lost though because Myst went on to sell more than 12 million copies. Not bad for a game without guns.

The Myst Lineage (Minus Uru)

Myst (1993). You find a book called *The Book of Myst* and, after opening it, are transported to a beautiful deserted island. Have fun!

Riven: The Sequel to Myst (1997). Riven was a lot like Myst; the only major gameplay difference being that the graphics were animated. The game was a very fitting sequel to the original game and it sold extremely well.

Myst III: Exile (2001). Set a full 10 years after the events of Riven, Myst III was a success, but you could tell that the fan base was starting to shrink a bit. Myst III introduced a 360° panoramic view, allowing you to scan the scenes rather than looking at them one at a time. This was the first game in the series not made by Cyan. It was instead developed by Presto Studios.

Myst IV: Revelation (2004). The best-looking game of the series and the first to be ported to the Xbox, Myst IV used 3D effects and loads of animation along with the 360° view from Myst III. PC and Mac fans loved it. Xbox gamers, well, not so much.

MYST OBSESSION
The guys at **Myst Obsession** (www.mystobsession.com) have what could best be described as a Myst fetish. Kidding aside, this is a great site with a highly active fan forum and tons of background info on the series.

DID YOU KNOW

There are three Myst novels written by the Miller brothers in conjunction with David Wingrove. Their titles are *Myst: The Book of Atrus*, *Myst: The Book of Ti'ana*, and *Myst: The Book of D'ni*.

NHL 2K6 and NHL 06
The Crown Jewel Versus the Armpit

Image courtesy of GameSpy.com.

If NHL 06 played as good as it looked, hockey fans would be in heaven.

DOSSIER

Genre: Real Hockey, Arcade Hockey **Publisher:** 2K Games/EA Sports **Developer:** Kush/EA Sports **Platform:** Xbox, PS2, 360, Cube, (PC: NHL 06 only) **Metacritic Metascore:** 84/78

This is the story of two hockey games. One strives for realism, whereas the other strives to look like hockey but plays like roller-ball. One appeals to die-hard fans of the sport, whereas the other appeals to people who watch hockey only when *SportsCenter* highlights force them to. One costs $20 and the other costs $30.

NHL 2K6 looks good, but it's not like you can play the game from angles like this.

Image courtesy of GameSpy.com.

Other than that, NHL 2K6 is the clear and decisive winner. In NHL 2K6, you have to cycle the puck; one-on-one hockey is rarely effective and more importantly you have to get yourself into good position to get off a quality shot. Just trying to set up a one-timer every time down the ice is not going to work. You will not find an 85MPH backhand shot in NHL 2K6.

I think the best part of NHL 2K6 is that each period feels like its own mini-drama. The CPU will adjust to what you are doing, so even if you have a 3–0 lead after the first period, that doesn't mean you're in for an easy victory. The AI is smart enough to see *how* you scored those goals and adjust to counter it.

Head-to-Head Comparison

Whether you enjoy NHL 2K6 or NHL 06 will depend, almost exclusively, on what you want out of a hockey game. Do you want a game of fast break hockey with lots of shots on goal and spectacular animations? If so, NHL 06 is definitely for you. There's nothing at all wrong with wanting a hockey game to play this way as long as you understand it ain't exactly NHL hockey.

In fact, there are areas that NHL 06 has the edge over NHL 2K6. The rosters that ship with EA's game are infinitely better. In fact, NHL 2K6's rosters are so out of date that it's absurd. Also, the graphics, particularly on the PC version, are better in NHL 06.

ON THE WEB

> "We are really trying to promote cycling the puck, looking for that small opening in the defense...we are really trying to promote real hockey. Every year we try to take that next step with our AI." **—Ben Bishop, Project Manager of NHL 2K6 in an interview with IGN.com**

When you toss in the fact that NHL 2K6 supports brilliant online league play via Xbox Live, you come up with a package that is perfect for true hockey fans despite some glaring bugs in the gameplay. Oh, and the $20 price tag? Yeah, that's NHL 2K6, too.

THEY SAID IT

> "NHL 06 is all about the rush. It's all about the offense and it's all about superstars scoring incredible goals." **—NHL 06 Producer David Littman in an interview with Team Xbox.com**

2KHOCKEY.NET

You can grab updated rosters for the Xbox and PS2 versions of NHL 2K6 from **2kHockey** (www.2khockey.net), which is a first rate community site for NHL 2K fans.

DID YOU KNOW

Although there is nothing like watching live hockey in person, according to Nielsen Ratings, regular season NHL TV ratings in the United States are truly horrific. They're on par with sports talk shows like *Pardon the Interruption* and ESPN's *Cold Pizza*. Folks, that's bad.

Indigo Prophecy
Adventure Games Live!

DOSSIER

Genre: Genre Revival **Publisher:** Atari **Developer:** Quantic Dream **Platform:** PC, Xbox, PS2 **Metacritic Metascore:** 85

Now I know that some of you reading this will think I'm certifiably nuts for saying this, but there was a time when graphic adventure games were popular forms of entertainment. These games, for the most part, shied away from shotguns, zombies, gibs, exploding head shots, and enemies that yelled, "Suck it down!"

Lucas is busted by the cops.

The graphic adventure was about telling a story with you in the middle of it—and they were *really* popular. Now, they're all but dead. The industry has simply turned its back on the interactive story and has instead focused primarily on action games, sports games, and games with orcs. I like a good orc game as much as anyone, but with today's technology, adventure games could (and should) offer amazing ways in which to spin a good yarn.

Indigo Prophecy is that good yarn.

THEY SAID IT

"Indigo Prophecy tries to put the story at the center of the experience, make it the core engine, the reason why you want to play more. It is not an added layer to justify action, it is the experience itself." —**David Cage, writer of Indigo Prophecy in an interview with PC Gamezone.com**

Lucas gets to work cleaning up his crime scene.

Grab Your Popcorn

It's unfair to label this as an old school graphic adventure. It's not like games such as Myst and its ilk. This is more like an interactive movie where you get to play the lead roles. There are no evil monsters, exploding buildings, and very few puzzles to solve. This is a supernatural murder mystery—with you as the murderer. You actually get to control three main characters throughout the tale, and you get to experience the story from their own points of view. These characters are fully realized, complete with top-notch voice acting and dialogue, and not cardboard cutouts.

The choices you make during the game have an enormous impact on how it plays out. Your character's mood changes, his actions affect those around him, and so on.

As for complaints, well, the graphics aren't out of this world and the character control is a bit clunky at times in conjunction with a twitchy camera that likes to move too much. But as far as being a good interactive movie, this is as good as it gets.

A Man Walks into a Diner...

The story starts out with you, as Lucas Kane, in a bathroom stall at a New York City diner. Kane kills a man in the bathroom for no apparent reason; even Lucas has no idea why he did it. But there's no time for reasoning through this—you have to escape.

There are a lot of things to consider, and even this first scene of the game gives you insight in what you can expect in Indigo Prophecy: There's blood on you, so you'd better clean up first. Oh, and that body sitting in the middle of the floor? Better hide that in a stall, too. Then there's the pool of blood on the floor. Get a mop. You go out of the restroom and see a cop in for a quick bite. Do you talk to him? Ignore him? Run out of the diner doing your best Michael Corleone impression? It's up to you.

INDIGO HOME PAGE

Read up on the story and the cast on the **Indigo home page** at www.atari.com/indigo.

DID YOU KNOW

Quantic Dream's first major project was the 1999 high-profile Dreamcast adventure game Omikron, which featured the voice and likeness of musician David Bowie.

Dragonshard
D&D in Real-Time

Image courtesy of GameSpy.com.

DOSSIER

Genre: Fast and Furious RTS **Publisher:** Atari **Developer:** Liquid Entertainment
Platform: PC **Metacritic Metascore:** 80

The marketing plan for Atari's Dragonshard claims that it's the "First D&D Real-Time Strategy Experience." Technically, that's not true. Interplay released a game back in 1996 called Blood and Magic and even though it was a fairly rotten game, it was in fact a licensed D&D product that played in real-time. Pity the guy who had to review that steaming pile back in the day.

Dragonshard is part 3D real-time strategy, with great graphics and fast gameplay.

Also, it's important to note that Dragonshard is a D&D game only because of its setting and not because it uses the D&D rule set. What does makes the game more D&D'ish is that you not only control large armies above ground, as in a typical RTS, but there is also an underground portion in which your heroes do a little bit of D&D-style dungeon crawling.

THEY SAID IT

> "Dragonshard is still an RTS game, so it isn't going to replace those hardcore RPGs on everyone's favorites list as the new hardcore RPG. But it is a fantastic RTS game that has lots of RPG elements, so I think that makes it attractive to any type of gamer that likes RTS games or RPGs." —**Designer Jasen Torres, in an interview with IGN.com**

The Building Nexus. You don't build cities wherever you want. Instead you build them in predetermined areas. You have a large keep in the middle, surrounded by empty squares on which you can build a specific number of structures. With limited build space you are forced to make tough choices during the course of a game. Do you build an extra Barbarian building to advance your units to a higher level or do you build a structure that adds to their health or combat ability?

What's to Like

Dragonshard slipped into stores in late September without much fanfare. In fact it took most major websites a week or so after release to even get a review posted, which is rare in today's climate. Some aspects worth noting include

Eberron is cool. Eberron's world was forged by magic; it's a living, breathing part of the landscape rather than just a medieval world with spells, so it fits the game perfectly.

The RPG stuff. Although managing both above- and below-ground sections of the game is challenging, the RPG portion that takes place below ground is a heck of a lot of fun.

Designed for free-for-all multiplayer. Dragonshard is a good cut-throat multiplayer game as well as a great single-player skirmish game. On the downside, there is no direct IP support—and it's not a good team-based game.

It's pretty. The visuals are fantastic if you have the horse-power to run it.

Image courtesy of GameSpy.com.

Dragonshard is part underground dungeon crawl....

Why You Might Hate It

There isn't anything technically wrong with Dragonshard if you are the type of real-time gamer that Liquid is targeting. But it does come up short in a couple spots.

Speed Kills. The above-ground real-time battle portion of the game is lightning fast and there's no speed control setting at all. You also cannot pause and issue orders, which is something that might frustrate those without quick hotkey reflexes.

The Solo Player Shrift. The two single-player campaigns are fairly short, each running seven missions in length. If you play it consistently, and are not into skirmish or multiplayer games, you'll be finished with it within a week.

DID YOU KNOW

The demo that is available for Dragonshard does an extremely poor job of showing you how the game really plays. It only has the fist two campaign missions and is best ignored or just used to gauge the graphics and interface.

Ultimate Spider-Man
As Faithful to the Comic As It Gets

Image courtesy of GameSpy.com.

The fight with Rhino is just plain cool.

DOSSIER

Genre: Comic Book Spidey Game **Publisher:** Activision **Developer:** Treyarch **Platform:** Xbox, PS2, GameCube, PC, DS, GBA **Metacritic Metascore:** 81

Last year, Treyarch developed the Spider-Man 2 game (see p.118) which had a ho-hum storyline, a great fighting model, and a revolutionary web-slinging system. This time around, Treyarch has gone in a different direction.

The Ultimate Spider-Man comic was launched roughly five years ago as a modern reboot of the Spider-Man universe, taking Peter Parker back to his roots as a teenager discovering his strange new gifts. Treyarch brought in the creators of the comic to write the dialogue, form the story, and provide character designs. By doing so, Ultimate Spider-Man is, without question, the most authentic Spidey game ever created.

It's important to understand that Spider-Man 2 and Ultimate Spider-Man are two *very* different games in both style and playability. Ultimate Spider-Man doesn't use the same fantastic web-slinging system, which is admittedly a real bummer, the city is scaled down a bit, and the combat model is stripped down and doesn't make use of the insane number of upgrades and combo moves that were in last year's game. However, the graphics, story, and the missions themselves, including the boss fights, are all spectacular and help make Ultimate Spider-Man arguably a better game.

THEY SAID IT

"Spider-Man in the Ultimate line is a different character than in the Amazing line. He's still a kid in high school who JUST got his powers and isn't really all that good of a fighter. This helped us to key in the basis for our combat, a frenetic combat with Spider-Man doing his best work when he is punching, kicking, and flipping about the area, just like he does in the comics." —**Chris Busse, Creative Director, in an interview with Nintendojo.com**

Famous Faces

There are a *lot* of characters in Ultimate Spider-Man, some of them are bosses and some are there in cameo appearances. (Although Aunt May is nowhere to be found, oddly enough.) Here is the roster of foes you'll meet during the course of the story.

Shocker. Lifelong criminal Herman Shultz is back as Shocker, a villain with vibro-guns that carry some punch.

Wolverine. It's Marvel Comics, so of course they find a way to include Wolverine. He's used mainly as an early tutorial boss and isn't a part of the story.

Rhino. The Rhino is not a dumb-as-a-stump bad guy in a plastic costume in the Ultimate universe. Alex O'Hirn is a super

genius who built the powerful battle suit that he now uses to beat the snot of out people.

Image courtesy of GameSpy.com.

Wolverine and Venom...this is going to get ugly.

Electro. I always liked Electro in the old Spidey comics but here he's even better. Controlling electric energy and traveling on power lines is just cool. The twist is that you fight him as Venom in a battle to see who gets to kill Spider-Man.

Beetle. Both Spider-Man and Venom do battle against Abner Jenkins, AKA The Beetle. Jenkins is a master thief who created his flying beetle costume that gives him super strength.

Silver Sable. Sable makes her Ultimate debut in the videogame. She doesn't have any superpowers, per say, but she's a hell of a hand-to-hand fighter.

Green Goblin. Green Goblin is also very different in this universe. He's not dressed up in a Halloween costume flying on a glider. Here, Norman Osborne is a *real* monster. As is the case with Rhino, this boss fight kicks all kinds of butt.

DID YOU KNOW

Developer Treyarch has worked on several titles from sports games like NHL 2K3 and Triple Play Baseball to old-school PC action games such as Die by the Sword.

X-Men Legends II: Rise of Apocalypse
It's Much Better Than the Comics

Image courtesy of GameSpy.com.

Mutant powers fly around like bullets during most missions.

DOSSIER

Genre: Dungeon Crawling with Mutants **Publisher:** Activision **Developer:** Raven Software **Platform:** Xbox, PS2, Cube, PC, PSP **Metacritic Metascore:** 84

I still clearly remember the days whenever a video or computer game was announced with any kind of comic book theme that it meant its inevitable doom. Then Freedom Force broke the curse and now all of a sudden you can't walk five feet in a game store without tripping over a box with a superhero on the cover.

The original X-Men Legends, also from Activision and veteran developer Raven Software, was a wildly entertaining game, a combat-oriented role-playing game where you were able to team up members of the X-Men and beat down some bad guys.

It was such a hit that they decided to do it all over again with X-Men Legends II: Rise of Apocalypse. This time around there's a twist—you get to team up with the villains from The Brotherhood to stop Apocalypse from destroying the Earth.

THEY SAID IT

"My favorite thing about online multiplayer is that you can use your save games from offline. So, if you want to jump into a quick match with your friends, you don't always have to start at the beginning of the game or at level 1. Or, if you've been playing online with your friends and they can't continue playing, you're not stuck with a useless save game." — **Producer Mathew Paul in an interview with IGN.com**

have more fighting power? You also unlock powers as the characters gain levels. Unleashing Magneto's Magnetic Grasp is worth the wait whether or not you're an X-Men fan.

Image courtesy of GameSpy.com.

Admit it, we all love Magneto.

Building a Better X-Men Game

Despite some rumblings in the press that X-Men Legends II is just more of the same, I think nothing could be further from the truth. I mean yeah, it's still a team-based combat-oriented role-playing game with a bunch of mutants running around blasting each other. However, Raven has made the sequel a much better game from top to bottom. Here's why.

More characters. Sequels usually mean that things get bigger and that's definitely the case with X-Men II. There are 16 characters in the game as well as some that can be unlocked as you play (like Professor X). The roster includes Cyclops, Storm, Nightcrawler, Colossus, Iceman, Rogue, Magneto, Juggernaut, and Deadpool. The idea of playing as the "bad" mutants is a stroke of genius. Even Toad is fun.

Your characters evolve throughout the game, allowing you to customize them, turning them into the kind of character that you want. Do you want Nightcrawler to be super nimble or

Taking it online. This addition alone is worth the price of admission. Four-player co-op mode on Xbox Live is just sweet and dreamy.

Graphics. X-Men II isn't the best-looking comic book game ever made but it does look a lot better than last year's game and the cel-shading isn't quite as extreme.

Teammate AI. The biggie, for me at least, is the improved teammate AI. Last year, you couldn't get your teammates to help much, if at all, when things got hot and heavy. Raven juiced up the intelligence of your CPU buddies, which makes the solo game experience a *whole lot* better.

OFFICIAL GAME SITE

Read up on the characters (including the list of enemies) and hit the forums on the official **X-Men Legends site** at www.xmenlegends2.com.

DID YOU KNOW

The movie *X-Men 3* finally started shooting in the fall of 2005 in anticipation of a 2006 release. Director Bryan Singer has moved on to make a Superman movie, so Fox appointed Brett Ratner (*Red Dragon*, *Prison Break*) to the helm.

Ninja Gaiden Black
Black Is the New Gold

Image courtesy of GameSpy.com.

The hand-to-hand fights in Ninja Gaiden Black are the straw that stirs the drink.

Genre: Good Gaiden Update **Publisher:** Tecmo **Developer:** Team Ninja **Platform:** Xbox
Metacritic Metascore: 94

The most important thing to understand about Ninja Gaiden Black is that it's not a sequel to the superlative 2004 action game, Ninja Gaiden. It's basically a gold edition of Ninja Gaiden, with a handful of additions, tweaks, and changes. So, let's talk about Ninja Gaiden.

Despite the fact that it was one of the best Xbox games of 2004, it did have its problems. The biggie was the fact that it was almost sadistically difficult. You more or less had to be a real ninja to be able to play and complete the game.

The lack of an "easy" difficulty setting only compounded the problem. I know there are a lot of Gaiden fans out there that revel in the game's challenging gameplay. There is definitely something to be said for the feeling you get when you finally get past a tough battle. Still, there's a line that got crossed with this one and Ninja Gaiden Black tries to fix that.

THEY SAID IT

"One of the things that motivated us to work on Ninja Gaiden Black is the idea of leaving the best and the ultimate action game on the current console before we move on to the 360. We desired to do that. When I play those other games and the control just doesn't feel right, I get sick. At Team Ninja, we describe those as games that will give your fingers cancer." —**Team Ninja's Tomonobu Itagaki in an interview on Xbox.com**

Image courtesy of GameSpy.com.

It's not all hand to hand. Even ninjas use bows, right?

New Stuff

Ninja Gaiden Black is more or less the original Ninja Gaiden with the goodies from the Xbox Live Hurricane Pack download-able expansions. You also get more costumes, an enhanced story, and a new gameplay mode focused on scripted missions. Best of all, there's the "Ninja Dog" mode, which is the game's way of saying the "easy mode." Funny thing is that the easy mode is not available at the start—you have to die a few times before the game realizes how much you suck and only then does it ask you whether you want to abandon the true way of the ninja and take the easy road. Yes, Ninja Gaiden Black calls you a wuss.

Ninja Dog mode aside, the new Mission Mode is really the biggest selling point for fans of the series. The missions are really rough but at the same time, they're also exhilarating. The idea is simple: You are thrown into a scenario with a ton of bad guys and you have to do your ninja thing and kill them. It's fast, bloody, and a complete and total blast. Remember the House of Blue Leaves scene in *Kill Bill: Volume I* with The Crazy 88s? Well, here you go, Uma. These missions are not available at the start, though; you have to earn the right to be able to try them. They're that hard.

NBA 2K6 and NBA Live 06
The Cream Versus the Crop

The animations and player authenticity is second to none in NBA 2K6.

DOSSIER

Genre: A Tale of Two Hoop Games **Publisher:** 2K Games/EA Sports **Developer:** Visual Concepts/EA Sports **Platform:** Xbox, PS2, 360 (PC, GameCube, PSP: NBA Live only)
Metacritic Metascore: 86/80

As with their hockey offerings, EA Sports is going after a slightly more arcade, fast-paced design whereas 2K Games and Visual Concepts' design is more simulation oriented. But unlike the NHL games, NBA Live isn't a total waste, even though it, too, is not as good as its 2K counterpart.

THEY SAID IT

"We have improved the open court transition game with our fast-break and we eliminated the stop-and-go feel of previous versions of NBA LIVE with a new passing and receiving system that allows you to make these plays on the move." —**NBA Live Producer Dean Richards on EA.com**

Head-to-Head Comparison

Superstars. This is really the "big new feature" of NBA Live 06. The star players are labeled as a certain kind of Superstar (Shooter, Stopper, High Flyer, and so on) and as a result they have access to moves that help separate them from your average player. So, a guy like Steve Nash has access to no-look behind-the-back passes, whereas a slower, defensive guard like Lindsey Hunter doesn't.

Fast breaks. EA begrudgingly earns points here for *finally* allowing true fast breaks in an NBA Live game. That only took a decade.

Graphics. Most EA Sports games look the part, but NBA Live 06 is a truly beautiful basketball game, particularly on the PC. NBA 2K6, I think, has better animations, but NBA Live's PC graphics are a cut above.

You can finally run the break in Live 06.

Image courtesy of GameSpy.com.

Dynasty. NBA Live 06's Dynasty mode is nearly identical to the one in last year's game, with the only meaningful addition being assistant coaches that help players develop. Compared to other games in the EA stable, like Madden, Live's Dynasty mode continues to lag behind. On the other hand, NBA 2K6's Association mode is surprisingly deep. You can drill players in specific categories such as quick shooting, post moves, and so on. Team chemistry also plays a role, and assigning a weekly practice schedule to get everyone on the same page is vital to your franchise's success.

THEY SAID IT

"We have rewritten nearly every piece of the game to make it smarter, better looking, better animated, and with better feeling in general. ISO Motion was rewritten; blocking, rebounding, stealing were all rewritten. What you played last year compared to this year will be completely different." —**NBA 2K6 Project Manager Rob Jones in an interview with GameSpot.com**

New Controls. Let's be honest, the old ISO motion in NBA 2K games sucked. Thankfully, it has been scrapped and in its place is a system that is just as good, if not better, than NBA Live's Freestyle mode. When used in conjunction with the new right analog shot-stick you have complete control over the kind of shot you want to attempt. It's designed brilliantly but requires a lot of practice.

Challenge. Being the sports game junkie that I am, I am confident in saying that NBA 2K6 is the most challenging sports game of 2005. The AI in this year's game will kill you if you give it the chance. This is really the reason why I prefer it to Live 06. The single player game requires you to bring your A-game night in and night out. This is not a game for a casual fan that doesn't know a 3-2 Zone from a Box and One.

DID YOU KNOW

In late September 2005, the NBA turned down a deal offered by EA Sports that would have granted the company an exclusive basketball license, which would have effectively killed the 2K6 series. Cheers to the NBA!

Top Ten PS2 Games
Metacritic's Ten Best Reviewed PS2 Games

Winning Eleven is the undisputed king of hands-on soccer.

Of all of the Best and Worst of the Metacritic lists, this one surprised me the most. The top ten PS2 game list is dominated by Tony Hawk and Grand Theft Auto, almost to a ridiculous degree.

There are some A-list games that failed to crack the top ten. However, all it takes is one sub-par review to knock a great game out of the running. God of War, Sony's brilliant Greek gore fest, received a 94, one point away from being listed. Devil May Cry better than God of War? That's a tough sell. But then every point counts when you are talking about top ten lists. Like for example how NCAA Football 06 missed out because some guy at *Computer Games* magazine gave it a 2.5/5.

Oh wait, that was me.

10. Winning Eleven 6 (Score: 95). The Rolls Royce of soccer games, Winning Eleven absolutely puts the FIFA series to shame. If you're still drinking the Kool-Aid and playing EA's game over this, seriously—give it a try. If you enjoy soccer, you're going to get hooked.

9. Devil May Cry (Score: 95). I was surprised that Devil May Cry received such widespread praise, not because of a lack of quality, which was great, but rather because the game was so damn hard.

8. Madden 2003 (Score: 95). The cash cow just keeps chuggin' along, and this is considered the best PS2 version of Madden, although I'd argue that 06 is the best of the bunch.

7. Grand Theft Auto: Vice City (Score: 95). Palm trees, pink undershirts, and cheesy songs all wrapped up in a glitzy and gritty Grand Theft Auto game. Vice City is easily one of the best PS2 games ever made.

6. Tony Hawk's Pro Skater 4 (Score: 95). Tony Hawk 4 was a spectacular game, even if you don't like the whole skater scene thing. With more game modes than you can shake a half-pipe at, including online multiplayer, Tony Hawk 4 is easily deserving of its spot on this list.

5. Gran Turismo 3: A-Spec (Score: 95). Lots of cars, new tracks, spectacular graphics, and a very approachable driving model means big, big sales for Sony.

4. Grand Theft Auto: San Andreas (Score: 95). Scoring the same as Vice City, the latest game in the series is not a letdown in any way, shape, or form. Hot coffee not withstanding....

3. Metal Gear Solid 2: Sons of Liberty (Score: 96). Sons of Liberty is without question one of the best console games ever made. Solid Snake's journey as a member of Philanthropy truly shocked a lot of gamers as it showed just how compelling a game on the new PS2 could be.

Tony Hawk shares the stop spot with the thug from GTA.

2. Grand Theft Auto III (Score: 97). GTA III was an enormous leap from the previous 2D GTA games and took the gaming world by the throat and squeezed. Living the life of a street thug not only provided hour after hour of entertainment, but it also provided politicians with an easy talking point about the evils of the hobby.

1. Tony Hawk's Pro Skater 3 (Score: 97). When the Tony Hawk series switched to the PS2, it was met with open arms. This is also the only Top Ten game that received one very low score—a 70% at the All Game Guide.

DID YOU KNOW

This month in 1999 Sega of America launched the Dreamcast to North American retailers. It had some truly great games, but was ultimately a failure that drove Sega out of the console hardware business.

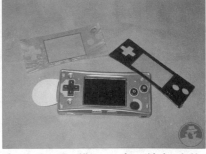

Image courtesy of GameSpy.com

Game Boy Micro and the New GBA SP Because It's All About Looking Cool

Grab Bag

The new Game Boy Micro, complete with detachable faceplates

Nintendo is either a company full of brilliant executives who know gaming trends better than any other group on the planet, or the game industry boat left port without them on it. Maybe it's actually somewhere in the middle?

Regardless, Nintendo's new Game Boy Micro and the "updated" version of the Game Boy Advance SP are new takes on old ideas that aim to keep those platforms alive and kicking despite the presence of the technologically superior Game Boy DS.

The Micro

Nintendo says that the Game Boy Micro ($99) was created for "image-conscious folks who love video games, the ones who want the look of their system to be as cool as the games they play on it." As a gamer of some 20-odd years, I can honestly say that I have no idea what that means. You can only look so cool playing video games (see p.124), and if you're really just looking for a slick little trinket to show off, get an iPod mini and be done with it. Music will always be cooler than games no matter how much street slang you learn from playing Grand Theft Auto.

Anyway, the system itself makes Mini-Me look like the Jolly Green Giant. It's like a Game Boy that is the size of a cell phone and weighs about the same as a 100 paper clips with a *two-inch* backlit screen. It's so small that if you have large hands, you're going to have a hell of a time using it. Highly advanced two-year-olds, however, should in gaming nirvana.

You can play any GBA game on the Micro, so you aren't going to have to buy new software for your little hip gaming system. It will not play old Game Boy and GB Color games, though. In keeping with this trendy style, the system has a detachable faceplate so that you can buy more colorful plates rather than being forced to use the standard black and silver that the system comes in because nothing says "cool" like a camouflaged Game Boy Micro.

Game Boy Advance SP

Whereas I'm obviously not sold on the tiny GBM, the updated version of the GBA SP is all together different. Nintendo updated this system without any fanfare at all. No press releases, no official announcements—it just sort of happened.

Image courtesy of GameSpy.com

The new GBA SP brightens things up...a lot.

Although this new version is identical to the 2003 GBA SP, the updated model has a fully backlit screen that looks fantastic and brightens everything up (some might think too much). If you thought the old SP was a bit too dark, this is almost a must buy, even at $80.

DID YOU KNOW

This month in 2001: Nintendo releases the GBA to retail stores across North America. It was a monumental success.

Warhammer Games
Closet Classics

Image courtesy of GameSpy.com.

Games Workshop's popular Warhammer universe has seen its fair share of PC and console adaptations. That's not too surprising, really, because the Warhammer Fantasy and Warhammer 40K tabletop miniatures world is extraordinarily popular both overseas and in the United States. Here's a quick rundown of Warhammer videogame ports.

Dawn of War is like watching a miniatures game come to life.

Fire Warrior was basically a run of the mill FPS that just happened to use the 40K setting.

Image courtesy of GameSpy.com.

The Warhammer Lineage

Space Hulk (1993). The first Warhammer board game to make its way to a computer was Space Hulk. The idea was simple: You controlled a squad of Terminator Space Marines (of the Deathwing Chapter, in this case) boarding a floating space ship (a space hulk, get it?) and attempting to eradicate all that dwelled inside it. It's kind of like the movie *Aliens*, only the Deathwing marines are a lot tougher than the guys from the movie. Even Hudson.

Blood Bowl (1995). Microleague published the official computer version of one of the most popular and beloved board games in the Games Workshop line. As a big Blood Bowl fan myself, this was a big, big disappointment.

Warhammer: Shadow of the Horned Rat (1996). The first Warhammer Fantasy game to make it to the PC, Shadow of the Horned Rat was a real-time strategy game that loosely used the rules of Warhammer Battle. Its incredible difficulty turned off a lot of gamers.

Space Hulk: Vengeance of the Blood Angels (1996). Three years after the first Space Hulk, Electronic Arts published this updated version with much better graphics and more action-oriented gameplay.

Warhammer 40K: Final Liberation (1997). This was based on the Epic 40K game, which uses tiny miniatures to represent enormous battles rather than the skirmishes of a normal 40K game. Final Liberation was a turn-based strategy game that pitted the Imperials (you) against the Orks.

Warhammer: Dark Omen (1998). Dark Omen was a sequel of sorts to Shadow of the Horned Rat. It used pretty much the same design although it looked better and wasn't as sadistically hard. If a game ever deserved another sequel, it's this one.

Warhammer 40K: Chaos Gate (1998). A turn-based squad level game that had you, as the Ultramarines, battling the forces of Chaos through a long and pretty tough campaign. Think X-Com in the 40K universe.

Warhammer 40K: Rites of War (1999). This should have been a no-brainer. Take the classic Panzer General turn-based design and throw in cool Warhammer 40K units and races and the game can't miss, right? Wrong.

Warhammer 40K: Fire Warrior (2003). After a rash of games in the mid to late '90s, Warhammer games were few and far between until Fire Warrior hit the scene. Unfortunately the game, well, reeked.

Warhammer 40K: Dawn of War (2004). The boss of Warhammer games, Dawn of War reminded gamers just how cool the Warhammer universe can be when it's done right. It was arguably the best real time strategy game of 2004.

> ### BLOOD BOWL JAVA
> Okay, so the 1995 version of Blood Bowl was an atrocity. Thankfully, you can play Blood Bowl the way it was meant by hopping over to **Ski Junkie's Java Blood Bowl** page at www.geocities.com/javabowl.

DID YOU KNOW

In March 2005, Namco purchased the videogame rights to Warhammer saying that "We plan to extend its rich characters, environments and lore to the video game arena, with some blockbuster titles for the PC." They are currently working on Warhammer: Mark of Chaos (see p.277).

Kohan II: Kings of War
Bargain Bin Special

Image courtesy of GameSpy.com.

DOSSIER

Genre: Slow Paced Real-Time Strategy **Publisher:** Global Star **Developer:** Timegate Studios **Platform:** PC/Linux **Metacritic Metascore:** 81

A battle at a snowy mountain pass in Kohan II.

Yes, I realize this is an older game, but the Kohan series of real-time strategy games is the poster child for games that didn't sell as well as its quality would indicate. This is my way of reminding strategy fans: Go buy this.

Kohan has the pacing and the tactics of a serious wargame and the playability of a classic real-time strategy game, all wrapped up in a unique fantasy setting. It also has some of the best AI this side of Deep Blue. It's not a "build and rush" type of game, but rather one where formation makeup, proper maneuvering, and using smart tactics rule the day.

If you're a real-time strategy fan and you don't own either Kohan or Kohan II, you should be ashamed. You're the reason why it didn't sell like gangbusters! They're in the bargain bins and can be found for sale online from anywhere from $8 to $20.

THEY SAID IT

"Some real-time strategy games use a scripted AI; other games use AI that cheats by having access to increased resources or lower cost units. Our AI does not cheat because of its ability to adapt." —**Ian Klimon, Timegate Studios**

Kohan History

Kohan: Immortal Sovereigns (2001). Kohan: Immortal Sovereigns was released under the Strategy First publishing banner in 2001 and introduced gamers to the idea of the Kohan—immortal heroes that have awakened to battle the forces of The Shadow. The Kohan can't "die," but when their hit points reach zero, they are put back to sleep inside their Kohan Amulet and you have to wake them up again (at a price). Hokey? Maybe, but trust me it works.

Serious strategy fans loved the game's fresh approach. You didn't have peasant or peons running around chopping wood and mining for stone; instead the game focused primarily on the building and the forming of small regiments. These regiments moved as a group and not as individual units. In another twist, you were not responsible for spell casting and healing units. If you had a mage in your regiment, he'd do all the work of casting fireballs, summoning elementals, and so on. This simplistic style put a premium on building the proper regiment with well-balanced units and reduced the amount of babysitting and ultra-quick reflexes that most real-time games require.

KOHAN ON THE WEB

Check out the **Timegate Website** (www.timegate.com) for news, updates, patches, and all other official Kohan stuff.

This **Awakening: Kohan and Kohan II Fan Site** (www.strategyplanet.com/kohan) is a fabulous fan site that is updated regularly with new maps, tips, walk-throughs, tournaments, mods, and a fan forum. If you're a Kohan fan, bookmark this sucker.

Kohan: Ahriman's Gift (2001). Later that same year, Strategy First and Timegate released this standalone sequel that was fun, but wasn't anything radically different from the original.

Kohan II: Kings of War (2004). The latest release added a spiffy new 3D engine that allowed you to zoom in and out, rotate around, and view the proceedings from pretty much any point that you wanted. You got new heroes, a fantastic 32-mission campaign, enhanced multiplayer support, and new factions and races. It was really the ideal sequel to the original game.

Image courtesy of GameSpy.com

Kohan does a great job of depicting the ebb and flow of a real battle.

DID YOU KNOW

In 2002, Timegate released a Special Awards edition of the original Kohan that ran on the Linux operating system.

♟ The Games of Battlefront.Com
Vintage Wargaming Is Alive and Kicking

Combat Mission is one of the best wargames ever created.

It's frustrating to see good gaming genres fall by the wayside. Genres that once flourished such as the graphic adventure game, flight sims, and wargames are now extremely hard to find at your local game shop.

These days if you take a lower-budget game to most publishers, you're going to get laughed out of the room. Try walking into EA with a new design for a turn-based Revolutionary War game and watch as the executives scan the room for the *Candid Camera* crew.

As frustrating as it is to see this genre marched off into the sunset, so to speak, there are still some quality alternatives. Battlefront.com is a company founded in 1998 by industry veterans that share a passion for historical wargames. It was one of the first online game retailers, and when the industry started to shy away from hardcore simulations, Battlefront was there to provide old warhorses with an outlet to continue their hobby.

If you're really into naval sims, Dangerous Waters should fill the bill.

The Battlefront Lineup

Combat Mission series. This is the flagship series that helped put Battlefront on the map. Its three games include: Combat Mission: Beyond Overlord, Barbarossa to Berlin, and Afrika Corps. Each game follows the same basic turn-based design in a full 3D environment. The games go pseudo real-time when final orders for the turn are given so that you see the action happen, technically, in real time, although all the planning is turn based.

Dangerous Waters. This recently released game is a modern day naval simulation. It's bliss for the hardcore gamer, but unless you really have a love for modern day submarine action or have a willingness to learn, you might want to steer clear.

On the Horizon

T-72 Balkans on Fire. Set in the period of Yugoslavian civil wars from 1991 to 1995, this 3D tank simulation places you in the role of a Russian tank officer.

Down in Flames. This is a World War II dogfighting simulation using cards as the engine (see p.210). The company is also working on another card game port called Modern Naval Battles.

Drop Team. This is a futuristic real-time tactical simulation of armored ground combat. Who said Battlefront only does historical stuff?

> **COMBAT MISSION HQ**
> A fantastic fan site for Combat Mission, **Combat Mission HQ** (www.combatmission.com) hosts dozens of user-made mods. The news feed has slowed, but the mods are all there ready for download.

DID YOU KNOW

Most consider the 1952 board game Tactics to be the first modern-day tabletop wargame. It was designed by Charles S. Roberts, who went on to found Avalon Hill in 1958.

Red Baron
Closet Classic (1991)

The planes look sort of decent even today, but the scenery, well, okay, that looks bad.

Flight simulations, for whatever reason, are not as popular as they used to be. Back in the days of Falcon and the Jane's line of flight sims, the genre was booming. Today, however, fans are left with a much smaller pool from which to choose.

Back in 1991, however, the genre was doing just fine and it was at this time when Dynamix released its epic World War I flight sim: Red Baron. This was the golden age of PC gaming, back when MS-DOS was king and it could take hours just to get your soundcard configured properly. Ah the memories.

Red Baron was such an engaging game because although it wasn't an arcade sim, it didn't forget that a great flight sim can also have a great *game* behind it as well and not just an accurate flight model.

In Red Baron, you could fly for the Germans or the RAF (Royal Air Force) in the game's brilliant campaign mode. You could face the Red Baron himself if you were flying for the Brits, or fly along side him when flying for the Germans.

Bombs away!

When Biplanes Were Cool

The game sported a whopping 28 World War I–era aircraft and a vast array of mission types including straight up dogfights, escort missions, scouting, zeppelin attacks, balloon busting, and so on. It remains one of the best designed flight sims of all time that was hardcore enough for the serious sim fans, but easy enough for mainstream gamers to hop in and shoot down Germans with a Sopwith Camel.

The jewel of the game was its campaign mode, which told the story of the war though the eyes of your pilot. You could earn promotions and then see friends and wingmen perish and get scratched off the duty roster. After you earned your stripes in

the air, you could even request newer aircraft that were coming right off the assembly line.

The AI of the enemy planes (technically the enemy pilots) was by today's standards not all that good, but for 1991, it was something we were willing to live with. The game used 256-color VGA graphics, which was pretty darn spiffy looking at the time. I know that it pushed my Intel 486 33MHz PC to its very limit.

In 1997, Sierra shipped the greatly anticipated Red Baron II, which was released with a lot of fanfare but unfortunately it was nowhere near as fun as the original. Other games that tried to recapture the sprit of the original included Curse You Red Baron and Red Baron 3D. I'd love to say they carried the torch, but sometimes you really never can go home again.

In fact, the only other classic WWI flight sim worth mentioning in the same breath as Red Baron was Wings of Glory from Origin. I played this game on the defunct Amiga platform back in the early 1990s and I found it almost as good as the original Red Baron and certainly it was prettier to look at.

PLAY RED BARON TODAY
You can download the 1991 classic from The Underdogs at www.the-underdogs.org/game.php?id=4845. Curse you, Red Baron and DOS emulators!

DID YOU KNOW

On April 21, 1918, the real Red Baron (Manfred von Richthofen) was shot down and killed over the Somme Canal in France. A debate still rages over who shot the Baron down. Some claim it was Canadian pilot Roy Brown, but others credit Australian ground forces. My money is on Snoopy.

GBA SP Accessories
Have More Fun with Your GBA SP

What the heck is it about the Game Boy that makes us want to accessorize it? Sure, it's small, cute, and portable, but so is a kitten in a lunchbox, and nobody ever gets the urge to stick lights, magnifiers, and cameras on one of them.

But I digress. The fact is that people love their Game Boy Advance SP accessories. And even though the GBA SP corrected the two major problems with the Game Boy by adding a front light screen and a rechargeable battery, there are still plenty of nifty add-ons that can exponentially improve your experience, stretch your GBA SP, and generally help you achieve coolest-kid-on-the-block status. Here are some of the coolest.

Top 10 Accessories

Game Boy Player ($50; www.nintendo.com/systemsgbplayer). If you have a GameCube, why get stuck playing your Game Boy games on that teeny screen? Just hook up the Game Boy Player to your GameCube and play them on your TV in all their big-screen glory.

GameCube–Game Boy Advance Cable ($9.95; www.gameboy.com/sp/accessories.jsp). The GC-GBA cable lets you unlock secret stuff hidden in your GameCube games by linking your GBA to your Cube.

Game Boy Advance Game Link Cable ($9.95; www.gameboy.com/sp/accessories.jsp). If you're going to play multiplayer on your GBA, you're going to need this cable.

GBA Movie Player ($34.90; www.lik-sang.com). You can play movies, music, and e-books on your Game Boy Advance using this player and your PC.

GBA Camera (Cost varies; www.gamestech.com). Yup, a camera for your GBA. Just plug it in, take your pictures, and transfer them to your PC.

Advanced Music Player ($39.99; www.codejunkies.com). The GBA Advanced Music Player allows you to play MP3 files right on your Game Boy. After uploading your files, you can plug in your earphones and go.

Game FM Radio ($9.99; www.inteclink.com). Plug this puppy into your GBA SP and listen to your favorite radio stations.

Game Boy Advance SP Game Changer ($9.99; Amazon.com). Some might call you lazy for buying this nifty accessory that lets you play three games at a time without changing cartridges, but they're just jealous newbies who don't appreciate great accessories.

Pro Gamer's Kit ($39.99; www.inteclink.com). Not only do you get the very-secret-agent-like aluminum carrying case, but you also get everything else you need for gaming on-the-go, including a screen lens, a multiplayer cable, ear phones, a 12V car adapter, and even cases for your games.

Free Flash and Shockwave Games
Free Doesn't Mean Bad

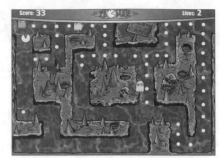
Pac-Man 2005. The little bugger just won't die.

Playing games doesn't always have to be about playing the latest and greatest and most expensive games money can buy. Sometimes you just need a quick little fix.

Thankfully, an almost unlimited number of free games are available online at various websites that use Flash or Shockwave. Some are classic arcade games from the past, whereas others are crazily addictive games that are a fantastic way to kill time at work because let's face it—Excel is just flat-out boring.

The sites listed here are just some examples of the websites you can find that host free Flash and Shockwave games. If the game you are looking for isn't on these sites, there are plenty more from which to choose.

One More Level (www.onemorelevel.com). One More Level hosts dozens of free Flash and Shockwave games from classics like Asteroids, Pac-Man, and Pong to new games like the eye-straining game Avoider.

Avoider (www.onemorelevel.com/games/avoider.html) is a very simple game where the goal is to keep your mouse cursor from being captured. The ninja who is trying to grab your cursor is a sneaky little devil, though. He'll send guided rockets after it and even jump from one side of the screen to another. You think you're a master at the mouse cursor? Give it a try.

Miniclip (www.miniclip.com). Miniclip hosts a ton of free games. Heli Attack is a fantastic game with good graphics and a lot of weapons and tight controls. It's a platform-action game with you as a solider, shooting at attack choppers with flame-throwers, RPGs, mini-guns, and so on. If you're looking to kill 30 minutes, Heli Attack is a great choice.

Miniclip also hosts a multiplayer game called Runescape, which is worth checking out, and then there's Save the Sheriff which is like Super Mario, but with a little pig as the hero.

Free Flash Games (www.free-flash-games.com). Another popular Flash and Shockwave destination; just make sure to turn on your pop-up blocker because there are lots of ads on this site.

One game to check out here is called Clash'N Slash, which is a space-combat action game where you fend off a UFO assault force. It's like a modern day Asteroids, but with weapon upgrades...and color.

Flash Games 247 (www.flashgames247.com). Another free game site with games broken into categories, Flash Games 247 hosts a lot of original content. A particular favorite here is Thin Ice, an action game based on Fro-Zone from the movie *The Incredibles*. You can also play a very faithful Flash rendition of Super Mario Brothers here.

Heli Attack is a must-play free-bie.

2FlashGames (www.2flashgames.com). Don't be fooled by the name. 2Flashgames hosts about 2,000 free games.

There is some really cool stuff here like the 2005 version of Pac-Man, with environmental levels and some tricky advances on the basic gameplay of the original.

There are games here with, well let's just say "questionable" taste, such as Baghdad Bowling, and some movie clips that are more teen-oriented, such as "Pregnancy Test" (which is pretty funny, actually), so some of the stuff here is hit-and-miss and an acquired taste.

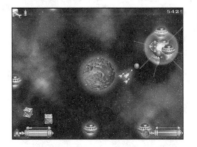
Clash'N Slash is another great way to kill some time.

Addicting Games (www.addictinggames.com). A well-organized site with a ton of games from which to choose, such as a really cool mini-golf game; I like Addicting Games because everything is easy to find and there are no pop-up ads, which is rare for a free game site.

DID YOU KNOW

My daughter, Ashley, is an expert Save the Sheriff player. She's only five, but she can beat the first five levels without dying once. Think it's easy? See if you can top that, buddy!

Sly 3
Honor Among Thieves

Sly, Bentley, and "The Murray" together again.

DOSSIER

Genre: Raccoon Thievery **Publisher:** Sony **Developer:** Sucker Punch Productions
Platform: PS2 **Metacritic Metascore:** 84

The Sly Cooper series, just like LEGO Star Wars, are fantastic games for kids. Even though Honor Among Thieves is rated E10+, it's really not very hard. In fact, its ease is really one of the game's shortcomings for older gamers. For the younger crowd, this is a wonderful platform action game with colorful characters and a witty and fun (although technically criminal) hero. Members of Sucker Punch Productions, the game's developer, have said repeatedly in interviews that the target demographic for all the Sly games is not the usual 14–21-year-olds age group, but younger gamers as well as their parents. They call it the "anti-Madden." Mission accomplished, boys.

Kids love the cel-shaded graphics and the funny and interesting characters and adults love the subtle (and sometimes not so subtle) pop culture references and the platform action itself isn't half bad either. If you like this one, keep in mind that you can still grab the 2004 release, Sly 2: Band of Thieves, for $20 at retail stores across the country. It's an ideal Bargain Bin game.

THEY SAID IT

"We've upgraded the main characters, and the number of playable characters has more than doubled from three to eight; we've got vehicles, including trucks, boats, and biplanes. Different mechanics gives players different ways to play. Sly's universe is like a huge amusement park—you don't want to be on the same ride all the time..." —**Brian Fleming, co-founder of Sucker Punch Studios in an interview with GameSpy.com**

Sly has a very unique art style; it's like a living comic book.

The Guru. Guru, a new recruit, is a pacifist Koala Bear that doubles as an Australian shaman. He has some mind-control ability and is able to turn himself into a rock or a bush, just for kicks.

Penelope. She's a cute mouse mechanic who Bentley has a crush on. She's also an expert pilot.

The Sly Character Roster

The cartoon graphics are part of what make Sly so much fun, but the real soul of the game rests within the game's characters. Here are some of the more prominent figures in Sly 3.

Sly Cooper. The leader of the Band of Thieves, Sly is both quick on his feet, with his cane, and with his tongue. (Yes, the ladies love him.) In Sly 3, he tries to break into the Cooper Vault, which holds a lot of the loot his ancestors had collected over the years.

Bentley the Turtle. Bentley is a computer whiz who is now in a wheelchair (a highly modified, adventure-ready wheelchair) following the events at the end of Sly 2.

Murray the Hippo. "The" Murray left the gang after events from previous games, and still blames himself for Bentley's injuries. Sly recruits him in Venice as an expert getaway driver and hired muscle.

Panda King. Panda is a demolitions expert and former member of the "Fiendish Five" who Sly recruits in China, forming a delicate alliance.

Dimitri the Lounge Lizard. Former member of the Klaww Gang and enemy of Sly, Dimitri is recruited to be the team's frogman.

Carmelita Fox. She's a nimble inspector for Interpol who has been chasing Sly and his gang for quite a while. You actually get to play as her in Sly 3 for the first time.

SLY IN 3D
Sly 3 comes with a pair of 3D glasses inside the manual that are required for a few segments of the game, something that most younger kids think is amazing. For an adult, wearing 3D glasses went out of style around 20 years ago with bad movies like *Jaws 3D*.

DID YOU KNOW

Often game titles, as well a character titles, are different in North America and Europe. For example, Sly Cooper is known as Sly Raccoon overseas. Why companies do this, I have no idea.

October 2005

Big Names, Varying Results

As October arrived, so did the promise of several very high profile games. The release of Age of Empires III, Quake IV, and Civilization IV dominated the PC headlines. Civ IV more than lived up to the hype, Age of Empires III was well received but didn't blow people away, which was something of a surprise, and Quake IV proved to be better than DOOM 3, but not quite as good as many had hoped.

Still, as much as those old heavyweights dominated the headlines, plenty of other games captured the attention of both casual and hardcore gamers. Whenever a new Soul Calibur game is released, it's a huge deal; Serious Sam returned and we found out that he still isn't all that serious; Tony Hawk went the open-ended route; SSX went on tour; Blitz the League gave the NFL the finger (among other things); The Warriors came out to play-ayeee; F.E.A.R. scared the ever-loving crap out of us; and Grand Theft Auto "Got Small." By the time October was over, many gamers didn't have enough money to buy anything but Ramen noodles.

Flops of the Month:

- **Black and White 2:** Calling Black and White 2 a flop might be a bit of an overstatement, but it was the first time that a Peter Molyneux game was released and no one seemed to care. Black and White 2 was an okay game, but compared to the level of buzz that the other high profile October games received, Black and White 2 got lost in the shuffle.

- **L.A. Rush:** Now this was a flop. In a genre (arcade street racing) full of top-level games, L.A. Rush fell on its face by not offering any online play, no huge jumps, and repetitive (boring) gameplay. Do yourself a favor and stick to Midnight Club.

Soul Calibur III
Screw the Xbox

Image courtesy of Gamespy.com.

DOSSIER

Genre: PS2 Exclusive Fighter **Publisher:** Namco America **Developer:** Namco America
Platform: PS2 **Metacritic Metascore:** 85

There are fighting games and then there is Soul Calibur. The series actually began in 1995 when Namco released its arcade classic, Soul Edge, which was a fighting game based around bladed combat with a heavy medieval theme. It wasn't until the 1998 version on the now defunct Sega Dreamcast that the franchise reached classic status with its eight-way running ability and 3D weapons.

It's good to see that Voldo looks as bizarre as ever.

The Dreamcast version of Soul Calibur was a true system-seller; people actually bought the gaming system just to play the game. It was the best fighting game of its generation due to its smooth, fluid animation, responsive controls, and almost unlimited number of unique combos for each of the game's many larger-than-life characters.

In 2003, Namco released PS2, Xbox, and GameCube versions of Soul Calibur II, which was just as fun, but not as groundbreaking as the original.

THEY SAID IT

> "The PS2 is the single most prolific hardware that is out there, but in order for us to add as much new content as we have added we needed to focus on one platform rather than spreading ourselves out too much." —**Hiroshi Tanaka, Manager, Namco Inc. in an interview with IGN.com**

Soul Calibur III Features

First off, Soul Calibur III is a PS2-only release. There is no Xbox, Xbox 360, or GameCube version available. Namco says this is because it has added so many new features that the company wanted to focus on one platform.

There is also no online support. The new Chronicles of the Sword mode is a complete waste of time; it's a pseudo strategy game that just doesn't fit the Soul Calibur theme at all. The new Create-a-Character feature is actually pretty cool. You pick a base "class" and as you play through various parts of the game you unlock new weapons, clothes, and so on. (In fact, there is an *ungodly amount* of content to unlock in Soul Calibur III.) After a while, your character takes on a life of its own. The only problem with this is that the graphics for the custom characters are not as sharp as the established ones. They don't look bad, but sometimes the armor and weapons don't jive together.

Although it might sound like Namco dropped the ball this time around, the truth is that Soul Calibur III is just as addictive

and enjoyable as ever and it remains the best pure fighting game around, particularly when battling against another human opponent. The characters (of which there are now a staggering 33) have all received much-needed tweaking, and there are three new ones to boot (Zasalamel, Tira, and Setsuka).

So, what we really have is a great fighting game marred by some silly single-player design decisions and a lack of online support. If you want to beat the snot out of your roommate, brother, sister, or spouse, though, there is no better game than Soul Calibur III.

SC3's New Fighters

Zasalamel. A scythe-wielding terror also known as "The Enigma," who continues to reincarnate throughout the ages; his arch nemesis is Siegfried and his ally is Nightmare.

Tira. This 17-year-old, 94-pound fighting machine is a nimble little minx armed with a large ring blade that she uses to great effect.

Setsuka. She wears a red kimono and has a sword hidden inside an umbrella (seriously).

Zasalamel looks a bit, um, Iyeah... spooky is the word.

DID YOU KNOW

Rumors continue to swirl about an Xbox 360 version of Soul Calibur III. Namco has remained silent on the issue but hasn't denied the rumor, either. Let's all hope it becomes a reality.

Blitz: The League
Midway Moons the NFL

DOSSIER

Genre: Unlicensed Pro Football **Publisher:** Midway **Developer:** Midway Chicago
Platform: PS2, Xbox **Metacritic Metascore:** 78

Image courtesy of Gamespy.com.

See what happens when a game company (EA Sports) and a professional sports league (the NFL) get together to shut every other company out of the market? (See p. 143.) Chaos is what happens!

Without an NFL license, Blitz developers got creative with team names and uniforms.

Competitors are forced to make a decision: Do they simply drop the sport from their lineup or do they decide to *get creative*? Midway decided on the latter and the result is the wildly over the top football game called Blitz: The League.

THEY SAID IT

"The League's season is quite brutal—it consists of 33 games, three divisions of ten games each, including three playoff games to reach the top. So one season of The League is almost double that of the NFL season. Once you're done with the Campaign "Story" Mode, you can still edit your team, use them in Quick Play, or bring them online. I personally can't wait to see the sort of uniform designs that people come up with. Being able to bring your team online also means you'll be able to see how everyone did in Campaign Mode by how powerful their team is." —**Kraig Kujawa, Lead Designer of Blitz: The League in an interview with GameShark.com**

commercial featuring half-naked women wrestling in a fountain, would rather not admit that Blitz exists.

Unfortunately, there are two substantial problems with Blitz the League. First, although the game is fun to play, it's more of a novelty than a satisfying sports experience. The games take no time at all to play and yet there is more scoring in a game of Blitz than in an Arena League game. There's also a bug that disallows touchdowns when you run a play as time expires, and with so many points thrown on the scoreboard this happens *a lot*.

Image courtesy of Gamespy.com.

Blitz the League—where Personal Fouls are encouraged!

All About the League

Midway's NFL Blitz series has always considered itself the "bad boy" of football games. Always quick to ignore the simulation elements of the sport, Blitz is about back-breaking tackles and a lot of smack talk, so losing the NFL license is something of a boon to the series. Blitz: The League, which is set in a fictional world with teams like the Chicago Marauders and Arizona Outlaws, is the most violent, over-the-top football game ever made.

Midway went all out by adding even more controversial content, such as allowing you to inject shady drugs into an injured player in order to keep him on the field and the game's single-player "storyline" is ripped right out of ESPN's *Playmakers* TV series. Due to its tactless portrayal of football, the NFL, the same group of gents who approved a beer

Finally, there is a question of replay value. Sure it's fun to create a team from scratch and throw it into the game's story mode or take it online, but after you play through the single-season story mode, the single-player game is pretty much over. There's no franchise mode in Blitz and that hampers its effectiveness. As it stands, Blitz doesn't have a lot of long-term play value unless you want to live online after you're done with the solo game.

DID YOU KNOW

Sony was working on its own nonlicensed football game in 2005 called Road to Sunday. After months of development, it was mercifully cancelled.

Half-Life 2
Keeping It Real with Mods

The CTF mod looks fantastic.

DOSSIER

Genre: Best Shooter Ever **Publisher:** Vivendi **Developer:** Valve **Platform:** PC
Metacritic Metascore: 96

I'm not going to waste a whole lot of time describing Half-Life 2 to you. If you've played it—and if you're a PC gamer you probably have—you know how great it is. If you haven't played it, please put the book down and go buy a copy of HL2 post haste. Seriously. Go. Right now. We'll wait.

...

Okay, now that you're done with the game, there are more options available to you other than shelving it or playing online. There are lots of excellent third-party mods and total conversions out there for Half-Life 2; so many, in fact, that they'll keep you busy for a long time to come, maybe even until Half-Life 2 Aftermath is released. Hey, it could happen.

Finished Mods

As I like to say in all the mod entries—this is just a small smattering of what is out there. Just check out some of the Half-Life 2 mod and community sites to find what you are looking for.

HL2 CTF (hl2ctf.com). This is a multiplayer Capture the Flag mod that is extremely popular and wonderfully designed. It includes custom maps along with special rules to help make the games a bit more fair and fun.

Antlion Troopers Deuce Mod (antlions.hl2world.com). A single-player mod with an all-new storyline.

HL2 Substance (ludus1942.ngi.it/index.html). This mod is a single-player "enhancement" mod. It's still basically the same game, but this ups the difficulty and adds a few other new gameplay twists.

Sven Co-Op (www.svencoop.com). A really slick mod that allows two players to play together as team; it also includes new maps.

Plan of Attack (www.planofattackgame.com). This popular modern combat mod is based on multiplayer team tactical gameplay. This is one of the best mods around.

Art of Ascension (www.planethalflife.com/aoa). Another very cool mod; AoA incorporates RPG elements like character development, level increases, etc.

Zombie Panic (www.zombiepanic.org). In this great multiplayer mod, zombies are coming after the last remaining humans and you have to fight them off. The cool part is that some of the players are humans and some are zombies. When a zombie is killed, it simply respawns back into the game, but

when a human dies, it turns into a zombie. Each round lasts until one human is left standing.

Half-Life 2 Dodgeball (mods.moddb.com/5428). It's pretty straightforward, really. This total conversion mod replaces Half-Life 2 with the game of dodgeball. It supports 32 players (up to 16 per side) and is an absolute riot.

Plan of Attack is one of the best mods around for HL2.

Mods in Development

Goldeneye Source (www.goldeneyesource.com). This mod tries to convert the classic GoldenEye 007 N64 game to the Half-Life 2 Source engine, complete with all the maps, weapons, and so on.

Dystopia (www.dystopia-game.com). This is a multiplayer cyberpunk-themed total conversion of Half-Life 2. You'll even get to experience being jacked into cyberspace—check out the screens on the website.

Rogue Threat (eqxp.com/rogue2). In this mod, you play the role of a Half-Life 2 combat soldier. I have to admit that I have no idea if this Half-Life 2 single-player campaign mod is going to be good or not but it does have one of the coolest websites around.

Black Mesa Source (www.blackmesasource.com). This mod attempts to re-create the original Half-Life using the new Source engine.

DID YOU KNOW

Half-Life nuts might want to check out the book called *Half-Life 2: Raising the Bar* by David Hodgson. It's a great coffee table book complete with interviews, artwork, and more.

Serious Sam II
Innovation on Hold; Just Keep Shooting

Image courtesy of GameSpy.com.

DOSSIER

Genre: Serious Sam with Better Graphics **Publisher:** 2K Games **Developer:** Croteam
Platform: PC, Xbox **Metacritic Metascore:** 75

Serious Sam, at a bargain price of $20, was a throwback shooter. Released in March of 2001, the first Sam was *all* about action. Detailed story? Intricate dialogue? Stealth? Hah! They're for pansies and Girl Scouts. Serious Sam was about grabbing the biggest gun you could find and mowing down innumerable enemies all with a style and humor that was sadistically refreshing. In fact, GameSpot.com awarded Serious Sam its 2001 PC Game of the Year (make of that what you will).

Killer clowns...I hate these guys.

Serious Sam II, released in October of 2005, is actually a whole lot like Serious Sam I, but with better graphics. The 75 Metascore is fair given that Sam doesn't push the envelope of design in any way, shape, or form. It's still all about running around and blowing the hell out of wave upon wave of bad guys. As long as that's your cup of tea, you're good to go.

THEY SAID IT

"When we set out to create Serious Sam II we realized it would be really hard, impossible even, to connect our engine to any of the existing level editors available on the market. Since our engine uses so many advanced technologies that aren't in other games and editors, we had to custom-make a level editor. We even decided to abandon the original Serious Editor and build a new one from scratch to be able to implement all the advanced features of the Serious Engine 2." — **Roman Ribaric, CEO of Croteam in a developer diary on Seriouszone.com**

Image courtesy of GameSpy.com.

Have chain gun, will travel.

Why You Should Care (Seriously)

It's Seriously Big. The original game wasn't terribly long. It was a fast-paced romp—a quick adrenaline burst of a game. Serious Sam II, on the other hand, is huge. Sam visits seven different worlds that encompass more than 40 levels of gameplay. Sam travels to jungle worlds, a city made of wood, a level that looks like Hong Kong, and a world full of giants where the grass is as tall as a tree. You have to admit the folks at Croteam have vivid imaginations.

Adding to the gameplay is fantastic co-op play, so you and some friends can tackle the game together over the Net or via Xbox Live.

The game is longer than the original and the Second Encounter combined, so maybe that's the reason for the $50 price tag? Well, that and the fact that the budget for the sequel is a wee bit more, as well.

It's Seriously Gorgeous. Serious Sam II is a great-looking game. It looks nice on the Xbox, but it truly shines on a good PC. The new engine and game editor make the difference between the 2001 original and Sam II shocking. It still has the bright and colorful worlds and over-the-top creatures, but now it looks realistic. Hey, making a game with monsters that have bombs for heads realistic is hard work. Seriously.

It's Got Serious Weapons and Serious Bad Guys. The original was known for its wicked weapons and a colorful cast of monsters and the sequel carries on that tradition. There's even a parrot weapon that drops bombs on enemies from overhead. How can you not like a game with a bomb-dropping parrot? Toss in more than 40 monsters along with some enormous level bosses, and you've got one insane 3D shooter on your hands.

THE SERIOUS ZONE
At www.seriouszone.com, you'll find a great fan site dedicated to all things Sam.

DID YOU KNOW

Croteam's first game was a soccer game called Football Glory, which was published back in 1993.

Virtua Tennis: World Tour
Handheld Tennis for the Masses

Image courtesy of GameSpy.com.

A little clay court doubles is a nice way to spend an afternoon.

DOSSIER

Genre: A Good PSP Sports Game! **Publisher:** Sega **Developer:** Sumo Digital **Platform:** PSP **Metacritic Metascore:** 84

One of the best games on the old Dreamcast console was Sega's Virtua Tennis. It had great graphics, tight controls, and addictive gameplay that made it one of the best sports games available for the ill-fated system.

The move to the PSP has proven to be a fantastic decision as Virtua Tennis: World Tour is easily one of the best sports game available for Sony's new handheld wonder. Granted, it's basically the same game as it was on the DC and PS2, only in handheld form. But in this case that's a good thing.

THEY SAID IT

"I think players will enjoy the portability of the simple and addictive gameplay that has been translated from the arcade and Dreamcast versions. Now they can take it anywhere they go. The PSP has allowed for improvement on the multiplayer perspective to where all players will be facing the court at the bottom front of the screen, making it more intuitive to play." —**Carl Cavers, Chief Operating Officer at Sumo Digital in an interview with IGN.com**

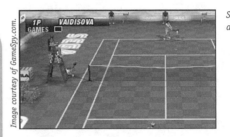

Image courtesy of GameSpy.com.

Several real tennis stars are also in the game.

The Gameplay

Controls. Like most PSP games, Virtua Tennis: World Tour is easy to just pick up and play. The controls are simple and intuitive. You control your player via the analog controls or via the directional pad, which is actually the easier of the two methods. The buttons control the three stroke styles: the lob, slice, and ground stroke. Deep it's not, but it's also easy to get into and a nice fit for the PSP platform.

Graphics. The graphics don't disappoint. Full of robust color, replay cams, and multiple playing surfaces, Virtua Tennis is the ideal PSP sports game. In fact, it looks an awful lot like the PS2 version.

Multiplayer. Even though the World Tour single-player mode is a lot of fun (and almost identical to previous editions of the game), the real fun starts when you're playing against another human opponent (or opponents; the game also supports doubles matches). The only downside to multiplayer is that it's

available only in Quick Match mode and not a multiplayer World Tour, and is supported only via an ad hoc network and not online.

World Tour. This is really the meat of the game. You simply create a player (either male or female; you create one of each during the game) and off you go. There is a strict calendar schedule in this mode, and the tournaments pop up at a designated time, so make sure not to train your players so that you miss an upcoming event.

This is basically a tennis RPG mode because your players start out as no-name tennis rookies with little skill who eventually turn into stars capable of playing against the Davenports and Federers of the world. That is, unless you suck at it.

You get better by playing matches (to earn cash to buy more stuff), but also by completing certain mini-games. By doing a mini-game, you get a boost to a particular attribute. It's not unlike the training camps in Madden. By focusing on particular traits via the mini-games, you can create a player with specific abilities from a fast court coverer to a power hitter.

DID YOU KNOW

The Virtua Tennis series has been around the block a time or two. Not only was it a huge hit on the Dreamcast back in 2000, but it was also ported to the Nokia N-Gage in 2004.

Castlevania: Dawn of Sorrow
Soma Cruz Kills on the DS

Image courtesy of GameSpy.com.

The top screen character sheet/map combo is the best part of the DS version.

DOSSIER

Genre: Dracula: 2036 **Publisher:** Konami **Developer:** Konami Tokyo **Platform:** Nintendo DS **Metacritic Metascore:** 89

If you're a veteran of the wonderful Castlevania platform action series, you're probably already hacking away and enjoying the latest adventure on the Nintendo DS. If not, here's a brief synopsis: It's the year 2036 and the lead character, Soma Cruz, is still basking in the glory of his victory in the previous game (Aria of Sorrow on the GBA). This lovely downtime is interrupted as he is thrust back into the fight to stop a cult from resurrecting Dracula.

Basically the gameplay consists of you hacking and slashing and solving the occasional puzzle as you make your way across 2D maps in classic platform action style. And, just as in Aria of Sorrow, you collect the souls of your dead enemies and (potentially) get new powers from them. There are *lots* of different enemies in the game, so you won't get bored with the bad guys.

THEY SAID IT

"Well, I'm not sure if you know this title, it's a Japanese game series called Tokimeki Memorial, which is a dating sim about being in high school, that I used to work on. I was a programmer and a scenario writer at that time. Then came Castlevania: Symphony of the Night, where I was director, programmer, and scenario writer. And I've been the producer of Castlevania: Harmony of Dissonance and Castlevania: Aria of Sorrow for GBA." —**Producer Koji Igarashi in an interview with Nintendo of Europe**

Image courtesy of GameSpy.com.

Even though it doesn't take full advantage of the DS, Dawn of Sorrow is still one fantastic platformer.

Live by the Stylus, Die by the Stylus

The DS is a cool little handheld capable of adding a lot of unique twists to how a game plays. Just take a look at games like WarioWare and Kirby: Canvas Curse to see what I mean. Castlevania: Dawn of Sorrow, on the other hand, although undoubtedly a great game, doesn't really *need* to be a Nintendo DS game. For example, the stylus is used primarily as a way to finish off level bosses.

There are more than 15 bosses in Dawn of Sorrow and some are ridiculously easy to beat, whereas others are a bit trickier. You have to use the DS stylus to "draw" magic seals to finish them off. If you fail to draw the seal successfully, it breaks and the boss can continue to fight. It's more of a pain than a fresh gameplay idea, but hey, they had to find something to do with that pen, right?

Neither is the touch screen really taken advantage of. You can solve certain puzzles using it, but it's not really something that needs to be in the game. I think the only cool part of playing the game on the DS is the system's dual screen. The top screen doubles as a handy map or can be switched over as a character sheet. Having the map readily available at all times is by far the number one bonus to having the game on this system and not the GBA. Even the graphics aren't as good as this system is capable of delivering.

DS ranting aside, that doesn't strip away the fact that Dawn of Sorrow is a fantastic 2D platform action game. If you already have a DS and like these kinds of games, it easily fits into must-buy territory. Just don't go running out to buy a DS only to play this game...unless you've got a serious Castlevania fetish. (In that case, however, therapy might be money better spent.)

DID YOU KNOW

The Castlevania series returns to the big consoles (in this case, the PS2 and Xbox) in the winter of 2005 with a new hero and a new story in Castlevania: Curse of Darkness.

Trauma Center: Under the Knife
Playing This Does Not Make You a Doctor

A lacerated lung! Woo hoo!

DOSSIER

Genre: Making Surgery Fun! **Publisher:** Atlus Software **Developer:** Atlus Software
Platform: Nintendo DS **Metacritic Metascore:** 82

Trauma Center: Under the Knife is a clever little game from Atlus Software that makes use of the Nintendo DS functionality as well as any game on the market. It's like a handheld version of the old board game Operation, only this time you get yelled at by the staff when you mess up, which is somewhat preferable to the big, noisy red nose of Operation's patient.

Complete with a storyline right out of *General Hospital* and some surprisingly gory graphics (in a professional, surgical sense), Trauma Center is strangely enjoyable. You're not quite sure *why* you're having fun, but it manages to lure you in with its unique gameplay.

It's important to point out that the game takes quite a bit of concentration so don't play it if you're likely to get bothered by nonmedical personnel. Remember, it's not the flight attendant's fault if she asks you whether you'd like a bag of peanuts when you're right in the middle of a tricky heart procedure.

Yes, yes, I know! Stop yelling at me!

Paging Doctor Styles

It is the year 2018, and you play a young doctor named Derek Styles who has just finished his residency and is now officially part of the surgical team at Hope Hospital.

The first portion of the game is basically a tutorial and the staff holds your hand through some of the early medical procedures. After this trial period, you're pretty much on your own, though.

As the story unfolds, an outbreak called GUILT (Gangliated Utrophin Immuno Latency Toxin) takes a grip on the city. It's a rare affliction and the meat of the story revolves around trying to find a cure for it. The story, though, is secondary to the surgeries themselves, some of which are *really* hard! Both the touch screen and the stylus are used to perform operations.

Tools of the Trade

In Trauma Center you have access to lots of different tools when performing surgery. Here's a taste of these instruments of pain...er...healing:

Antibiotic Gel. Don't forget to disinfect any small wounds with this healing salve. A little dab will do ya.

The Drain. Use this device to suck out fluids, usually blood, during tricky procedures when you need to see a bit better. Ugh.

Scalpel. Your numero uno surgical tool when you need to slice open a patient. Use your stylus and have fun!

Forceps. Use the forceps to remove small objects from a patient; they can also be used to pull back skin and to extract delicate tissue material.

Syringe. Morphine!!! Stat!!!

Scanner. The scanner is used to find hidden tumors inside a patient.

Hand. Yep, your hand. Use it to massage a heart that has stopped. Too bad you can't also use it to smack your assistants when they give you the wrong tool. Ingrates!

Stitches. One of the most important, and most challenging, parts of the game is sewing up your mess. It takes a steady hand.

Bandages. When you think you're done, use the bandages to finish the procedure. Good thing for you they can't sue for malpractice.

DID YOU KNOW

A trauma center should not be confused with an emergency room. If you need emergency surgery, you are sent to a trauma center. If you're 12 and cut your leg open taking out the garbage because your mom put a broken applesauce jar in the trash, *then* you go to the ER.

Shattered Union
So Much for the "One Nation" Bit

Image courtesy of GameSpy.com.

A battle breaks out on Route 54!

DOSSIER

Genre: Twenty-First Century Civil War **Publisher:** 2K Games **Developer:** PopTop Software **Platform:** PC, Xbox **Metacritic Metascore:** 79

PopTop Software, best known for strategy games like Railroad Tycoon II and III and the Tropico series, is at it again this time with a beer and pretzels turn-based strategy game called Shattered Union. PopTop has called it a mix of Advance Wars and Panzer General and such a comparison should pique the interest of strategy fans across the board.

There isn't a whole lot of hype surrounding Shattered Union, but that's to be expected. Showing off a brand new, turn-based game to the press is tough to do because you can't show real-time explosions and advanced physics engines. Turn-based games are slow and methodical, and that just isn't all that eye-catching at first glance. There's a reason that people don't watch chess on TV. That said, this game has sleeper written all over it because defying expectations and gamer apathy is what PopTop does best.

THEY SAID IT

"I think people will find it has that 'one-more-turn' feel. We hope that Shattered Union will not only appeal to strategy gamers but hopefully to those that have been reluctant to try such games due to steep learning curves or boring graphics." —**Franz Felsl, Art Director at PopTop Software in an interview with TeamXbox.com**

Image courtesy of GameSpy.com.

A nation divided....

New England Versus Texas

The setting of Shattered Union is a near-future America in which several years of unpopular national elections have seen both political parties falling apart and sinking into corruption and chaos. Civil rights begin to erode and the American people are fed up to the point of becoming violent. It's the stuff of science fiction, I tell ya!

The incumbent president wins another corrupt election, which clearly goes against the will of the people. It all comes to a head when a terrorist nuke following the president's inauguration wipes out our elected officials. The country splinters as legal battles are waged to determine who will lead the nation. No agreement can be reached and nationwide secession from the union begins. After the dust settles, six factions remain: The Republic of Texas, New England Alliance, Great Plains Federation, Pacifica, California Commonwealth, The Confederacy, and The European Union.

Structure

As interesting as the back story is, when you get right down to it this is still just a good old-fashioned turn-based strategy game with simple game mechanics and a lot of personality. The campaign isn't mission-based; instead, it's an open-ended game in which the goal is for your faction (and you can control any of them) to control all 24 United States territories.

The combat takes place on a 3D grid complete with U.S. highways and buildings. The battles themselves aren't complex, though. Units are assigned ratings for attack, defense, movement, and so on. You also get a lot of toys with which to play, from M1 tanks to Apache helicopters.

Finally, each "nation" has its own political reputation that shifts throughout the course of the game, which has an impact on how other factions treat you as well as the types of random events your nation receives.

There's a lot of hidden depth here, which is the case with most games from PopTop. It won't be for everyone, but with the turn-based options dwindling, it's nice to see a major publisher such as 2K Games still backing one.

DID YOU KNOW

In Shattered Union, The Republic of Texas is actually formed by Texas, Oklahoma, New Mexico, Arkansas, and Missouri. Texas and Oklahoma on the same side? That's a first.

Tony Hawk's American Wasteland

Damn Skater Punks

Image courtesy of GameSpy.com.

DOSSIER

Genre: From Zero to Hero **Publisher:** Activision **Developer:** Neversoft Entertainment
Platform: Xbox, Xbox 360, PS2, PS3, GameCube **Metacritic Metascore:** 79

Cops hate skaters.

The success of the Tony Hawk franchise, and it's easily one of the most successful gaming franchises in the history of the hobby, is admittedly a shock to me. I grew up right at the dawn of the whole skater-scene thing, and maybe it's because I'm from Ohio, skateboarding capital of the world, that I'm just a bit surprised at just how much that culture has crossed over into the mainstream. I am so old.

Cultural phenomena aside, the Tony Hawk games are popular because they contain great graphics, control, and gameplay and Tony Hawk's American Wasteland is another notch in Neversoft's belt. While the game is still a fun diversion, the gameplay formula is starting to grow stale. How many ways can you flip a skateboard, ya know?

THEY SAID IT

> "The game is situated in the city of Los Angeles and it's a huge, streaming city. What that means is that you will be able to skate from downtown LA to Hollywood to Beverly Hills and then to Santa Monica and never have to see a load screen." —**Producer Jennifer O'Neal in an interview with GameSpot.com**

Little Man on Campus

In American Wasteland, you play a young teenage nobody fresh off the Greyhound from Smallsville, USA. Your home life is crap and your girlfriend has left you, so where better for a fledgling skater to go than LA?

Off the bus, you run afoul with some locals and then meet your tour guide, Mindy. She takes you under her wing, gets you some clothes, and introduces you to the local skater scene.

You start the game off with minimal skills (basic flips, grinds, and grabs) and have to work your way up to learn more advanced tricks from other skaters in the city; this is perfect for a newbie to the series, but not so much for a veteran who doesn't want to waste time with the basics.

As the story progresses, you and your crew find an abandoned skater park (dubbed the Skate Ranch) and you decide to refurbish it and deck it out with city landmarks. Legal? Well, no, but it sure will look cool.

Getting Tricky

There are all sorts of new and improved tricks in the game, as well as the capability to hop on a BMX bike. Neversoft has gone out of its way to make sure that the way the bike handles is very different from how your regular board handles. It takes some practice to be effective on the bike, but it's well worth it.

Some of the new (or enhanced) tricks include the Natas Spin (you can now do Natas handstands as well as one-footed spins), tail taps, one-footed grinds, stall maneuvers, and the new Bert Slide, which emulates surfing and is, according to Activision, a tribute to old-school skaters.

Graphically, this is a bit of a conundrum. It looks fine on the PS2, if a bit jaggy. It's a bit better on the Xbox, but looks drool-worthy on the Xbox 360. It really does look significantly better on Microsoft's new toy.

Regardless of which system version you end up checking out, American Wasteland is an effective blend of the Tony Hawk Underground (with its story-driven design) and the old school Tony Hawk Pro Skater series (with a lot of great moves) that focuses more on the skating than the dialogue. Toss in a little Rise Against covering Black Flag on the game's soundtrack and you're good to go.

Image courtesy of GameSpy.com.

You can walk into shops and get new boards, tattoos, or a hair style change.

DID YOU KNOW

American Wasteland marks the first time that a Tony Hawk game has shipped with Xbox Live support. Not only that, but multiplayer is easily one of the most enjoyable ways to play American Wasteland, particularly in co-op mode. Not a bad debut.

Shadow of the Colossus
16 Colossi. You Have a Sword. Good Luck.

Image courtesy of GameSpy.com.

Yeah he's big...but you're quick!

DOSSIER

Genre: 16 Fights **Publisher:** Sony **Developer:** SCEI **Platform:** PS2 **Metacritic Metascore:** 92

Who said the PS2 is dead? Shadow of the Colossus is another reason to keep the system in the rotation. You won't find it on any other system and it's a game that you really *need* to play. Sony started the year off with God of War and has now book-ended it with Shadow of the Colossus. Nicely played, Sony. Shadow of the Colossus is the simple story of a boy and his steed...and of his unconscious beloved, and of 16 enormous ancient creatures that he needs to kill in order to somehow save his darling from her slumber. The story practically writes itself, doesn't it?

THEY SAID IT

"The Colossi are extreme and varied. They have taken inspiration from anything from historical creatures... you have Minotaurs, you have giant sea creatures, you have Clockwork Beasts, but each one has this natural feel to them, some are made out of stone and fur, and there's moss growing out of them like they have been around for a thousand years. We have multiple bipeds, multiple quadrupeds, multiple flying creatures, and multiple sea creatures. Some are enormous and some are smaller. I think the smallest one is like a giant bull—and he's...really fast." —**Producer Kyle Shubel in an interview with GameSpot.com**

Image courtesy of GameSpy.com.

Sometimes it's best to avoid hand-to-hand fighting all together.

No Minions, Just Bosses

Shadow of the Colossus is one wild game. It's unique in that it consists of, literally, 16 boss fights. Reaching each fight is half the fun, and the "adventure" part of the game comes in as you ride across sweeping plains, do some basic platform jumping, and so on. Part of the game is actually finding the enemy. You carry with you a magic sword that also acts as a beacon that shows you the way to the next fight.

Riding on horseback over huge, wide-open terrain adds to the epic scope of the game because in the back of your mind you start thinking, "I'm on my way to fight one creature, which just happens to be the size of a three-story building." There are no minor fights. It's *all* about the Colossi.

The graphics and the animation are fantastic, even for a late-generation PS2 game. In fact, the horseback riding segments are the best I have ever seen in a videogame. You really feel like you're riding a horse and you are independent of the animal, so you can move around on its back, fire arrows while riding full speed, leap off to reach a ledge—it's just really, really, sweet.

Even though the horse is cool and all, the stars of the show are the 16 Colossi. Each one is very different (some are in the ocean, some fly, some are just big) and you need to find out where each one's weak spots are. As you climb onto a large beast's back, a weak spot starts to glow to indicate where you need to stab him. After a successful hit, the spot might go dead, meaning you need to find the next spot.

One caveat: The game can get a bit frustrating because you really are fighting 16 boss battles, and with that you are talking about a lot of reloading and figuring out how to win. Patience is a virtue here and if you get easily flustered, perhaps it's best to rent the game first.

DID YOU KNOW

The internal team at Sony developing Shadow of the Colossus is the same group that developed the highly underrated 2001 action adventure, Ico.

Grand Theft Auto: Liberty City Stories
GTA Hits the PSP

Toni has access to more than just cars....

DOSSIER

Genre: GTA On the Go **Publisher:** Rockstar Games **Developer:** Rockstar Leeds/Rockstar North **Platform:** PSP **Metacritic Metascore:** 91

When I first heard that Rockstar was taking the GTA series to the Sony PSP, I thought that the company was going to take a stripped-down version of the game and port it over into handheld form. After all, a lot of companies do just that and not always unsuccessfully. Thankfully, Rockstar decided to actually make Liberty City Stories a new, full-featured Grand Theft Auto title rather than a quick money-making port.

Not only is this little PSP game a brand new GTA experience, but it also comes packed with six-player wireless support, making Liberty City Stories the first ever multiplayer-ready Grand Theft Auto game.

THEY SAID IT

> "The designers actually stepped things up from GTA III graphically. It's the little things like reflections and draw distances, lots of small differences which all combine to make a huge difference to the whole gameplay experience. We're not seeing this game as a cut-down version of any of the other GTAs for the PSP, but the next GTA in the series. Just to put the size in perspective, if you think back to when GTA III came out on the PS2, it was a massive game to fit on the disc. We've got equal geographic size on the UMD for Liberty City Stories, and it's full 3D." —**Rockstar Team interview with Eurogamer.net**

The controls, one of the potential snafus, might take some getting used to but they're still not all that convoluted.

Liberty City's finest.

Fortunately, the driving works just fine. Outside the car you control Toni via the analog stick, the select button changes the camera, and you target enemies by holding down the right shoulder button and cycling through targets with the directional pad. This method also ignores pedestrians; it just locks onto potential targets. Can't go shooting every stiff on the street now can we?

Yo, Toni

The game is set in 1998, roughly three years before the events of Grand Theft Auto III. You play Toni Cipriani, who was one of the mission-giving bosses in GTA III. In 1998, Toni is returning from exile after he whacked a made man. He's low on the mob food chain, and it's your job to get Toni back in the mix.

The structure of the game is very similar to your basic Grand Theft Auto design. Rockstar didn't skimp here—you get about 70 missions, some of which advance the story and some that are just there for fun and cash.

You get a lot of cars (all the rides from GTA III are in the game), motorcycles, several clothing alternatives, radio stations playing licensed tunes, and a *lot* of guns. Basically, everything you'd expect in a Grand Theft Auto title on a large console.

GTA Goes Multiplayer

Finally, Liberty City Stories allows for eight-player multiplayer sessions. There are several multiplayer modes: Liberty City Survivor (pretty much a basic Deathmatch but with full access to the city); Protection Racket, which is about blowing up limos; Get Stretch, which is GTA's version of Capture the Flag, but with cars; The Hit List, which involves killing the "marked" player as fast as possible; Street Race, a racing game where you can switch vehicles and shoot other players; and finally The Wedding List, a game that involves delivering cars to various shipping crates.

DID YOU KNOW

Liberty City Stories has a battery life of, approximately, four hours. Good enough for a plane trip from Columbus to Los Angeles.

SOCOM 3: U.S. Navy SEALs
Better Than the Charlie Sheen Movie

In SOCOM 3, you can hop into one of many vehicles.

Image courtesy of GameSpy.com.

DOSSIER

Genre: An IRC Chatroom with Guns **Publisher:** Sony **Developer:** Zipper Interactive
Platform: PS2 **Metacritic Metascore:** 85

SOCOM is one of the most popular online PS2 games of all time. Personally, I have some problems with it—mainly the fact that finding a good game is terribly difficult because of the smacktard level of many of its players (see p.18). Although every popular online game from World of Warcraft to Forza Motorport has its share of numbskulls out to ruin everyone's time, SOCOM's level of boorish behavior is about as bad as it gets.

Fortunately, there are a lot of SOCOM clans on the Net—people that like to play together rather than just getting into random games—and this is definitely the way to go if you have the time to devote to forming those kinds of online relationships (it takes time to weed out the doofuses).

The problem isn't always the way in which people play the game (even some of the smack-talkers are great players), but when you're sitting in your living room wearing a headset, about to storm into a terrorist stronghold and then some kid describes how drunk he got last weekend or how hot this girl at his school is...I dunno, call it the curmudgeon in me but I'd rather be playing Stubbs the Zombie.

THEY SAID IT

> "...it is important to note that all of the maps are designed around the players on foot, and the vehicles are designed to support and compliment these players on foot. All of the key objective locations in the maps require the player to be on foot before the player can interact with the objective. Whether this involves simply stepping out of the vehicle to take control of a hostage, or having to exit the vehicle and walk for a while on foot to an area that doesn't allow vehicles, this was intentionally done to keep the focus of the game on the players and not the vehicles." —
> **CJ Heine, Lead Designer, in an interview with Ps2.gamebattles.com**

Bad guys...dead ahead.

Image ccurtesy of GameSpy.com.

There are two new game modes in online play in addition to the old standbys like Breach and Extraction. The new games, Control and Convoy, are both welcome additions. In Control, the idea is to plant markers faster than the other team. After it's in place, a marker cannot be removed or destroyed, but each team can place a marker on the same zone. So, it's both a race and a war. Good fun.

In Convoy, the team playing the terrorists guards a convoy and the SEALs try to blow it up. If the convoy gets through, the terrorists win; if the SEALs destroy it, they win. The game requires teamwork which, well, isn't always possible in the land of SEAL smacktards.

One Last PS2 Firefight

As the PS2 begins its slow curtain call and the PS3 hype reaches its crescendo, SOCOM 3 tries to send the PS2 version out with a bang.

Here's the deal: If you love SOCOM, you'll love SOCOM 3. If you're a hater, this is not going to change your mind despite its improvements (encumbrance rules, vehicles, larger maps, 32-player support, the ability to swim, and so on). It's still SOCOM, and it's still primarily focused on the online experience, which as I said earlier, is both hit and miss depending on who you are playing with.

RED CELL SOCOM CLAN
At www.redcellsocom.com is an amazing clan website. If everyone that played SOCOM 3 took it this seriously, it would be an infinitely better game.

DID YOU KNOW

SOCOM actually stands for The United States Special Operations Command (USSOCOM) and is an official branch of the Department of Defense.

Stubbs the Zombie
...In "Rebel Without a Pulse"

Image courtesy of GameSpy.com.

Stubbs may be a pretty funny game, but it's still for older gamers only.

DOSSIER

Genre: Hip Zombie Sim **Publisher:** Aspyr Media **Developer:** Wideload Games
Platform: PC, Xbox, Mac (yes, Mac!) **Metacritic Metascore:** 80

Zombies are suddenly experiencing something of a rebirth, even a renaissance in both games and movies. I'm not entirely sure why that is; classic Hollywood zombies are slow, die easily with a bullet to the head, and are quite frankly getting cliché. Despite its short length (5 to 7 hours), this is part of what makes Stubbs the Zombie so appealing. Not only do you get to play as Stubbs as he tries to munch on the brains of terrified humans...but you get to do it with style.

Back in the 1930s, when Edward Stubblefield was a regular joe, he was a salesman trying to survive during the Great Depression. Sadly, Stubbs was murdered and buried in a makeshift grave in Pennsylvania. And there he remained—for 20 long years. That is, until a billionaire named Andrew Monday decided to build a futuristic city called Punchbowl on his gravesite. Now, Stubbs is ticked off, confused, and he has an insatiable hunger for human brains. To make matters worse, his clothes are hopelessly out of date.

THEY SAID IT

> "Perhaps the most obvious ability is that of converting your enemies into zombie allies. Eat a brain, make a friend. Eat a lot of brains and you'll make a lot of friends. Friends who will take a bullet for you—several bullets, actually. Friends who will help you swarm enemies you couldn't handle alone. Good friends to have."
> —**Stubbs the Zombie's Lead Writer Matt Soell in an interview with Computer and Videogames.com**

Braaaaains!!!

This is the basic idea of the game: You, as Stubbs, must chow down on human brains to keep chugging along. In addition, when you eat humans, they turn into zombies and continue to chase humans alongside you. You can't give them orders, but you can whistle to them if you want them to follow you.

Stubbs has a few basic attacks, but by far the most humorous is his "undead flatulence," which stuns enemies, thus making them more susceptible for a chomp attack. Yeah, it's gross. In addition to his Gas O' Death, Stubbs can remove his innards and use them as makeshift grenades or remove his arm and use it as a club.

Stubbs can't shoot a gun, so he has to use his possession ability to take control of a human for a short period of time if he wants to indirectly use any firearms.

As for enemies, Stubbs and his zombie horde fight through run-of-the-mill cops, cops in riot gear, shotgun-toting locals outside the city, and chainsaw-wielding farmers, among other partisans. There have been no *Shaun of the Dead* sightings to date.

Image courtesy of GameSpy.com.

The lesson here is never build a city over a dead guy named Stubbs.

The gameplay can get a bit repetitive (you're really just out for brains here folks), but the star of the show is the dialogue and sense of humor. One-liners from Stubbs, the people he kills (after ripping off a human's arm you can hear one say, "How can I juggle?" or ""My brain! It hurts!"). The gameplay can be a bit gruesome, but it's all tongue-in-cheek.

Finally, if you have a buddy sitting around, you can play in split-screen mode on the Xbox as your partner in zombie-dom takes control of another Stubbs-like character...two Stubbs for the price of one. That's a lot of gas.

DID YOU KNOW

Stubbs the Zombie in "Rebel Without a Pulse"—it might surprise some to discover—uses Bungie's Halo engine. Maybe the Master Chief will eat some brains in Halo 3?

Quake IV
Picking Up Where Quake II Left Off

Image courtesy of GameSpy.com.

The graphics in Quake IV are sure to please.

DOSSIER

Genre: FPS Stuck in a Time Warp **Publisher:** Raven Software/id Software **Developer:** Activision **Platform:** PC, Xbox 360 **Metacritic Metascore:** 83

If you're a fan of first-person shooters, you are all too familiar with id Software's Quake and its importance to the history of our wonderful hobby. Quake was one of the very first games that showcased just how amazing a game could look. 3DFX Voodoo video cards were flying off of store shelves mainly due to how stunning Quake looked when running on a powerful chipset. Through a fantastic sequel and a multiplayer-only version called Quake III: Arena, the series has sold more than four million copies.

THEY SAID IT

> "We really want multiplayer to be skill-focused, with the emphasis on movement and shooting, the pure elements of what multiplayer gameplay is like. We've really focused on a fast pace, where you fly across the levels really fast via bounce pads and acceleration pads and those sorts of things, as opposed to needing a vehicle to propel you along." —**Todd Hollenshead, CEO id Software**

Well, It's Better Than DOOM 3

Many took it as a good sign when id Software handed the development reigns of Quake IV over to long-time collaborator Raven Software, makers of games such as X-Men Legends, Jedi Knight II: Jedi Outcast, and the classic Hexen series (see p.240). Unfortunately, the game still comes up a bit short.

The problem with Quake IV is that it feels like it's stuck in the past. The first-person shooter genre has come a *long* way since the days of Quake II, and yet Quake IV's single-player game feels a lot like an old-school shoot 'em up in nearly every way aside from its graphics and sound (which are both first rate). Half-Life this is not.

Quake IV is a direct sequel to Quake II and picks up right where the old game left off. The Stroggs are on the run but regrouping, and mankind has launched a huge invasion force to attack the Strogg home world. You are part of that invasion force. For the first time ever in a Quake game, you are not playing a nameless marine fighting the Strogg menace; instead you play a space marine named Matthew Kane, a member of the new Rhino Squad, and a man with a checkered past (what that past is, we never really find out).

For the first third of the game, you're running around with Rhino Squad doing led-by-the-nose missions taking it to the Strogg. It's FPS 101. Then Kane is captured by the Strogg and is about to suffer the fate of many a solider who land in such a situation: The Strogg are about to turn Kane into one of them. The process is nearly complete but Kane is rescued—now he's half-man, half-Strogg! He's stronger, a bit faster, and can interface with Strogg technology. He's Super Kane!

Image courtesy of GameSpy.com

Rhino Squad in the house!

The rest of the game is basically you killing fairly unintelligent enemies, doing things you have done in other games many times before. I was rather bummed to say the least. I was hoping for greatness, but instead Quake IV's single-player game is merely decent.

Fortunately, multiplayer, as is the norm with many id Software games, saves the day. The game is at its best when playing Capture the Flag, Deathmatch, or Team Deathmatch. There is also a new Tourney mode that takes every player on a server and breaks them off into brackets for a Deathmatch Tournament. Very cool.

QUAKE 4 ONLINE

The **Official Quake 4 Website** (www.quake4game.com) has trailers, screenshots, news and more.

PlanetQuake (www.planetquake.com) is *the* place to go for Quake news. Period. Keep an eye on this site for Quake IV mod updates, as well.

DID YOU KNOW

The original 1996 Quake design involved a fantasy character who wielded a giant hammer. Early screenshots of the game even showed medieval environments and mythical beasts.

Civilization IV
Play It or We'll Smack You

DOSSIER

Genre: Turn-Based Strategy **Publisher:** 2K Games **Developer:** Firaxis **Platform:** PC
Metacritic Metascore: 94

Image courtesy of GameSpy.com.

The world map still has a Civ look, but it's a lot more detailed...and pretty.

Sid Meier's original strategy game of nation building and world conquest still ranks as one of the most important and influential games of all time. In an industry where "turn-based" is a four letter word, the Civ name still carries a lot of weight among PC gamers. The fourth version of this esteemed series carries on the tradition in a huge way. This is arguably the best game of 2005. It's *that* good.

THEY SAID IT

> "Civilization 4 will be the most moddable version of Civilization ever. Players can edit basic stats and attributes in XML files. Modders will be able to edit events and have more control over how the game works. On an even higher level, we are planning to provide an AI SDK to allow experienced programmers to dig very deep into customization." —**Barry Caudill, Producer of Civ IV, in an interview with IGN.com**

Why You Should Care

The obvious answer is that you should care because it's **Civilization**! It has 18 civilizations! Nine levels of difficulty! People, come on—what more do you need? If the name alone isn't enough for you, here's some of what makes Civ IV special.

Scaled Back. Civ IV doesn't follow the kitchen sink path of game design. Yes, there are a lot of civilizations, but the tech trees are smaller than in Civ III as are the army lists. This makes each advance very important. The idea is not to overwhelm players with innumerable choices, but to force them to make tougher decisions with fewer options. And it works.

CIVILIZATION EXISTS ONLINE

Many of us have been infected by the Civ bug, and the people at **Civ Anon** (www.civanon.org) understand your disease.

Civilization IV @ Apolyton is a fan site dedicate to all things Civ IV. If you want the latest info on the game, visit civilization4.net.

Image courtesy of GameSpy.com.

The military units, however, are nothing like we have seen in a Civ game until now.

All 3D, All the Time. The most obvious change from previous editions is the switch to a 3D graphics engine, the same engine used in Sid Meier's Pirates! remake (see p.121). You can now zoom in to see the landscape or zoom out and rotate the camera to get a complete look at the game world.

Time for New Rules! Although there are several new rules and rule tweaks, there are a few specific ones that really stand out. First off, religion plays a more vital role. Each of the game's seven religions is tied to a specific technological advancement; you can even to convert other cities to your religion with missionaries.

Another new twist is the addition of Great People, such as a famous artist, holy man, or engineer. These Great People all have special abilities, such as being able to finish off a building project or provide instant tech advancements.

Combat has also been revamped. Units have a single combat stat and not several stats such as attack and defend. However, you can now train units and assign specific upgrades to help differentiate the units even more than before. There will be no spearmen taking out tank divisions in this game.

Multiplayer in Mind. Offering a standard marathon format for the truly sadistic, you'll also be able to hop into a quickie pick-up game on the Civ IV servers. Still, even the standard games work online because turns are taken simultaneously and people can come and go as they please.

DID YOU KNOW

Sid Meier is famous for designing such games as Civilization and Pirates!, but he also has developed games in other genres, like F-15 Strike Eagle and F-19 Stealth Fighter flight sims.

SSX On Tour

She'll Be Shredding Around the Mountain When She Comes

Image courtesy of GameSpy.com.

Do not try this at home.

DOSSIER

Genre: Sports—to the Xtreme! **Publisher:** EA Sports BIG **Developer:** EA Canada
Platform: PS2, Xbox, GameCube, PSP **Metacritic Metascore:** 83

The SSX series has proven to be very popular on the EA Sports BIG label. Who knew that if you made a slick-looking snowboarding game that allowed you to perform impossible tricks on a snowy mountainside, people would buy it in droves? The fact is that people cannot get enough of this series, which is why EA Sports is publishing a fourth game.

THEY SAID IT

"The way to think about SSX On Tour is to imagine you wanted to throw the biggest, cheesiest hair-metal rock and roll party ever, on the side of a mountain. We've got this living sketchbook design aesthetic that really captures the '80s rock and roll ideology and the guys on the team are really feeding from that. It's really tongue-in-cheek, a little bit sarcastic, but very good natured as well." —im Fields, Producer of SSX On Tour in an interview with computerand-videogames.com

Why You Should Care

If you're a fan of the series, you should care quite a bit because it's bigger, better, and loaded with more options (still no online play, though). If you're tired of SSX at this point, well, you probably still will be, but this list of features might just pique your interest.

It's Customizable! One of the niftier features this year is the ability to totally customize your character. You can deck out your shredder with all sorts of official and nonofficial gear; you can even choose a basic personality that affects how your rider behaves.

Career Mode. A staple of the series, the career mode (Tour Mode) this time places you in the role of an unknown—a nobody on the mountain. You now have to catch the eye of someone in order to get a spot on the tour with the ultimate goal of becoming a Mountain Rockstar. When you hear the music tracks, you'll understand.

Graphics and Speed. Obviously, the graphics are better, that sort of goes with the territory of a new release, but what is really cool is the true sense of speed that you get when flying down the mountain. The edge of the screen begins to blur as you gain speed and obstacles whip past you. On Tour does an amazing job of putting you in the boots of a snowboarder or a skier.

Image courtesy of GameSpy.com.

Skiing is new to the SSX series, but is optional if you want to stick to your trusty board.

Skis! Skiing is another new feature this year. However, this isn't a leisurely jaunt down the slopes; this is trick skiing, which is becoming extremely popular with extreme sport enthusiasts. Clamping on your skies is optional though, so you can just stick to boarding if you want.

New Tricks and Tracks. There are 12 new tracks on the mountain, each providing unique challenges and which can be attacked via day or night. There are tons of new tricks in the game, but what truly stands out are the new Monster Tricks, which send you dozens of feet into the air as the scenery slowly vanishes, leaving you alone to pull off an insane trick that earns you serious points.

DID YOU KNOW

Sierra Sports tried its hand at skiing in the game Front Page Sports: Ski Racing. Skiing, fishing, and bull riding, evidently, were higher priorities than basketball. I need Maalox just thinking about it.

Star Wars Battlefront II
Because Lightsabers Aren't for Slicing Bread

Attacking Yoda with a blaster? Come on....

DOSSIER

Genre: Online *Star Wars* Shooter with Jedi **Publisher:** LucasArts **Developer:** Pandemic Studios **Platform:** Xbox, PS2, PC **Metacritic Metascore:** 88

Star Wars Battlefront, released in 2004, proved once again that despite the best efforts of George Lucas, *Star Wars* still has a legion of followers. Even though a lot of middle-aged *Star Wars* fans hated the new movies, the idea of playing a game in a galaxy far, far away remains too tempting to pass up.

The original Battlefront took the basic idea of the popular Battlefield games (objective-based online team play; see p.106) and slapped it inside the *Star Wars* universe. It was fun, for the most part, but it also lacked a lot of what makes *Star Wars* what it is—famous characters, epic space battles, and the ability to play as a Jedi. Battlefront II's design goal is to fix this and to make the game more than just about no-name Stormtroopers and Rebel soldiers.

THEY SAID IT

"The single-player campaign is more directed in terms of the factions you play. The objectives will relate to what's going on within the larger battle, but they won't always follow the exact events from the movies. There was a lot of action going on behind the scenes in the *Star Wars* movies and in other *Star Wars* fiction, so there's plenty of great material to draw from." — **Producer Shara Miller in an interview with Teamxbox.com**

Step Off, Punk. I'm a Jedi.

Even though Battlefront II still has the same four factions from the original (Republic, Separatists, Rebellion, and Empire), the ability to play as a Jedi is a huge selling point for the new game. Last year, Jedi were in the game but they were AI controlled, which was annoying because it looked as if the computer was having all the fun. Of course, you also don't want the game plagued with 50 player-controlled Jedi running around dominating a battlefield.

Pandemic's answer to this potential problem is to limit the time that a player can play as a Jedi. For example, if a team captures a specific map goal, one player gets to turn into Darth Vader for a short period of time complete with Force Chokes and a flashy red lightsaber. Luke Skywalker, Darth Maul (never has a bit character gotten so much pub), Obi-Wan, Mace Windu, Yoda, and a host of other special characters

(including non-Jedi like Han and Chewie) are also in the game. Although a fight between Chewie and Vader might sound a tad unfair, the non-Jedi characters all have some special gear or ability.

Image courtesy of GameSpy.com.

"All too easy."

Space Battles. The space battles play a big role in the sequel, as well. Not only can you hop in the cockpit of a TIE Fighter, but you can also board capital ships and fight out a ground battle in space on board a large vessel. Most of the classic ships from the films are in the game, from A-Wings to the TIE Interceptors.

Solo, Not Han. Battlefront II has several modes of play for the solo gamer. There's the Historical Campaign with a linear story-line and objective-based gameplay. There's also an open-ended mode that allows you to conquer planets in the galaxy one at a time. Pandemic has compared this mode to the board game Risk. Sign me up.

DID YOU KNOW

With all of the great *Star Wars* videogames released over the years, the original Battlefront is the best-selling *Star Wars* game of all time.

The Warriors
Time for a '70s Revival

Sometimes even The Warriors need to high-tail it!

Image courtesy of GameSpy.com.

DOSSIER

Genre: '70s Gang War **Publisher:** Rockstar Games **Developer:** Rockstar Toronto
Platform: Xbox, PS2 **Metacritic Metascore:** 87

I was a bit surprised when Rockstar Games announced that the company was going to publish an action game based on the 1970s cult classic film *The Warriors*, which is the story of a New York gang trying to flee the city after being wrongly accused of assassinating a gang messiah named Cyrus. It just didn't seem like a license that many 20-somethings would care about.

Several gangs chase The Warriors through the streets: female gangs, gangs dressed up like baseball players, gangs on roller skates, and so on. It was a very violent movie for its day, and also had a unique style ripped right out of the late '70s. It was *Welcome Back, Kotter* with knives.

As entertaining as the film was, it's hardly a known entity with today's younger audience. For an older guy like me, I'm all for a little '70s gangland warfare, but others might find the style a bit corny. Then again, this is Rockstar we're talking about; the company that made the *Miami Vice* scene cool again.

THEY SAID IT

> "*The Warriors* has a huge cult following. Die-hard fans are not going to be disappointed. We are keeping true to the story of *The Warriors*. We're not raising Cyrus from the dead or anything crazy like that. It's pretty much true to the film. We went crazy to make sure that we were accurate and nearly everything is in there for people familiar with it." —**Producer Jeronimo Barrera in an interview with Prodigious Gaming**

Unlike other fighting games, the environments are wide open and you can use the scenery to your advantage. It's not a game like Soul Calibur or Mortal Kombat where you are pitted against your enemy face to face. It's open in the sense that you can run around and use the terrain.

Image courtesy of GameSpy.com.

The Warriors against a bunch of mimes. I like the Warriors.

Fighting in the City

The Warriors is a third-personal brawler. It's basically a fighting game that emphasizes hand-to-hand combat, be it with your fists, a knife, or a two-by-four. The game follows the theme of the film as the goal is to get back to your home base in Coney Island. Several of the gangs from the movie are in the game, like the Turnbull ACs, The Orphans, the Moon-runners, the Baseball Furies, and so on.

The Warriors is also mission-based and not open-ended, as are other Rockstar Games like Grand Theft Auto. Some missions are simply a matter of trying to fight rival gangs and fleeing for your life (sometimes you are heavily outnumbered; after all, there are a lot of gangs after you), whereas others involve spraying graffiti or ripping off car stereos. Hey, you are in a gang, you know.

In addition, if you have two controllers, a second player can enter the fray as another Warrior simply by pressing the Start button. The screen splits in two so that you can play alongside your buddy. You can enter and leave as you choose, so there's no fear of screwing up another player's solo game.

Warriors History

In some of the early screenshots of the game, the leader of The Warriors was seen running around the city streets, which seemed odd because he gets killed in the first five minutes of the movie. It turns out that the game contains a few flashback sequences that try to flesh out the history of some of the gang members and even that of the gang itself.

DID YOU KNOW

Set for a release sometime in 2006, Paramount Pictures is remaking *The Warriors* (the movie), only this time it takes place in Los Angeles and all the characters are different. Other than that, it's just like the original!

F.E.A.R.
The Ring Meets Half-Life

Image courtesy of GameSpy.com.

F.E.A.R. isn't just a psychological thriller. It's also quite bloody.

DOSSIER

Genre: Ghostbusters Without the Laughs **Publisher:** Vivendi/Sierra **Developer:** Monolith **Platform:** PC **Metacritic Metascore:** 89

I love the feeling of being scared. Actually, let me clarify that. I love the feeing of being scared when I know I am in no real danger. Haunted houses, ghost stories, a good scary movie, or a suspense-filled videogame are all right up my alley.

Enter F.E.A.R. from developer Monolith Productions (No One Lives Forever, Tron 2.0, Blood), a game that combines elements of games like Half-Life and the film *The Ring*—the idea being to play with the lights turned off and then to watch The Weather Channel afterward just to calm down.

THEY SAID IT

"It probably sounds like an obvious and not especially daring thing to do, but it's been the biggest challenge I've faced as a writer. Trying to tell a story almost entirely in-game from the first-person perspective with a silent protagonist is, quite frankly, a hell of a thing. All the devices I've always relied on as a storyteller went right out the window, because there was no way to guarantee players would be looking in the right place at the right time to see what I needed them to see." —**Lead Designer Craig Hubbard in an interview with GameSpot.com**

Image courtesy of GameSpy.com.

Just your standard day as a member of the F.E.A.R. team.

Little Girls Are Creepy

In the game, you play the role of an anonymous new recruit to the *First Encounter Assault Recon* (F.E.A.R.) team—a government unit created to deal with paranormal threats. You are no ordinary solider, though. You possess the ability to go into a hyperactive mode that makes everything else around you slow down for a short period of time (think bullet-time).

On your first day on the job, a man by the name of Paxton Fettel, the subject of a classified research experiment, is freed from his "captivity" by cloned elite troopers that he can control with his mind. These bizarre soldiers massacre the ATC guards in particularly gruesome ways. Enter the F.E.A.R. team.

You and your team are sent in to stop Fettel and to find out just what in the hell is going on. You are beset by weird visions about both Fettel and a dark-haired little girl who literally looks like she was ripped off the screen from the movie *The Ring*. This is no ordinary prison break. Just one look at that freaky little girl and my skin starts to crawl.

Making It Scary

Making a scary game isn't easy. It's particularly difficult when the designers deck you out with all sorts of military firearms. It's tough to be frightened when you're walking around with an assault rifle. F.E.A.R. manages to frighten not only because of the weird visions and gory scenes of untold mayhem that you stumble on, but also for what you don't see.

You'll hear weird noises echoing around you and you aren't quite sure where they are coming from. Shadows flicker all around you. Footsteps come and go, but you don't see anything. The game's engine allows for a cool strobe effect when you shoot down darkened hallways, so you aren't sure what you are seeing. There's also a wonderful use of empty space and mood music. Sometimes walking down a long, dark abandoned hallway and encountering nothing is just as scary as being attacked.

Finally, what makes F.E.A.R. succeed, apart from its tension-filled setting, is that the enemy AI is fantastic. This isn't Resident Evil, where zombies come right at you waiting to get plugged. These enemies hide behind cover, lob grenades, blind-fire over boxes, and generally try to lure you out in the open.

DID YOU KNOW

According to Dr. Robert Plutchik, fear is one of the eight basic human emotions, the others being joy, acceptance, submission, sadness, disgust, anger, and anticipation.

MUDS and MOOs
The Oldest of Old School

They might not be much to look at but MUDs like this remain popular, even today.

Online multiplayer roleplaying games such as EverQuest and World of Warcraft have become wildly popular over the past few years. But with the attention they've received, it's easy to forget that they're not the first of their kind. In fact, online multiplayer RPGs have been around since 1979.

Yup, believe it or not, gamers have been able to log on to remote servers, explore strange new lands, battle monsters, and hang out with other people since the earliest days of the Internet. And even though these games didn't have the graphics (and the big company support) that today's MMOGs have, the online worlds of MUDs (multiuser dungeons) and MOOs (MUD, object-oriented) have been compelling diversions for millions of players for decades.

Fun with Text

Of course, if you're used to the graphical richness of today's MMOGs, you might be surprised when you enter your first MUD. Created in 1978 by Roy Trubshaw of Essex University in England, the first MUD (called MUD1) was designed as a multiplayer version of the early text-based game Adventure. Players connected to the MUD server using the Telnet program (a command-line, terminal-based application) to remotely access other computers and were able to move through a virtual dungeon by typing commands, reading descriptions, and interacting with objects and monsters.

Over the years, MUDs have developed far beyond their original adventure game roots. Various MUD server types have allowed the creation of increasingly sophisticated gaming systems, including *MOOs*, MUDs with an object-oriented architecture that allows players to actually create new objects, write scripts to control them, and otherwise alter the virtual world they inhabit. This might seem like a bunch of mumbo-jumbo, but if you've ever spent a lot of time roleplaying on an MMOG, you probably know what I'm talking about—it's easy to lose yourself in one of these worlds.

MUD LISTS

Looking for a MUD? Here are some places to start:

MUDConnect—www.mudconnect.com

Top MUD Sites—www.topmudsites.com

MUDMagic—www.mudmagic.com

MUD CLIENTS

If you want to get the most out of your MUDding, a MUD client can make your life a lot easier. Here are some of the best:

TinyFugue for Windows and Mac—www.druware.com

SimpleMU for Windows—Simplemu.onlineroleplay.com

Fire Client for Windows—www.firebolt.com

Cantrip for Mac OS X—www.solidsun.com/cm/

DID YOU KNOW

Back in my college days, I was hopelessly addicted to a MUD called Tsunami. 12 years later, that MUD is still alive and kicking at tsunami.thebigwave.net.

Command & Conquer and Red Alert
Closet Classics

Image courtesy of GameSpy.com.

Explosions are everywhere in a C&C game.

DOSSIER

Genre: Cash Cow RTS **Publisher:** Virgin Interactive **Developer:** Westwood Studios
Platform: PC

The Command & Conquer (C&C) series is the most popular real-time strategy (RTS) game series of all time, selling in excess of 36 million units. Of course that spans a legion of games, but still, 36 million is 36 million.

Many consider developer Westwood Studios the father of the real-time strategy genre. Back in 1992, the company developed Dune, which wasn't particularly popular but laid the RTS groundwork for what was to come.

In 1995, Westwood blew the doors off the gaming world with the release of Command & Conquer, a real-time strategy game that became a gold mine for the company and challenged Blizzard Entertainment as king of the genre. A year earlier, Blizzard had released the original WarCraft: Orcs and Humans; and in 1995 had released the staggeringly popular follow-up, WarCraft II: Tides of Darkness.

The graphics were pretty darn good for 1995.

Image courtesy of GameSpy.com.

The Setting

C&C was set in modern times following the impact of a comet (or maybe it was a meteor) that spread a highly hazardous resource material called Tiberium across the planet. The two warring factions, the GDI—Global Defense Initiative—and the Brotherhood of NOD, fought to the death over the resource. The GDI was sort of like the United Nations, whereas NOD was a terrorist organization run by the infamous bald menace known as Kane.

You could play the campaign from both sides, and how it was done was the very essence of cool. You would really see the point of view of each faction through the use of full motion video cut scenes. This was about the time that developers finally realized that full motion video could be used as part of a game, without trying to make it the game itself.

The graphics, for a 1995 DOS game, were very good. Whereas WarCraft went for larger, cartoony units, C&C units were smaller but there were more of them and they packed a lot of punch. Explosions were everywhere in a C&C game, and

although it doesn't look too hot by today's standards (the lack of 3D video card support will do that), it's still a very playable game.

C&C was amazingly popular but the C&C: Red Alert series, which started a year later in 1996, has proven to be an even bigger hit with RTS fans. Red Alert takes place in an alternate history where Allied forces must defend Europe from an overly aggressive Soviet Union. In Red Alert, World War II never happened. Instead, Einstein invents a Chronosphere, which allows him to go back in time where he meets a young Hitler and by shaking his hand, breaks the chain of time, so Hitler never comes to power. Instead Stalin gets the bright idea to invade Europe. Pretty cool for a videogame plot, eh? The game itself takes place 20 years after the failed Soviet offensive.

Red Alert gameplay was very similar to that of C&C, with a few exceptions. It looked better and had a wonderful interface that allowed you to control as many units at one time as you wanted, and you could queue unit orders, which was unheard of before Red Alert. Both games are considered pioneers of the RTS genre and many of the basic design elements of these decade-old games are still in use today.

C&C DEN
This veteran website (at www.cncden.com) has been covering C&C for going on ten years. Tons of info and downloads here for everything C&C.

DID YOU KNOW

Petroglyph Games is a developer founded by many former Westwood members. The company's first game is Star Wars: Empire at War, a real-time strategy game slated for an early 2006 release (see p.268).

News You Can Use

The Best Gaming News Sites on the Web

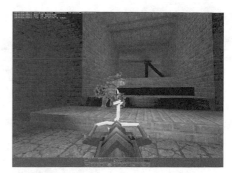

The original Quake spawned many a game site as well as news sites like Shacknews.

The day-to-day happenings inside the game industry can be fairly mundane, at times pretty darn funny, but usually it's a lot like any other entertainment industry—games are announced, patches released, reviews and previews posted, interviews conducted, and mods released. Keeping on top of all of this stuff can be pretty daunting, to say the least. Thankfully, there is an almost-innumerable number of gaming news sites on the Net to help keep you informed. The problem is that some are better than others, some rip off news from other websites, and some aren't updated as often as they need to be. The following is just a very small sample of some of the better news sites on the Internet; some are general news sites, whereas others cater to a specific genre.

Blue's News—www.bluesnews.com. Blue's News is one of the most respected and most read news sites on the Net. Blue has been at this since 1996 and this is his full-time job—so you know a lot of people read this website. It is continually updated, 365 days a year. If you want to stay informed, this is a great place to start.

Shacknews—www.shacknews.com. This is another enormously popular general news site. Although this site isn't quite as old as Blue's News (The Shack started in 1999) a lot of the same news is covered and Shacknews breaks things down by genre. It really depends on which layout and writing style you prefer because both Blue's News and Shacknews are grade-A news sites.

RPG Dot—www.rpgdot.com. RPG Dot has been around since 1999 and is an indispensable news resource for role-playing fans. It also hosts sites dedicated to specific role-playing games, but the core website is updated every day and carries every piece of RPG news you could want.

Operation Sports—www.operationsports.com. Operation Sports is dedicated to sports gaming on both the PC and consoles. Aside from offering daily news, there is an active forum for sports gamers as well. This is also a good place to find updated rosters.

Just Adventure—www.justadventure.com. Just Adventure focuses on, obviously, adventure games. The site has been around since 1997 is has proven to be extremely popular with fans of role-playing games, MMOGs, and graphics adventures.

Team Xbox—www.teamxbox.com. If you are looking for daily news specifically on the Xbox and Xbox 360, this is the site for you. It also provides other Xbox resources such as cheat codes, previews, reviews, and so on. But it's a really good news site for the MS console.

The Wargamer—www.wargamer.com. Founded way back in 1995, it's one of the oldest gaming websites around. This isn't just a news site, but it covers every aspect of military war games and general strategy games, including reviews of board games and books.

SimHQ—www.simhq.com. Want to stay current on the world of flight sims, driving sims, and naval games? SimHQ is the place to go.

Evil Avatar—www.evilavatar.com. Evil Avatar is a general news site that covers a lot of what the other sites do, but tends to do it with a bit more sarcasm. It's an acquired taste, so make sure to check it out to see whether this kind of news is up your alley. Personally, I find some if it hilarious. There's also an incredibly active forum here—enter at your own risk.

DID YOU KNOW

Shacknews was called Quakeholio when it was launched and covered mainly news about the game Quake. It was later called Shugashack, but was changed to Shacknews because too many people thought Shugashack was a porn site.

Gamer Lingo
It's English...Of a Sort

Image courtesy of GameSpy.com

Large gatherings in World of Warcraft tend to take on a weird life of their own.

So, you're new to this whole gaming thing, or you're a parent (or guardian) that wants to feel a shade more hip—or you fear your child is talking in some sort of bizarre code—fear not!

When your son calls a buddy a mule, it's not slang for jerk, or if he likes to rant that his friends are all low-ping bastards, he's not mad at them...he's mad at *you*. This is his way of saying you need to get out of the Stone Age and order a fast broadband connection and to give your crusty dial-up modem the old *Office Space* fax machine treatment.

Common Online Gamer Speak

Here is some basic vernacular that a lot of gamers use when playing certain games. Of course you could probably write an entire book on the slang that gamers and general tech-geeks use, but this is a good sampling. These phrases are generally used in first-person shooters and MMOGs.

Fragging. This is a simple term meaning to kill an opponent in a first-person shooter. The term itself comes from the military. Remember the line in the movie *Platoon* when Bunny says, "We should frag his ass!"?

Buff. A *buff* is an enhancement of some sort. If a player finds a magic potion that increases his abilities or a friendly spell-caster casts a spell that temporarily boosts an attribute, it's called a buff.

Role-Play Versus Roll-Play. There are two schools of thought when playing a role-playing game (RPG). There are people that like to role-play and those that, well, don't. A role-player stays in character and a roll-player just worries about stats and hard numbers (see www.cybermoonstudios.com/8bitDandD.html).

Power Gamer. This term is used to label a person who plays a game, usually an MMOG, simply to build up a powerful character as fast as possible. Generally speaking, power gamers are roll-players, and they tend to get extremely annoyed at role-players.

PK. PK is short for *player-killing*. When someone says, "I just got PK'ed!" It means he or she just got killed by another player. Along these same lines, a PK Specialist is someone who is very, very adept at killing other players.

Reduce! In a lot of MMOGs, people like to complain about certain skills, items, classes, or races. Usually it's a skill, class, or race that they didn't choose. So when you hear a Rogue yell "Reduce Paladins!" it means he thinks the Paladin class is in and of itself too powerful.

Exploit. To use an exploit is to find a game loophole and exploit it for your own gain. If a moderator finds out you are using an exploit, you'll usually get banned from the game or at least be given a stern talking to.

Noob, Newbie. This refers to a player brand new to a particular game. They are usually taken advantage of by veterans. Noobs are usually ignorant, wide-eyed, and tend to get lost a lot. They're cute, though, in their own way.

Mule. A term used to define someone that is willing to carry your extra loot when you don't have anymore room. Mules tend to be noobs.

Tank. When grouping during an MMOG, a tank is usually a fighter-class character that can handle the close combat while ranged players attack from a distance.

Rez-Kill. To use a spell or scroll to resurrect a dead player, only to immediately kill them again.

Griefer. The worst type of gamer, a griefer is the kind of person that makes it his/her life's mission to simply annoy and make games more difficult for other people. If you have ever had a kill deliberately stolen in an MMOG, you have been the victim of a griefer. Griefers tend to be social misfits with very little contact with the outside world. Do not get angry at the griefer; you should pity and then rez-kill them.

DID YOU KNOW

Will Wright's first game was the 1984 C-64 title, Raid on Bungeling Bay, which was a pretty basic action shoot 'em up game. Wright would later go on to make classic games such as SimCity and The Sims.

Let's Talk Sales
...And Is PC Gaming Dead?

Image courtesy of GameSpy.com.

GT4 is a venerable cash cow for Sony.

Here's a look at the best selling games for the first half of 2005.

On July 28, 2005, the NPD Group (www.npd.com), a marketing/retail tracking service, released a report on retail sales of video games in the United States for the first half of the calendar year. In that time frame, the U.S. market saw hardware (consoles and handhelds, mainly), software (the games), and accessories (everything else) sales up 21% compared to 2004. In fact, sales related to gaming shot up from 3.4 billion to 4.1 billion. Why?

What a Difference a New Console Makes

According to NPD, the year-over-year growth in sales can be attributed to the release of the Sony PSP and the Nintendo DS. Take a look at this, though. Console game sales saw a boost of a meager 3%. So, take away the release of the new handhelds and the rate of sales seems to be staying roughly the same.

Then there's the PC, that poor, old, and lonely computer sitting in a corner looking for something to do besides surf the Internet and check email.

Sales for the first half of 2005 dropped 10.5% (from 453 million down to 404 million). Even though 404 million dollars is a lot of loot, a 10% drop is pretty significant. Blockbuster PC games are getting more rare each year and when there isn't a huge release during a particular quarter, sales suffer tremendously, whereas there are more console games being released that appeal to a wider range of gamers, so the numbers are a lot better as a result.

It's not like every PC game released fails at the cash register. Half-Life 2 sold more than 1.7 million copies in its first two months back in 2004 (and that number doesn't include Steam purchases). World of Warcraft was a huge hit for Blizzard—but those mainstream mega-hits are few and far between on the PC.

Just look at the list shown here. How many PC games do you see on this list? Yep, that would be a big, fat zero. A big reason for this is that there were very few big name PC games released for the entire first six months of the year.

According to NPD, the top selling PC games for the first half of 2005 were Guild Wars (which is great), World of Warcraft (also great, but it's been out since 2004), The Sims 2 University (an expansion), Empire Earth II (a mediocre real-time strategy game), Stronghold 2 (a very mediocre castle-building game), and Half-Life 2 (a 2004 release). It's so bad that the #16

game on the top selling PC games list is a game called Dungeon Lords, which is an abysmal action-RPG. If Dungeon Lords is cracking your top 20, even briefly, then there's a problem.

FIRST HALF 2005 (JANUARY–JUNE) TOP SELLERS
1. Gran Turismo 4 (PlayStation 2: SCEA)
2. Pokemon Emerald (Game Boy Advance: Nintendo)
3. MVP Baseball 2005 (PlayStation 2: Electronic Arts)
4. Star Wars Episode III: Revenge of the Sith (PlayStation 2: LucasArts)
5. Grand Theft Auto: San Andreas (PlayStation 2: Take-Two)
6. God of War (PlayStation 2: SCEA)
7. Zelda: The Minish Cap (Game Boy Advance: Nintendo)
8. Resident Evil 4 (GameCube: Capcom)
9. Midnight Club 3: DUB Edition (PlayStation 2: Take-Two)
10. Star Wars Episode III: Revenge of the Sith (Xbox)

Where does this leave the PC? My take is that as long as there are PCs there will be PC games. Of course, the PC industry and its sales are also hampered by the shadow of game piracy, which is a story for another time.

Selling games over the Internet, I think, is the future of the hobby on the computer. I doubt we'll see a resurgence anytime soon that puts the PC back in the running in terms of sales, but I hope with this book I have highlighted some of the fantastic PC games that are either on the shelves or should be by the time you read this.

There's a lot of good stuff out there, you just need to look for it.

DID YOU KNOW

The number one selling video game of all time is Super Mario Bros. for NES. To date it has sold more than 40 million units. Yeow, that's a lot of Luigi!

Scary Games
Play with the Lights On!

Image courtesy of GameSpy.com.

I have always been of the opinion that there are very few scary games; the kind of game that from start to finish creeps you out like a late-night showing of *The Exorcist*. (*That movie scares the ever lov'n #$@! out of me.*) That's rare. However, there are a lot of scenes or specific parts of games that are out-and-out heart-pounding.

Fatal Frame is about an 11 on the creep-o-meter.

Image courtesy of GameSpy.com.

The haunted hotel in Vampire: Bloodlines is one of the best missions in any game, ever.

The Scariest Moments in Gaming

Vampire Bloodlines: The Haunted Hotel. Released in 2004 by Activision and Troika Games, Bloodlines had a few macabre scenes, but the mission in the abandoned haunted hotel scared the bejeezez out of me. This scene, which is ripped straight from *The Shining*, was so tense that I had to keep reminding myself, *"Dude, you are playing a vampire...you're the monster here, you idiot."* As you wandered the hotel, you discovered clues as to what happened there and why. Best of all? There are no monsters in the hotel. It's you, a ridiculously creepy setting, some atmospheric sights and sounds, and your worst enemy of all—and your imagination.

Unreal: Meet the Skaarj. Released in 1998 by GT Interactive and Epic Games, the original Unreal was a gorgeous game, but it wasn't particularly frightening. That is, except for the first time you meet the Skaarj. If memory serves, this scene takes place when you are running through a cave, chasing an unknown enemy. You walk past a certain trigger zone, and a log falls behind you, blocking your way out. Then the light goes out. It's deadly quiet for a few agonizing seconds. You can't see *anything*. Then you hear the Skaarj growl...right behind you. It was one of the best staged scenes that I can remember.

Resident Evil 4. I've spoken at length about this game's greatness (see p.8). And really, if you like horror-action games, you simply must have this in your gaming library. There are two main reasons why I mention this over the other games in this series. First off, zombies, although scary, aren't as terrifying as real people like the chanting monks and brain-washed villagers in RE4. Blasting a farmer in the face with a shotgun—his reaction is a bit spine-tingling to say the least. Second, RE4 makes use of sound like no other RE game before it.

Fatal Frame. Tecmo's classic horror game from 2001 is truly scary not because of monsters popping out from behind walls, but because of its wonderful use of setting and sound. It's more about what you *don't see*, which is usually far more frightening than when the bogeyman actually shows his face. Plus, you play a young girl in a huge mansion full of cultists. Where's my vampire when I need him!

DOOM 3: The First 30 Minutes. I have to say, even though I wasn't a huge fan of DOOM 3 (in fact I thought it was fairly mediocre), the first 30 minutes were sheer brilliance. It was tense, scary, creepy, and just plain perfect. The first few times a demon hopped out of his monster closet, it was genuinely frightening. Of course, after the fiftieth time...not so much.

System Shock 2: SHODAN Says Hello. Two of the best games ever made, I give the nod to SS2 because of the improved graphics and because the way that you meet SHODAN in that game is wonderfully executed. (It's a huge spoiler, so I'll spare you details.) You know what else creeps me out about that game? The fact that you see these mutated people, all former employees of the station, wandering around while the cheery elevator music can still be heard throughout the complex.

Age of Empires III
You Have the Right to Bear Arms

Image courtesy of GameSpy.com.

DOSSIER

Genre: Really Popular Game **Publisher:** Microsoft **Developer:** Ensemble Studios
Platform: PC **Metacritic Metascore:** 82

Yeah, it looks this good.

Every year, a handful of games are considered slam dunks; games that the public is just dying to get its collective hands on. Age of Empires III (AoE3) is one of those games. If you're a veteran of the series, you're already playing it and most likely enjoying it.

Yeah, I know it's not perfect. It's more evolutionary than revolutionary and plants its roots firmly in the past, when managing your economy was by far the most important aspect of an RTS game; whoever has the most peasants wins! Despite the stunning graphics, the gameplay is vintage Age of Empires. For many, this will undoubtedly be enough, but those looking for a huge leap forward in terms of gameplay may feel a bit underwhelmed.

THEY SAID IT

> "We learned a lot developing Age of Mythology. It was our first attempt to do a 3D game, and we used the opportunity to try and put a new spin on some of the sacred cows of the Age of Empires series.... We think our fans will really be blown away by the amazing visual detail of Age of Empires III. No RTS game, and few games period, have ever looked this good." —**Age of Empires III designer Greg Street in an interview with GameSpy.com**

Image courtesy of GameSpy.com.

The New World never looked so good!

A New Era

Age of Empires III picks up where Age of Empires II: Age of Kings left off. This latest edition spans, roughly, from the year 1500 to around 1850 and is set primarily in the New World. This age of discovery and colonialism is a new twist for the series because in earlier games everything was about ancient phalanxes or medieval knights. This also marks the first time an AoE game has focused on the age of gunpowder. Musketeers are available almost right off the bat and the technology just grows from there; you'll even see railroads and stagecoaches.

The countries vying for a spot in the New World are the Brits, French, Spanish, Ottomans, Spanish, Portuguese, Dutch, Germans, and Russians. Each has its own technologies, unique units, and so on, just like in a traditional AoE game. On the continent you'll run across several Native American civilizations, like the Lakota and the Aztecs, with whom you can establish alliances, form trade agreements, and even use their technology and lore.

Home Cities

Perhaps the most obvious change in this version, aside from the new time period, is the idea of the Home City. You are there as an extension of your home country and you get to call on the capital for fresh supplies during the course of a game. You can send troops, technology, food, gold, and so on. It's the home city card deck that really makes this feature tick, though. Your deck of 20 cards is custom built and allows you to predefine what kind of shipments you will be able to send during the course of the game. You can even take this deck online and play in skirmish games.

When you finish a game, you can upgrade your city to a higher level (100 being the max) which provides more cards from which to choose; as the city level increases, more valuable cards become available. Your home city is like a character in a role-playing game in that it gets stronger the more you play.

AGE OF EMPIRES HEAVEN
AoE Heaven (aoe3.heavengames.com) is a fantastic website dedicated to the new version as well as the rest of the series. It's also a great place to talk with other players and read about strategies.

DID YOU KNOW

In 2003, the original Age of Empires (first released in 1997) was released on Microsoft's Pocket PC. It's not gaming nirvana, but it's a fun diversion on the road.

Call of Duty 2
Suit Up and Gear Up

Image courtesy of GameSpy.com.

I don't think a wooden crate is gonna help....

DOSSIER

Genre: Another WWII Shooter **Publisher:** Activision **Developer:** Infinity Ward
Platform: PC, Xbox 360 **Metacritic Metascore:** 86

Call of Duty 2 (CoD2) once again puts you in the uniform of a World War II soldier, fighting your way across Europe. The first game was a huge success when it was released back in 2003, and whenever you try to follow up a popular game with a sequel using the same basic concept, you had better bring some distinctly improved features to the table.

For the most part, developer Infinity Ward accomplished that goal; it's still basically more of the same but it's such as *exhilarating* experience that the sameness of it doesn't matter all that much. Call of Duty 2 is an absolute blast, particularly online with 32 people on a server.

THEY SAID IT

"I would say the linearity and lack of choices was one of the few complaints that we got (about Call of Duty). We like to take on challenges, so we decided that would be one of our goals: to give the player more choices and let the player use more tactics." —**Lead designer Zied Rieke in an interview with GameSpy.com**

Image courtesy of GameSpy.com.

War is hell.

The Campaigns

Just like the first game, the campaign is broken down into three parts: the American, Russian, and British campaigns. The twist is that this time you can move around the campaigns at your own discretion. So, after finishing the 1942 Russian campaign, you can move on to 1943 or jump into the British portion of the game.

The British campaign takes place in, as you'd expect, North Africa. The Russian segment runs from Moscow to the climax at Berlin. The American campaign goes from D-Day to the end of the war. The missions are heart-pounding adrenaline rushes. During most missions, you have fellow soldiers fighting, and dying, by your side. You aren't fighting this war all by your lonesome. You don't issue orders a[ag] la Brothers in Arms, but your AI "teammates" do a good job of fending off the German attacks. They aren't there just for show and they aren't cannon fodder. They're there as real soldiers.

The Sound and Tech Factor

Call of Duty 2's sound is amazing. Not only do the sounds of war (explosions, gun fire, and artillery) permeate the battlefield, Infinity Ward upped the amount of battlefield chatter during combat, which adds an entirely new level of atmosphere. This also goes for the Germans, too. Imagine being in a firefight with your buddies screaming that they need another bandolier while the Germans yell at each other in their own language. Sounds intense, eh? It is.

Infinity Ward stated that it used nothing from the original game (including the Quake III engine) technology-wise. It has been built from the ground up and looks incredibly realistic.

The game's enemy AI is also very good. It's not quite up to Half-Life 2 standards, but the Germans will lob grenades and generally behave in a believable fashion, especially when you ramp up the difficulty level.

CALL OF DUTY BOARDS
Call of Duty has a very loyal online following and the **CoD boards** at www.codboards.com is arguably the best place to talk shop about it on the Net.

DID YOU KNOW

Call of Duty 2: Big Red One, also due out for the various consoles in time for the 2005 holiday rush, is developed by Treyarch, not Infinity Ward, and is not a port of the PC game but a standalone product all its own.

Holidays 2005

Sleigh Bells, Mistletoe, Stuffed Turkey, and the 360

Do you even need this book to tell you that the Xbox 360 was the big news this holiday season? Of course, I had to finish this little tome before the system was released. So, here are two quick reactions to the launch. By the time you read this, you'll already know how it went, so pick the reaction that is appropriate.

1) The Xbox 360 launch was totally wicked-awesome! Every 360 game was just as good as advertised and we can all die happy now that it has been released! I never dreamed gaming heaven would be like this. Thank you, Microsoft.

2) What in the hell was *that*? That's it? I was promised that the Xbox 360 would not only iron the collars, but that *ample* starch would be applied. This is what we get? I say good day to you, sir! I say, good day! Friggin' Microsoft.

What if you don't care about the 360? Well, I guess that's possible. For those who refuse to play Microsoft's reindeer games, there's always College Hoops 2K6, Call of Duty 2 (for PC) or Call of Duty 2: Big Red One (for Xbox, PS2, and GameCube), City of Villains, Lord of the Rings: Tactics, and other non-360 stuff.

Still, you really don't care about the Xbox 360?

Before we move on, I need to make it very clear that the entries in this section are speculative looks ahead at games that as of this writing are not yet released. Some of these games will undoubtedly slip into 2006 and miss the holiday season altogether, and a few might even end up as vaporware. Such is the nature of the game industry. Still others might fall way below expectations. This is my way of covering my rear if a particular game that sounds cool on paper ends up being as much fun as watching a documentary on the history of felt. (Apologies to any felt lovers out there who feel that the fabric's fascinating history is tragically misunderstood.)

College Hoops 2K6
The Madness of March Begins Here

Throwing down with the Carolina blue.

DOSSIER

Publisher: 2K Sports (Division of Take 2 Interactive) **Developer:** Visual Concepts
Platform: PS2, Xbox, Xbox 360

Of all the high profile sports games due this fall and into next year, College Hoops 2K6 is at the very top of my "gotta play" wish list. I realize that later in this chapter (p.238) there is an essay about how sports games are a big rip off—a scam job that milks people out of their money on a yearly basis. For the time being, you should ignore that essay.

Why You Should Care

College Hoops 2K5 was the best basketball game released in 2004 and there are many that feel it is the best basketball game ever released—period. I'm excited because the College Hoops series has yet to reach that inevitable "it's starting to get stale" stage that most sports game franchises reach after several years of development on the same platform.

From the sound of it, the folks at Visual Concepts are aware of last year's shortcomings and are ready to repair them. College Hoops 2K6 uses the same engine as will NBA 2K6 on the Xbox 360; as a result, the player models and the crowd look significantly better. Visual Concepts even includes school pep bands in the crowds, and there are more than 300 accurately modeled arenas and 150 authentic school fight songs as well. (If that sort of thing floats your boat).

The meat of the new version is in the gameplay. The focus is on having teams play more like their real-life counterparts. This means, in theory, that teams that love to run and gun will show more of this tendency in the game (and vice versa).

The "Strip and Rip" and shot stick features from NBA 2K6 make an appearance in College Hoops this year, which is sure to add to the game because they were both cool new additions to the pro game. There's also a new Lead Pass system in which you can tell a player to cut to the basket so that you can attempt to zip the ball in to him on the fly. It works seamlessly when used properly and looks to be a pretty tough move to defend.

Other new features include a Selection Sunday show that lists off the teams that qualify for the tourney, more detailed player ratings (like confidence and focus), practice sessions that increase player skill, and a Coach's Clipboard that allows for greater use of strategy during time outs.

The one caveat is that nearly every 2K Sports game released over the past three years has contained egregious bugs that have caused major headaches for sports fans across the board. College Hoops 2K5 wasn't immune from this, and if Visual Concepts fails to release a tight game without any major bugs, confidence in this series, as well as the other 2K Sports games, will continue to wane.

Spotting up for a trifecta!

COLLEGE HOOPS ROSTERS
So, you have the Xbox version of College Hoops along with an Action Replay device and you want the real player names? Point your browser to **Codejunkies** (www.codejunkies.com) or **Operation Sports** (www.operationsports.com) and get real.

DID YOU KNOW

In College Hoops 2K5, there was a bug that caused all in-season recruiting data to be lost. Data could sometimes be recovered by powering off your Xbox without saving and then restarting it.

City of Villains
Because Bad Guys Are Cool

Image courtesy of GameSpy.com.

Super Bad Guy Ninjas! How cool is that?

DOSSIER

Genre: Dr. Doom Simulator **Publisher:** NCsoft **Developer:** Cryptic Studios
Platform: PC

City of Villains is the standalone sequel to NCsoft's popular City of Heroes online RPG. (You do not need to own City of Heroes to play City of Villains.) City of Villains starts out with your villain being busted out of jail by the evil Lord Recluse. He takes you to a chain of islands outside the jurisdiction of International Law, where bad guys fight each other to prove their worth to the evil lord. After that, all hell breaks loose between the super villains and the heroes of Paragon City.

The number one issue with most MMOG "sequels" is the price structure and that's really the only thing that is still a mystery at this point. NCsoft has stated that the game will require an additional monthly fee, even for those that already own City of Heroes. There should be a discount for CoH owners, but just how much of a discount is anyone's guess at this point. But enough of all that. Let's get to the fun stuff.

THEY SAID IT

> " we want to capture the more proactive nature of villains. Comic book heroes generally react to situations, but villains tend to scheme and plot." —**Lead designer Jack Emmert, Cryptic Studios, in an interview at IGN.com**

Image courtesy of GameSpy.com.

Now THIS is a super villain!

City of Villains Super Bad Guy Features

Super Evil Bases. This is one of the coolest features in the game. A secret base is where you and your group mates can go to rest, plot, and scheme and generally hang out without fear of attack. You get to design and construct it, even selecting the basic appearance (cave, secret lab, whatever) using drop-down tiles to form your base as you see fit.

Base Raids. Okay, so there actually *is* fear of attack. The base leader designates a time when the base can be raided by other teams. The idea is that if you are in control of a super item of power, it can be stolen during a base raid.

Villain Costumes and Powers. City of Heroes is famous for its nearly endless combinations of costumes, and City of Villains should allow for *even more* possibilities as well as tons of new powers and abilities specifically made for villain-like behavior.

Enhanced "Powers" Graphics. Although the game itself looks a lot like CoH, the power effects are far superior. Cryptic Studios has stated that the new graphics will be available for City of Heroes users at some point, but in what capacity the developers do not know.

Player Versus Player (PvP) Combat. Even though City of Heroes now has an Arena for good guys to test their battle prowess, City of Villains will be all about battling it out against the goodie-goodie superheroes in four PvP-specific regions.

SUPERGROUPS
SuperGroups are an important aspect of City of Heroes and **cityofheroes.gameamp.com/team/viewTeams** lists several that are currently recruiting. You can expect a City of Villains list to pop up soon after release.

DID YOU KNOW

Marvel Comics filed a lawsuit against the makers of City of Heroes saying that the game encouraged players to create heroes based on copyrighted material. A judge dismissed the case, calling it "false and sham."

Down in Flames
WWII Dogfighting with Cards

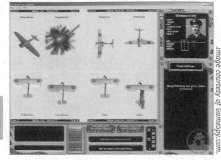

It won't win any awards in graphics, but Down in Flames has it where it counts—it's a lot of fun.

Image courtesy of GameSpy.com.

DOSSIER

Genre: Under-the-Radar Strategy Game **Publisher:** Battlefront.com **Developer:** Battlefront.com **Platform:** PC

In writing this book, I'm trying to give you a heads up on all of the high profile titles that are either on the shelves or that soon will be when you read this. However, it's also important to keep lesser-known games that might not get as much ink as some of the blockbusters on your radar. Down in Flames is one such game.

Card games that are converted into video games are nothing new; games like Magic: The Gathering and even more standard games like poker and bridge have done fairly well when ported to the PC. Down in Flames, on the other hand, is a converted card game that is also a wargame. It tries to simulate World War II–era dogfighting in a fun, fast, and yet moderately realistic fashion.

THEY SAID IT

"I think that at the present time the computer gaming world is dominated by a small group of game types. There are the first-person shooters, the first-person fantasy games, and the real-time strategy games. While all these types of games are fine, what I want to do is expand that list with easy to learn, flavorful, strategy games." —**Dan Verssen, Designer of Down in Flames in an interview with Wargamer.com**

Image courtesy of GameSpy.com.

Having an experienced pilot can make all the difference in a tough fight.

The Planes

In Down in Flames, you get to pilot classic planes from World War II such as the British Spitfire, the U.S. P-38 Lightning, and the German Bf 109. There are several campaigns, from the Battle of Britain to the Solomon Islands, so basically every major theatre in the Western Front and the Pacific is represented.

Each plane has unique statistics that highlight its strengths and weaknesses. The planes are rated in Performance, Horsepower, Bursts, and Airframe. These basic traits, combined with the skill of the pilots, really help differentiate the planes from one another.

Easy to Learn, Hard to Master

The design uses what is called the *Action/Reaction system*, which means that some cards that you draw allow you to perform an action (like an attack or a maneuver), whereas others allow you to react to another card played by your opponent.

Each dogfight is split into six turns that pit two or four elements (which are a lead pilot and his wingman) against one another. The turns are further broken down into phases where you can change altitude, attack another aircraft, or draw/discard cards. What makes it fun (and tough to master) is deciding when to you use specific cards and how best to use your wingman.

New to the PC version is the experience system that allows pilots to get better as they complete missions. Skills earned through this experience provide pilots with special abilities or the capability to draw more cards during a battle.

DOWN IN FLAMES HOME PAGE
Not only does **www.battlefront.com/products/dif** give more specifics about the game, it also provides a detailed walkthrough of how the battle system works.

DID YOU KNOW

Battlefront is also working on another card strategy game called Modern Naval Battles—World War II at Sea. It's set for an early 2006 release.

Marc Ecko's Getting Up: Contents Under Pressure
The Fine Art of Spray Painting

Image courtesy of GameSpy.com.

A look at our hero, Trane, "bombing" a subway car.

DOSSIER

Genre: Marc Ecko Is Everywhere! **Publisher:** Atari **Developer:** The Collective
Platform: PS2, Xbox, PC

What if graffiti could change the world? That's the question that Getting Up: Contents Under Pressure asks.

Well, sort of.

The game is like a blend of Tony Hawk Underground and Jet Set Radio with a dash of stealth-action game tossed in for good measure. But instead of using a sniper rifle or rocket launcher, your primary tool is a can of spray paint.

Graffiti 101

Whether or not you're a fan of Marc Ecko's clothing line, he does come with some legitimate street kred. The guy definitely knows the culture of the graffiti world and it really shines through in the landscape and the overall flavor of the game. You can even unlock famous graffiti artists (also known as taggers).

You play a "toy" graffiti artist named Trane, voiced by rap artist Talib Kweli, in the fictional city of New Radius. (A toy is slang for a novice graffiti artist.) Trane travels through 11 large levels in an attempt to get his message out to the people via graffiti (what that message is, we'll have to wait and see). It isn't as simple as grabbing a can and spraying wherever you please; you need to find the best spot. Each goal area is marked with a blinking red X, so you always know where best to make your mark.

THEY SAID IT

> "It's not a graffiti simulator. It's something that takes the graffiti narrative and the lore of graffiti and the ideas of the risk of life and limb that gives you some intimate and close-up experiences of what it's really like if you are into street bombing. What's cool about it is that if you're not, it's still a great game. You'll never look at a piece of graffiti the same way again." —**Marc Ecko in an interview with GameSpot.com**

Finding the blinking red X is really half of the struggle because some of the locations are in seemingly impossible areas. Reaching the locations requires a lot of coordination

(jumping subway cars, for example) as well as a lot of stealth. Rival gangs try to snatch you up at every turn. You can fend off these foes by using items from the environment (boards, crowbars, and so on) as well as using your spray-paint can in an inventive way to create a makeshift flamethrower comprised of your can and an everyday lighter.

Image courtesy of GameSpy.com.

Our man Trane—locked and loaded...with paint.

The art itself is actually a very important part of the game. You'll get to use stencils, rollers, aerosols, custom stickers, and so on. You also need to watch how much paint you use in order to avoid drips or blurs, which can ruin any creative piece of graffiti. It's going to take practice to master, so patience is an important virtue.

Truth be told, I don't know how good or bad Getting Up will be in November. I saw it and played the PS2 version at E3 and from the little I was able to see it was a lot of fun, but I have to wonder whether people will actually want to spray-paint walls rather than blast bad guys with a plasma rifle. Regardless, you have to give Ecko and the team at The Collective a thumbs-up for trying something so utterly novel.

GETTING UP HOME PAGE
Head over to **www.atari.com/gettingup** to get the latest info on Getting Up and, with a PC version in the works, some cool mods, I hope.

DID YOU KNOW

Mark Ecko is a 32-year-old fashion designer, of a sort, who got his start as a graffiti artist in the New York area while still in college.

The Movies
Mr. Lucas, Eat Your Heart Out

On the set of a classic Western.

DOSSIER

Genre: Lights, Camera, Action: The Game **Publisher:** Activision **Developer:** Lionhead Studios **Platform:** PC, PS2, Xbox, GameCube

The Movies has been in development for quite a while now. In fact, the press has been writing about it since early 2003. Still, it's such a cool idea that if it all comes together the way developer Lionhead Studios wants it to, it'll be worth the wait. I mean really, who doesn't want to run their own digital movie studio and deal with the mammoth-sized virtual ego trips of a fake cast and crew?

THEY SAID IT

"We really see this as being almost three separate games. The first is a simulation of running a movie studio. The second is taking care of your stars. And the third is actually making the movies. There are lots of things to consider, and the player can do pretty much whatever he wants. The game isn't all about making the biggest studio. You can create your own small cult studio if you wish." —**Peter Molyneux of Lionhead Studio in an interview with GameSpy.com**

World War II movies are all the rage!

The Games Within the Game

Cool ideas are pretty rare in the industry these days. Sure, there are a lot of great games out there—many of them highlighted in this book—but there aren't many truly original ideas. This is one of them.

The Movies starts in the 1920s. You're the head honcho at a movie studio during the silent film era. As you continue to play the game, the eras change and you'll see different classic themes such as war movies and westerns and science fiction thrillers capture the public's eye.

The game is actually divvied up into three distinct parts.

The Studio. The first part is the day-to-day grind (a fun grind) of running a movie studio. You hire the staff for the marketing department, along with everyone else, from writers to stunt people. It's here where the studio actually functions; the "little people" are just as important as the superstar actress. You can pick up and place people and get them to work on specific tasks.

The Stars. What is a game about movies without movie stars? As head honcho, you have to cater to the needs of the stars.

What if the actress you signed for a role hates the cameraman? You have to deal with it. The press is hounding your star and driving him Tom Cruise–crazy! Deal with it. The stars in the game all have very distinct, and surprisingly complex, personalities. Some are easy to get along with and will work well with practically everyone; others define the term *egomaniacal*.

The Movies. This part is really intriguing; you actually get to create your own mini-movies. People will be able to share their creations with one another via the game's home page. The Movies comes with more than 8,000 scenes, props, and special effects so that you can really personalize your creation. You can even add sound and music.

The movies you make also fit into the context of the game. People (little computer people) review your movies (you need to create at least five per year) and if you create a poor one, they *will* let you know about it. On the other hand, if your film is great, it might even win an award.

> ### THE MOVIES HOME PAGE
> **The Movies website** (www.lionhead.com/themovies) hosts player movie files and provides hints and tips on how best to run your studio.

DID YOU KNOW

For a firsthand look at how movies get made, check out the HBO show *Project Greenlight*, which is now available on DVD. Just don't watch the *Project Greenlight* movies. Have you seen *The Battle of Shaker Heights*? *Cringe*

The Chronicles of Narnia
The Lion, the Witch and the Wardrobe

Image courtesy of GameSpy.com.

The gang's all here—battling wolves.

DOSSIER

Genre: Closet to Another World **Publisher:** Buena Vista Games **Developer:** Traveller's Tales **Platform:** PC, PS2, Xbox, GameCube, GBA, DS

I realize that a recurring theme in this book is that the gaming industry is pretty darn predictable. Still, when you see a new action adventure movie based on a famous novel, comic book, or anything that involves kids, you can bet your last nickel that there will be a video adaptation attached to it. The problem is that most of these short development cycle knock-offs, which are produced solely to cash in on the current popularity of the movie in question, are usually pretty awful games.

Sometimes, however, these games are actually fun. The Chronicles of Narnia: The Lion, the Witch and the Wardrobe has the potential to be the rare game that takes a movie license and turns it into a cool game.

Image courtesy of GameSpy.com.

You have to start somewhere, in this case—head for the attic.

Image courtesy of GameSpy.com.

Some of the bad guys are really menacing-looking and could be a bit much for really young kids.

Why You Should Care

A big reason to care about the Narnia videogame is that Traveller's Tales is developing it. This is the same company that made LEGO Star Wars for LucasArts, which is one of the best co-op games around, especially if you want to play a game with your child (see p.51).

Just like LEGO Star Wars, you can play co-operatively at any time. So, if you're playing the game solo, player two can come in and click the Start button and join the fray. You also have the ability to switch characters at any time.

Obviously, the movie is based on the classic C.S. Lewis books. If you haven't read them, put down this book and go buy the entire series. (Feel free to come back to this book when you're done.)

Narnia itself has been frozen by the evil White Witch. (That's something I love about Lewis: How many White Witches are evil?) The true ruler of Narnia, the lion Aslan, invokes the ancient prophecy that four young siblings will save the day and end the reign of the witch. That's where you come in.

The game, following the arc of the film, has you play as all four children: Peter, Susan, Edmund, and Lucy, and each has certain skills. Peter has his sword, Susan her trusty bow (along with sleep-inducing panpipes), Lucy is a healer, and Edmund is more of a rogue-climber type. You get to do battle with all sorts of creatures, such as Cyclopes, werewolves, centaurs, minoboars, wraiths, and many more; in fact, there are more than 30 creatures in all.

The game itself feels like a blend of LEGO Star Wars and the action-oriented Lord of the Rings games. This is a button-mashing action fest with some tricky puzzles tossed in for good measure—and it looks beautiful, with gorgeously animated characters and tons of environmental detail that captures the beauty and spirit of Narnia.

It seems like the ideal game for young teens who want to play a game co-operatively, or with a gaming parent that enjoys action-oriented adventure games.

NARNIA WEB

At **www.narniaweb.com** you'll find a fantastic website that discusses not only the video game but the film as well.

DID YOU KNOW

The Lion, the Witch and the Wardrobe movie and game are based on the classic C.S. Lewis book of the same name. There are seven books in the Chronicles of Narnia series, which were written between 1950 and 1956.

Perfect Dark Zero
Going Back to the Beginning

Image courtesy of GameSpy.com.

Perfect Dark Zero is both a stealth game and a full-blown classic shoot 'em up.

DOSSIER

Genre: Gorgeous 360 Shooter **Publisher:** Microsoft **Developer:** Rare Ltd. **Platform:** Xbox 360

Perfect Dark, released back in 2000 on the N64, is considered the spiritual successor to the classic 1997 console shooter, GoldenEye 007. That's no coincidence given that Rare Ltd. was the developer of that game, too. Now it has set its sites on Perfect Dark Zero.

Even as late as October 2005, Perfect Dark Zero was supposedly going to be one of the Xbox 360 launch titles even though by the start of November Microsoft had yet to confirm this. What can be confirmed is that this first-person shooter "prequel" to the classic Nintendo 64 game looks sharp.

You play the role of special agent Joanna Dark, codename: Perfect Dark. In Perfect Dark Zero, among other things, you'll find out how she became an agent in the first place.

THEY SAID IT

"We wanted to find out more about Joanna. Where did she come from? How did she turn into this "perfect" agent? What makes her tick? Setting the game a few years prior to Perfect Dark meant we could ground the universe better and keep Jo on planet Earth. It also meant we could use weapons inspired by those in the real world, to balance against the high-tech hardware available to Jo, her allies, and enemies." —**Rare Ream interview with Xbox.com**

Image courtesy of GameSpy.com.

There are roughly 20 weapons in the game, each with primary and secondary functions. Most just blow stuff up.

Supposedly up to 50 players will be supported via Xbox Live, but you'll also be able to play co-op on the same machine, which is something every game should allow.

Pretty, Pretty Pictures

The Perfect Dark Zero tech demo that Microsoft unveiled at E3 in May 2005 showed some of the multiplayer capabilities of the game as well as some of the early graphic renderings. It's safe to say that that the game is going to look disgustingly good. Early pictures of Joanna had an "anime-ish" look, with a chest that would make Elvira jealous. Thankfully, things changed and the graphics now have a very realistic edge to them. At the show, the game was running on an alpha kit of the 360 and it still looked remarkable. It uses a technique called *parallax mapping*, which is an alternative to the usual bump-mapping technique that takes graphical realism to a new level.

As with most Xbox 360 titles, Perfect Dark Zero will be multiplayer friendly. Several new modes will be available as well as games like standard Deathmatch, Capture the Flag, and King of the Hill. Multiplayer games will also feature vehicles. So far, three vehicles have been announced: the jet pack, hovercrafts, and two-man motorcycles.

Big Guns

There will be nearly 20 different weapons in the game from pistols to crossbows. Some of the confirmed weapons include

- **The Phantom.** An energy gun that also acts as a cloaking device.
- **The Laptop Gun.** A favorite from the original, it's a gun disguised as a laptop and can be used as a sentry device.
- **The Shockwave Rifle.** A deadly sniper rifle that also gives you the ability to see through walls.
- **The Psychosis Pistol.** Another favorite from the earlier game, this allows Joanna to turn enemies against one another for a short time.

In addition to these weapons, other toys include personal teleporters similar to those in Quake III, X-ray devices, and other spy tools.

DID YOU KNOW

Developer Rare Ltd. is an U.K.-based company that was founded way back in 1985. Rare was a second-party developer for Nintendo for years, but Microsoft acquired the company in 2002.

NBA 06
Live the NBA Life

DOSSIER

Genre: Risky NBA hoops game **Publisher:** Sony **Developer:** SCEA Sports Studio/989 Sports **Platform:** PS2, PSP

Although The Life is the big new feature, there is also the usual NBA option.

Yes, yes, I know. Sony and 989 Sports's track record with basketball games has been, shall we say, less than stellar. You could probably call it downright abysmal, but look at it this way: 989's baseball game improved dramatically over the past few years, so maybe its basketball game will do the same?

Last year Sony skipped the NBA season by shelving the NBA Shootout series (thank God). With an additional year of development and a unique story-centric game design, dubbed The Life, NBA 06 could very well turn some heads. The jury is definitely still out, but the idea is actually pretty cool and unlike a game like Blitz (see p.181), the other basic modes like online play and franchise support will still be there.

THEY SAID IT

"Well, as you know, we took a year off and did not ship an NBA product last year. We completely retooled this engine from the ground up, you know, everything, so that we could do with AI and animations the way we felt it was necessary. And we had to add an entirely new cinematic engine to support the whole story mode aspect." —Scott Rohde, Sony Director of Product Development in an interview with GamerFeed.com

The Life

In NBA 06's new RPG-style The Life mode, you create a player from scratch using the usual methods of selecting basic traits, gear, and so on. (You must create a point guard, however.) After that you pick your favorite team that you'd like your new star to play for via the NBA Draft.

From here you go to the predraft workouts, which is more of a basic tutorial. You go through a series of basic drills like passing, dribbling, shooting, and so on, which end up determining your basic attributes. It's like Madden's Superstar mode, only (hopefully) not nearly as lame.

After your initial skills are set, you are introduced to your new agent, who also serves as a mentor of sorts. You also meet other characters during the course of the game—even your mom makes an appearance. It's unclear if she's there to encourage you or to hit you up for a new house.

You'll soon be drafted to your team where, after a few practice sessions, you'll replace the current point guard, the cocky former Rookie of the Year winner and one of the story's main antagonists.

It's an interesting premise but because the story and the season itself are totally scripted, it could end up feeling sort of canned. It's important to understand that this mode isn't like your typical franchise mode where you play your games at your own pace. Everything is staged and done in sections.

Showtime!

The new Showtime Gameplay is also adds an intriguing twist. There are two aspects to this concept. First is the team component, where if you hog the ball all game long, your teammate's skills suffer while yours improve (if you play well). This is all temporary to that particular game, though.

A style factor also plays a part, and this is where the Showtime feature comes in. There are Showtime buttons on the gamepad such as Showtime Pass and Showtime Dunk. A Showtime Pass might be a no-look toss or a behind-the-back pass on a fast break. Performing these moves excites the crowd into a frenzy and gives a huge temporary boost to your players. Mess up a Showtime move, and your ratings drop like a rock.

The Life takes the action off the court.

DID YOU KNOW

The PSP version of NBA 06 is very different than the one released on the PS2. There's no "life" mode, and it's basically just an average sports game from top to bottom. (72 Metascore)

King Kong
What Could Possibly Go Wrong?

Image courtesy of GameSpy.com.

No, this is not Jurassic Park.

DOSSIER

Genre: Ape-Sized Action **Publisher:** Ubisoft **Developer:** Ubisoft **Platform:** PS2, PS3, Xbox, 360, PSP, GBA, DS, GameCube, PC

Geez, you make one little movie trilogy involving a ring, a wizard, and a few orcs, and all of a sudden you get to make whatever movie you want. Peter Jackson, of *The Lord of the Rings* fame, loves King Kong. A lot. Too much to be healthy, really. He loves The Kong so much so that he brought the big galoot back to the silver screen in 2005.

Consequently, just like clockwork, the gaming industry has hopped on board to create the videogame version because that's simply what the gaming industry does. Here's the kicker, though: The potential for this game looks really, really good.

THEY SAID IT

> "I'm really enjoying the collaboration with these artists, and all the creative possibilities we're discovering. By working closely with the development team, Ubisoft is enabling me to help shape the kind of gaming experience that I will be proud to associate with this new version of King Kong, a story that began my life-long love of film." —**Peter Jackson, Director of King Kong the movie as quoted on IGN.com**

Kong! Kong! Kong!

Peter Jackson is sort of overseeing the project, in a sense, and he has given the game his blessing so that's a pretty good sign. More importantly, producer Michel Ancel designed the terribly underrated game Beyond Good and Evil and the popular Rayman platformer, so with his experience, Kong's foray into videogames hopefully will be a good one. Also involved in the process is Weta Ltd., the visual effects studio behind both *King Kong* and *The Lord of the Rings*, so you can expect the game to look the part.

I never have been quite sure what it is about King Kong that captures our imagination. I guess as a society, we just like big gorillas. Regardless, you'll have a chance to play King Kong in the game as well as other characters. As Kong, the action switches to a seamless third-person mode, so you'll be able to see Kong in action rather than just through his point of view.

When playing as other characters, such as Jack Driscoll, the game switches back to first-person and you have to use your team members because each person has unique skills. It's not just a run-and-gun action game.

Image courtesy of GameSpy.com.

Be very, very quiet; we're being hunted by a huge gorilla.

Loud, Proud and HUD-Less

The theater demonstration at E3 showcased some of the most impressive sound effects of any game at the show. Kong's roar, for instance, was deafening, but the ambient sound effects were also remarkably well done. It was like actually being on Skull Island (I assume...).

Equally impressive are the graphics. Although it will be available for the next-gen platforms, the game was designed with the current systems in mind. Even so, the level of detail in the visuals was staggering. It wins the best looking videogame dinosaur award, hands down. (Sorry, Turok.)

One of the reasons the graphics stand out (aside from the giant screen the game was running on at E3) is that there is no onscreen interface clutter. There's literally no HUD display, so all you see is the action itself. I admit that this could pose a problem if not handled properly, but it certainly did add to the atmosphere by not having health meters and ammo displays cluttering up the foliage.

> ### KONG ONLINE
> Get up-to-the-minute details on the new Kong flick at **Kong Is King** (www.kongisking.net). The **Kong Home Page** (www.kingkonggame.com/us) is worth visiting just for the sound effects.

DID YOU KNOW

The 1933 classic *King Kong* film has a sequel that was made in the same year. Titled *Son of Kong*, it features an expedition that heads back to Skull Island and finds that Kong left behind an albino son. Seriously, I'm not making that up.

Gun
Call It *Deadwood*: The Game

Image courtesy of GameSpy.com.

I got 'em right where I want 'em.

DOSSIER

Genre: Six-Shooter Action **Publisher:** Activision **Developer:** Neversoft Entertainment
Platform: Xbox, Xbox 360, PS2, GameCube, PC

Gun is a rare bird in that it's set in the American West, but it's also not a supernatural fantasy. Most games set in the Wild West of the 1800s, going back to the days of the Alone in the Dark series, have some kind of supernatural angle, like Darkwatch. The West was wild enough on its own; it doesn't need an appearance from Cthulhu or a vampire to spice it up. Gun is a gritty and gory first- and third-person Western shoot 'em up. It's more *Deadwood* than *Bonanza*, more *The Outlaw Josey Wales* than *Rooster Cogburn*.

You play the role of Colton White, a former Civil War soldier with no home to go back to who heads west after the end of the war. From there you go on a quest to find out the truth about the man you thought was your father. There's a pretty cool storyline in Gun; it's not just a "grab your six shooter and go blasting" type of game.

THEY SAID IT

"Right now we are in a very exciting position as a company. The Hawk franchise is probably stronger than ever and we are sitting on the makings of a totally new franchise, which we plan to establish and sequel just like we have with the Tony Hawk games. We have a really solid system in place here for getting great games on the shelf each year, so it is really just a matter of finding more great people to work into our teams." —**Joel Jewett, President of Neversoft Entertainment in an interview with GameSpot.com**

Image courtesy of GameSpy.com.

The Lone Ranger you are not.

The West Comes Alive

The world of Gun is huge and you're free to explore it. From small towns and dusty saloons to desert canyons, you get to investigate a wide variety of classic western locations. The world is also streaming, so when in a town, you can walk the streets and enter a saloon and there's no load screen to slow down the game.

There is obviously the main plot thread, but you can also accept a huge number of side missions to acquire the money needed to upgrade your guns and so on. Again, this is all classic western fare from stagecoach shootouts and Pony Express missions to playing a cool hand of seven-card stud. The world is also alive with activity and not all of it revolves around you. Bar fights break out, gun battles might litter the streets—you just never know.

Quick Draw McGraw and His Trusty Steed

The Quick Draw feature is a lot like Bullet Time. It slows down the action (after your Quick Draw meter is filled) so that you can aim with more precision and see slow motion blood fly out of an outlaw's skull. It's sort of like Neo with a cowboy hat and a six shooter.

In addition, what would a western be without horses? One of your main forms of travel in the game is on the back of your stallion. You can jump over obstacles, rear him up on his hind quarters, fire on a chasing posse, and generally ride him like a classic western hero. You can also spur him to get some extra speed, but if you do this too much, you can exhaust your mount—possibly killing him, if you drive him too hard.

A word of caution: This is an **adult** game with not only a ton of limb-flying graphic violence, but also several adult situations concerning prostitutes, opium, and other *Deadwood*-ish vices. That's all great for adult fans of the genre, but not so great for a wide-eyed ten-year-old.

DID YOU KNOW

Neversoft is also the developer of the ultra popular Tony Hawk series. Wild West shooter...skateboards...there has to be a connection in there somewhere.

The Matrix: Path of Neo
You Know You Want to Be Keanu

Neo and Trinity, together again, with guns.

DOSSIER

Genre: Dying License Action Game **Publisher:** Atari **Developer:** Shiny Entertainment
Platform: Xbox, PS2, PC

I know this franchise isn't the meal ticket that it was back in 2002/2003, but you shouldn't immediately dismiss the talent at Shiny. This is the same company behind such games as Sacrifice and Earthworm Jim. Shiny knows how to make a good game, despite the fact that Enter the Matrix was a rush job released to coincide with the release of the film. This time there is no such rush.

THEY SAID IT

"…it's a great example of how the story can change. If I was just to walk out in front of these security guards I would be captured, and the footage would continue with me being put in the car in the street exactly like it happened in the movie. Basically I can follow the path of the movie and be Neo from the movie, or I can do it my own way, which means I can try my hardest to get the hell out of the office and not fail where Neo failed. In the game you can get to the same window ledge and you can decide what you want to do." — **David Perry of Shiny Entertainment in an interview with Eurogamer.Net**

There are a lot of role-playing elements in this action game, too. Neo can learn several new skills and abilities throughout the course of the game, allowing you the chance to develop your own special Neo character. Code Vision (allows you to see the world as a computer program), Weapon Strips, Bullet Dodge, and Tornado Throw are just some examples of the basic skills you can learn.

Neo and Smith doing the Matrix Tango.

Tearing It Up As Neo

This is perhaps the biggest selling point. For years, fans have wanted to play as The One and not some anonymous "dude" inside The Matrix. Well, here's your chance. The game spans the length of all three films, retelling the story with you, as Neo, as the hero. From the beginning as a hacker/programmer on the run from nameless agents and into the arms of Morpheus and the rest of the gang to the final showdown, you're the star of the show.

The combat model is similar to that of God of War. Although not a carbon copy of it, the sheer number of vicious combo moves will remind you of Sony's PS2 classic. For example, if you get good enough, you can grab an enemy, smash him against a wall, shoot him, fling him up in the air, land a kick, throw him to the ground, and kill him with your sword—all in one flashily cool sequence.

Flip the Script

Finally, you will have some sense of freedom even though the game is based on the films. You can try to approach problems from various angles; you don't have to do things the same way Neo did them in the movies. Maybe you can do them better? This branching story element will add entirely new plotlines. In the game, you have the ability to dramatically alter the way the Matrix saga is told, which is in and of itself pretty cool.

DID YOU KNOW

Early in the game, as Neo chooses his fate, you can take the Blue Pill—at which point the game ends, making Path of the Neo the shortest game ever.

Lord of the Rings: Tactics
Turn-Based Strategy Hits the Little Screen

Image courtesy of GameSpy.com.

Tactics isn't hurting in the graphics department.

DOSSIER

Genre: REALLY Small Hobbit Strategy **Publisher:** EA Games **Developer:** EA Games
Platform: PSP

The *Lord of the Rings* license has a lot of staying power. The movies simply reinvigorated the already huge fan base while introducing the story of Frodo to the masses. I think this series is now on par with *Star Wars* in terms of marketing. There will always be room for new *Star Wars* games, just as there will always be room for more games set in Middle-earth. Gandalf is just that cool.

Lord of the Rings: Tactics has the potential to be one of the very best games released on the PSP. I say this not because it has the licensing from both the films and the books, but because it has the look of an A-list game. If I'm wrong, well, it wouldn't be the first time.

Tactics is a turn-based strategy game in which you get to play as the major heroes (as well as the villains) in the race to destroy the One Ring. The Tactics games are played on a chessboard-like isometric grid, complete with terrain and other obstacles. Each "team" tries to either wipe out the opposing team, a particular character, or accomplish another specific goal. It's ideal for a handheld system like the PSP.

THEY SAID IT

"We loved Final Fantasy Tactics for sure. But the thing that struck us is that lots of RPG franchises have been turned into good tactics games. And looking at everything, our feeling is that tactics games are really well suited to handheld platforms. Being turn-based really works on a handheld because you can put it down whenever you need to." —**Tactics Producer Jeff Lind in an interview with GameSpy.com**

Old Friends, New Evils

The campaign spans all three of the books and uses roughly 45 minutes of film footage from the movies to set the scene for each battle. So, as you'd expect, you get to use all the main protagonists, as well as several secondary players. There's even a new storyline in place specifically for the Mordor battles to provide you with specific "bad guy" story elements. (As if the "We need that damn ring" approach weren't enough.)

Each character also has a skill set and special abilities that can be upgraded throughout the course of the game. Gandalf has spellcasting abilities, Legolas still has that bow that he apparently never misses with (seriously, did he miss *anyone* in the movies?), and Aragorn has leadership skills and can learn how to summon the army of the dead (a skill I think we all could use).

Ready, Set, GO!

Perhaps the most intriguing gameplay element is the fact that characters move simultaneously and not in your standard turn-based fashion. There is a movement phase and a combat phase. During the movement phase, you give the move order to all your characters while, at the same time, your opponent

Image courtesy of GameSpy.com.

You can view the landscape from several points of view.

is doing likewise. After all the orders have been given, everyone moves. The trick is that there is a "zone of control" in place so that characters cannot simply run past each other, which would look ridiculous. The combat phase follows the same idea, but instead of moving, you are trying to decapitate the other guy rather than move near him. This should not only speed up multiplayer play, but should provide for a much better and more streamlined game.

DID YOU KNOW

In the movie *The Lord of the Rings: The Two Towers,* Viggo Mortensen (Aragorn) kicks an orc helmet and appears to scream in frustration. Actually, the scream was real. Viggo broke his foot, but stayed in character to salvage the shot.

Ghost Recon 3
Advanced War Fighter

DOSSIER

Genre: Near Future Solider Sim **Publisher:** Ubisoft **Developer:** Ubisoft **Platform:**
Xbox, 360, PS2, PC, GameCube

GR3 is one sweet-looking game.

Although Advanced War Fighter (AKA Ghost Recon 3) is available on every main platform, the gorgeous graphics of the Xbox 360 and PC versions take it to the next level.

The story sets the game in Mexico City around the year 2013 during North American trade treaty talks. During the summit, Mexican insurgents storm the gates and kidnap the presidents of Mexico and the United States. What's a country to do when presented with such a scenario? Call the Ghosts, of course. In this case, four of them.

This looks like a no-brainer shoot 'em up sort of game, but I do wish that the series would go back to a more stealthy approach (hence the name "ghosts") rather than a game about killing tons of bad guys. Still, it will shock me if GR3 isn't a success.

THEY SAID IT

> "There has always been a focus for our Tom Clancy titles to ensure that the stories, characters, and equipment are as authentic as possible. We wanted to ensure that this tradition continued, as fans of the brand have always enjoyed the realism that we convey in our games. As this is a next-generation title, we also wanted to give players the ability to play as the next-generation soldier, not sci-fi but the kind of soldier you will see on the battlefield in the next 10 years." —**Christian Allen of Ubisoft in an interview with GameSpot.com**

Ten Years Later...

GR3 is set roughly ten years in the future and therefore you and your squad get to play with some new toys. This isn't a "sci-fi" game by any stretch, but Ubisoft has gone the extra mile by collaborating with military consultants to provide likely technology for the soldier of the future.

Some of the new trinkets include a Warrior Physiological Status Monitoring System, which monitors stuff like your heart rate so that medical personnel can always view your vitals. It's kind of like in the movie *Aliens* when Gorman and Ripley could always see when team members bought the farm. Hot damn, but that movie was cool.

Among other new items, you also get a new helmet. This new dome can withstand fragmentation impact (grenade bits bounce off) and also has a radio and antenna built in for easy

communication. You can even use the helmet as a digital cam-era—and it comes with spiffy night- and thermal-vision capabilities. Cool, eh?

These ghosts are in serious trouble.

Hot! Hot! Hot!

The graphics, particularly on the 360 and PC, are jaw-dropping, but they also serve a purpose: Ubisoft wants to use them as part of the setting and not just as pretty pictures. For example, the city is extremely bright because Mexico City is freaking *hot*. The idea is to get a true sense of just how hot it is on the surface while your team tries to find the presidents.

Shoot That Hub Cap!

The environments are also almost completely destructible. You can shoot out individual windows or lob a grenade at a street sign, and even shoot individual hub caps off of cars. Not only is this just plain neat-o, but it also can have an impact on how the game plays and can alter your tactics in specific situations.

A game like this will be only as good as its AI, and I hope the team at Ubisoft will pull it off. On the surface it sure looks good, even if the whole idea of being a stealthy ghost is no longer as relevant.

DID YOU KNOW

Advanced War Fighter will have four-person co-op mode so that you can play multiplayer games as a team with your buddies.

Project Gotham Racing 3
These Cars Corner Like They're on Rails

Image courtesy of GameSpy.com.

First rate scenery...check.

DOSSIER

Genre: Glitzy Car Racing Game **Publisher:** Microsoft **Developer:** Bizarre Creations
Platform: Xbox 360

Some gamers just want to race fast cars and that's really what Project Gotham Racing (PGR) has always been about. It doesn't try to be the ultimate driving simulation. That's what MotoGP and Forza Motorsport are for.

The plan for PGR3 was to launch with the release of the Xbox 360. My guess is that it did, but you never can tell. In any case, by the time you read this, the game will most certainly be available—that is, unless agents from Sony have stolen the code and are holding it for ransom. (I kid, I kid.)

THEY SAID IT

"We're going for 80 cars—it's a figure we thought a lot about. We didn't want too many that you'd never get to own them all, or too few that everyone's tastes weren't being met. Also, when we looked at what cars people played on the PGR games, almost all of them were super cars. With 360's increased graphical bar, each car takes months to make, so we wanted to make sure we made each one count. But obviously you need variety too, so there are still five classes within the game's structure. Some of our cars are pretty much road-legal go-karts, whereas others are big and heavy muscle cars." —**Bizarre Creations team interview with Computer and Video Games.com**

Image courtesy of GameSpy.com.

Come on, you know you want one.

Fast Cars

There are several new features and design tweaks in this latest installment. First off, there are no set car classes in PGR3. Of the 80 licensed cars in the game, all are high performance sports cars capable of hitting speeds of at least 170MPH. There's still lots of unlockable content, and you'll still need to earn enough loot to afford the better cars (each of which has realistic price tags), but the entire class structure has been removed. Even the cars that you can buy from the get-go aren't *bad*—they're just a shade less prestigious. When you're used to driving a Ford Contour that starts to rattle at around 85MPH, any car that can do 170 is fun to drive in my book.

Mode Bonanza!

PGR3 has a lot of game modes from which to choose. The career mode, which works both online and offline, is still the meat of the game. The solo mode consists of 23 championships in four separate cities; at this time, only New York, Tokyo, and London have been revealed. Even though four cities sounds like a rip off, there are several distinct locations inside each city and they are all meticulously detailed.

There's also a "playtime" mode where all user-made tracks are used and there's no rating/stat tracking—it's just for fun. The game's Route Creator gives you access to all four city maps from which you can easily mix and match sets to form your own circuit.

Finally, there's Gotham TV (Batman not included), which just sounds downright cool. It allows you to monitor races for everyone on your XBL Friends list, so you can click a button and watch your friend's race. However, the developers have stated that they will hold "televised" events of high-ranking players that will allow up to (hopefully) 30,000 people to "tune in" and watch. Very cool.

DID YOU KNOW

PGR3 is supposed to have online tournament modes soon after its release via a free download from Xbox Live. Be sure to check the service options to see whether it's ready.

Must-Play Wargames
Grognards of the World Unite

Wargaming is a fascinating part of our hobby. These games don't get the kind of attention that they deserve because, quite frankly, they don't appeal to the mainstream videogame audience. They are more for military history buffs who value authenticity over flash-bang graphics.

Korsun Pocket isn't the best-looking game ever made, but it's a fantastic wargame all the same.

Still, if you like deep strategy games, wargaming might be something you should investigate. The problem with a lot of wargames, though, is that they tend to get bogged down with rules and minutiae and this can really turn off a casual gamer just looking for a quick 30-minute gaming fix. But if you're willing to learn and have an interest in military history, the PC games listed here are a good place to start.

The Ardennes Offensive by SSG (1999). SSG's classic wargame series started back in 1999 with this amazing hex-based wargame based on the infamous Battle of the Bulge. If you're a World War II buff, this is a no-brainer. SSG made it easy on you because the company made the game freeware and you can download the entire game from www.ssgus.com/ardennes-download.htm.

Korsun Pocket by SSG (2003). Korsun Pocket is the next game in the series and it is arguably the best turn-based wargame ever designed. With ruthless AI and wonderful multi-player functionality, this is 2D wargaming at its very best. The next game in the series, Battles in Normandy, is also definitely worth checking out and Battles in Italy is due out in late 2005.

The Operational Art of War Series by Talonsoft (1998–2000). The Operational Art of War (TOAW) is a classic wargame series from developer Norm Koger. It tries to re-create many of the most famous land battles of the entire twentieth century rather than focusing on one conflict. It also does things on a much greater scale (the operational level).

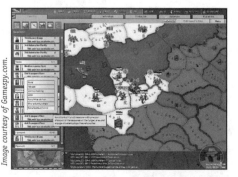

Hearts of Iron II is incredibly deep and not for the faint of heart.

Great Battles Series by I-Magic (1997–1999). This is a bit tougher to find because these games are out of print; I found some on auction sites such as eBay for next to nothing, so if you're lucky enough to score a copy, don't hesitate to get them. There are three games in the series: The Great Battles of Alexander, Hannibal, and Caesar. The games re-create every famous battle of these great generals and are fantastic multi-player games even today—close to a decade after the fact. (Note: Alexander might not work with Windows XP.)

Hearts of Iron II by Paradox (2004). This is World War II on a massive scale (see p.11). This is a complex game, so don't jump in unless you really want to re-create World War II in minute detail.

Combat Mission: Beyond Overlord by Battlefront.com (2000). One of the finest wargames ever designed, Combat Mission broke the mold by using good graphics and both turn-based and real-time gameplay without sacrificing realism. Folks, it just doesn't get much better than this.

> ### THE WARGAMER
> You can find what is quite simply the best wargaming resource on the Internet at **www.wargamer.com**.

DID YOU KNOW

If you want to get into this genre of gaming, check out some wargame publishers like Battlefront.com and Shrapnel Games (www.shrapnelgames.com).

Painkiller and Far Cry Instincts
PC Games Ported to Consoles (No, Really)

Image courtesy of GameSpy.com.

Eat this!

DOSSIER

Genre: Kick Ass Shooters **Publisher:** Dreamcatcher/Ubisoft **Developer:** People Can Fly/Crytek **Platform:** Xbox

There's an obvious reason why these two games should be lumped together into one tidy little essay. Both were fantastic PC shooters released in 2004 that have now made their way to the Xbox. In fact, Painkiller was *Computer Games* magazine's runner-up Game of the Year, losing out to World of Warcraft. Far Cry, too, was a widely praised shooter and received a Metacritic score of 89.

These are not 100% direct ports of the PC games, however. Whether fans of the series like the degree of the changes varies, but if you strictly play console games and didn't get to experience these shooters, you should definitely give these Xbox versions a whirl.

THEY SAID IT

"Far Cry Instincts AI is based on the Far Cry PC version, and has been adapted for the console version. Having enemies tracking you is a major point. We kept the wide open environments we had for the PC, allowing the AI to go anywhere the player goes. This is very important because in the first part of the game, the player will be a prey." —**Laurent Mascherpa, Technical Creative Director of Far Cry Instincts**

Image courtesy of GameSpy.com.

The graphics in Instincts will not disappoint.

Painkiller: Hell Wars

Painkiller is not a stealth game. In fact, it is one of the most in-your-face, run-and-gun games of the past decade. This is the game DOOM 3 should have been, but wasn't. The storyline involves double-crossing demons, angels, and your fight out of Purgatory where you battle it out in seemingly random, incoherently stringed levels that have nothing to do with each other than to allow the developers to stretch their creative minds and create monsters the likes of which you have never seen in a shooter.

The game is a bit different than it was on the PC. There are some new levels, monsters, and weapons and People Can Fly has taken the best levels from the original and the expansion and made a "best of" for the Xbox version. Best of all, Dreamcatcher has stated that the game will sell at a "budget" price, so you won't have to shell out $50 for it.

Far Cry Instincts

In terms of approach, Painkiller and Far Cry could not be any more different. In Far Cry, although you do get to blow a lot of stuff up, there are also several stealth sequences and vehicles to ride. This is also as far from Purgatory as you can get, with the game taking place on a tropical island paradise. The game's developers are also talking up its AI, whereas the AI in Painkiller consists of the enemies yelling "CHARGE!"

In the Xbox version, you still get to play Jack Carver, but the vastly drawn maps have been scaled back a bit for the Xbox. You also get to use some new "powers" after being experimented on during the game—stuff like enhanced strength and vision, self-healing, that sort of thing.

Both games should make a good splash on the Xbox, even if they don't look quite as good as they did on the PC. Xbox gamers should get to experience these great games, just like PC gamers should one day get to play Halo 2. Right, Microsoft? Halo 2 is coming out on the PC one day, right?

DID YOU KNOW

During the development of the original Far Cry, German police raided the offices at Crytek on suspicion that the company was using unlicensed copies of Maya and 3D Studio Max.

Full Auto
It's Burnout with Guns

The action in Full Auto is freaking insane.

DOSSIER

Genre: Car Wars Standard Barer **Publisher:** Sega **Developer:** Pseudo Interactive
Platform: Xbox 360

Full Auto is the kind of game that loves a nice TV screen. It's also the kind of game, particularly if you have a nice TV, that you want in your gaming library simply to show your friends how sweet the Xbox 360's graphics can be. You are certain to get a lot of "oohs and ahhs" from the peanut gallery when you show this to your buddies. It's also pretty safe to say that if you like combat-racing games with a tremendous amount of explosions, guns, and collateral damage, Full Auto is right up your alley.

THEY SAID IT

"I think almost everyone on the team is a fan of the Burnout series—as any self-respecting gamer should be. I had the pleasure of meeting one of Criterion's producers at this year's E3 and recently sent her an e-mail to congratulate the team on going gold with Burnout: Revenge. She was nice enough to respond and say how excited she was to play Full Auto. The team here at PSEUDO considers it an honor that editors sometimes label our game as Burnout with guns."
—**Cord Smith, Producer at Pseudo Interactive in an interview with Prodigious Gaming**

Um, yeah, these guys are out of the race. Ouch.

Wanton Destruction

This is a game in which you can leave your brain at the door; it's not a "thinking man's" racing game. It is, however, a pyromaniac's dream. The setting is the modern-day city of Staunton, a fictional city composed of five districts: the industrial zone, entertainment district, the garment area, and so on. Every one of the unique locations inside the city is ripe for destruction. You play a "death racer," one of many gang-affiliated thugs who race the streets of Staunton. That's pretty much the story.

Full Auto sports 20 different cars, more than 10 weapon types such as machine guns, missiles, grenades and even shotguns all with unlimited ammo, several game modes, and more than 60 events in the game's career mode. Multiplayer is supported through XBL, as well as in two-to-four player split-screen action on the same machine.

This is all well and good, but what truly makes Full Auto tick is the absolutely stunning amount of destruction that takes place during a race. Not only is the destruction inevitable—it's encouraged. You are rewarded by blowing stuff up via the Unwreck Meter. This works a lot like the Sands of Time in Prince of Persia wherein you can rewind time by a few seconds to try a shot again, undo a timely death, reattempt to make a tough turn, and so on.

Still, it's the physics, graphics, and explosions that steal the show. Everything—and I mean everything—can be blown to bits in Full Auto. Telephone poles, supermarkets, gas stations, office buildings, trees, bridges, hotels, statues, road signs, you name it: No piece of scenery is safe. Best of all, the destruction of Staunton happens in real-time—nothing is scripted or predetermined and at times blowing up one building causes a chain reaction and leads to massive carnage. Blowing up a gas station, for instance, can cause complete havoc as the district catches on fire.

Really the only question about the game is whether the frame rate will be as good as the developer says. Running on an E3 Alpha kit of the Xbox 360, the game never quite reached the promised 60 frames per second. If Pseudo Interactive can pull that off, combat racing fans should line up for this one. I mean really, who doesn't like exploding gas stations?

DID YOU KNOW

In 1999 Pseudo Interactive announced (but never released) a car combat game for the PC—it, too, was called Full Auto.

Kameo: Elements of Power
A Potential 360 System-Seller

Image courtesy of GameSpy.com.

DOSSIER

Genre: Another Gorgeous Rare Game **Publisher:** Microsoft **Developer:** Rare **Platform:** Xbox 360

Pummel Weed...the battling botanical.

Kameo: Elements of Power has been in development for a *long* time. Originally planned for the GameCube, the game shifted to the Xbox with a planned release date of 2003 after Microsoft snatched developer Rare Ltd. Obviously, that didn't work out, either. Finally, after more design tweaks and revamps the game has landed on the 360. (I hope.)

Look, Kameo might end up being a fantastic 3D action-adventure game. It certainly looks the part. But when a game goes through such a long and winding road during its development, it raises a red flag. I do hope Rare succeeds but gamers should proceed with cautious optimism.

THEY SAID IT

"One of the key features is thousands of enemies fighting on the field at the same time, which was something that never could've been done on the Xbox and was something we definitely wanted in the game.... The folks at Rare are amazing, they were able to port this from the Xbox to the Xbox 360 in just an insane amount of time." —**Dave Johnson of Microsoft in an interview with Koin.Com**

Why You Should Care

The storyline of Kameo: Elements of Power revolves around several key players. The Troll King, Thorn, has escaped from his stone prison (actually he's freed by Kameo's sister, the wench!) with plans to make life rather hellish for every other creature of the Elfin Empire. From engaging in acts of murder to forcing a mass exodus, Thorn attempts to create a society for his troll army. Kameo (that's you) is charged with stopping all this from happening. Piece of cake, eh?

Kameo sets out on an adventure where she must free her three trapped Ancient Ancestors, whom Thorn has imprisoned in different parts of the world. She also must track down the old spirits of the Elemental Warriors and convince them to join the cause. (Aragorn, you have a call on line one.)

Kameo has the ability to morph into the form of an Elemental Warrior, thus gaining the powers of that particular form. She can transform into Chilla, a yeti-like creature who is immune to ice-based attacks or Ash, a fire-breathing dragon. She can also morph into more bizarre creatures such as Pummel Weed, a vicious plant (yes, a plant, just like *Little Shop of Horrors*, sans the singing), and a giant rollerball armadillo.

Image courtesy of GameSpy.com.

If this looks sort of Nintendo-y, that's not by accident.

It's a mistake, however, to think of this as just another wildly inventive console action-adventure game. Some of the battles in this sucker are huge—flat-out enormous. The trolls and the elves are really at war here, and you certainly get that sense in the game as hundreds of units are on the screen at the same time battling it out. Kameo has to navigate this war-torn landscape to reach her goals and it's up to you to figure out how best to do it.

Kameo is a unique game with stunning landscapes and overall aesthetics. Will it live up to its vast potential? Well, it's a tough call. I hate to see games go through so many transformations, but it's hard to argue with what I've seen of it thus far.

DID YOU KNOW

In November 1983, Microsoft Windows is formally announced as a graphical operating extension to the MS-DOS operating system.

Infected
The Bird Flu Has Nothing on This

Another day, another dead zombie.

DOSSIER

Genre: Zombie-Killing Sim **Publisher:** Majesco **Developer:** Planet Moon Studios
Platform: PSP

It's a testament to the people at Majesco that I still vividly remember the 2005 E3 advertising campaign for Infected, a PSP shoot 'em up from developer Planet Moon Studios. Majesco grabbed a bunch of people (actors, I assume, because they were damn good at this) and painted and dressed them up to look like infected zombies. These *Night of the Living Dead* cast-offs stalked the E3 escalators, hallways, and the food court looking for brains. The make-up job was outstanding and I have to admit I was a bit wigged out when they started following me into the cafeteria. If I had known that I was supposed to *shoot* the zombies, it would have made E3 a hell of a lot more fun. At the same time they stood out enough that I wanted to find out more. Advertising mission accomplished.

THEY SAID IT

"The largest combo I have seen is a 15X. The Infected are vomiting on you, hurling their guts at you, they are swiping at you with their claws, biting at you, so to actually be able to carefully dodge these things and to get the perfect shot off to get an ultimate combo like that is quite challenging, but I have seen it done." —**Aaron Loeb, Producer of Infected in an interview with 1Up.com**

Infect Your PSP

The premise of Infected couldn't be any more straightforward. It's Christmas Eve and New York City has fallen under a shadow of, well, zombies. The Infected have taken over the city and it's up to you, of course, to kill them while saving the noninfected from a grizzly demise. That's pretty much it. I know this doesn't sound like the da Vinci of game design but hey—sometimes you just want to kill zombies, right? Your character has also been infected but, rather than zombifying, your blood has turned into a substance that can kill the zombies. With your viral gun in tow, you go out on a zombie hunt. Good, clean, family entertainment.

The single-player mode is fast and furious with roughly 50 game levels of zombie-killing fun. The multiplayer mode, however, is where things get interesting. Supporting up to eight players via ad hoc or local mode, when you lose a multiplayer game, your game gets "infected." This means that your custom-made character (from the single-player campaign) is replaced by the character that beat you. To disinfect the game, you need to either play through parts of the single-player campaign again (with your old character as an Infected) or beat three others in a multiplayer game and pass the infection along to them. You can then log on to the Infected website (www.infected.com) to see how the virus is spreading.

Infected might not be the best game to show your seven-year-old cousin who is visiting for the holidays....

Mad Cows!

Infected features a Mad Cow multiplayer mode in which one person runs into a cow, and thus becomes the cow. You still get to use all of your weapons and you walk on two legs, sort of like a Werecow. You earn points each second you remain the cow, so you actually want to be the cow for as long as possible because everyone else in the game is going to be gunning for you. You want originality? Name me another game where you get to be a chainsaw-wielding bovine.

DID YOU KNOW

Other stuff named zombies: A potent mixed drink with pineapple juice, lime juice, and rum; an emotionless poker player; and of course, there's the snake god of Haiti, which is where the term originated.

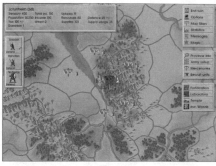

Dominions II is an awesome game to play via email. It's damn hard, though.

Play by Email Games
The Best in PBEM Gaming

Grab Bag

If you're an old-school gamer, you have almost certainly heard of play by email (PBEM) gaming. Playing games via email used to be a fairly common way to play multiplayer games prior to the days of the broadband connection. In fact, a lot of high profile games supported play by email right out of the box. Today? Well, not so much.

Still, playing a game leisurely by email is a lot of fun; it obviously takes a long time, in most cases, but it can also be surprisingly addictive. It's also a very convenient way to play a game with a group of friends. For many grown-up gamers, it's tough to get a group of buddies together, particularly if they are scattered throughout the globe. PBEM gets by the usual time zone issues and the simple fact that it's hard to pencil in a few hour long blocks just for online gaming unless you don't have a job and have nothing else to do.

PBEM games help alleviate the pressure of actually showing up at a designated time. You can play almost anything via email: strategy games, war games, role-playing games, sports games...you name it. Here are a few examples of the kind of games that you can play via email as well as a few websites to help you hook up with fellow gamers looking for a similar experience.

Ab Initio Games (www.pbmsports.com). This is a company located in the U.K. that specializes in the production of PBEM games. You can play (for a small fee) all sorts of original games here. You can join a PBEM baseball league, hockey league, soccer league, and even an NFL football league. The site also offers games in other areas, such as Barbarians at the Gate and a sci-fi strategy game called Star Chase.

KJC Games (www.kjcgames.com). This is another company that offers up original content for PBEM gamers. From modern-day strategy games like Warlord, soccer sims like Extra Time, and epic sci-fi games such as Phoenix, KJC offers a small, but high quality game list from which to choose.

Lords of the Earth (www.throneworld.com/lords). This old-time wargame has been around for more than a decade. You play as the king or queen of a real-world medieval or totally fictional fantasy nation, battling it out via war and diplomacy to rule the land. This is a very popular game and there are always several games running, so finding a spot is very easy.

Empire Forge (empireforge.com). This is another world-conquest fantasy game that is very popular and will remind people of the classic Axis and Allies board game (mixed with a splash of Diplomacy), only without the WWII angle.

Chess Here (www.chesshere.com). Chess was probably the first game to be played via email. Playing the classic game this way is called *correspondence chess* and Chess Here.com is a great way to find players, even highly ranked players, for a game of chess via email.

Dominions 2 (www.shrapnelgames.com). A retail game that just so happens to support PBEM play, Dominions II: The Ascension Wars is one of the most highly detailed, complex, and yet highly rewarding strategy games ever designed. It has a very steep learning curve, but if you love fantasy strategy games, you owe it to yourself to give this a look.

Age of Wonders: Shadow Magic (www.ageofwonders.com). Not only was AoW one of the best fantasy turn-based strategy games since Master of Magic, it also supports PBEM gaming right out of the box. If you can score a copy, don't hesitate to grab it.

PBEM RESOURCES

If you're looking to expand your PBEM horizons, be sure to check out **PBEM News** (www.pbem.com), the **PBM Home Page** (www.pbm.com), **Web Grognards** (grognard.com/pbem.html), and **Email Games** (members.shaw.ca/emg.pbm/emg.htm).

DID YOU KNOW

Although many think of email as a fairly new technology, it has actually been around since the mid-1960s on mainframe computers.

Condemned: Criminal Origins

These Guys Make Hannibal Look Like a Boy Scout

Image courtesy of GameSpy.com.

DOSSIER

Genre: Hunting Serial Killers **Publisher:** Sega **Developer:** Monolith Productions
Platform: Xbox 360, PC

Battling a lunatic with a 2 × 4.

Condemned: Criminal Origins is all about serial killers. In the game, you play FBI agent Ethan Thomas, a member of the organization's Serial Crimes Unit who himself has been accused of murdering two police officers. The rest of the game consists of you tracking down the maniac and his faithful minions who are actually responsible for the slayings.

Monolith is shooting for a first-person horror game with intense up-close action elements, but also for a game that oozes mood, atmosphere, and general creepiness while requiring you to use your noodle to solve the mystery. It's also a game best played with the lights out after the kids have gone to bed.

THEY SAID IT

> "Condemned heralds the coming of next-generation consoles with a frightening presentation of psychological horror. The next-gen Xbox lets us create detail, atmosphere, and game systems that approach a level of realism previously unattainable. For example, in our game, we have an enemy who berserk attacks at an extremely close range. The detail in his face, the spit and blood flying from his mouth, and his hands with dirty fingers clawing into your eyes is really something to experience and is quite disturbing—but in a good way!" —**Producer David Hasle in a Developer Diary on GameSpot.com**

From .45 to Mannequin Arm

Condemned is technically a first-person shooter, but a lot of the combat is done face to face. There's no hiding in another building with a sniper rifle in this game. Here's a list of some of the weapons that are at your disposal during the course of the game.

Standard Issue Weapons:

- **.45 Auto:** Your basic FBI handgun, the .45 automatic is a trusty weapon capable of taking down enemies with one shot.
- **Stun Gun:** The nonlethal stun gun might be the most important tool in the game. Incapacitating your target can be just as important as blowing him to bits.

Street Guns:

- **.357 Magnum:** Getting hit at close range by this leaves a mark.
- **12 Gauge:** The classic pump action shotgun is absolutely devastating at close range.
- **Sawed-Off:** This one only carries two shells. After that, you can either use harsh language or use it as a club.
- **Submachine Gun:** Obviously, using this 20-round machine gun will kill a lot of bad guys—finding ammo for it, well, good luck.
- **.308 Rifle:** The best long-range gun in the entire game. Use your ammo wisely.

Image courtesy of GameSpy.com.

Have shotgun, will travel.

Hand to Hand:

Although there's plenty of firepower in the game, a lot of your combat will be done at very close range. Condemned is cool because you can use nearly anything you can get your hands on as a weapon. A rusty locker room door, a lead pipe, a 2 × 4 with nails protruding from it, even a mannequin arm can be used to conk enemies over the head. In addition to improvised weapons, you'll be able to use hand axes, sledgehammers, and crowbars to beat on the psychopaths.

DID YOU KNOW

Many scholars believe that creatures such as vampires and werewolves were created in part based on the acts of medieval serial killers, going back as far as the 1500s.

Girls and Games
Wanted: Women in Game Design

Image courtesy of GameSpy.com.

Lara Croft: Heroine or Harlot?

Despite the fact that more girls (and women) are playing video and computer games, this is still for the most part a big boys club. Need proof? I have referenced the L.A.-based electronic entertainment expo trade show throughout this book (see p.87).

I have attended six of these shows over the years and one thing I am certain of is that few girls are allowed. Oh, they're there. You'll see female PR people (usually young and attractive). They work their tails off, but they aren't really there *for* the games. There is a small smattering of female journalists, too, but they are drastically outnumbered. Then there are the booth babes: Women that are there specifically to attract men to a company booth. Again, these women work hard. It takes a lot of resolve to wear a ridiculously revealing costume and have your picture taken with umpteen hormone-filled 20-year-olds and a gaggle of dirty old men for eight hours a day, but gamers they're not.

Image courtesy of GameSpy.com.

The Soul Calibur 2 version of Ivy was a bit um, yeah....

Breaking Up the Boys Club

Games are designed with men in mind, plain and simple. Even the so-called female heroes of the industry, such as Lara Croft, have the figure of a supermodel. What's worse is that over the years, Lara's chest size grew as Tomb Raider game sales started to plummet.

Look at Soul Calibur II as another example. Was there anything wrong with the art in Soul Calibur on the Dreamcast? Can we agree that it was a gorgeous game? Was there really a need to pump up the bra size of practically every female character? Don't even get me started with the hackery that is Dead or Alive: Extreme Beach Volleyball. There's almost no game at all in that game, just pixilated T&A.

To help alleviate this, the industry needs more female game developers. I know there are some out there, but they are few and far between. To me, this is the crux of the issue. If women aren't making games, how can we expect women to want to play them?

The Parent Factor

One reason why I think girls aren't into games as much as boys is the parent factor. I speak from some experience here. Parents treat girls differently than boys and it isn't that girls are disinterested in games, it's that they aren't exposed to them.

My daughter just turned five and she *loves* video games. From LEGO Star Wars and Spider-Man 2 to kid software like Winnie the Pooh Adventures, she loves to play games. The problem (if you want to call it that) is that parents get their son a console game system as soon as he's able to wield a gamepad, but girls for the most part get left out of the equation even though they'll have as much fun as the boys. Videogames are imprinted on a youngster's brain at an early age and if girls don't grow up playing them as a way to have fun or as a learning tool (like the Pooh games), by the time they turn into teenagers, videogaming will forever be a hobby that's foreign to them.

If you're a parent who is also a gamer, there's no reason to feel that your daughter will be less inclined to like videogames than your son. For me, it's a great bonding experience to play co-op LEGO Star Wars with my daughter, and she loves it so much that she begs to play several times a day.

I wouldn't have it any other way.

> ### SITES FOR "GIRL GAMERS"
> **GRRL Gamer** (www.grrlgamer.com), **GameGirlz** (www.gamegirlz.com), and **GameGal** (www.gamegal.com) are all sites that are operated solely by "girl gamers" and provide an insight on the hobby that is overlooked by many in the industry.

DID YOU KNOW

The "real" Lara Croft is actually the Duchess of Saint Bridget, a wealthy British aristocrat born in 1968. Lord Henshingly Croft, her father, appeared in the *Lara Croft: Tomb Raider* movie starring Angelina Jolie.

Panzer General
Closet Classic (1994)

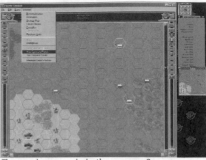

The opening scenario in the game as Germany invades Poland.

Genre: Beer and Pretzels Strategy Game **Publisher:** SSI **Developer:** SSI **Platform:** PC

Panzer General, the enormously popular 1994 turn-based strategy/wargame was one of the few wargames that actually reached a wide audience that included more than just hard-nosed military history buffs. Of course, some of those same hard-nosed war gamers scoffed at the game's lack of "true realism," but as a game and not as a WWII simulation, it was utterly engrossing.

It was also the first time I had ever heard the phrase *beer and pretzels* wargame. This is a term used by wargamers for a game that isn't bogged down in rules, but rather is the kind of game you can sit down and play while eating pretzels and drinking beer. Yes, wargamers are a weird lot.

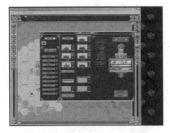

Purchasing new toys was half the fun. I want the Tiger Tank!

Birth of a Series

Panzer General was such a success that an entire franchise of "General" games spawned as a result of its success. Allied General, Pacific General, Star General, Fantasy General, Panzer General II, People's General, Panzer General 3D: Assault, Panzer General III: Scorched Earth, and Warhammer 40,000: Rites of War (which used the Panzer II engine) are all relatives of this "simple" war game.

The game's campaign system, which allowed you to play only as Germany, was brilliantly designed. Starting with the invasion of Poland, the game took you on a tour of Europe and Africa. A German official speaking to you in a demanding tone, offering little praise, and continually warning you that failure was not an option precluded each mission. He wasn't kidding, either. If you lost too many battles, the official would address you one last time right before you heard the cocking of a pistol.

Graphically, Panzer General was a real looker by 1994 standards. The maps were bright and colorful and easy on the eye. The 2D units were so highly detailed that you could easily recognize a Bf 109 from a Spitfire. Even the interface was grade A. Everything you needed was right at your fingertips.

Conversely, the sequel, Allied General, was one of the first games made exclusively for the Windows 95 platform and it was an absolute mess.

The branching campaign presented the gamer with several options. Would you travel to Africa to battle the Brits and Americans? Or would you take part in the invasion of Russia? This added a ton of replay value to the game because you could try a different route the next time you played. If you amassed enough Major Victories early in the war, you even had a chance to invade England in Operation Sea Lion, a real plan of Hitler's that never took shape due to Germany's loss in the Battle of Britain over the English Channel. Eventually, you either had to defend Berlin (which would end the war in a draw), take Moscow in a ridiculously short amount of time (if you took too long it would result in another draw), or, if you were really good, you would get a chance to invade the United States.

It was a wargame for the masses and remains a game that is a blast to play today, if you can find a way to make it play nice with Windows XP.

PANZER ONLINE
Head over to The Underdogs and check out **Play Panzer General for WIN95** (www.the-underdogs.org/game.php?gameid=4758) to see why this is still such a great game today.

JP's Panzer General Forum
(ep090.ezboard.com/fjpspanzersfrm17) shows you how popular the game is—there are still active forums such as this where people discuss the entire Panzer General line.

Allied General was one of the very first games ever released on the then-new Windows 95 operating system.

Gaming Threads
It's Better to Look Dorky Than to Be Dorky

There's plenty more where this comes from.

What do gamers wear? On the one hand, it's sort of a ridiculous question: What do *people* wear? On the other hand, you know what I'm talking about. Now I don't want to stereotype anyone here, but I think I'd probably get a big "amen" from the audience if I was offering free T-shirts, hoodies, wacky ties, or baseball caps to the next 10 people who emailed me. (I'm not, by the way.)

The bottom line is that you've gotta wear something. The only problem is that the stuff at the local Malleria is pretty lame. No, if you want cool gaming threads, you have to go online. Here are some of the best sources.

T-Shirts
Who doesn't love T-shirts? There's no better way to look cool, stay cool, and tell the whole freakin' world your point of view on whatever you want.

Game Goons Gift Shop (www.mallasch.com/videogames/gift_shop.php)—The Game Goons shop has tees with wacky sayings like "One More Level," "eat.sleep.game," and "game over"—just the thing to get comfortable for your next LAN party sleepover.

Hackerthreads (www.hackerthreads.com)—Shirts. Lots of shirts. That's the only way to describe Hackerthreads.com. These are the kinds of cool shirts that I guarantee will satisfy the inner geek in anyone.

Inkplosion Gamer Store (www.cafeshops.com/thegamer)—I was sold on the Inkplosion store the minute I saw the first shirt on its list: "Jesus Saves! Everyone else takes 5d6 points of damage!" If you don't get the joke, you don't deserve to be reading this book.

Everything Else
If you want to move beyond tees to something a little less casual, several stores will oblige. Sure, they sell T-shirts, but if you peruse their virtual aisles, you'll find cool ties (yes, there is such a thing), hats, hoodie sweatshirts, work shirts, golf shirts, and even patches.

ThinkGeek (www.thinkgeek.com)—One of the all-time greatest one-stop-shops for geeks, ThinkGeek has a huge line of T-shirts and (as they call it) "other apparel" for those with a tech frame of mind. From hoodies to ties (my favorite says "ties suck" in binary!) to hats and patches, you can probably outfit both your summer and your fall wardrobes with one visit.

Jinx (www.jinxhackwear.com)—T-shirts. Sweatshirts. Hats. Baby clothes. Even girl stuff...it's all here at Jinx. Although the merch isn't exclusively gamer, it's definitely got that techo-cool edge that'll make you stand out in a crowd.

ON THE WEB
For the ultimate in mobile electronics fashion accessories, check out the **eHolster** (www.eholster.com). Basically a shoulder holster for electronics, the eHolster keeps your gear safe while giving you that satisfying bulge under your jacket that can deter those with unsavory intentions. I'm not sure what airport security will think, however... .

DID YOU KNOW

At the 2003 GenCon, the hosts of the live-action RPG gme True Dungeon (www.truedungeon, com) would secretly let your party's thief choose between a "I screwed over my friends for this T-Shirt" shirt or give your party extra hit points. My editor's thief took the free shirt.

Grab Bag

The Xbox 360
Anatomy of a Weird Launch

I love my Xbox. I wouldn't go so far as to call myself an Xbox fanboy because I just don't understand the fanboy mentality. (My multibillion dollar corporation's console is better than yours! Huh?) That said, if a game is released on both the Xbox and PS2, I'm going to buy it for the Xbox. It's just better hardware, so I mainly use my PS2 to play games that are exclusive to that console (God of War, Shadow of the Colossus, Gallop Racer, and so on).

The first Xbox was black. The Xbox 360 is white. I think Microsoft has a whole yin-yang thingie going here.

Because of my affinity for the Xbox, I am totally jazzed about the Xbox 360. But that is despite, rather than because of, all Microsoft's best efforts to hype its new console as the best thing since the wheel. Despite all its attempts to deter me from buying one, I'll be waiting in line like the rest of you when it's released on November 22.

Defining Surreal

As I write this essay, it is early November 2005. The Xbox 360's launch date is a mere three weeks away. I'm excited by much of what I've seen, but I'm also worried that the Xbox 360 launch isn't going to go as planned, particularly if you are into sports games. EA Sports has already announced that games like NBA Live 06 for the Xbox 360 will ship without basic features like Dynasty mode. Oh, but we're to believe they're still worth a premium price tag of $60. They're like The Grinch before his heart swelled 16 sizes and broke that little measuring device in his chest.

The Xbox 360 controller has a hip "x" design on it, which doubles as the new Guide button.

The weirdness of the Xbox 360's hype started right off the bat when it was unveiled to the MTV-watching public on May 12th. The show was described by Microsoft as the public's first chance to really see the 360 in action. I watch MTV about as often as I watch reruns of *The Golden Girls*, but I couldn't resist tuning in. It was the next-to-worst 30 minutes in television history, right ahead of the final episode of *Blossom*. In 30 minutes, we actually saw about 5 minutes of game footage (Perfect Dark Zero, in this case). The rest was filled with songs by The Killers and some guys from the show *Pimp My Ride* talking about how to customize the Xbox 360. They couldn't even give us a straight answer on which Xbox games the 360 would be compatible with (a question to which we still don't have an answer). It was painful to watch.

New Levels of Gouging

A few months after E3, at the Leipzig Games Convention in Germany, Peter Moore, Microsoft's VP of Worldwide Marketing and Publishing for the Xbox made the announcement that the company would ship two separate versions of the Xbox 360: A bare bones unit for $299 and a deluxe edition for $399. The latter has a 20GB hard drive, component HD A/V cable (for HDTV support), a wireless controller and headset, and simplified version of the Xbox Media Remote (the retail version is larger and has more buttons). The bare bones model has the console, a wire-bound controller, and I guess a big red sticker that says "SUCKER" that you can slap on the front of the machine for all to see. Why? Because at some point you're going to want, even need, the stuff in the premium version and buying it separately will set you back far more than an extra 100 clams.

There is an amazing amount of confusion and speculation surrounding the console's launch. I'm sure the Xbox 360 will be a cool toy (yes, it's a toy), but Microsoft did a terrible job of providing necessary information leading up to its release.

Game Resources for Kids

Family Friendly Websites

Image courtesy of GameSpy.com.

This book is primarily about "adult" games, be they for very adult audiences, like Saint's Row and Resident Evil, or even "safer" games that simply require a bit more agility to play well, like Winning Eleven Soccer.

However, kids games earn a lot of loot every single year as parents try to find something for little Jimmy (or Jane). Sometimes it's an educational game that teaches the ABCs, or it could be a game just for fun but that caters to a much younger audience.

We all know Backyard Baseball is perfect for young-sters, but some games are a bit trickier to label.

The problem many parents have is finding a place on the Internet that focus on gaming for kids. Thankfully, there are several great websites out there; you just need to know where to look.

The ESRB (www.esrb.org). A good place to start for parents who want to know more about the games their kids are playing. The ESRB (Entertainment Software Ratings Board) assigns every game a rating based on its content. There is a lot of good info on the site, but it's very important to remember that not all M games (for mature audiences) are the same. You need to know *why* a game got the rating that it received. Was it for foul language? Violence? Mature themes?

Websites like Edutaining Kids review hardware like the Leapster handheld.

Edutaining Kids (www.edutainingkids.com). Click on the Games section to enter the videogame portion of the website. Edutaining Kids reviews nothing but kid-oriented console and PC games as well as hardware ranging from the Nintendo DS to the Leapster handheld. This is a very good site for parents to see whether a kid's game is actually *worth playing*; the games reviewed here are all safe in terms of content.

Gamerdad (www.gamerdad.com). Gamerdad is more is of a hardcore gamer site rather than one that focuses solely on kid's games. Gamerdad reviews pretty much everything from Backyard Baseball to F.E.A.R. It's a great website for parents who are gamers and want to share the hobby with their children. There is also a very active community forum for parents to get together and talk about games, which games to get for a child, and so on.

Noggin (www.noggin.com). As a parent of a five-year-old, I am all too familiar with the Noggin cable channel, but my daughter has just as much fun on the website playing mini-games with her favorite characters. Some of the games here also take you to www.nickjr.com.

Superkids (www.superkids.com). Superkids focus mostly on educational software. Still, it's an important website because I cannot count how many times I have wandered into the kid section of a game store only to be bombarded with all the educational games. Even as a hard-line gamer and member of the maniacal press, I get overwhelmed. This website helps alleviate the stress of choosing the right math game for your preschooler.

Sesame Street (www.sesameworkshop.org). Sure, there are a lot of cool games to play on the Sesame Street website but I add this mainly because I am amazed at how many parents, many of whom grew up watching Big Bird, have no idea that the website even exists. It's a great place for kids who love the show to play games with their favorite character and being *Sesame Street*, it's all educational as well as entertaining.

DID YOU KNOW

Sesame Street first aired on PBS way back in 1969 and still runs to this day, despite declining ratings and several company lay-offs in 2001.

Hammer and Sickle
Capitalist Pig Dogs Must Die

Be very, very quiet....

Image courtesy of GameSpy.com.

Genre: Obscure Strategy Game **Publisher:** CDV **Developer:** Nival Interactive
Platform: PC

Silent Storm, a World War II strategy/RPG hybrid was a vastly underappreciated game from 2004. Critically acclaimed, it has an 83 Metacritic score, but it barely registered a blip on North American sales charts (it was a bit more popular in Europe). But that's not stopping developer Nival Interactive, (developer of Etherlords and Heroes of Might and Magic V) from having another go at it with a pseudo-sequel called Hammer and Sickle, which would also make a great name for a two-man rock band, sort of like Ashford and Simpson, but with guitars.

THEY SAID IT

"Initially Hammer and Sickle was created as a fan mod to Silent Storm: Sentinels and we saw that this mod had a huge gaming potential. It was just about the time when we were opening a producer department inside of Nival to support interesting projects from other studios and teams. So we offered the creators of the mod, Novik&Co, all the required support to make Hammer and Sickle a real game." —Dmitri "Zak" **Zakharov of Nival Interactive in an interview with Gamecloud.com**

There's a lot of NPC dialogue in the game, just watch out for weird Russian translations!

Image courtesy of GameSpy.com.

Cold War "Politiks"

Hammer and Sickle is set in 1949 during the initial phases of the Cold War. You play a Russian agent who is assigned (more like forced) into a top-secret mission to infiltrate American- and British-held sections of Berlin. In short, you're a spy, and if you get caught, the Russian government isn't going to help you.

As you'd expect in a game revolving around the Cold War era, the plot involves political intrigue and the new threat of nuclear war. You'll meet a lot of dark shadowy figures as the plot unfolds. You have goals presented to you by accepting basic quests, but the game isn't broken down into missions like most other strategy games. Instead, you are a part of the scenery. Take Berlin, for example—there is plenty there to keep you busy. The NPCs, both the ones you need to talk to as well as regular citizens, follow a day/night cycle pattern. If it's 2:30 a.m., you can't go to the local grocery store to pump a contact for information. You have to wait until morning.

You're free to do what you want, but this isn't Grand Theft Auto in 1949 Germany. You do have a clear objective, but it's entirely up to you as to how to go about completing it.

Strategy + Role-Playing

Strategy fans will appreciate the Action Point (AP) system used during combat. When you're just walking around everything happens in real-time, but when combat occurs, the game shifts to a tactical turn-based mode. You, and your enemies, have a set number of action points from which you can walk, crawl, run, shoot, throw grenades, and so on. Everything you do costs AP during the round, even basic things such as looking in a certain direction. (Think Fallout.)

But the game goes a bit deeper than that by adding a ton of role-playing elements to the mix such as the ability to pick a basic character class like scout, sniper, or soldier and to customize his abilities by earning experience points and spending them on unique skills like marksmanship and explosives. Your character develops a great deal during the course of the game.

Hammer and Sickle won't appeal to everyone, but for those who love strategy/RPGs, it looks like a certified winner.

ON THE WEB

S2 HQ (www.strategycore.co.uk/s2hq) is a great fan site for Silent Storm—a game that is a bargain today at under $20.

Keep updated on Hammer and Sickle at the **Nival forums** (forum.nival.com/eng).

DID YOU KNOW

Although Nival Interactive is best known for its Etherlords series as well as the fact that it's developing Heroes of Might and Magic V, it also developed the World War II RTS series, Blitzkrieg.

Saint's Row
The 360's Grand Theft Auto Clone

Image courtesy of GameSpy.com.

I like his green shoe laces. Oh, the explosion is kinda cool, too.

DOSSIER

Genre: Unofficial GTA Sequel **Publisher:** THQ **Developer:** Volition **Platform:** Xbox 360

It's still up in the air as to whether the Grand Theft Auto series will make the leap to the Xbox 360 any time soon. For those unwilling to wait, I present Saint's Row—THQ and developer Volition's take on modern-day urban thug life.

THEY SAID IT

"The city is controlled by three other gangs. Each gang controls one territory and each territory is made of a number of neighborhoods—you control Saint's Row. There are a number of activities in each territory. You choose which ones you want to play and how often you play them. Completing activities—such as randomly killing enemy gang members—earns you respect, which in turn unlocks story missions and reveals stronghold locations. Each story mission or stronghold conquest earns you one neighborhood. Conquer all the neighborhoods and you win." —**Jacques Hennequet, Senior Producer for Saint's Row, in an interview with Gamepro.com**

From Humble Beginnings

Although Saint's Row has a fairly robust character creation model that allows you to alter nearly everything about your appearance, one thing that doesn't change is the fact that you start out as a low level hood in the 3rd Street Saint's gang. As you play through the main campaign—and there is definitely a central storyline—your reputation and gangland fame increase through completing side missions. When your respect is high enough, rival gang hideouts and other previously locked locations become available to help advance the main story.

The side game activities include stuff like shooting random rival gang members, fleeing from chasing cars, running drugs, car jacking, and even kidnapping a prostitute. Hey, what can I say—one man's disgusting form of entertainment is another man's dream game.

Saint's Row isn't mission based like the GTA games; it's a bit more open ended than that. Part of the game is simply roaming the streets looking for stuff to do. Completing tasks earns you money, which can then be spent on clothes, accessories, car decals, and so on. You can even buy customized underwear.

Image courtesy of GameSpy.com.

You can buy better cars than this, I promise.

You can also call a homie. Really, that's what Volition calls this feature. Basically this allows you to call up fellow gang members in your personal address book to join your posse as sidekicks, drivers, and so on.

The Tunes

Music is a very important part of Saint's Row. You get an in-game MP3 player that allows you to import as many tunes as you want via your iPod (or whatever device you have). You can then use those songs as part of the soundtrack as you roam the streets. How cool will it be to cruise the city to some Air Supply? There are also ten radio stations you can tune into that carry more than 100 original artist music tracks.

Multiplayer Thug Life

Finally, there's Xbox Live support, which is where things might get very interesting. Volition is planning to allow up to 12 people online at the same time, forming their own gangs, earning online loot to unlock more stuff, and playing in several online modes such as basic Deathmatch, Big Ass Chains (where you try to collect as many chains as you can), or even two-player co-op modes.

DID YOU KNOW

The term *volition* actually means the study of will, choice, and decision. Does that not sound like the perfect name for a videogame developer?

Prince of Persia: The Two Thrones
More Trouble Playing in the Sand

This Prince of Persia is still all about fighting and playing acrobat.

DOSSIER

Genre: Spilt Princely Personalities **Publisher:** Ubisoft **Developer:** Ubisoft Montreal
Platform: Xbox, PS2, GameCube, PC

Is Ubisoft ever going to give the Prince a name? I mean come on! You'd think someone would slip up and say his name at least once during all of these damn games, right? An evil swordsman charges and says, "Death to Prince Jones!" or something like that. But no, he's still just the Prince, and I guess we're just going to have to live with that.

The story in The Two Thrones sees the Prince return from the Isle of Time to Babylon only to find it under attack. Kaileena, the Empress of Time from The Warrior Within, is murdered and the Sands of Time spill out and curse everything in their path. As usual, the Sands turn everything that is alive into lovely demonic-looking monsters. This time the Sands even affect the Prince himself. Seriously, at some point the Prince is going to have to move somewhere, *anywhere*, where's there's no sand.

While it's not *required* that you play both The Sands of Time and Warrior Within, it is highly recommended if you care at all about the game's storyline.

THEY SAID IT

> "Speed Kill is about killing your enemy BEFORE being detected. This new system made us rethink the whole AI of the enemies in the game, and the results so far are very impressive. Patrolling enemies will be able to detect the Prince, either by seeing him or by hearing him. If the Prince goes undetected, he will be able to trigger a series of Speed Kill attacks that lead to spectacular finishing moves." **—Ubisoft team interview at TeamXbox.com**

The Dark Prince

The exposure to the Sands of Time has a Dr. Jekyll and Mr. Hyde, Good Ash–Bad Ash impact on the Prince. Sometimes the Prince is the swashbuckling loveable hero, and at other times he's the sinister Dark Prince, who looks, moves, and even attacks differently than when he's in normal Prince Mode.

The Dark Prince is sarcastic, reckless, and pretty much a total jerk who is bent on revenge. However, he also has some wicked attacking abilities.

You can't change into the Dark Prince when you want to; certain circumstances trigger the change and there are scripted times that the transformation takes place in order to continue the story. Water soothes the prince, however, so if you turn into the Dark Prince, you can get back to normal by finding water or wading in a pool.

Another point about the Dark Prince is that he's not healthy; the Dark form is cursed with the disease from the Sands of Time so his health slowly deteriorates over time and finding a healing water source is important. If the Prince stays the Dark Prince for too long, the Sands consume him, turning him into one of the Sand minions. That's not good.

Umm. OUCH!

The Dark Prince also uses a different weapon than the Prince, the Daggertail, which is a barbed-chain weapon capable of doing serious damage. He can use it to activate switches from afar, strangle enemies, or to swipe at enemies from a distance.

When you combine the fact that The Two Thrones looks amazing, offering up a wider variety of landscapes and enemies, it looks like a can't-miss game for fans of the earlier titles. Still, I strongly suggest playing the first two games before jumping into this one. What? You have something better to do?

THE SWORDSMEN
www.theswordsmen.net/swordsmen is by far the best community site for PoP on the Net.

DID YOU KNOW

The Two Thrones uses the "alternative" ending from The Warrior Within as the true ending of that game. Don't worry, it's all explained at the start of the new game.

Energy Drinks
Because Gatorade Is for Pansies

A few chugs of Bawls and LAN fatigue just melts away.

Sometimes coffee and soda just don't cut it anymore. You know what I'm talking about: It's about 2 a.m. and your LAN party is going strong. You've been kicking serious butt for hours, but you're losing your edge. Your friends might be chugging soda by the gallon or downing mega-cups of coffee. You? You're a little smarter. Just when you feel yourself starting to slow down, you dip into that minicooler by your feet and yank out your secret weapon—energy drinks so advanced, so packed with brain-tweaking goodness that those Red Bulls or Cokes your buds are chugging look like 486s by comparison.

It used to be that if you needed a caffeine rush, you had your choice of soda, coffee, caffeine tabs, or possibly a particularly strong cup of tea. Jolt soda came along in 1986 featuring "all the sugar and twice the caffeine" and become a favorite of hackers and coders worldwide. But you probably want more, and you should. If you take a second and read the labels on most energy drinks, you'll discover that the "energy" part really just comes from super-high levels of sugar.

If you want a real edge, you need to go a little off the beaten path and check out where commercial energy drinks and nutraceutical drinks (also known as *smart drinks* or *nootropic drinks*) collide. These not only provide good stuff like caffeine and sugar, but also kick their brain-tweaking powers up a notch by including substances that make you smarter and more alert, better able to concentrate, and more responsive—just what you need when the action gets hardcore at 2 a.m.

Bawls

Bawls's blue knobby bottle has become a favorite of gamers everywhere; check out www.bgcg.net for details. Bawls gets its kick from guarana, a seed from a vine that grows in Brazil and a longtime ingredient in drinks found south of the border. The active ingredient is still caffeine, but because guarana provides 2.5 times the kick found in regular caffeinated beverages, a 10-ounce bottle of Bawls is a little buzzier than what you get in regular soda. Bawls has a fair amount of sugar in it, but sugar-free Bawls Guaranexx is also coming to the market. Visit www.bawls.com.

BongWater

Besides having the obvious beneficial side effect of irritating authority figures with its name, BongWater (www.drinkbongwater.com) energy drinks can provide that serious competitive edge. With minimum levels of sugar and carbonation coupled with high caffeine content (105 milligrams), loads of vitamins, natural fruit flavors, and loads of B vitamins, BongWater drinks can really help you keep going strong long after your friends are comatose from their sugar crash. These drinks are a little tough to find, but you can order from the site or find a retailer near you with the handy locator.

Dark Dog

Although you can't say much for the spelling on their site at www.darkdog.com (anyone ever heard of spell check?), you can say a lot for their drinks. Available in several fruity flavors, Dark Dog drinks contain guarana, dextrose, taurine, five vitamins, and loads of caffeine. Sold in more than 30 countries around the world, Dark Dog is what you drink when you want to lift your (metaphorical) leg to your competition with their mainstream energy drinks.

Life-Enhancement Energy Drinks

If you seriously want to kick it up a notch, check out the drink mixes at Life-Enhancement.com. Brought to you by nutraceutical gurus Dirk and Sandy Shaw, these pricey drink mixes go far beyond caffeine, offering supplements from phenylalanine (which some people think helps them deal with lack of sleep), creatine (for physical stamina), vitamins, taurine (the active ingredient in Red Bull), and other brain boosters. In fact, if you're really interested in brain-tunage, be sure to poke around the site for other products. It'll blow your mind.

DID YOU KNOW

Jolt Cola actually has fewer calories than Coke or Pepsi. Seriously. Read the label.

Sports Games
The Big Rip Off

I love sports games. I cut my teeth on classics like Intellivision Baseball, Hardball, Dr. J and Larry Bird One-on-One, right down the line. I have been playing sports video games since there *were* sports video games. So, it pains me to admit the fact that today's sports games are the biggest rip-offs in the entire industry. It doesn't matter how good some of them are, compared to other genres, sports games offer less bang for your buck. The weird thing is that as consumers we don't really seem to mind all that much.

If you have bought a new Madden game every year on the PS2, has it really been worth $300?

What's really frustrating is when a series takes a step backward, like the MLB series did last year. Sports games should at least be better each year, right?

It's not that today's games are bad; quite the contrary, modern-day sports games are amazing pieces of software. Anyone over the age of 30 would have absolutely killed to have been able to sit down with a copy of Madden 2005 back in 1984. If I were 12 years old today, I wouldn't leave the house!

However, the rush to get sports games to market on a yearly basis has caused the genre to stagnate to the point of absurdity. You really can't blame the developers for this. These guys are under the gun because they have to crank out games on a standard cycle and we expect them to be "new," which is totally unrealistic.

The rip-off is the price. If you are going to make a football game every 10 months that consists mostly of roster updates, badly implemented new features, and features that were broken in previous editions but still aren't fixed, you can only expect so much, right? Then why do we gladly pay $40 or more for games that are usually nothing more than rehashes of games that we bought a year ago?

This is all about money, obviously. When Take 2 released its 2005 sports lineup with a price point of $19.99, it was the greatest thing to happen to sports games since 3D graphics. By lowering the price, it forced EA Sports to drop the price of Madden and its other games, and both Take 2 and EA Sports sold a huge number of copies and gamers saved a few pennies in the process. It was a joyous time. It also lasted precisely one year.

With exclusive sports license agreements all the rage (see p.143) you can expect Madden NFL 07 to retail at the usual highway robbery price of $50 (or more) and don't be shocked if Major League Baseball 2K6 retails around $50 as well. When you eliminate the competition, the prices go back up.

I never have understood why sports games get such a free pass with the media, and again I am guilty of this, too. Can you imagine if Blizzard released a "new" version of WarCraft every 10 months and with each release the same engine was used with only minor graphic tweaks, a few new gameplay wrinkles were added, and maybe some new spells and new hero units thrown in, and charged *full price* for it?

It is, quite simply, a rip-off.

Paying $40 as year for a hoops game is almost as scary as Richard "RIP" Hamilton's mask.

Lord of the Rings Games

Image courtesy of GameSpy.com.

The Good, the Bad, the Gollumesque

The videogame industry is always quick to jump on a popular movie license. *The Lord of the Rings* trilogy screamed for a videogame adaptation, right? Oh, admit it. When you saw the scene in *The Return of the King* when they were dodging the big elephants, you didn't think, "That looks like a videogame?"

Return of the King, or as I like to call it: Return of Sadistic Game Design.

The problem is that when you take a great movie and try to pigeonhole it into videogame form, it usually loses something in the translation. The best *Star Wars* games, for example, use the *Star Wars* universe as a base rather than trying to make the movies into a game. So it goes with games based on *The Lord of the Rings*. There's some good, some bad, and some that should be cast into the fires of Mount Doom.

Image courtesy of GameSpy.com.

The Battle for Middle-earth is one of the best LotR games ever made.

The LOTR Lineage

LOTR: The Fellowship of the Ring (2002; Xbox, PS2, PC, GBA). This was a complete mess. The game is based on the book and not the film, so you get to see characters such as Tom Bombadil, but even that couldn't save the game from its own poor design.

LOTR: The Two Towers (2002; Xbox, PS2, GameCube). This was a better effort, but was nothing more than a 3D hack-and-slash fest; an orgy of combat that just happened to be placed in the realm of Middle-earth. Still, compared to Fellowship, this was a five-star bonanza.

LOTR: The Return of the King (2003; PC, Xbox, PS2, GameCube, GBA). Even though it's generally regarded in the press as a good game (84 Metascore), it broke one of my personal game design rules in that it forced you to replay sections over and over until you got past it. A "save when you want" design would have made this a lot more fun.

LOTR: The War of the Ring (2003; PC). A real-time strategy game from developerf the Ring was a very standard RTS that failed to use the Tolkien license to full effect.

LOTR: The Third Age (2004; Xbox, PS2, GameCube, GBA). A full-blown turn-based role-playing game from Electronic Arts, The Third Age was at least an original idea and not a video adaptation of the movies with its laundry list of famous characters. If you don't mind that, this is still worth picking up and at a bargain price of $20 to boot.

LOTR: The Battle for Middle-earth (2004; PC). Widely considered as the best Lord of the Rings game to date, this real-time strategy game from EA and the creators of Red Alert 2 and C&C: Generals didn't redefine the genre but made extremely good use of the license and provided some huge battles which fans of the series (and RTS games in general) appreciated.

Lord of the Rings Online: Shadows of Angmar (PC). See page 259 for a full write up on this Middle-earth MMOG from the makers of Asheron's Call.

The Hobbit (2003; PC, Xbox, PS2, GameCube). Technically not a LotR game, but it is based on another Tolkien classic set in Middle Earth. The game was awful, though...just dreadfully awful.

DID YOU KNOW

The games mentioned here are just the most recent games based on Tolkien's writings. You can go back as far as 1982's Shadowfax on the C-64 to find a game based on the books. In all, there are more than 15 games based on the books and films.

Heretic and Hexen
Closet Classics (1994/1995)

DOSSIER

Genre: FPS Getting Medieval **Publisher:** id Software/Activision/Atari **Developer:** Raven Software **Platform:** PC, Mac

Heretic doesn't get its due despite it being one of the pioneers of the shooter genre.

DOOM gets all the press, but back in the day, Heretic was its equal. I truly believe that. No one can possibly deny DOOM its place in the history of videogames, but Raven Software's classic first-person shooter, which also used the DOOM engine, was just as good a game, if not better.

Heretic hit the scene in January of 1994. Raven followed this up with a 1995 sequel called Hexen: Beyond Heretic, which was also a fantastic shooter and is vastly underappreciated today. These games deserve a lot more attention because when people discuss the golden age of the first-person shooter, these games are invariably left out—along with other games such as Rise of the Triad—which is a real travesty.

Hexen was another revolutionary game in the series.

Heretic

Chickens. When someone mentions Heretic, I cannot help but think of chickens because during multiplayer games you could find a weapon that turned people into little white cluck machines. This had nothing at all to do with the rest of the game, which had a medieval-mystical theme, but just the fact that you could zap someone into a foot-tall chicken is something I'll never forget.

Aside from morphing a buddy into a flightless bird, Heretic was the first shooter to offer basic inventory management. You could cycle through your inventory to use potions and other objects. In DOOM, you grabbed your gun and took off. Heretic allowed you to use your goodies later by carrying them around.

Here's another bit of trivia: Heretic was the first game to allow what is called *gibbing*, which is a way to describe shooting an already dead body in a multiplayer game and watching it explode into tiny bits. Heretic started that. Surely that deserves a cookie.

Hexen: Beyond Heretic

In October of 1995, Raven released Hexen, the sequel to Heretic. It, too, used a modified version of the DOOM engine but it was also ported to console systems such as the PlayStation, N64, and even the Saturn.

Hexen upped the ante a bit by allowing you to pick a basic character class (Warrior, Cleric, or Mage) as well as supporting eight players in a multiplayer game. Pretty hot stuff for 1995. Not only that but the game had a fantastic CD audio soundtrack.

It was basically a bigger and better version of Heretic with more weapons and monsters, larger levels, better visuals, and it was, for its day, one of the best multiplayer games in existence. I still vividly recall the weapons in the game from the countless hours of playing it over a LAN at college. Talk about funds being put to good use!

Late in 1998, Activision and Raven released the long-awaited sequel, Heretic II. Heretic II, driven by the Quake II engine, although considered a very solid game, was a third-person/first-person hybrid rather than just a straight-up shooter. If there was ever a first-person shooter franchise that needed to be resurrected, it's this one. Hexen III, anyone?

HEXENWORLD

All you need to give these old games a spin is at **www.hexenworld.net**—Raven even released the source code for Heretic, Hexen, and Hexen II several years ago, allowing gamers to go nuts.

DID YOU KNOW

id Software, makers of DOOM, not only published Heretic but helped make some of the levels.

Black Isle Studios (1998–2003)

Corporate Graveyard

Icewind Dale II was bigger and better than the original, and also used the then-new 3rd Edition D&D rules.

The PC role-playing genre (the non-online kind) is literally like a rollercoaster. It goes up, peaks, and then drops almost out of sight only to reappear again just when everyone else thinks it's dead.

Back in mid- to late '90s, it was on the downswing. Going to a game store and trying to find a good single-player RPG was nigh impossible. It was at this time that a division of Interplay, dubbed Black Isle Studios (BIS), along with BioWare, reshaped the role-playing landscape by creating some of the most beloved games in the history of the genre.

Black Isle's fall was a sad one. What did the company in was mainly its parent company, Interplay. Interplay was losing money like a fat man at a doughnut shop. In fact, Interplay had lost more than 20 million dollars at one point in 2003, according to Gamespot.com. When a game publisher loses that kind of dough, developing role-playing games, which usually take a long time to create properly, is a risky proposition.

Interplay laid off Black Isle's PC games staff in December of 2003, effectively ending an amazing run for one of the most respected developers in the RPG genre. The good news is that a lot of former BIS employees made their way to other companies such as Obsidian Entertainment, the developer of Star Wars: Knights of the Old Republic II, and the soon to be released Neverwinter Nights 2.

> "It took about a year for us to come up with a name—one of the reasons we didn't launch the division until late in 1998. We threw everything around from 10 Gauge, to Monolith (we found out that one was taken), to Colostomy Bag Food Fight. Good name for a punk band—bad name for a brand that needs to be on the shelves at Wal-Mart." —**Feargus Urquhart, former director of Black Isle Studios**

Fallout 2—it just doesn't get much better than this.

The Black Isle Lineage

Fallout 2 (1998). The original Fallout, the post-nuclear spiritual successor to the classic Wasteland, helped reinvigorate the stagnant RPG genre. Fallout 2 kicked the genre into overdrive and is considered one of the very best RPGs in existence.

Planescape: Torment (1999). This is considered by many to be the best of the Infinity-engine-driven games (this includes the Baldur's Gate and Icewind Dale franchises). Planescape: Torment has one of the best storylines for any game ever made and if you can get your hands on a copy, it plays just as well today as it did then.

Icewind Dale (2000). Icewind Dale was a lot like Baldur's Gate, only with more combat and a lot of snow. Unfairly criticized as just a hack-and-slash game, it might not have been Baldur's Gate's equal, but it was a fun romp regardless.

Icewind Dale: Heart of Winter (2001). The first expansion for Icewind Dale added more stuff and a new story, but it was criticized for being too short.

Icewind Dale: Trials of the Luremaster (2001). In response to criticism over Heart of Winter, Black Isle released Trials of the Luremaster as a download expansion that wasn't sold in stores.

Icewind Dale II (2002). A sequel that took place 30 years after the original, it was pretty much more of the same, but the fact that it used the 3rd Edition D&D rule made it a must-have for many fans.

Torn. An RPG in a new non-D&D world, it was cancelled in 2001.

Lionheart (2003). Black Isle was involved but the true developer was Reflexive Entertainment. It was pretty abysmal and was a black mark for the company.

Baldur's Gate: The Black Hound. A Baldur's Gate game for the consoles. Cancelled in 2003.

DID YOU KNOW

Black Isle was famous for codenaming its projects using the names of United States presidents. Icewind Dale II was project Madison and Fallout 3, before its cancellation, was project Van Buren.

Developers: Please, I Beg You...
Game Design Pet Peeves 101

Hurdles are cool, but why can't I save a game in progress in NCAA 06?

I am not a game designer. Being a gamer or even a game critic does not make anyone an expert on how best to design games. In fact, I subscribe to the John Cleese (Monty Python, *Fawlty Towers*) theory of criticism. Cleese said, and I'm paraphrasing here, that most critics are critics because they can't actually do what they are criticizing. If they could, they'd be doing it rather than writing about it. Believe me, if I could program and design games I would not write about games for a living.

That said, I do have a few suggestions for developers and would-be developers. As a gamer for more than 20 years, I feel that I have the experience necessary to offer educated opinions on why a game is good or bad and what can potentially cause a gamer to chuck a game out of the window of a fast-moving car. Without further ado, I present to you, dear reader, five basic design lessons that I wish every game followed. If they were, the world would be a much better place.

Lesson #1: Allow us to skip every cut-scene. There are some really wordy games being made today. Now I know that there are story writers out there that cannot stomach the idea of a gamer skipping over their Asimov-esque prose, but these are games first and novels second. Every time a character starts to give a speech, let us skip it with a press of a button. Never force players to watch something that they don't want to watch. It's boring.

Lesson #2: Always create a good save game system. The best way to do this is to simply allow players to save when and where they want. And don't tell me game-controlled save points add necessary challenge. Baloney. It's called "making a short game seem longer." The world's on to your little secret. (Lord of the Rings: Return of the King, I am looking at you.)

Lesson #3: The less puzzle-y, the better. This is true unless, of course, you are designing a puzzle game. If so, go for it! If not, try to allow players multiple ways in which to achieve a goal. The best games are the ones where the experience that I have might not be the same as yours.

Lesson #4: Make the difficulty levels matter. Gamers come in all shapes and sizes and what is hard for me might be terribly easy for my wife. When you offer multiple levels of difficulty, they should have an actual impact on the difficulty of the game. I know this sounds obvious, but a lot of games fail miserably in this regard. If I want to play Painkiller on Easy, even people like my editor should be able to navigate it with relative ease. This point actually leads me to lesson five.

Lesson #5: *Super Hard* does not mean *Super Fun*. Although hardcore gamers love to spout about how easy Game X was and that they beat it in a matter of days, the reality is that most people who buy games buy them for the experience of playing them and not necessarily to get a mental workout. This doesn't mean that programming inept AI is fine or should be ignored, but making a game ultra-tough just for the sake of it is a really bad idea. The number one reason that a gamer will quit playing an otherwise fun game is out of frustration...especially if there's a cut-scene that they can't skip tossed in for good measure!

DID YOU KNOW

In what is perhaps the worst design decision of all time, 3DO shipped the PC version of High Heat Baseball 2004 without *any mouse support* whatsoever. Lesson #6: Add Friggin' Mouse Support!

Board Game Conversions
From Video to Cardboard

Civilization the board game uses a beautiful high color map.

It's not all that uncommon for classic board games to be ported over to the PC or other gaming platforms. Board game staples such as chess, Monopoly, Risk, and Axis & Allies have all been converted to video game format at one time or another. But there are actually quite a few instances where it's worked the other way around. Games that were initially designed as computer or video games later were were converted into tabletop board games. Here's a look at some of the more popular titles that have been turned into kitchen-table entertainment.

THEY SAID IT

"Civilization was relatively easy to do. We streamlined Age of Mythology, boiled it down, and then built it back up so that it took about two hours to play a game, which is about where we like it. A game like Pirates!, on the other hand, takes a lot more work because it's not a goal-oriented strategy game. It's more of a nonlinear adventure game, which makes turning it into a board game and keeping the same Pirates! flavor much more challenging."—**Glenn Drover, CEO of Eagle Games in an interview with Gamespy.com**

Civilization. Eagle Games publishes this remake of the Sid Meier classic. It was actually popular enough to warrant a second edition. The game starts in 4000 BC when you found a small village and build your empire up from scratch, just like the PC game. In fact, the idea is almost identical to the original Meier design, aside from the fact that you need at least two players in order to play.

World of Warcraft. Fantasy Flight Games publishes the official board game conversion of the Blizzard smash hit. The board game and its expansion set use an adaptable board that ensures you never play the exact same game twice. You can choose to play as the Night Elves, Humans, Orcs, or Undead. It tries to stay true to the game by using many of the same spells and creatures from the PC game.

Age of Mythology. Eagle Games took on a tougher challenge with the Age series. Converting a turn-based game is a bit easier than converting a real-time game. An Age of Empires III

board game conversion is still in development, but the company already proved it can handle the challenge because the Age of Mythology port has been extremely successful since its release. The game sticks to its roots as you control the Greek, Egyptian, or Norse cultures.

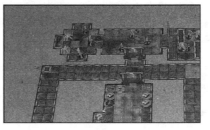

DOOM the board game is actually a hell of a lot of fun. Pun totally intended.

DOOM. Admit it. When you first played DOOM you thought, "Wow, this would make a great board game!" Okay, maybe not. The folks at Fantasy Flight Games apparently thought it was a good idea and it seems to have paid off as the DOOM board game has proven to be very popular. All of the trappings from DOOM 3 are here, from the weapons to the monsters. With tons of cards, multiple dice, and a wide array of maps, it's as close to DOOM 3 as you can get without mouse in your hand.

In the Pipeline. Eagles Games is close to releasing board game versions of both Age of Empires III and Sid Meier's Pirates!. Look for Pirates! to ship (har har) in the fall of 2005.

BOARD GAME GEEK

If you're interested in board games, and not just the ones mentioned here, you need to check out **Board Game Geek** at www.boardgamegeek.com. It's by far the best board game resource on the Net.

DID YOU KNOW

Eagle Games also makes a Lord of the Rings boardgame for kids ages 6 and up. It's a neat little game and perfect for a youngster who likes the movies.

Fixing Your Xbox Controller
It Can Be Done

The Xbox S-controller is one of the best designed in the biz.

If you really think about it, the controller might just be the most important part of your Xbox. Sure, the guts of the Xbox are pretty cool, pumping out some sweet graphics and killer sound, but without a controller you're just going to be sitting there watching the opening credits and CG cut-scenes from your game. Not so cool.

So, when your controller goes on the fritz, you need help fast. What do you do? You take matters into your own hands (pun intended)!

Basic Troubleshooting

First, be sure that you actually have an Xbox-compatible controller. You don't have to worry if you're using the one that came with your machine or have purchased a controller from a reputable third party. (Mad Catz, Logitech, and Thrustmaster are all good brands.) If you bought a cheap controller "as good as the Microsoft one" from some guy in some dark alley, you've probably got troubles enough already.

Next, make sure it's actually plugged in. Usually your Xbox will tell you if the cord becomes unplugged (either at the breakpoints or at the console), but if you start up your machine with the controller unplugged, everything will seem fine until you try to actually play a game.

While you're checking the cables, be sure everything's snug. Push on the connector where it meets your Xbox and test the breakpoints (called the *Inline Safety* by our buds at Microsoft) to be sure they're together.

If you have a DVD adapter, take it out. If that doesn't work, make sure that everything's plugged in and restart the machine.

WARRANTY MELTDOWN

As with any hardware repair, after you crack the case and start yanking screws, you void your warranty. You should usually think two or eight times before opening your Xbox. Of course, when a new controller costs only $30, why not give it a shot?

Going Deeper

This basic procedure is fine if you have a controller that generally won't work. If you have other problems (like sticky but-tons, a broken or eaten-by-your-mutt cord, or a problem with your stick), it's time to take out the screwdriver.

In most cases, sticky buttons can be resolved by cleaning the inside of your controller. By simply disassembling the controller, removing the buttons, and giving everything a bath, you can reverse the effects of too many late-night soda spills or peanut butter sandwiches.

Total Teardown

There's really not enough space here to go into all the details. But if you want to go deep, *deep* into your controller's guts, go to Llamma's Adventures in Xbox: www.llamma.com/xbox/Repairs/original_xbox_controller_repair.htm. Here you'll get detailed, high-res pictures and step-by-step instructions that'll make you a first-rate Mr. Fixit of Xbox controllers.

SHOCKING!

Now that you've lost your controller-disassembly virginity, you might want to check out an article written by TechTV nutcase Kevin Rose. It seems that ol' Kevin wasn't satisfied by the rumble in his controller. Kev wanted to actually receive an *electrical charge* when he got smacked in Mortal Kombat. Go figure. Enlisting the skills of a professional electrician (or at least claiming to...I have my doubts), Kevin married a 20,000-volt pest shocker (the kind to frighten off dogs) with his controller to create what he calls the "Xshok." Apparently it works, although no one's seen Kevin for a while....

If you want to check out how to do it yourself, go to www.techtv.com/screensavers/howto/story/0,24330,3450946,00.html.

DID YOU KNOW

The Xbox was released in November of 2001, but Xbox Live support was not available until a year later. By July of 2004, XBL had more than one million subscribers. That's a lot of Halo.

244   Holidays 2005

No One Lives Forever 2
Bargain Bin Special

Image courtesy of GameSpy.com.

DOSSIER

Genre: Hip Spy Shooter, The Sequel **Publisher:** Sierra **Developer:** Monolith Productions **Platform:** PC **Metacritic Metascore:** 91

The No One Lives Forever Series (NOLF) from Monolith Productions is easily one of the most underappreciated first-person PC shooters of all time. I really cannot explain why these games didn't sell more copies. They didn't *tank*, but they certainly undersold compared their level of quality.

Cate not only whups all kinds of ass, she also wears clothes in sub-zero temperatures. Lara Croft, eat your heart out.

In both the original, released back in 2000, and the 2002 sequel dubbed A Spy in H.A.R.M.'s Way, you play the role of Cate Archer, a member of the secret organization called Unity, which constantly tries to thwart the dastardly plots of the evil secret organization called H.A.R.M.

Both games are a mix of first-person shooter and first-person stealth-action rolled up into a very hip and ultra colorful 1960s backdrop—it's James Bond meets Austin Powers, but with a gorgeous female in the lead role.

Image courtesy of GameSpy.com.

Hold it! I have a crossbow and I am not afraid to use it.

What Makes It Great

As in every good spy yarn, you get to play with a wide assortment of gadgets such as body-removing spray, lock picks, and even an electronic dog that is used to distract guard dogs. It's campy, funny, but above all else—fun.

The sequel, which is really the Bargain Bin entry topic because the first game is getting a shade long in the tooth, can be found at some retail stores for as little as $10 and is still a lot of fun today.

Set about a year after the events of the first game, NOLF2 once again pits Cate against the evils of H.A.R.M. This time around the super-secret group is working on something called "Project Omega," which is an operation to allow Russia to take over a small island called Khinos, which would then set up a communist island resort—with casinos.

Cate is sent off to a lot of wildly different locations from Siberia to Akron, Ohio, from India to the Antarctic. In fact, there are roughly 15 chapters in the game, which span more than 40 levels.

What's truly great about the NOLF games is that they perfectly blend stealth and action. There are levels when, in true *Monty Python's Flying Circus* fashion, you are trying not to be seen. At other times, Cate has no choice but to grab an automatic weapon and go a shootin'.

There's even some role-playing in NOLF2. As you complete objectives, you gain skill points, which can then be assigned in one of eight categories, such as stealth, marksmanship, and stamina. Assigning points to various skills can result in better weapons handling, faster searching of bodies, and so on.

Both games can be a bit difficult to find, though. So, if you have trouble, you can always try contacting Chips and Bits or using an online auction site such as eBay, which usually has the games for as little as five bucks. For a stealth-shooter fan, it might be the best five bucks you spend all year.

A word of warning: The raves for NOLF and NOLF 2 are specific to the PC. The PS2 editions are really, really bad, so avoid the temptation and save the 10 bucks. Also, a spin-off game called Contract J.A.C.K. was released on the PC. It received a lot of attention while in development, but ended up being a monumental disappointment, so avoid that one at all costs as well. However, if you never got around to playing the NOLF games, they are two of the best shooters of the new millennia.

> ### NOLF GIRL
> This community site (www.nolfgirl.com) for the entire series is still active with regular news updates and a fan forum for all things NOLF.

DID YOU KNOW

This game should not be confused with the 1986 James Bond novel by John Gardner called *Nobody Lives Forever*. Of course, I'm sure Monolith is aware of its existence.

Ultima
Closet Classics

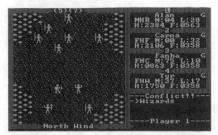

The Ultima III combat screen. This was awesome stuff for 1983.

If you are one of those young pups who grew up during the Age of the PlayStation rather than the Age of the C-64, you have probably never played an old-school Ultima game. It's hard to describe what it was like back in the early days, when the hobby of computer gaming was still in its infancy and designers were allowed to stretch their imaginations more than they are today.

Ultima, created by Richard Garriott (a.k.a. "Lord British"), is one of the most important, if not *the* most important, names in the history of computer role-playing games. It's a shining example of what was possible, even back during the primitive 1980s, when designers were allowed to make the games that they wanted to make, often in their basement or garage.

The Age of Darkness

Ultima I (1981). The original Ultima was a kill-the-foozle type of game where the goal was to destroy the Gem of Power, which was held by an evil wizard named Mondain. They'd get better.

Ultima II: The Revenge of the Enchantress (1982). A weird game, Ultima II had space travel, a map that looks just like earth, and locations such as San Antonio and the United Kingdom. If the series had stopped here, Ultima would be a footnote in the history of RPGs.

Ultima III: Exodus (1983). This is where Ultima started to earn its stripes. It is arguably the most important RPG ever made. It sported animated characters (totally new for 1983), a full party of heroes of varying races and classes, puzzles, and a cool story. Exodus was simply amazing.

The Age of Enlightenment

Ultima IV: Quest of the Avatar (1985). Ultima IV was another huge hit. The series took a turn here from the combat, hack-and-slash design of the first three and into a more cerebral, moralist approach. The goal wasn't to kill the evil boss man at the end; rather, you needed to become the virtuous Avatar (think Eagle Scout). Garriott himself considers this game the high watermark of the series.

Ultima V: Warriors of Destiny (1988). My personal favorite, Warriors of Destiny is a big reason why I had a rough sophomore year of high school. Not only did my grades suffer because of this game, but when a nongamer would ask me, "What did you go this weekend," I'd reply, "I finally killed one of the three Shadowlords! Death to Blackthorn!" I lost a lot of friends that year.

Ultima VI: The False Prophet (1990). The Avatar battles gargoyles that started plaguing the land. This was another technological advance (NPC portraits were used) and the story was well developed. It wasn't Ultima V, but that's a high bar to reach.

The Age of Armageddon

Ultima VII: The Black Gate/Serpent Isle (1992, 1993). Released in two parts, Ultima VII was an amazing game with highly detailed NPCs, and a brand-new real-time combat system. Many fans consider Ultima VII the best game of the series.

Ultima VIII: Pagan (1994). Pagan was the beginning of the end. It shipped about 3–4 months early, according to Garriott, to appease stockholders at the behest of Electronic Arts. But it's hard to imagine that a bug-free and finished version would have faired much better. Longtime Ultima fans mocked its console-esque gameplay by referring to the game as *Super Avatar Brothers*.

Ultima IX: Ascension (1999). Someone could write a novel about the insane development of Ultima IX. The development team was shuffled back and forth between it and Ultima Online. The original code was sacked and started from scratch. In the end, it was just another buggy, incomplete product with a weak story.

ULTIMA ON THE WEB

Tons of great info on the Ultima series can be found at the **Ultima Web Archive** (www.owo.com/archive).

EA might have killed the official Ultima line, but Ultima fans continue to work at reviving the existing games. Keep tabs on the fruits of their efforts at **Project Britannia** (www.projectbrittannia.com) and **Ultima: The Reconstruction** (reconstruction.voyd.net). Great stuff.

DID YOU KNOW

Richard Garriott chose Sierra Online to publish Ultima II because it was the only publisher to let him not only put his game in a box (instead of a plastic bag), but also include a cloth map.

Looking Ahead to 2006

I Am The Amazing Kreskin!

In the future, there are no bad games. As gamers, we can be eternal optimists. The Sony PS3 and the Nintendo Revolution will change the way we play games, and every handheld and PC game will be just as good as the public relations department claims. In short, 2006 will be a great year for games!

Okay, I really have no idea whether 2006 will be a great year for games. I do know that there are some cool ideas being bandied about—new game franchises waiting in the wings and old stand-bys about to get another fresh coat of paint. Fact is some of these games will end up disappointing us; it's just the way the industry works. It's easy to get excited about a great idea that is still in development, but to say without hesitation that every high profile game set for release in 2006 will hit a home run is irresponsible and really kind of silly. We know better, right? Still, previews are fun because the games are always great when they're still in development.

The entries in this chapter are obviously not a complete list and I'm sure you're reading over this thinking, "What about Super Cool Sequel VIII!?" Lighten up, Francis. If enough of you buy this book then that, and more, will be covered in the *2007 Gamer's Tome of Ultimate Wisdom*. For now, turn the page and take a peek at some of the games we know a bit more about that are coming soon to an overly crowded store shelf near you.

The Godfather: The Game
Mr. Coppola Does Not Approve (Seriously)

Image courtesy of GameSpy.com.

The cityscape definitely looks like 1945 New York, right down to the mom and pop shops

DOSSIER

Genre: Old-School Mobster Sim **Publisher:** Electronic Arts **Developer:** EA Redwood
Platform: PC, Xbox, Xbox 360, PS2, PSP

The vast majority of games that are based on official movie licenses, well, kind of suck. Honestly, how many "movie games" can you name that were worth the price of a used napkin? (We will ignore any cool *Star Wars* or Indiana Jones games for the sake of this exercise. I guess the Riddick game was good, too.)

The Godfather game is different for many reasons. First off, and most important, it looks really, really good. Seeing the game first-hand behind closed doors at E3 2005 proved that EA Redwood is not out to cash in on a movie license; it's trying to make a great game. This leads into the next point. A license for *The Godfather* isn't really a hot commodity. As fabulous as those films were (let's pretend *Godfather III* never happened), they were made more than 30 years ago. This isn't like trying to make a quick rip off of Ice Cube's *XXX: State of the Union* or a boxing title called Cinderella Man.

Image courtesy of GameSpy.com.

Take that you dirty rat!

Mob Stories Rule

We love mobsters. We can't get enough of mobsters. From Tony Soprano to John Gotti, we love mob stories and mob movies. So, when you take that premise and combine it with the level of care being put into The Godfather, the chance to play an aspiring member of the Corleone crime family is a very attractive idea for a game.

The Godfather game has a lot of violence from gunplay to beating guys up with baseball bats, but a very complex story unfolds during the game and the decisions that you make will have a dramatic impact on how it gets told. In fact, Mark Winegardner, the author of *The Godfather Returns*, is on board to help with script development and James Caan, Robert Duvall, and even Marlon Brando recorded voice work for use in the game.

The story, which runs from 1945 to 1955, is open-ended, so you're free to do as you please and approach missions from a variety of perspectives. You can try to be a Tom Hagan diplomat or go the Sonny Corleone route and fly off the handle and shoot first and let Fredo sort out the damage.

It's All About Respect...And Guns

During the course of the game you can earn Vengeance points, which means other crime families will be after you. You might also tally a few Crimewatch points if you blatantly disregard innocent bystanders or decide to rob the local fruit seller. Achieve a high Crimewatch score and the cops will be looking for you at every turn. If you play your cards right, however, you can actually have the cops on your side in typical mob movie fashion.

The game's combat model is also spectacular. You can aim at a particular area of the body and then get even more precise by using the Pressure Point Targeting system that allows you to shoot someone in the kneecap to hurt them, but still leave them able to spill the information that you need. The melee combat system is equally nifty. EA calls it "black hand" control and it allows you to punch with varying degrees of strength or even pull a punch in order to simply threaten someone.

DID YOU KNOW

Before Coppola decided on then-newcomer Al Pacino, James Caan was set to play the role of Michael in the film. How weird is that?

Supreme Commander
It Puts the *World* in World War

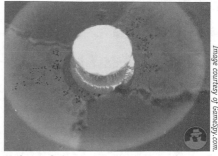

Image courtesy of GameSpy.com.

Nuclear explosions are sure to get everyone's attention.

DOSSIER

Genre: Total Annihilation Circa 2006 **Publisher:** THQ **Developer:** Gas Powered Games
Platform: PC

Supreme Commander is one of the most hotly anticipated titles for 2006, and even though Gas Powered Games has not set a firm release date, I cannot wait to get my hands on this thing. Even hardnosed game critics get excited every now and then. If this sucker comes together like the designers envision, we are all going to be in for a real treat.

One thing we know is that Chris Taylor knows how to design an innovative real-time strategy game. This is the man who was the driving force behind Total Annihilation (see p.144) and it's wonderful to see him back in the RTS ring again. This time he's taking real-time strategy to a scale no one has attempted.

You play as the "Supreme Commander," an overseer of a futuristic army on a truly global scale. This isn't WarCraft III or even Rome: Total War. This is global war where you will be controlling thousands of units across vast land masses, endless oceans and in the sky above the fray. This is real-time strategy turned up to 11.

THEY SAID IT

"…we call this genre 'Real-Time Strategy,' it should have been called 'Real-Time Tactics' with a dash of strategy thrown in. The goal with Supreme Commander was to really deliver the strategy, by opening up the game to an enormous theatre of war, with some incredible, never-seen-before Super Units, that absolutely require the player to think strategically before attempting to deploy them into the field." —**Chris Taylor of Gas Powered Games in an interview with GameSpy.com**

Think Globally

In Supreme Commander you can use the mouse wheel to zoom in and out of the action. Zoom in and you might see small units exchanging small arms fire as hand-mounted lasers fire back and forth at one another. Zoom out a bit and you then see a hulking tank emerging from the forest area. Zooming out even more, you see a hulking spider-like machine coming from the opposite direction toward the tank...the spider is about as big as a New York City block—it makes the tank look like a speck of dirt on the ground.

Another zoom out and you can see the coast and the enormous fleet of ships sitting on the shoreline. Bombers fly overhead, escorted by wicked-looking jet planes. Finally a full

zoom out reveals the globe and you can see little colored dots that represent your units. You can control the entire war from this viewpoint, zooming in and taking over when you want to see a particular battle.

Image courtesy of GameSpy.com.

A zoomed-out view of a section of the globe with your units as just dots. That big cloud is a nuke, which can cause tsunamis as well as destroy land masses.

The only fear I have is that it could be too much to handle. The game has only two resources (mass and energy), but controlling units on such a huge scale is a concern. Chris Taylor has repeatedly stated that you can automate enough to make it as manageable as you need it to be, but it's still something we'll have to wait and see to understand how that's all implemented.

Still, a truly epic grand-scale, real-time strategy game is long overdue, and fans of the genre must give this a look when it hits shelves sometime in 2006.

DID YOU KNOW

In 2002, GameSpy.com named designer Chris Taylor the 30th most influential person in the game industry. (Shigeru Miyamoto was number one.)

Hellgate: London
Part London, Part Diablo, Part Whup Ass

The weapons and monsters promise to be very...unique.

DOSSIER

Genre: Demon Killing RPG **Publisher:** Namco **Developer:** Flagship Studios
Platform: PC

Hellgate: London is the first title from Flagship Studios and it looks like a can't-miss game. It's an action-RPG in the spirit of Diablo but instead of top-down 2D graphics, the game is in full-blown gorgeous 3D. It has the look of a first-person shooter, but Flagship insists that it's an RPG first and an action game second.

I love it when developers try to create something new rather than building off of already established licenses. In an industry full of sequels and clones, we need more games like this. As you'll see here, there are lots of reasons to get excited about Hellgate.

THEY SAID IT

> "As a gamer, I personally don't like to be told what to do. I don't like looking up solutions on the Web. I don't like having to jump through the same hoops everyone else does. For this reason, we like to shake up the gameplay as much as we can. You won't be able to look up maps online to find where some monster drops what loot." —**Erich Schaefer, Chief Creative Officer at Flagship Studios in an interview with GameSpot.com**

The Story

Hellgate: London relies heavily on its story; this is not just a "go kill some demons" kind of game. It takes place in London in the not too distant future. Foul demons have emerged from Hell to take over the Earth and you are one of the defenders trying to stop them. On the surface that doesn't sound too original, but the backstory is actually very detailed. In this alternative reality, demons have tried many times in the past to enter this world, only to be thrown back by mankind. Demons were responsible for the London fire and the great plague, both of which were failed attempts by demons to destroy the world. As time went on, the Age of Science replaced the Age of Mysticism, people let their guard down, and the demons took advantage of it and stormed through the Hellgate.

Thanks to ancient secret societies such as the Knights Templar and the Freemasons, there are still some demonic defenses such as the London Underground. The subway stops are "demon-resistant" and are used as a HQ for mankind as they fight the hell spawn.

Leaping Frog Demons...from Hell!

The Random Factor

Practically everything in the game is randomly generated, so my experience playing the game will most likely be different than yours. The weapons are randomly generated as is the layout of each area. This is a lot like the design of the original Diablo in that each area is whipped up on the fly, except that this is done in 3D.

The weapons are also customizable. There are custom slots for each item so that you can upgrade your base weapon in many different ways. And because regular firearms don't hurt the demons at all, you can expect some wildly inventive weapons to be at your disposal.

Another example given by Flagship is that you could be fighting demons in the street when a Knight Templar comes running down the street; if you help him fight off his attackers, he might join you and become your companion. What makes this commonplace cool, however, is that the event is completely random encounter and not scripted.

Although the game is in 3D with a first-person perspective, it's not a shooter. There are stats, items, and inventory management just like an RPG. Again, think 3D Diablo in London with inventive futuristic weapons and you get the idea.

DID YOU KNOW

Flagship Studios is made up of several former key members of Blizzard Entertainment, many of whom worked on Diablo I and II, including industry veterans such as CEO Bill Roper.

Tabula Rasa
From the Mind That Brought Us Ultima

DOSSIER

Genre: Lord British's MMOG **Publisher:** NCsoft **Developer:** Destination Games
Platform: PC

It's going to take teamwork to bring this sucker down!

Sometimes it's hard being an "unbiased" member of the gaming media. At E3 2005, I was in a small room with a few other members of the press when Richard Garriott walked in to demo his company's upcoming MMOG, Tabula Rasa. I have interviewed and talked shop with dozens of big names in the game industry over the years, but Garriott is different. This was Lord British! This was the guy who was responsible for me nearly missing all of seventh grade because of Ultima III (see p.246).

At first it was hard to focus on what he was saying about Tabula Rasa because I wanted to raise my hand and ask him whether he really had trap doors in his house, how he came up with the Avatar idea for Ultima IV, and who, in fact, was responsible for Ultimas VIII and IX? Fortunately, I'm a professional. No, really.

Tabula Rasa has been in development since 2002 and what was shown at E3 was vastly different from what anyone had seen in the years prior. The old design, even though it was still an MMOG, was a very eclectic game with bards who could damage you by spouting poetry. It was "out there."

The new Tabula Rasa is a science-fiction blast-fest in which humanity was almost annihilated by an alien race called the Bane. Fortunately, a friendly alien race (the Logos) has taken in the surviving refugees and they're organizing a resistance. You're part of that resistance. It's part RPG and part first-person shooter, all wrapped up in a persistent online world thanks to publisher NCsoft, who is apparently taking over the MMOG planet with games like Guild Wars, Lineage II, Auto Assault, and City of Heroes.

THEY SAID IT

> "Building worlds means just that, creating real spaces for people to live in with their own unique history and culture and believability." —**Richard "Lord British" Garriott** in an interview at GameSpy.com

There is a reason why the Bane is winning the war....

The Gameplay

The action is fast paced and the control similar to that of a first-person shooter, but the core of the game is pure role-playing. Although you can manually aim your crosshairs at a target, your chance of hitting that target doesn't depend on your manual aim, but rather on your skills and stats.

The game comes with built-in voice chat capability and is just as much about tactics as it is action. Teamwork, just like Guild Wars, will be vital when confronted by Bane forces.

Tabula Rasa supports lots of players at one time, and when the Bane attack a human outpost (or vice versa), you're going to see scores of people fending them off. Attacks from the sky as well as from ground forces really make you feel like you are part of a living, breathing war.

Beautiful, Dynamic Worlds

By far one of the best features in the game is the idea that the things that happen during a fight have an impact on the rest of the world. The tide in the struggle is constantly shifting and when one faction controls a particular area, benefits are gained as a result. There's a reason for attacking locations beyond just because the bad guys are there. And the world itself. It's really something to see.

OGAMING

tr.ogaming.com is a Tabula Rasa fan site with a lot of good info on the game and an active news page and forum section.

DID YOU KNOW

"Tabula Rasa" (which is Latin for *blank slate*) is also the name of an episode in the *Buffy the Vampire Slayer* TV series. Seriously, I didn't make that up.

Scarface: The World Is Yours
The Original Miami Kingpin

Image courtesy of GameSpy.com.

DOSSIER

Genre: Grand Theft Auto with Pacino **Publisher:** Vivendi Universal **Developer:** Radical Entertainment **Platform:** PC, Xbox, Xbox 360, PS2, PS3

Scarface: The World is Yours is sure to cause a stir with antigaming groups because of its over-the-top violence and the fact that the goal of the game is to become the crime lord of Miami by killing rival gang members and selling illegal narcotics. Hey, if you're going to rule the Miami underworld, selling Girl Scouts Thin Mints is not going to cut it!

Yep, that's Tony Montana all right.

THEY SAID IT

> "We've already recorded over 30,000 lines of dialogue; just tons of dialogue. It's great to go to different places in the open world to see what Tony says, how people react to him, etc. This was very important to us so we've done a lot of work in that area. Gamers will have a lot of fun just with the entertaining dialogue and conversation all over the place." —**Cameron Weber, Scarface Producer, in an interview with TeamXbox.com**

It's Scarface!

This name alone is perhaps the game's biggest draw. Let's face it: If this were just another unlicensed game, everyone would simply dismiss it as a Grand Theft Auto clone. However, throw in Al Pacino's likeness (no word yet on whether Al will lend his voice), real Miami landmarks, and all the other movie tie-ins and you have the makings of a game people can relate to. You can also buy the upcoming Godfather game to get the full retro mobster effect.

The game is open-ended, just like GTA, but Tony operates a bit differently than a normal street thug. Tony doesn't kill random people; you have to cross him to feel his rage, so shooting innocent bystanders is a huge no-no (Tony might even refuse to do it). That said, you can still go where you want when you want. You can take Tony to a disco and boogie the night away, do a side mission, or just drive around in your sports car.

Business, Blind Rage, and Blood

In Scarface, Tony has to run his business which is under constant attack from rival gangs and those that are after his head. This isn't a game where you simply wander the streets

looking for trouble. It usually comes to you. Tony is all about money, not random violence; he's the mobster with a heart! Just don't make him mad.

Image courtesy of GameSpy.com.

Say hello to my little friend! (Come on, you know I had to go there.)

"Blind Rage" happens when Tony goes into the "zone" and pretty much turns into a violent killing machine. It's kind of like a bullet time effect because the game slows down and allows him to wipe out multiple enemies. In fact, the game starts off like this, with an opening scene that is actually the final scene of the film when thugs are attacking Tony's mansion. But in the video game he survives the attack.

There's no way around it: This is a very violent game. You can target body parts, shoot off legs, you name it. There's also a whole lot of cursing, which makes sense if you have seen the film. I'm not going to tell you how to raise your kids, but I'd avoid playing this with junior after he's finished with his multiplication tables. Still, Scarface looks like a promising addition to the genre. I just hope they get Pacino's voice.

SCARFACE MODS

scarmods.com is a well-designed Scarface fan site that is part of the MafiaMods game network.

DID YOU KNOW

Scarface the movie was written by famed director Oliver Stone, who reportedly named the title character, Tony Montana, as a tribute to 49ers football great Joe Montana.

The Witcher

Getting Paid to Lay Waste to Retching Undead

Geralt battling some soon-to-be mincemeat ghouls in an underground sewer system.

DOSSIER

Genre: Hacking and Slashing in 3D **Publisher:** CD Projeckt **Developer:** CD Projeckt
Platform: PC

The Witcher is a third-person action-oriented role-playing game from Polish publisher CD Projeckt. The game is actually based on the works of popular Polish fantasy writer Andrzej Sapkowski's series of novels. (Popular in Europe, that is.)

After seeing a private showing of the game at the E3 trade show in May of 2005, my personal anticipation for it went up tenfold. The Witcher looks like it could be a sleeper hit, with great action sequences and a lot of potentially deep role-playing all wrapped up in an open-ended "do what you want" setting.

THEY SAID IT

"We're constantly in touch with BioWare and they have supported us greatly with their knowledge and experience since the very beginning. We've received numerous hints and suggestions concerning not only the Aurora Engine, but also the most vital issues concerning the mechanics of an RPG design process." —**CD Projeckt spokesperson in an interview at Gamebanshee.com**

A New Hero, an Old Engine

The Witcher himself is an anti-hero of sorts. No one trusts him because of his shady past, but the people need him to defeat the enemy presence. The lead hero, Geralt, is actually one of many Witchers in the game world; they are monsters hunters who have been trained since birth to track down and annihilate evil. However, our hero isn't out to save the world: being a Witcher is his job. He's in it for the money, not to save peasants from werewolf attacks.

The game uses a heavily modified version of BioWare's Neverwinter Nights engine, called Aurora. It's amazing how much CD Projeckt has tinkered with things because Neverwinter Nights never looked this good with its highly detailed underground areas and sprawling outdoor environments. The cool thing about using this engine is that BioWare has offered to lend a hand when necessary and anytime BioWare touches a game, it turns into RPG gold.

Real-Time Combat

This isn't Knights of the Old Republic. This is a real-time combat engine that allows you to duck, jump, spin, and use your sword to amazing effect. The Witcher is supposedly one of the most deadly hand-to-hand fighters in the world and the game does a fantastic job of showcasing this ability. Toss in Criterion's Karma Physics Engine (so that a zombie's head falls off *just right*...) and you potentially have a combat system that role-playing fans as well as action fans will be drawn to.

The game isn't all about hacking up bad guys. There's a huge and highly detailed storyline to follow.

Quests Out the Yin-Yang

This isn't a "grab your sword and hack your way to glory" kind of game, although you will certainly be doing a lot of fighting. This is a role-playing game first and an action game second. You can approach quests in various ways. Your actions during the game will also determine NPCs' attitude toward you, and just like in Sapkowski's books, you're never quite sure who to trust.

THE WITCHER HOME PAGE

For up to the minute info on the game's development as well as an active fan forum, head over to www.the-witcher.com. You can also sign up for a newsletter for more detailed info on the inner workings of the game and the world of The Witcher.

DID YOU KNOW

Founded in May of 1994, CD Projeckt, publisher of The Witcher, was the first ever international game publisher to be located in Poland.

Heroes of Might and Magic V
A Legend Returns

The Haven units on glorious 3D!

DOSSIER

Genre: HoMM Goes 3D **Publisher:** Ubisoft **Developer:** Nival Interactive **Platform:** PC

The Heroes of Might and Magic series (HoMM) of turn-based strategy games is one of the most beloved of all time. The games have been leisurely with bright, colorful 2D graphics, outstanding music, and a charm that was all its own. Its design was fairly simple: You recruited heroes who led armies across a large map, picking up resources and magic items along the way. When armies met, the game shifted to a tactical battle mode in which creatures battled it out while the heroes sat back and cast spells and provided moral support for the troops.

The series started (officially) in 1995 and went though three sequels along with several expansion packs. When publisher 3DO declared bankruptcy in 2003, many thought the series was dead forever. Ubisoft, however, announced plans to revive the franchise with the help of developer Nival Interactive and the fifth installment of this classic series is set for a spring of 2006 release.

THEY SAID IT

> "The concerns I've read regard more the number of creatures. I was very interested in reading fans' calculations, including upgrades and add-ons. I think it ended on around 130 creatures in Heroes III. I dare say we will easily top that." —**Fabrice Cambounet, Producer of HoMMV, in an interview with CelestialHeavens.com**

What We Know

A lot of the intricate details for HoMMV have not been released yet. For example, we know that the Inferno town type will return (think Mordor) along with a Holy Knight town type (called The Haven), but the other four are still a secret. Here's some of what we do know.

Heroes goes glorious 3D! Hard-line gamers will tell you that graphics are always secondary to gameplay but it's impossible to deny the fact that Heroes V looks stunning. If you are familiar with the series and its staple cheery 2D graphics, to see the new version in full-blown, highly detailed 3D graphical splendor is quite a shock.

Back to the future. Heroes V pretty much removes everything that was done in Heroes IV, which was considered the low watermark of the series. Instead, Nival is going back to the spirit of Heroes III, which means that the hero characters will not take part in the actual combat, but rather will play a supporting role, casting spells, providing combat boosts, and so on.

Dynamic combat. A brand new, but optional, feature is the ability to switch from basic turn-based combat to a dynamic model that is being described as "not real-time, but close to it." It involves gathering action points to take multiple actions and it happens in pseudo real-time, so you have to act quickly.

Inferno versus Haven...in glorious 3D!!

Ghost Mode. Playing a multiplayer turn-based game is a real pain because there's a lot of downtime between turns. The new Ghost Mode allows you to take actions while it's not your turn so that you aren't left twiddling your thumbs while your opponents take five minutes weighing their options.

CELESTIAL HEAVENS
All Heroes all the time, **www.celestialheavens.com** is by far the best HoMM resource on the Net. Along with Heroes V info, you can get new maps and campaigns for the older games.

DID YOU KNOW

The 1990 release King's Bounty is often referred to as the original Heroes game because it used very similar game mechanics and was also developed by New World Computing, the developer of Heroes I through IV.

Parkan II
From Russia with Love

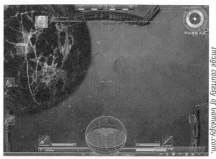
Image courtesy of GameSpy.com.

Exploring the vastness of space in Parkan II.

DOSSIER

Genre: Genre Blending Space Sim **Publisher:** 1C Company **Developer:** Nikita
Platform: PC

I'll understand if you have never heard of Parkan, let alone Parkan II. The original was released in Russia several years ago and never made it stateside. Publisher 1C Company has stated that the sequel will "without question" be released in the U.S., so finding it shouldn't be a problem. This is one of those games that might turn out to be great or could turn into an overly ambitious mess. It looked pretty damn nifty at E3 last year.

The idea is to take a science-fiction first-person shooter and combine that with a space flight sim like Freelancer or Privateer. If it all comes together, it could be a sleeper hit because although space sims are pretty much a dead genre to the industry at the moment, they still have a loyal fan base desperate for something new.

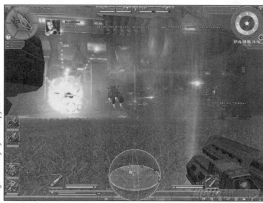
Image courtesy of GameSpy.com.

The action gets particularly hot during first-person land battles.

Roam Wide, Roam Free

Taking place in the vacuum of space has its advantages. Parkan II is a *huge* game with more than 500 star systems and 300 individual planets, all of which have environments varying from mountains to lush jungles. It's safe to say that exploring the entire game world will take a really, really long time and for a game that allows you to go where you want when you want, that's a definite plus.

You play the role of a star pilot of a Corvette-class star cruiser. There's a main storyline that you can follow or you are free to freelance your way to big money and bigger fame. You can simply play the role of space merchant or go a bit more militant and take part in huge planetary battles to take over an entire set of planets and declare yourself warlord of that system. You may then develop colonies on the planet or turn it into a factory world that just cranks out military units and weapons.

Unlike other games of this ilk, you can't buy new ships; you're pretty much stuck with your Corvette, but you can add a slew of upgrades, from armor to weaponry, to your ship as you earn more loot. You'll also be able to upgrade the droid units that help you when attacking a planet or defending your ship from a pirate assault.

First Person...In Spaaaace!

This isn't just a ship-to-ship game, though. You can drop into first-person mode when boarding enemy vessels or when pirates decide to try to take over your Corvette. Also, when you attack other planets with your Warbot army, you do so in first-person mode. This is the part of the game that will make or break the design: If the engine can convincingly handle the first-person side of things, then the game has a chance to be something special.

The game isn't catching a lot of press here in the States but it's hotly anticipated in Russia, and is definitely an under-the-radar game that is worth keeping an eye on. In fact, word is that it might not even ship to the U.S., so check out the game's homepage at www.parkan.ru/p2en for details.

DID YOU KNOW

Parkan II was actually released in Russia in May of 2005. A U.S. release date is still not set in stone.

The Lord of the Rings
The Battle for Middle-earth II

Image courtesy of GameSpy.com.

DOSSIER

Genre: Big Budget RTS Sequel **Publisher:** Electronic Arts **Developer:** EA Los Angeles
Platform: PC

I'm extremely excited about this one. Even though the first game was hardly ground-breaking, I was still a fan and this sequel takes that basic gameplay and adds layer after layer of cool new toys and creative ideas into the mix.

Check out those ships! The graphics are remarkably good.

Electronic Arts now has the exclusive rights to the content from the novels as well as for the movies, so there's absolutely no holding back when it comes to what it can and cannot use for this game.

THEY SAID IT

> "The single most requested Lord of the Rings character people wanted to see in the sequel was Tom Bombadil. He sings and kicks ass." —**Mike Verdu, franchise lead of Lord of the Rings at Electronic Arts in an interview with *Computer Games* magazine**

RTS Advanced

The most notable addition is that of unique naval units. You can build shipyards and unleash highly detailed ships to either transport units or engage in large naval battles. Also unlike the original, the units themselves act like they are part of a war machine rather than individual units. Taking a page from the Total War series, units form into organized regiments, and if a closed-rank regiment is attacked from the rear or on the flank, it has a devastating effect.

The old campaign system has been scrapped and in its place is a more Total War–style campaign with large Risk-style map of Middle-earth. It's not linear at all—this truly is the battle for Middle-earth, one province at a time.

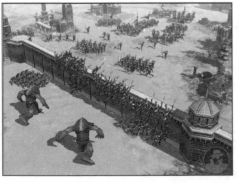

Image courtesy of GameSpy.com.

A glorious siege battle between goblins and elves.

There is a lot going on in this game, and RTS novices should take note of that before diving in; this is a game that will appeal to hard-core real-time strategy fans.

The Obligatory Extra Stuff

There are a lot of new goodies in the sequel. First off, the men of Rohan and Gondor have been consolidated into the Men of the West. However, there are new playable races such as the goblins, dwarves, and elves.

In attempt to make them all as different as possible, each race has a unique retinue of units; the goblins, for example, can recruit wicked-looking spider riders and the elves can field expert archers. The goal isn't to have each race play the same way, but with different graphics.

The forces of both Sauron and Saruman also get new toys such as the infamous Black Riders, boulder-wielding giants, The Watcher of the Water (the big octopus), and terrible blue dragons. Finally, there are more than 30 hero units in the game, including new faces such as Elrond, Arwen, Glorfindel, and the gruesome Mouth of Sauron.

This is just a sampling of what's new in the game. If you like real-time strategy games and love The Lord of the Rings, this seems like a no-brainer. It really could be something special. One game to rule them all and in the darkness bind them!

> ### THE MIDDLE-EARTH CENTER
> Battle for Middle-earth II will be very mod-friendly, so keep an eye out at **middleearthcenter.com** for some custom-made content.

DID YOU KNOW

Battle for Middle-earth II was originally planned as an expansion pack, but was turned into a full-blown sequel when EA was granted the full license for the novels.

Dungeons and Dragons Online
It's About Bloody Time

I would not want to be that skeleton right about now....

DOSSIER

Genre: Geek's Online Paradise **Publisher:** Atari/Wizards of the Coast **Developer:** Turbine **Platform:** PC

At what point does the massively multiplayer online role-playing genre implode on itself? How many customers are out there who are willing to pony up $15 *per month* for World of Warcraft, Tabula Rasa, City of Heroes, and EverQuest II at the same time?

Regardless, one game that should find absolutely no trouble in finding an audience, if it can live up to the name, is Dungeons and Dragons Online. Developed by the folks at Turbine (makers of Asheron's Call), D&D Online could conceivably sell more units than a Jessica Simpson CD at an all-girl middle school. Or, if Turbine screws it up, could bring down the wrath of obsessive D&D fans everywhere, and believe me—no one wants to see that.

THEY SAID IT

> "Most quests will be given out in town but at this point, there's no plan to make players wander over-world in search of the dungeon entry point. The focus is more about giving players as much actual party and dungeon time as possible." —**Lead Designer Ken Troop in an interview with Gamesdomain.com**

What's Unique

Taking a page from Guild Wars and a few other MMOGs, D&D Online will use nothing but instanced dungeons. What this means is that if your party is heading to the Dungeon of Doom, other players not in the party can't come in and steal kills. If another group goes in the same dungeon, they'll be playing in their own personal area, as well.

Another area in which I think D&D sets itself apart is that the experience points awarded to each player is determined by completing objectives and not sitting around bashing skeleton heads for 30 minutes. Just killing a monster earns you no experience; you need to complete your objectives.

Combat is another area where the game is a tad different. It's in real-time and also a bit more hands-on than your run-of-the-mill MMOG. You have to learn how to master the controls to attack, dodge, and so on. It's not an action game, but it requires a bit more mouse/keyboard skill than your standard RPG—there are even basic targeting controls and the ease of using them depends on your character's skills.

Tell me this isn't every D&D fan's dream!

D&D 3.5

The game uses the core 3.5 D&D rules but there are a few differences worth noting. You can play a human, elf, dwarf, halfling, or warforged. The available core classes are barbarian, bard, cleric, fighter, paladin, ranger, rogue, sorcerer, and wizard. (Sorry, no monks yet.)

Spellcasting works a bit differently, too. In D&D Online, spellcasters receive a number of spell points based on class, attributes, and so on. Spell points are used whenever a spell is cast, and are restored by resting. You also cannot craft magic items—yet.

Turbine has stated many times that if the game is a success (and with that license it is hard to imagine the game tanking), expansions will add more and more core 3.5 rules to the design.

DID YOU KNOW

Eberron, the setting for D&D Online, is a land created by Keith Baker and was the winning entry for Wizards of the Coast's Fantasy Setting Search, a competition run in 2002 to establish a brand new backdrop for the pen-and-paper D&D game.

The Legend of Zelda: Twilight Princess
Link Grows Up

Link, you handsome devil.

DOSSIER

Genre: GameCube Money Maker **Publisher:** Nintendo **Developer:** Nintendo **Platform:** GameCube

The Legend of Zelda series is one of the oldest, most successful, and respected in the entire gaming industry. There just are not too many franchises still alive and kicking that were around in 1986, and Zelda has not only survived since then, but it's flourished. There have been no fewer than 13 Zelda games, which in and of itself is a remarkable achievement.

The latest Zelda adventure portrays the heroic Link as an adult. Actually, more like a grown-up teenager, but the point is that he's not "little Link." Gone is the overly cartoony cel-shaded look from Wind Waker, and in its place is a more dark, realistic, and admittedly more violent game. This is an edgier Link tossed into a darker world, but not so dark as to lose its core audience.

THEY SAID IT

"We always think about how we are going to express Link. So in Ocarina Of Time we tried to express him as both a child and as an adult; in Majora's Mask, Link was a child; and we changed the style of art in Wind Waker, using toon-shading, and we expressed him as a child again. But this time we thought about it and something we hadn't done yet with the property was to express Link as an adult, so we tried to focus on that." —**Eiji Aonuma, Producer of Twilight Princess in an interview with Edge magazine**

Wow, Link's supposed to beat this guy?

Staying True to the Legacy

It's important to note that although the game definitely has a darker tone it's not trying to be anything other than a Zelda game. This is not Link meets the Master Chief. It's still the same old mute hero with the green tunic, only this time he's a bit older and has to face some really grown-up bad guys.

With the more realistic—albeit still anime—look comes superb animations. Link and his virtual surroundings have never looked this good. Along these same lines, the full orchestral score is wonderfully implemented as are the ambient sounds of rustling trees, goats, birds, and so on. It's safe to say that this is the best-looking and best-sounding Zelda game ever made.

Link and His Animal Friends

Link deals with all sorts of critters in the game; some good and some bad. He tends goats, pets cats, feeds dogs, and so on. Here are some other examples of Link dealing with wildlife. I sense a theme here....

Werewolf Link. Link has transformed himself in other games (such as his bunny transformation in Link to the Past) so this shouldn't come as a huge shock. And no, Link isn't wolfing out like Lon Chaney and slashing up innocent maidens. Link can travel to the Twilight Realm where he transforms into a wolf.

Link and Epona. Epona has been with Link for a while now but in Twilight Princess, you don't technically have to call her Epona. You can rename the horse whatever you want, but Link without Epona is like Hall without Oates.

Link and the eagle. Link can control an eagle this time around, which is just plain cool. He can tell it to do a myriad things such as retrieve objects.

The monkey. Certain parts of the game team Link up with a wily monkey. No, I have no idea why either, but he does.

DID YOU KNOW

Epona, Link's trusty steed, is actually named after the Roman goddess of horses (technically of horses, donkeys, and mules).

Lord of the Rings Online:
The Shadows of Angmar

Image courtesy of GameSpy.com.

DOSSIER

Genre: Bride of Geek's Online Paradise **Publisher:** Turbine **Developer:** Turbine
Platform: PC

Formerly known as Middle-Earth Online, Shadows of Angmar is being developed by Turbine, which is the same developer of the MMOG Asheron's Call and D&D Online. One has to wonder whether Turbine can pull off releasing *two* big-time licensed MMOGs around the same time, which is quite an undertaking. The game will have a monthly fee, but Turbine has not released official info on a price model. My guess is that you're looking at $15 a month.

Giant spiders are part of the bestiary.

There's a lot of pressure on a developer when it tries to take an enormously popular franchise like *The Lord of the Rings* and turn it into game form because if you mess something up, you can rest assured that Tolkien fans will let you know about it. It's not like World of Warcraft where Blizzard can just create stuff. If Mt. Doom isn't right, everyone will know it.

THEY SAID IT

> "We're designing a game that will last for many, many years. To keep people from having to upgrade constantly, we're creating some very high-end graphics. The Turbine G3 Engine does allow us to scale down the graphics for lower-end cards, and then if people do upgrade, the engine will be ready for them." —
> **Christopher Taylor, Producer of LOTR Online in an interview with ToTheGame.com**

The Timeline

The Shadows of Angmar takes place, as far as a basic timeline is concerned, during the *Fellowship of The Ring*, roughly around the time that the fellowship flees the Mines of Moria. As the game continues to grow, events will continue to transpire and you'll meet famous characters from the books. How that's going to play out, we don't really know. I mean really, isn't Aragorn busy enough during the trilogy as it is?

Because you can't be a bad guy (bummer), PvP combat is going to be a tad tough to pull off given that the playable races include only humans, hobbits, elves, and dwarves. You'll also get to choose a basic class such as ranger, warrior, and so on.

The World and Its Landmarks

One thing that should help separate LOTR Online from many other MMOGs is that the world will be constantly evolving; it's not going to be the same static world for months at a time. As you complete quests, you'll see the world change, but if you are a new player who hasn't completed those same quests, to you, the world looks normal. The game is broken down into "instanced" areas that help make it easy to portray areas differently to multiple characters with varying experience. It also helps make the game world seem real and not staged.

Image courtesy of GameSpy.com.

Boy, I hope we don't have to fight these guys....

Although you aren't dealing with the One Ring (that's Frodo's story, after all) you will visit many famous locations such as Bree, Hobbiton, Weathertop, Rivendell, Angmar, and Mt. Doom, among others. The idea is to release more of the Middle-earth map through expansion packs. There are approximately 60 creatures in the original game, although more are planned if the game proves popular enough.

Finally, you can create groups of characters to create your own fellowship. Fighting as a group provides huge bonuses, so the game is really trying to push players to form partnerships.

DID YOU KNOW

Sierra had first crack at an online version of Tolkien's world, but Turbine bought the rights from Vivendi in 2003 after Vivendi decided Sierra's progress on the game wasn't going quite as planned.

Full Spectrum Warrior: Ten Hammers
Two Hammers Short of a Dozen

Image courtesy of GameSpy.com.

Incoming!!

DOSSIER

Genre: Brainy Tactical Shooter **Publisher:** THQ **Developer:** Pandemic
Platform: Xbox, PS2, PC

There are a lot of tactical military shooters on the market today, from modern-day inner-city games like SWAT 4 to World War II games like Brothers in Arms. Granted these games are more than just run-and-gun shoot 'em ups but, in the end, they're still action games first and tactical military games second.

Full Spectrum Warrior, on the other hand, is a true 3D strategy game that is all about giving orders and watching your units execute them. It's more about using your noodle than using your reflexes.

The follow-up title to the original Full Spectrum Warrior, dubbed Ten Hammers, has the potential to be a huge improvement over what was a solid, but not quite spectacular first attempt at simulating modern urban warfare in the Middle East.

THEY SAID IT

"Any game that claims to be about urban warfare that doesn't include civilians is being disingenuous because that is what urban warfare is about. It's about fighting in an area that is just full of non-combatants and that is really what we are trying to grab with Ten Hammers." —**Creative Director William Stahl in an interview with GameSpot.com**

How It's Evolving

Initial buzz on this one is very good. Here are some of the key changes from the original.

Squad control. In Ten Hammers you control up to four squads, not just one, and you can issue global commands to all four even though you are still in control of a specific squad. This is cool because you can keep your perspective from one squad while telling another to flank the enemy, issue covering fire, and so on.

In addition, your troops have more distinct personalities and will react differently to unique situations. The idea being that Pandemic wants to make each solider an individual and not just an automaton.

Scouting. Break your squads down further, into smaller mini squads of two or three troops in order to scout unknown positions.

Pulp fiction. Creative Director William Stahl describes the campaign as being like the classic Tarantino flick. No—Travolta doesn't make an appearance, but the narrative jumps around quite a bit. It tells the same story from the perspective of four different squads, who are at different locations and

during different time periods. So, you'll get to see how Alpha squad saw what happened during Bravo squad's raid, and so forth.

Image courtesy of GameSpy.com.

Everyone, quick, shoot that building!

Go inside. In Ten Hammers, you can enter abandoned buildings or clear out buildings infested with insurgents, and use them as a way to flank the enemy or gain other tactical advantages.

AI. This isn't a touted feature, but at E3, Pandemic reps stated repeatedly that the game's AI is a lot more refined (another way of saying the game will be more difficult) than it was in the 2004 original, and the AI was a big issue in that game.

He's dead, really. A big change from the original is that your troops can now get killed in action. In the original game, you always got a replacement after a fellow solider died. Not here. When Jones gets shot, Jones stays dead. This was done, according to Pandemic, to add another layer of authenticity.

Head-to-head multiplayer. Although co-op mode is still part of the multiplayer package, the new head-to-head multiplayer mode sounds very promising. One player takes the fully loaded Armed Forces while the other plays as the insurgents, who will outnumber the technologically advanced military units.

DID YOU KNOW

The name "Ten Hammers" refers to a bridge in the game that is the focal point of the single-player campaign.

Vanguard: Saga of Heroes
A MMOG for the Hardcore

Image courtesy of GameSpy.com.

What have you done with Frodo!

DOSSIER

Genre: Hardcore Online RPG **Publisher:** Microsoft **Developer:** Sigil Games
Platform: PC

Vanguard: Saga of Heroes is the offspring of many former members of Team EverQuest. Sigil Games has a very distinct vision when it comes to creating online role-playing games (open world, slower player progression, tons of content, tough death penalties, and so on). Whether you agree with that vision, well, I guess that's the proverbial $1,000 question.

THEY SAID IT

> "Certainly the quests will not be random, nor limited to taking an item from point A to point B. Our quest design involves a sophisticated flag system where characters can be marked by a number of events (including, but far from being limited by, picking up or being handed an item). NPCs will then react to that character depending on what flags he has on or off." —**CEO Brad McQuaid in an interview with IGN.com**

To Instance or Not to Instance

This design philosophy definitely gives you a sense that this is a real world; instanced dungeons are convenient, but highly unrealistic. Having 15 different groups entering the "same" dungeon and not seeing each other is kind of silly when you think about it.

However, instanced dungeons allow everyone to play the game and not sit around and wait for a monster reset. Also, kill-stealing is something that happens all too often in open play areas. It's the price you have to pay for having a totally open and free game world. Either you're cool with that or you're not.

There's also limited "fast travel." Again, a realistic way to do it, but it's a valid question as to whether or not it's going to work or just become plain boring. Sigil promises that the travel and exploration are huge part of the game and that many adventures await you along the roads. Hopefully that's the case. On the plus side, there are "vehicles" in the game such as horses and boats that will speed things up. Walking sucks.

Microsoft and Sigil are targeting both the hardcore MMOG player and the novice, but based on everything the company has shown to the media, Vanguard leans much more toward the hardcore side than the casual side. By Sigil's own admission, the game is going to be "challenging" by having a tough

penalty for dying and more realistic gameplay. I think as long as "challenging" doesn't equate to "tedious," this approach is fine.

Image courtesy of GameSpy.com.

Tonight on Vanguard: When Scorpions Attack!

Vanguard has an old-school EverQuest flavor blended with gorgeous graphics driven by a heavily modified version of the Unreal 2 engine. This pretty package is also an enormous one. It promises to be one of the largest MMOGs (in terms of land mass) ever made. Whew...walking is *really* going to suck.

Diplomacy is a big part of the game, too. You can alter your "stance" (aggressive, relaxed, and so on) and change your attitude to get a response out of an NPC. There are lots of options here, so the potential for some great interactions is endless. Your diplomacy choices also impact the kinds of groups you are most effective with; if you are a character who specializes in thuggery, you aren't going to get too far when dealing with royalty. Again, this is another way Sigil is trying to add realism to the game world.

Vanguard is loaded with potential, no question about it, but will it be too hardcore for the newbie MMOG player? The jury is still out.

> ### VANGUARD HOME PAGE
> There's a lot of good info at **www.vanguardsoh.com** as well as a roster of top-shelf Vanguard fan sites.

DID YOU KNOW

Sigil Games CEO Brad McQuaid started his career in the industry as the designer of the 1993 shareware RPG WarWizard before moving on to design the original EverQuest.

25 to Life
Jack Thompson Will Love It

I think we're going to need a little backup here....

DOSSIER

Genre: Cops Killing Gangsters (and Vice Versa) **Publisher:** Eidos **Developer:** Highway 1 Productions **Platform:** Xbox, PS2, PC

25 to Life is another game that is sure to get eager politicians drooling at idea of attacking the gaming industry. Sometimes we make it easy for them, don't we? Hey, let's kill some cops! The kids will love that!

25 to Life was slated for a summer 2005 release, but was delayed until February 2006, which is sometimes a bad sign because the multiplayer portion of the game, which is really the meat of the gameplay, has been playable really since E3. Still, there's a lot of potential here if you like the idea of cops and robbers in a modern urban environment with lots of rap music.

THEY SAID IT

"For the law enforcement side you get a more tactical set of weaponry and on the street side you get faster rate of fire weapons. Each side has strengths and weaknesses and you can customize your character how you want. You can play a DEA Agent or SWAT member or a member of a unique gang or a kingpin." —**Creative Director Jake Neri in an interview with GameSpot.com**

The human shield technique, as demonstrated by one of the bad guys.

Online Gameplay

Although there is a single-player campaign story mode, what makes 25 to Life tick is its eight-on-eight multiplayer mode. This is basically a cops and robbers frag fest. Think SOCOM (see p.191), but with police officers and gangsters and you get the idea.

An interesting twist to the online game is that the law enforcement side is rewarded for apprehending the bad guys with nonlethal weapons rather than just plugging them. If a criminal is caught, he's out of the game for 30 seconds; if he's killed, he's out for only 10, so there is incentive in taking them in alive. The gangsters, on the other hand, get to use civilians as human shields and have access to more "street" weapons like the AK-47.

There are various multiplayer games (deathmatch, territories, and so on) and 15 multiplayer maps in all, ranging from subway stations to all-out street battles.

The soloplay aspect of the game is rather troublesome because no one is talking about it. Even at the trade shows, the developers talk endlessly about its multiplayer capability, but details on the single-player game are rare to say the least. We do know that it tells the story from the point of view of both Detective Lester Williams and Andre "Freeze" Francis of the 22nd Street D-Boys. Freeze is trying to get out of the life, but gets sucked back in when a fellow gang member, who doesn't want him to leave the gang, double-crosses him on his "last job." Other than that, the solo game details are nil.

The Guns

There's a wide assortment of guns and weapons in the game (more than 40 in all). The types of weapons you have access to depend on what side you play on. For example, the law enforcement team gets to use a lot of standard issue weapons, like SWAT rifles, tasers, pistols, and even the Desert Eagle. The gangsters get to use stuff like baseball bats, automatic weapons, sawed-off shotguns, and Molotov cocktails. Each side is guaranteed to play differently, no doubt about it.

DID YOU KNOW

The meaning of the term *life sentence* varies from country to country. In Norway, for example, a life sentence is limited to 21 years. However, in The Netherlands, life imprisonment means literally until the prisoner dies. Just Say No, kids.

ToCA Race Driver 3
You Want Realism? You Got It.

Image courtesy of GameSpy.com.

The graphic detail in ToCA 3 is very impressive to say the least.

DOSSIER

Genre: Wonderfully Realistic Racing **Publisher:** Codemasters **Developer:** Codemasters
Platform: Xbox, PS2, PC

If you're a hardcore racing simulation fan, there are plenty of reasons you should be absolutely jacked up about ToCA Race Driver 3 from Codemasters, the makers of such gearhead classics as Colin McRae Rally and, of course, the previous ToCA (Touring Cars) games. ToCA 2 was a highly ambitious title, and Codemasters is taking that design and adding an amazing amount of new content that, if they can pull it off, will make ToCA 3 the kind of game to satisfy racing fans for years to come. It's *that* ambitious.

THEY SAID IT

"Players now have a Sim and Pro Sim option on every platform. For Pro Sim you get an extra level of simulation. For example with the tires, what happens when the tires break free from traction across different road surfaces, which is affected by time of day, road temperature, or even the height of sea level, absolutely every single nuance is basically in there." —**Designer Jonathon Davis in an interview with GameSpot.com**

Six Games in One

There is something in ToCA 3 for everyone. The game features 35 racing styles that are broken down into six distinct racing "spokes" with around 160 different championships and 80 different cars and 45 tracks.

You get Open Wheel, GT, Tour Car, Oval, Off Road/Rally, and Vintage Racing, and each spoke is a representation of that genre in its entirety; it's not just a truncated version of it. For example, if you start with the Rally spoke, you start off racing Baja Buggies and work your career up from there.

The damage model in ToCA 3 takes the model from ToCA 2 and adds more details like full tire wear, which can overheat, cool down, and so on. Radiators can overheat; oil can even catch fire and blow the engine if you abuse your car (buggy, truck, whatever). All of this stuff is modeled independently for each individual car. Everything that falls off the car, which is a big part of the damage model, can affect airflow and downfalls. Knock off a rear wing on an open-wheel car and it has a huge impact on the car's effectiveness.

The reason for adding a lot of this stuff, according to Codemasters, is that it adds depth to long races so that a player that jumps out to an early lead can still lose due to a

technical issue with the car as well as the need for more pit strategies. A player might go to the lead in a long race but the car may start to fall to pieces, which forces him or her to back off a bit to lessen the wear on the car.

Image courtesy of GameSpy.com.

Open-wheel racing with a full damage model—check out the flying debris.

AI Vs. Human Opponents

A big goal for Codemasters is to have competitive and realistic AI. CPU drivers, if it works as advertised, will respond to their standing in the championship so that their strategy in each race may change. They also have unique characteristics for turning, passing, and so on.

If you prefer human competition, however, ToCA 3 comes with full online support so that all the championships are available, including the qualifiers. It allows you to literally create your own online championships.

If Codemasters can pull this off, and this is a huge project, ToCA 3 is going to be the new Rolls-Royce of racing sims. Definitely keep an eye out for this one.

SIM RACING WORLD

Although not specific to ToCA, **www.simracingworld.com** is a great site for racing fans, regardless of the game. The site covers it all.

DID YOU KNOW

Touring Car is a generic term for a type of racing involving modified "street cars" in Europe and Great Britain.

StarCraft: Ghost
This Is No RTS Game

Image courtesy of GameSpy.com.

DOSSIER

Genre: Blizzard's Console Game **Publisher:** Blizzard **Developer:** Swingin' Ape
Platform: Xbox, PS2, GameCube

It's alive! StarCraft: Ghost is in fact a real game! The February 2006 release date for
StarCraft: Ghost is extremely tentative; in fact, the game has gone through a lot of changes, including a change of developer, since it was first announced back in late 2002. Yes, **late 2002.**

Nova would be advised to avoid attacks like this.

Swingin' Ape Studios is now at the controls rather than former developer Nihilistic, and it has expanded a lot on what the former team had done, while at the same time adding tons of new stuff. Ghost has been rebuilt from the ground up more times than the Las Vegas Strip.

Blizzard is well-known for shipping games "when they are done," so the delays shouldn't be a huge concern (or a surprise) simply based on the company's track record. Granted, the development of Ghost has been weird even for a Blizzard game, so watch this one with a skeptical eye.

THEY SAID IT

"Splinter Cell is a game that rigidly focuses on stealth, and that works well for that title. Ghost allows the player more latitude. While there is a stealth component to our game, it is only part of the game play. Gamers playing Ghost will find that at times, the best solution is using the intensive firepower of Nova's Gauss rifle, or a nearby machine gun turret, tank, or Goliath Combat Walker. The two games are set in different universes. Sam Fisher needs to deal with the problems of the present day. Our game is set in a version of humanity's far future, in the StarCraft universe." —**Producer John Lagrave in an interview with IGN.com**

The Story

In StarCraft: Ghost you play the role of Nova, a covert operative with wicked combat skills and psychic powers, called a "Ghost." Nova has access to several vehicles such as Siege Tanks, Vultures, and the new Fighter-Bomber called the Grizzly, along with lots of ranged weapons like the gauss rifle, sniper rifle, flamethrower, and so on.

Even though the game is hyped as a stealth game, it's more of an action-stealth hybrid. There are definitely missions when Nova needs to use her cloaking ability and thermal vision to sneak in and get out without being noticed, but there are several instances when she just needs to lay the smack down to some Zergs.

So, the basic premise—a stealth-action game set in the StarCraft Universe—is still intact, but there's a lot of new

stuff that should make it a much better game if it ever gets out the door.

Image courtesy of GameSpy.com

Yeah, it's safe to say that Halo was an inspiration.

A New Focus

The game is now set immediately after the events of the StarCraft: Brood War. You don't need to have played the real time strategy games to understand what is going on, for fans of the series, many characters from the old games will make appearances throughout the story-driven campaign.

Obviously, Swingin' Ape has used other games as inspiration for how Ghost is being developed. It's a splash of stealthy Splinter Cell, the over-the-shoulder, third-person combat-aiming system from Resident Evil 4 on the GameCube, and the vehicle driving mechanics of Halo. Personally I see nothing wrong with this approach. If you're going to use three games as inspiration, you could do a lot worse than Splinter Cell, Resident Evil 4, and Halo.

Ghost Goes Online

Finally, Ghost is going to be online-ready, which is another radical shift from its early development. The plan is to have eight players with varying classes, weapons, and vehicles in a team-based format.

DID YOU KNOW

According to NPD Data, StarCraft and its expansions have sold more than eight million units since the game's release in 1998.

Black

Just Think of It As Gun Porn

An explosion is a common sight in Black.

DOSSIER

Genre: Blowing Stuff Up **Publisher:** EA Games **Developer:** Criterion
Platform: Xbox, PS2

At E3 2005, I heard the term *gun porn* for the first time. Now, when you hear something called that, it's just human nature to see what it's all about.

What I saw was a tech demo for a console shooter from developer Criterion (the makers of Burnout) called Black. It was a riveting demo that celebrated guns, explosions, and complete and utter annihilation of the surrounding environment. After seeing it, "gun porn" really did make a whole lot of sense.

THEY SAID IT

"The game is about a black military operation. Largely this world has been seen in terms of stealth gameplay— being covert, sneaking around. All of the action in Black is *overt* not covert. Our focus is a strong single-player game. We're out to bring some innovation into this genre. We're out to do a few things very well. Not a lot of elements poorly." —**Criterion's Alex Ward in an interview with Eurogamer.net**

When in doubt, open fire.

The Buzz

I loved what I saw even in a limited tech demo, and based on what fellow members of the media have told me directly after seeing more of it in action at an Electronic Arts press event in late summer 2005, it's coming along nicely. It's still too early to say how much depth it's going to have, but if you like guns, explosions, and nonstop action—make sure to keep an eye out for Black.

Remember the scene in the movie *Predator*, when Jesse the Body dies and the rest of the troops open fire and shoot their guns for like two minutes into the jungle? Or the scene in *The Matrix* when Neo and Trinity blast the hell out of that office lobby? That's the general idea behind Black: lots of guns, lots of debris flying around, and a whole lot of noise.

There's a story, but it's really secondary. You play a member of a black-ops team, battling terrorists in a mission-based format, covering roughly 25 levels of solo gameplay (there is no online support at all).

It's not *all* about blowing things up; you have missions to accomplish and goals to reach, but the star of the show is the guns and the impact that those bullets have when they hit stuff.

It might come as a surprise, but your arsenal really isn't all that impressive compared to a lot of shooters, especially shooters set in the future. You've got the basics: AK-47, pistols, shotguns, RPGs, Uzi 9mms, grenades...that sort of thing. It's how the physics engine, combined with the distinct damage model, affects the gameplay that helps to make Black stand out in such a saturated genre.

Literally everything in the world of Black can be damaged or blown up. Street signs, poles, buildings, trees, cars, window glass, specific *floors* of buildings—you name it. Taking a rocket-propelled grenade and blasting the side of a stone building is going to cause more than just an explosion—it might take down the building itself.

I can't stress this enough: Black is truly an orgy of gunfire.

DID YOU KNOW

According to the Princeton Wordnet, the term *criterion* means "A basis for comparison; a reference point against which other things can be evaluated." I guess that means they are the measuring stick. No pressure there.

Prey
The Game That Won't Die

Prey's graphics are no longer circa 1995.

DOSSIER

Genre: The Return from Vaporware **Publisher:** 2K Games **Developer:** Human Head Studios/3D Realms **Platform:** PC, Xbox 360

Prey, a straight-up first-person shooter, was originally announced back in 1995. That's not a typo. It was supposed to be released during the second Clinton administration. Now that, folks, is the definition of vaporware. Or so we thought.

Jaws collectively dropped when at E3 2005 2K Games and developers Human Head Studios and 3D Realms had a tech demo of the "new" Prey showing behind closed doors. Despite the fact that the game was officially re-announced a month prior, to actually see a working model was quite a shock. Even more shocking—it looked *great*. Of course that's the idea behind these scripted E3 presentations, but still, it was pretty slick.

Although specific details on Prey (like multiplayer support) are being kept under lock and key, there are some things that we know that are worth highlighting.

THEY SAID IT

"Our creature design is probably more influenced by Clive Barker than by H.P. Lovecraft. The ship designs draw on a wide variety of influences, including (in no particular order) Geof Darrow's work on *The Matrix*, Frank Miller's *Ronin*, the work of Craig Mullins, Feng Zhu, Syd Mead, Masamune Shirow, and of course, H.R. Giger. We also derived a certain amount of material from studying anatomical photos of a huge array of tissues and organs, both healthy and diseased." —**Art Director Rowan Atalla in an interview with IGN.com**

The Story

You play the role of Tommy, a modern day Cherokee living on a reservation that he hates and doing a job he finds frustrating and unfulfilling. Tommy is not your typical shooter hero with oodles of testosterone and a machine gun; in fact, he has even lost faith in his Native American heritage and is quite the sullen sort.

Tommy's girlfriend is abducted by aliens who are bent on mass destruction, and Tommy's attempt to rescue her is the meat of the storyline. Being a Cherokee, Tommy eventually has access to cool powers that one might associate with Native American lore. Take Spirit Walking, for instance. You can leave your body for a brief period of time to slip past sentries, force fields, and other obstacles, which I'm sure Cherokee agree was the original idea behind the Spirit Walk. Ahem.

There is also the Death Walk, which is what happens when you die—you actually have to fight your way back to the living world. If you succeed, you are put back in the same spot where you died.

Whatever happened to little green men or the aliens with the big eyes? These guys look MEAN!

Portals

A big feature of the original Prey was the idea of using portals. Well, that's back for the "new" game, as well. These are basically rips in space that allow people to travel from one location to another in the blink of an eye. These portals serve as bridges to various parts of the game world—and monsters can even spawn from them. The idea is that you should never feel truly safe in Prey.

The DOOM 3 Engine

Prey uses a modified version of the DOOM 3 engine. The good thing about the E3 demo was that the game world was bright with color and not drab and exceedingly dark like that of DOOM 3. The demo did a wonderful job of showing how pretty this game is going to be.

There's a lot to like about the early Prey demo, particularly the cool use of gravity (wall walking, fighting during free floating, and so on) Still, it's Prey.

Fool me once....

DID YOU KNOW

Prey was originally supposed to be released at the same time as these other titles: Fallout, Mario Kart 64, Turok, Ultima Online, and Age of Empires. Prey is old.

Company of Heroes
Yep, Another WWII Game

Image courtesy of GameSpy.com.

Yep, this is a real-time strategy game and not a shooter.

DOSSIER

Genre: Cutting-Edge World War II RTS **Publisher:** THQ **Developer:** Relic Entertainment **Platform:** PC

Company of Heroes is a World War II company-based real-time strategy game. Yes, another one. But although the buzz surrounding it is huge, the lack of details on how it's actually going to play makes it hard to believe that it'll make its ambitious February/March 2006 deadline.

Even though the press went gaga over its demo presentation last year, any time a highly publicized game goes into information blackout mode, it's not an encouraging sign.

THEY SAID IT

"Up to now, we've all been playing RTS games on static (lifeless) maps. By adding fully destroyable, interactive environments we've changed the lifeless battlefield into something dynamic, which adds a whole new level of strategy to the game. Imagine a chessboard where now the board comes into play, and can be used and manipulated throughout the game. We're using Havok 3.0 for Company of Heroes, and the end result is an environment that is totally physics driven. Some examples would be units diving for cover along a road, when they come under fire, using craters that may have been left from an artillery attack that just happened." —**John Johnson, Lead Designer on RelicNews.com**

the level of detail is just ridiculous. You can see a sergeant giving orders via hand signals and yelling at troops, and so on.

By viewing the screenshots it's easy to mistake this game for Call of Duty or another next-gen WWII shooter. Using Relic's own Essence engine and the current version of the Havok physics engine, Company of Heroes looks like no other strategy game before it.

Image courtesy of GameSpy.com.

This is a zoomed-out view of an ongoing firefight.

The Relic Factor

This cannot be underestimated. Relic is a very hot developer with titles such as Homeworld and, more recently, the Warhammer 40K: Dawn of War line under its belt. Dawn of War and the Winter Assault expansion put Relic back in the forefront as one of the top real-time strategy developers around, so when it was announced that it was the team slated to do Company of Heroes, it caught a lot of people's attention.

Having Relic on board as the developer was great, but what really started the buzz was the game's stunning E3 showing. This is definitely a real-time strategy game, but it has the graphics of a first-class first-person shooter.

Many games have tried the "3D RTS" approach, but none have looked this good so early in its development. You can zoom the camera and see your soldiers up close and personal and

The Game

Here is where the details get sketchy. We know it's set in good old World War II and that it's a small scale, tactical squad-based real-time strategy game with your troops battling it out in smaller battles with infantry, jeeps, tanks, quick air raids, and so forth. It's sort of like the fight at the end of *Saving Private Ryan.*

Based on a few published reports, the game will use a "strategic point" system, similar to what Relic did in Dawn of War. This really helps to limit players from playing "turtle" and forces them to scout out the surrounding areas.

What we don't know is how the game's control will work in conjunction with its true 3D setting or how smart the AI will be. Relic promises that Company of Heroes will have some of the best unit AI ever seen in a strategy game, but that's just the company line; we haven't seen it yet.

DID YOU KNOW

In the summer of 2004, THQ acquired Relic Entertainment, which has firmly placed THQ on the map as a top-flight PC publisher. Prior to that, THQ was known primarily for wrestling games.

♟♟♟ Star Wars: Empire at War
Please, Oh Please, Let This Not Suck

Image courtesy of GameSpy.com.

Space battles are a huge part of Empire's design.

DOSSIER

Genre: *Star Wars* Strategy: Take Four **Publisher:** LucasArts **Developer:** Petroglyph
Platform: PC

You would think that the *Star Wars* universe would be the ideal backdrop for a great strategy game. Unfortunately, it hasn't worked out that way. It's not that LucasArts hasn't tried, but almost every time the company cranks out a *Star Wars* strategy game, it ends up being a huge disappointment. From Rebellion and Force Commander to Galactic Battlegrounds, it's been a rough ride.

You have to appreciate persistence, though. Star Wars: Empire at War is another attempt at recapturing the magic and the excitement of using *Star Wars* units, ships, and characters in a real-time strategy format. And although developer Petroglyph is a brand new studio, the company is made up of several former Westwood employees that have experience working on real-time strategy games such as Command & Conquer, C&C: Red Alert, and Battle for Middle-earth. If Petroglyph can pull it off, Empire at War will be the first of its brethren to boldly go where none has gone before...oops, wrong license.

THEY SAID IT

> "The galaxy is shaped around the actions you choose to take in your conquests, and you can go into battle with whatever forces you build. Those forces will be with you for the duration of the game until you lose them." **—Assistant Producer Dave Silverstein, in an interview with Gamershell.com**

Resources and Strategy

Empire at War's campaign is open-ended and not broken down into individual missions. You have a map of the galaxy and the goal is to capture/destroy planets and systems and defeat the Empire or the Rebels, depending on your point of view. The grand strategy map moves in real-time, so there's nothing turn-based about the game, although hopefully there will be an option to slow down time (or even pause it) if things get going too fast.

Resource management is a huge part of the game, but it's not a matter of asking a droid to chop down a tree or mine some gold. The planets you control are what affect your income, and different planets add specific resources and technology. (I'm just dying to know what possible benefit controlling Hoth has...maybe a never-ending supply of snow cones?)

Land and Space

Battles take place when armies meet on the grand strategy map. When that happens, the game shifts into its combat

mode which can take place on land (like the Battle of Endor) or in space (like the, um, Battle of Endor). The land and space settings are also intertwined so that if you have ships in orbit around a planet, you can ask for a planetary bombardment.

Image courtesy of GameSpy.com.

Tatooine attracts Stormtroopers like bees to honey. What is it about that place?

The space battles have everything from hulking Star Destroyers to nimble A-Wings, whereas the ground battles also have traditional units like Stormtroopers and AT-ATs. Even the Rancor makes an appearance.

Special hero units will be in the game and because it is set right before the first movie (the real first movie, Episode IV) and runs through the course of the film, you can expect to see famous faces from Vader to Solo. (What impact they'll have, we aren't quite sure yet.)

Finally, I'd be remiss if I didn't mention the fact that the Empire has access to the Death Star, and during the E3 presentation it actually blew up Tatooine! Sorry, Luke. That said, it does beg the question, how exactly do you lose a game if you have the freaking Death Star?

DID YOU KNOW

In addition to the C&C series, members of new developer Petroglyph have had a hand in creating dozens of games, from Eye of the Beholder to Sid Meier's Pirates!.

Auto Assault

It's Open Season on the L.A. Freeway

Cars and guns is the meat of Auto Assault.

DOSSIER

Genre: Cars with Guns Online **Publisher:** NCsoft **Developer:** Netdevil **Platform:** PC

Cars and guns seem to go hand in hand. Admit it, how many times has someone cut you off on the highway and you wished, just for a brief moment, that your Honda Civic had mounted 50-caliber machine guns attached to the hood? In Auto Assault, you'll get to live out your *Road Warrior* fantasies in a persistent online world with thousands of other road rage sufferers for $14.95 a month.

There's a very detailed backstory to the setting of the game, along with three playable races and several subfactions, but I'll hold off on that and just give you the guts of why Auto Assault is such a highly anticipated title.

THEY SAID IT

"The speed at which combat takes place is nothing like what players have seen before in an MMO. You are fighting and maneuvering throughout the entire combat experience, and all this with destruction flying all around in 5.1 stereo goodness!" —**Scott Brown, Auto Assault Project Leader in an interview with IGN's RPG Vault**

More cars blowing up! Eat that, Gibson!

Cars, Guns, and a Touch of Gravity!

In Auto Assault you play a character in the near future that specializes in vehicle combat. You drive through hostile territory collecting power-ups, fame, and money. In short, you're a road warrior with a much more deadly vehicle than Mel Gibson ever dreamed of driving.

The game uses a "reality-based" physics model, so your car behaves as it should, but this is by no means a realistic driving sim. There is no fall damage or anything like that. You can zoom off a mountain cliff and come crashing back to the surface and keep on truckin'. Everything in the world is destructible. There is no piece of scenery that cannot be blown to bits. There is also unlimited ammo, so you can shoot 'til your heart's content.

Items in Auto Assault are randomly generated. The stats and enhancements are created by the game on the fly, so seeing two cars decked out exactly the same should be rare. In fact, deciding which items to use is one of the best parts of the game, given that there is *lots* of cool loot to find in the wreckage of enemy vehicles....

The Gameplay

It should be understood that this is not just a "hop in your Car of Death and go blasting" game. Although it can be if you want to play that way, you are free to go to the "wasteland" area and just blast the hell out of other players. However, there is a very detailed story to follow and plenty of solo gameplay. The action is fast and furious, but there are tons of missions to do; there's some meat on this bone.

There are three races in the game—Humans, Mutants, and Biomeks—and each has strengths and weaknesses just like your typical RPG. Your choice of race also will have a dramatic impact on how others perceive you in the game world. Netdevil is doing all it can to make sure this is more than just a mindless action game, and this is yet another example of that.

Creating clubs or guilds is also an important part of the game and Netdevil will hold regular tournaments (both team and solo) and ladder events to keep things fresh.

AUTO ASSAULT HOME PAGE
Everything you need to know about the game can be found at **www.autoassault.com**, along with a list of fan sites worth checking out.

DID YOU KNOW

Netdevil, developer of Auto Assault, is a Colorado-based company that also developed the 2001 MMOG Jumpgate: The Reconstruction Initiative, published by now-defunct 3DO.

Titan Quest
Socrates Meets Diablo

Image courtesy of GameSpy.com.

Fireballs make for crispy spiders

DOSSIER

Genre: Diablo in Greece **Publisher:** THQ **Developer:** Iron Lore Entertainment
Platform: PC

Role-playing games seem to fit into three distinct categories. First you have the deep, highly detailed games with reams of stats, dialogue trees, and character development, all of which blend together to help tell a story, usually involving a really mean Foozle that needs to die because he/she/it wants to take over the galaxy/world/city. Games like Baldur's Gate and Knights of the Old Republic fit here.

You then have games that are totally open-ended where you can go where you want, when you want and do what you want. These games are typically also loaded with stats and details, almost to the point of absurdity. Games like Morrowind fit here.

Finally, there are the games where you fight stuff, kill stuff, and get stuff. The story itself is secondary to the action and the "phat loot" you acquire. Diablo, Fate, and Titan Quest fit snugly into this category.

THEY SAID IT

> "One of the great things about our game is our historical topic. This is new and refreshing for the role-playing genre. It is time for something new. Role-playing is such a great genre; it should not be restricted to just one topic. Questing in, around and under Athens and the Parthenon, the maze of Knossos, the great pyramids, the Hanging Gardens of Babylon while fighting a bunch of mythically inspired baddies—it doesn't get much better than this." —**Brian Sullivan, Iron Lore President and Lead Designer in an interview with IGN.com**

The Buzz

Titan Quest isn't a straight-up Diablo clone, though. First off, its setting is not your typical role-playing fare with knights, wizards, orcs, and dragons. The game is set in Ancient Greece (and also spills into Egypt and Babylon) and uses places such as the Parthenon, the Pyramids, and The Hanging Gardens as its canvas.

In addition, the monsters you battle are mythological creatures from this ancient time period. Creatures like mummies, harpies, cyclopes, satyrs, and everything in between are part of the 85-monster bestiary.

This is a really pretty game with amazing scenery; tall grass sways in the wind, sand blows up after a strong breeze, bugs infest murky swamps, and the city environments are bustling with detailed activity. The dungeons and other landscapes are

not randomly generated like in other action RPGs because Iron Lore wanted them handmade to look as good as possible. (The monster locations are randomly generated, though.) If you like eye candy to go along with your indiscriminate monster killing, Titan Quest aims to please.

Image courtesy of GameSpy.com.

Even the Greeks hated skeletons.

The character class system is unique due to its massive flexibility. Your hero can be either male or female, but there are no set classes like mage or fighter. You actually create your own class by choosing two mini-classes. This allows you to mix and match play styles: You can be the fireball-throwing rogue, or the self-healing fighter. This system will, hopefully, provide replay value by allowing you to try different combinations.

Finally, Iron Lore is taking a very "Pro Mod" approach and will ship powerful editing tools with the game so that fans can get to work on creating new adventures and even total conversions using the game's engine.

There is always a question of depth with these hack-and-slash games, and further details like multiplayer support are minimal at the moment, but fans of the genre should certainly follow Titan Quest's development.

DID YOU KNOW

Brian Sullivan, the President of Iron Lore Entertainment and lead designer of Titan Quest, was also the co-developer of the classic RTS Age of Empires.

Rise of Nations: Rise of Legends
From the Mind of Brian Reynolds

Image courtesy of GameSpy.com.

See? I told you it looks nothing like Rise of Nations.

DOSSIER

Genre: RTS Behemoth **Publisher:** Microsoft **Developer:** Big Huge Games **Platform:** PC

The level of prerelease hype a game gets is often dependent on the developer. Big Huge Games gets attention, mainly because of its founder, Brian Reynolds. Reynolds carries on his resume, Civilization II and Alpha Centauri, which in strategy circles is about as good as it gets. He's also one of the most genuinely friendly people in the industry. In talking to Reynolds you can just feel his excitement for not only his projects, but other games as well. As a "journalist" (I review games for a living, so I use that term loosely), I'm supposed to stay neutral but the fact is that it's really easy to root for a guy like Reynolds. Luckily, he also makes it easy because he makes *really* fun games.

Having Big Huge Games behind the wheel is reason enough to get excited, but there's more to it than that. First off, it isn't an historical strategy game; it marks Big Huge Games's first foray into the realm of fantasy. Second, the lush 3D graphics caused many an eyebrow to rise during its media presentation. This looks *nothing* like Rise of Nations, although it keeps some of that game's core gameplay elements (like border control and attrition damage).

THEY SAID IT

> "We were really excited to do a game that was not limited by reality, so we could concentrate on making our graphics be as incredible as our gameplay. Many of our past games have been inspired by history, and so it's refreshing to take the plunge into a bold new world. At the same time, all the races in our game have definite thematic roots in historical or literary archetypes, and so we still get to have a lot of the richness of a universe inspired by the 'real' world." —**Producer Tim Train in an interview with Gamecloud.com**

Not Your Typical Fantasy

This is not a fantasy game in the spirit of Tolkien; instead, Rise of Legends combines many themes from the designs of Leonardo da Vinci, steampunk, and tales of the Arabian Nights. It's quite the hodgepodge.

The game is set in the land of Aio. It's a land under assault by the forces of both magic and technology and the races in the game reflect this basic difference in philosophy.

At the time of this writing, only two of the game's four races have been revealed and Big Huge Games is keeping the other two under lock and key. Why that is, I have no idea. Here's what we know about two of the races:

The Vinci. Inspired by the designs of da Vinci, this faction uses workshops to build all sorts of wild contraptions, and their units are all steeped in technology from the basic musketeer to the deadly clockwork spider.

The Alim. Based on the Arabian Nights theme, the Alim are one of the "magic" races and are themed around fire, magic, and the desert sands.

Image courtesy of GameSpy.com.

A Vinci city goes boom.

In seeing the two races in action, it was clear that playing as the Vinci would require completely different tactics than the Alim, and hopefully this theme stays true for the two as-of-yet unannounced races.

The Campaign

The game's campaign will be both similar to the open-ended format found in Rise of Nations, but will also incorporate story elements to drive things along. Supposedly the solo campaign has three times the number of people working on it as worked on Rise of Legends, so let's hope that pays dividends.

Regardless of how the campaign shakes out, however, Big Huge Games is releasing the same toolset used in making the campaign so that modders can make campaigns and missions of their own.

DID YOU KNOW

Even though most known for his strategy designs, Brian Reynolds actually got his start at MicroProse doing graphic adventure programming for games like Rex Nebular and the Cosmic Gender Bender, Return of the Phantom, and Dragonsphere.

The PS3
The Games to Watch

The PS3...shiny!

Hardware talk bores the hell out of me. I can't help it. When people start talking about frame rates, overclocking, and all that jazz, I start to zone out like Homer Simpson daydreaming about hog fat and the little monkey that plays the cymbals. I care about the games more than I do the machines. Consequently, I'll be thrilled when all these next-gen consoles hit the streets so that we can stop focusing on their guts and start ragging on their games.

By now you surely have noticed that there has not been a whole lot of PS3 coverage (or Nintendo Revolution coverage for that matter) in this book. That's not by design, but rather by necessity. The PS3 is due to come in the summer of 2006 (we hope), and there just isn't a ton of detail about a lot of the games (Unreal Tournament 2007 and some others are the exceptions). In October 2005, at the TGS (Tokyo Game Show), the full list of known PS3 games was announced. Here's a sampling of some of the more eye-catching games you can expect to see in 2006 and 2007.

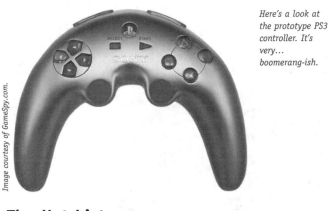

Here's a look at the prototype PS3 controller. It's very... boomerang-ish.

The Hot List

Gran Turismo Vision. Obviously, the GT series is going to make the leap to the PS3. Details are few but the plan is to have full damage modeling (one can only hope) and the ability to have 20 cars on screen at once. Multiplayer is also being bandied about as a potential feature, something that this fantastic series has sorely lacked.

Devil May Cry 4. Another series that was bound to make the jump to the new platform, Dante will be back again to kick more demonic booty.

Resident Evil 5. Few details are out there, but this official announcement made me smile. Rumor is that RE5 will take place in a brand new environment and not its usual creepy darkness, instead opting for a more bright color palette. Yeah, weird, eh?

Fight Night Round 3. I got a chance to see a brief clip of Fight Night Round 3 at E3 2005; it is the only confirmed EA Sports PS3 title, even though you can bet your last nickel that the other games will join Fight Night at a later date. New features include a one-hand push-off move to break a clinch and a totally new physics engine.

Final Fantasy. Another adventure in what is arguably the best console RPG series of all time will appear on the new PS3. Details aside from its official announcement are nil, however.

Metal Gear Solid 4. Set for a 2007 release, MGS4 takes place three years after the events in Sons of Liberty. Solid Snake is back as the main character and seven more characters have been "announced" via game trailers: Vamp, Meryl Silverberg, Revolver Ocelot, Otacon, and Raiden all appear to be in the game. Story details and new gameplay mechanics are top secret.

Tekken. Aside from the fact that Namco has announced that the company is working on another Tekken fighter, additional details are scarce. Still, it's more Tekken!

MotorStorm. This game's E3 trailer was wicked. No one said whether the images were renderings or "real" graphics, but it actually had people cheering—that's how cool this racer looked. You can pick from a wide variety of vehicles and take part in what is being called "extreme off-road racing," whatever that means.

PS3 NUTS AND BOLTS
The **Wikipedia PS3 entry** (en.wikipedia.org/wiki/PlayStation_3) has everything you need to know about the guts of the PS3.

DID YOU KNOW

The PlayStation 3 will be backward compatible with both PS1 and PS2 games. It will not, however, have a hard drive. Aren't memory sticks great!

The Nintendo Revolution
Don't Count It Out

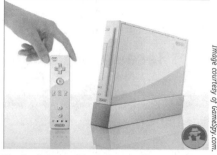

The Revolution and its funky controller.

It's hard to believe that a new console from Nintendo is considered the underdog in the "console wars" but that is exactly the situation Nintendo finds itself in with the Revolution. That's a shame because I still think that the GameCube has some of the most inventive pieces of gaming software available on the planet and the Revolution will most likely have the same quirky personality. And if you believe the company line that Nintendo is selling, the Revolution will be a sleek, affordable console without HD support, but one that will "revolutionize" (their word, not mine) the console gaming market. We shall see.

The Revolution will, thankfully, be completely backward compatible with all GameCube games. In addition, you can even download and play Nintendo 64, SNES/Super Famicom, and Nintendo Entertainment System/Famicom games on the new console. If you want to play a seven-year-old game on a shiny new console, I guess that's your business.

That Wild, Wacky, Controller

One controversial feature that we know is not a rumor is the unique controller that will ship with the console. This is definitely one of the "revolutionary" things about this unit; that doesn't mean it's going to *work*, but wow...it sure is different.

It looks like a remote control for your television or an iPod Shuffle, and I have to admit the first time I saw it I did that little puppy dog motion when they tilt their head to the side when they hear a weird noise. I had absolutely no idea what to make of it.

It's a motion-sensitive wireless controller which is designed to be used with one hand. Cordless motion-sensitive controllers are nothing new, although in gamepad form they never quite took off. This design is different, though. Let's say you are playing a fighting game and want to smack someone on the noggin with a bat. You would literally move the controller in

the same motion you want your character to swing the bat. Along these same lines you can use the laser pointer to aim a gun or fire a bow. It's a very hands-on, interactive experience.

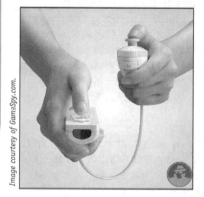

There are attachments for the new controller as well. I'm sorry, but it just looks weird.

There's an assortment of buttons and triggers, and even slots to fit it with additional attachments for use with certain kids of games. Based on published reports from people that have actually used the new controller, the aiming mechanism feels natural, and why wouldn't it? You're simply aiming the controller at a point on the screen. It's a very different and risky approach, so it's hard to say whether it'll be a revolution or a silly gimmick that no one buys into.

Oh, Yeah, the Games

With a release date of "sometime in 2006" the game specifics are few and far between. We do know that franchises like Metroid Prime, Animal Crossing, Final Fantasy, Mario, Splinter Cell, Zelda, and Super Smash Bros. will be making an appearance.

DID YOU KNOW

Nintendo continues to call *Revolution* their new console's codename and not the official name of the new machine.

Gears of War
Because Apocalypses Make for Good Games

The future is bleak on Gears of War.

DOSSIER

Genre: Survival Horror Shooter **Publisher:** Microsoft **Developer:** Epic Games
Platform: Xbox 360

Gears of War is, without question, one of the most highly anticipated Xbox 360 titles. It's expected to combine fast-paced shooter action, amazing graphics and sound, and a survival horror edge designed to scare the pants off of you.

The hype surrounding Gears of War is off the charts. After E3, and particularly after the game convention in Tokyo, Japan in October, the word from the gaming press was that it was a game that you would simply have to see to believe. Of course we in the press like to use hyperbole whenever possible, but Gears of War really does look fantastic and is easily one of the most impressive 360 titles to date.

THEY SAID IT

> "The Locust Horde are monsters, yes, but they are intelligent savages. They use a lot of the same moves against you, they are going to be blind firing against you, they will use grenades to flush you out, and they'll try to rush in for a melee encounter and try to break your neck. Using our dynamic AI allows us to make smarter and more entertaining enemies." **—Lead Designer Cliff Bleszinski in an interview with GameSpot.com**

An Epic Plot?

Most games from Epic are heavy on action and light on story (take Unreal Tournament, for example). Gears of War is not only an intense third-person action game but it also brings with it a supposedly fleshed out storyline.

It's set on a planet called Sera, a world rich in a substance called "Emulsion," which can be easily converted into pure energy. Countries that want the substance will do whatever they can to get it, whereas those who own it will die trying to defend it. Naturally, much fighting ensues.

What the people of Sera don't realize is that lurking underground lay the Locust Horde, who appear on the scene on "Emergence Day" to destroy mankind. A quick peace accord was drawn up to fight off this new enemy. Things don't go well for the humans; it's so bad that prisoners are released to stave off the threat. Here's where you come in—you play ex-solider and ex-con Marcus Fenix, a member of Bravo Company, part of a squad in the ongoing battle with the Locust Horde.

The folks at Epic are stressing the fact that Gears of War is not a typical run-and-gun shooter where he who shoots the fastest wins. You will need to make use of cover in order to succeed; there's even an evade button that is used to tuck-and-roll and duck behind certain pieces of cover (cars, buildings, whatever). You can even blind fire over a rock or from behind a wall. Just running around and shooting aliens is a surefire way to die—a lot.

Be afraid of the dark in this game. Bad things tend to lurk there.

Branched Linearity

The campaign uses an interesting system in which you can choose your own path as the story develops. The game presents you with options as to which path to take, sort of like the old Choose Your Own Adventure books. Better still, in co-op multiplayer mode you are still presented with these options and you can split up and encounter different things during the session. It's a classic example of "You take the high road and I'll take the low road and we'll meet in the middle and kill some aliens along the way."

Gears of War, according to Epic, will be a seamless world without any load times. You're just going to play the game and the story unfolds. There should be a good mix of play styles in the game. Missions will range from bug hunts to scenarios that are designed to scare you out of your wits. It looks like Halo meets Resident Evil with a staggering amount of graphic detail.

DID YOU KNOW

Gears refers to squads of humans in the Coalition of Ordered Governments, who are battling the Locust Horde. Thus, you play a Gear of war.

Age of Conan: Hyborian Adventures
A Different Sort of MMOG

Image courtesy of GameSpy.com.

Age of Conan isn't going to be a game for the squeamish.

DOSSIER

Genre: MMOG with Crom!! **Publisher:** Funcom **Developer:** Funcom **Platform:** PC

I'm excited about this one. Being an MMOG addict, I like it when a new game is announced that attempts to either take a different tack from a design standpoint or that is set in a fresh new environment.

With an interesting hands-on combat system and a significant solo-player experience all combined with the fact that it's set in the Hyborian Age of Conan the Barbarian—it's easy to see why this one could be a ton of fun.

After all, it *is* Conan. People still love the old roguish barbarian. Of course you don't actually play Conan in the game; the time period is set when Conan is King. The buzz, among online RPG fans, is one of intrigue more than anything else.

THEY SAID IT

> "I've always been of the opinion that PvP should be voluntary, fun, and available for everyone in an online game. Some players prefer to PvP all the time, others never. The majority of players, though, are in between these two extremes. Our goal is to create a system where you can PvP with your main character when you want to, without any permanent penalties." —**Director Gaute Godager in an interview with GameSpy.com**

Sticks and Stones...Yeah They Hurt

This is not a "high fantasy" game like D&D. The Age of Conan is the planet Earth roughly 10,000 years ago right after the end of the Ice Age. It's an adult (that is, graphic) game: brutal, dirty, and quite frankly, a prehistoric setting when "technology" consists of iron sword and mammoth skins.

Although the old *Conan* movies starring the Governor of California are great popcorn entertainment, they also do a fair job in capturing the style of the Hyborian Age: a lot of dust, dirt, mud, and primitive weapons and armor with some magic thrown in just for kicks.

This is an age of Old Gods (like Conan's Crom), of human sacrifice, black magic, and tribal wars. Doesn't this sound like a great place to spend your Saturday nights?

Goin' Solo

Here is where things get really interesting. The first part of the game is actually not an MMOG at all; for the first 20 levels you are playing solo, taking part in an adventure like a typical single-player RPG. After level 20, you are given the option to continue your adventure in the larger Hyborian world. The

idea, which is really cool I might add, is to remove the idea of "noobs" from the online world. By level 20, you should know what you're doing and the online world should consist of nothing but experienced players. The hurdle for Funcom is making the solo game fun, deep, and unpredictable. If Funcom can pull that off, Conan can succeed. If not, it's tank city.

Image courtesy of GameSpy.com.

The game certainly has an art style all its own.

A Combat Twist

Funcom's "Real Combat" system is very different than in other games such as EverQuest or even World of Warcraft. The idea is that player skill will play a role in the outcome of a fight in addition to his/her stats. For example, you need to manually aim when firing a bow or casting a spell. Your aim and your stats (as well as your target's defense/resistance) determine the outcome. The combat is in real-time, so when you click the mouse, your character swings his weapon or brings up his defenses. It's not just a matter of hitting the attack button and sitting back and watching the results. It's a hands-on experience.

Finally, the magic system is also a bit different in that you won't see typical magic spells tossed about. Magic is considered "foul" in this world. The magic, as a result, deals with summoning and the manipulation of objects (like when James Earl Jones turned that snake into an arrow in the first movie).

DID YOU KNOW

Author Robert E. Howard's Conan the Barbarian has been around since the 1930s, when he made his debut appearance in *Weird Tales* magazine.

Mage Knight Apocalypse
Namco's Foray into PC Gaming

Image courtesy of GameSpy.com.

You'll fight a lot of large enemies like this throughout the game.

DOSSIER

Genre: Combat Miniatures Go PC **Publisher:** Namco **Developer:** Namco/InterServ International **Platform:** PC

What in the world is Namco doing? Famous for action-packed console games like Soul Calibur and Tekken, Namco has entered the PC gaming arena with two officially licensed products: Mage Knight Apocalypse, an action-oriented RPG based on the fast-paced tabletop combat game, and an epic strategy game called Warhammer: Mark of Chaos (discussed on the next page), which uses the tremendously popular Warhammer license from Games Workshop.

Not that I am complaining. I'm a huge Warhammer fan and also enjoy the Mage Knight game but it's still quite a shift for Namco to say the least. At the time of this writing we didn't know too much about it to be quite honest. Most of what we do know is based on the fact that it's based off of a popular tabletop game.

THEY SAID IT

> "...if I was playing the nightblade character and continued to use vampiric attacks to defeat my enemies, my character stats would naturally gravitate toward those which contribute best to that skill set. Likewise, I will unlock new, more powerful vampiric skills and proficiencies as I progress. In addition to skills, stats, and proficiencies, my character will begin to take on a more vampiric appearance as she progresses up this skill tree." —**Senior Producer Chris Wren in an interview with GameSpot.com**

Image courtesy of GameSpy.com.

Say, that's a nice rifle you've got there....

About Mage Knight

The Mage Knight tabletop game (which is similar to the popular HeroClix franchise, also from WizKids, Inc.) has been around for a few years now and has since developed a strong fan base. The setting is a fairly typical fantasy universe complete with dwarves, elves, humans, trolls, wizards, and so on. In addition, you get a little technology thrown in with gunpowder and the like. (In this sense, it's not unlike Warhammer.) There is an ongoing storyline in the tabletop game, so it's not just about getting an army together and slapping each other silly.

The plot of the game surrounds the emergence of the Apocalypse Dragon, a creature who is increasing in power and is a threat to the entire land. (Think Smaug, only a lot worse.) Your hero is given the task of defeating the dragon and its chaotic allies before they destroy the world. Piece of cake, eh?

Diablo by Design

Based on discussions at E3, the game sounds an awful lot, at least in terms of pace, like Blizzard's classic action RPG, Diablo. There's a *lot* of fighting and a lot of mouse clicking.

You choose your character from a pool of five heroes; the four that you don't pick become members of your party, but they are all AI controlled. All you need worry about is the hero you selected. There's no word of whether you can issue orders, so we'll have to wait and see. The heroes include the following members.

Dwarf Rifleman. A typical dwarf gunner—good with TNT and his trusty rifle. His axe isn't bad, either.

Nightblade. She's basically a female vampire.

Elf Guardian. It's Legolas! No wait, wrong license.

Amazon Warrior. A fierce and speedy hand-to-hand fighter.

Draconum Mage. This mage deals primarily with elemental magic.

DID YOU KNOW

There are two Mage Knight novels in print—*Rebel Thunder* by Bill McCay and *Dark Debts* by Doranna Durgin—both of which were published in 2003 by Del Ray.

Warhammer: Mark of Chaos

Finally, a Return to the Fantasy Universe

Image courtesy of GameSpy.com.

Skaven attack the High Elves.

DOSSIER

Genre: Warhammer Total War **Publisher:** Namco **Developer:** Black Hole Games
Platform: PC

There are a lot of potentially great games coming out in 2006, but for me, Mark of Chaos is the one that I most want to see. The reasons are twofold: First off, it's a Warhammer Fantasy Battle game and being the unabashed Warhammer geek that I am, whenever a new 'Hammer game is announced, I tend to get as giddy as a schoolgirl. Secondly, it just happens to look *amazingly* cool.

It's been a while since a game based on the fantasy end of the Warhammer Universe has seen the light of day, making this game long overdue. Ever since The Creative Assembly started its Total War series, Warhammer fans have longed to see such huge, epic fights set in the Empire, the Border Princes, and in the Chaos Wastes. Well, the wait is almost over because Mark of Chaos is all about such battles. It's enough to make Warhammer fans explode with excitement.

THEY SAID IT

"Unlike a traditional RTS, Mark of Chaos puts the focus squarely on the battlefield. To succeed in Mark of Chaos, you must learn to command your army and defeat your enemies. Gameplay centers on taking territory, developing your army, strengthening the territories you have, and, if needed, defending them. In short, Mark of Chaos is all about war and giving you more control over the actual battling and not just the decisions that lead up to it." —**Senior Producer Chris Wren in an interview with GameSpot.com**

Image courtesy of GameSpy.com.

A Champion of Chaos stands tall.

Rats, Demons, Elves, and Man

Of the 17 Warhammer army races, four are fully represented in the game: The Skaven (twisted ratmen mutated by Chaos), The Empire (Humans), the High Elves (Elves from across the sea; arrogant yet powerful magic wielders), and the forces of Chaos (men and beasts that have pledged an oath to one of the powerful Chaos Gods). There is no word on whether the individual Chaos Gods will be represented, however.

Using only four races is a bit of a letdown, but units from the other races can be hired on as mercenaries, so we should still see regiments of dwarves, orcs, ogres, and so on.

More Than Total War?

The campaign map sounds very reminiscent of another Warhammer Fantasy board game called Mighty Empires, which was played on a Risk-style tile map with each race's army starting from a lone capital city and then branching out to conquer the rest of the territories.

In addition to the large-scale battles, you'll also take part in smaller skirmishes. The fights will, supposedly, have more purpose than just beating the snot out of the other side. There are side quests such as finding lost artifacts, which can lead to smaller and more personal encounters.

Of course the Total War series (see p.157) is what immediately springs to mind when you see the grand, sweeping real-time battles, and indeed it's not unlike those games in terms of its epic scale. Here, however, you also field powerful Champion units that not only lead your armies but might also enter a duel with another Champion during the course of a battle. These Champions earn experience, gain bonuses, new equipment—the works.

This level of personalization is ideal for a Warhammer game because the miniatures game is all about powerful identifiable hero units and just not the grunts.

DID YOU KNOW

If you're a Warhammer fan or just a fan of fantasy fiction in general, be sure to check out The Black Library, the publishing wing of Games Workshop. They can be found at www.blacklibrary.com.

Alan Wake
Whatever You Do, Don't Fall Asleep

Image courtesy of GameSpy.com.

Meet Christian Bale...er, Alan Wake.

DOSSIER

Genre: Puntastic Action Horror **Publisher:** Undetermined **Developer:** Remedy
Platform: Xbox 360, PS3, PC Undetermined 2006 Release

I'll be totally honest: I have no idea how Alan Wake is going to play. I can specu-late, but the nuts-and-bolts details on the way in which it plays are still under wraps. I know what you're thinking: So, why talk about it?

Despite the lack of a publisher, the E3 tech demo presentation was so impressive in terms of the graphics, atmosphere, and story that it demands that we keep at least one eye on it as it continues its development through 2006.

THEY SAID IT

"By far the biggest element in my opinion is how everything is so dynamic. Lighting is no longer static; objects in the world are dynamic and react to changes in the simulation. Effectively, we are building a mas-sive world simulation with unprecedented depth. Having said that, the visuals do make a huge differ-ence as well. There is simply no way that something like this could run on a 32MB PlayStation 2. It would be just as impossible to reach this level of versatile environments and visual fidelity with a 64MB Xbox 1."
—**Designer Petri Jürvilehto in an interview with Eurogamer.net**

Mr. King of Twin Peaks

Alan Wake is a successful horror author suffering from insom-nia (A. Wake, get it? Ha-ha) because his fiancé, who was Wake's true love and personal muse, has gone missing. Along with the insomnia, this trauma has apparently triggered some-thing in his head and he now feels as if he's losing his sanity. So he travels to Pride Falls, Washington to relax and to seek professional help.

As things start to get better, he sees a woman at the local clinic who could pass as his fiancé's identical twin. This starts the whole cycle over again and Wake begins to lose his grip on reality. He starts to see shadows at night—twisted shad-ows and hooded men that he feels are stalking him. Is this all in his mind or is Pride Falls a small town out of an H.P. Lovecraft story?

Environment to Die For

The quick demo at E3 unveiled the story, but also showed off the spectacular environments that Remedy has created. Pride Falls truly comes alive from detailed city streets to the people that inhabit them.

Image courtesy of GameSpy.com.

Night equals bad in Alan Wake's world.

Additionally, weather patterns change throughout the course of a game; when it starts raining, visibility is limited and driving is a bit trickier due to the wet pavement. Even the sound changes with the wind and rain. Remedy is trying to create a painstakingly detailed environment not only from a visual point of view, but with proper use of sound and physics as well.

As you play through the game, time passes. This in and of itself isn't groundbreaking because many games have day/night cycles. But in Alan Wake, it's going to play a huge role because the figures tormenting Alan emerge only at night and, in fact, light drives them away. So, you might be doing a side mission in the afternoon and get stuck in the middle of nowhere when the sun goes down. Not good.

All that is known at this point is that the game style will be similar to that of games like Grand Theft Auto. (I doubt we see any hookers, though.) There will be missions that advance the story, but it's an open-ended game world. This is also not a straight-up adventure game because Alan will do battle with the evil that haunts him; just don't expect Alan to be a Max Payne clone (at least I hope not).

DID YOU KNOW

Developer Remedy is the company behind the film noir shooter series Max Payne. Whether that's considered a plus is up to you.

Final Fantasy XII
Better Late Than Never

DOSSIER

Genre: It's Never Really the FINAL Fantasy **Publisher:** Square Enix
Developer: Square Enix **Platform:** PS2 Summer 2006 Release

Image courtesy of GameSpy.com.

Due to its long development, FFXII looks okay, but not earth-shattering. Most fans won't care.

Like Zelda, the Final Fantasy series is one of the longest-running game franchises in history. Starting back in 1987 on the NES, Final Fantasy has seen its share of ups and downs, but regardless of how the critics receive it, each Final Fantasy release induces long lines at the cash register. The FF fan base, particularly in Japan, is strong, loyal, and apparently loaded with discretionary income.

Final Fantasy XII, when it hits the street this summer, will undoubtedly sell like gangbusters. But will it be any good? The answer is a firm...maybe. The reason for the skepticism is that Final Fantasy XII was supposed to be released in the summer of 2004. It obviously missed that ship date (despite being playable at E3 2004) and then was a strange no-show at the 2005 E3. If that's not a red flag alert, I'm not an Ohio State grad.

THEY SAID IT

"These days, user demands and expectations for our games are very high. It's true that we still have do things such as, for instance, going to Turkey as we did for this project. The reason we went there is so we can see what's really out there. But if we just took that and made the game we wouldn't be able to satisfy everyone. So, we're still keeping true to creating something that's original and a fantasy world while referring to something that exists. We try to take something out of what exists and create our own original work." —**Background Director Isamu Kamikokuryou in an interview with IGN.com**

An E3 No Show

Funny story: The people at Square Enix stayed at the same hotel as I did for the E3 show. While waiting for the shuttle bus to pick us up, I started a little small talk with one of the guys in a Square Enix T-shirt. (They looked like they were part of a sports team.) After a few minutes of banter, I asked whether we'd get to see Final Fantasy XII at the show and when the fellow said no, I decided to go all "reporter" on him and try to find out why. Needless to say, it was a long and rather quiet shuttle ride to the Convention Center that day.

Despite not appearing at E3, Square Enix did in fact show the game at the Square Enix Party in the summer of 2005. According to IGN.com, which had staff members at the event, the game plays a lot differently than the other games in the series because of the new "Active Dimension Battle" system

that has replaced the old Active Time Battle standby. Gone are the familiar character columns with enemies on the left and allies on the right.

Image courtesy of GameSpy.com.

The new combat system will take some getting used to.

You can now go pretty much wherever you need to go during a fight and control only one character at a time, while issuing orders in real-time. You are basically managing three characters, switching back and forth to issue commands. Thankfully, the game still pauses when you bring up the command menu, so I don't want to give the impression that it's turned into an RTS.

The 12th Story

Changes aside, here's the basic plot of FF XII. Set in Invalice (the world from Final Fantasy Tactics and Final Fantasy Tactics Advance), the game deals with the Archadians, an evil empire bent on conquering all the land. The city of Dalmasca remains one of the last bastions of freedom. You play (among other characters) Vaan, a young boy from Dalmasca who rises up against the foreign threat.

DID YOU KNOW

Since its debut in 1987, the Final Fantasy games have sold more than 60 million units worldwide. At the equivalent of $50 a pop, that's some serious bank.

TimeShift
Time Traveling with Guns

That building doesn't look at all intimidating (gulp).

DOSSIER

Genre: Time-Traveling Shooter **Publisher:** Atari **Developer:** Saber Interactive
Platform: Xbox 360, Xbox, PC

Time travel is cool and all, but every story that deals with zipping to the future or backtracking into the past carries with it inevitable plot holes. Take the *Terminator* films. I love those movies, but really, why can't the machines just go back to 1885 and kill John Connor's ancestor and be done with it?

Needless to say, TimeShift also deals with time travel; in fact, it's really the entire premise of the game. It will most likely have similar plot irregularities, but unlike a movie, at least in a game you can mask the story gaffes with the fact that you get to blow stuff up.

THEY SAID IT

> "The game's story was inspired by classic time travel science fiction. Stories like *A Sound of Thunder* by Bradbury and *Time and Again* by Jack Finney. The story is about what could potentially happen if the power to travel through time was in the hands of the wrong man. It is about reversing the effects of an altered timeline. We hope that the story will spark a lot of debate and renewed interest in time travel literature." —**Saber Interactive CEO Matthew Karch in an interview with TeamXbox.com**

The Delays

TimeShift was originally scheduled for an October release on the Xbox and PC but suffered delays that pushed it back to Spring 2006. Every time the press gets a look at the game, it comes away impressed. But delays are usually the result of one or two things: the publisher (Atari) gave a silly release date it knew it couldn't keep (this happens all the time), or there are snags in the development.

Another potential issue is that Saber Interactive's only other known game was a shooter called Will Rock—which did anything but—of course that doesn't mean TimeShift will suffer the same fate, but it's a concern nonetheless.

Mr. Swift and His Suit

You play the role of Colonel Michael Swift (apparently a long lost cousin of Will Rock) who, after the tragic death of his daughter, agrees to be the guinea pig for a U.S. government time travel mission. Using a machine called the Chromonicon and a time-bending device called the Quantum Suit, Swift travels back to 1911 to plant an experimental probe. But when

he gets back to the present day, the world is a very different place. I guess he stepped on a butterfly. Swift is now an enemy of the state and his new mission is to not only survive but also to use his time travel ability to set things right.

At its heart TimeShift is still a shooter, even with the cool time travel stuff.

TimeShift has great graphics, a gritty steampunk setting, a surprisingly powerful physics engine, and a lot of trappings from every other shooter on the market. The hook, obviously, is the whole time travel thing. The Quantum Suit has three powers: It can slow, stop, and actually rewind time. It needs to charge up to use these abilities, so you can't just pause time forever.

Using this suit allows you to slow down bullets, escape from bad guys, and even avoid certain death. I know this sounds like a modern day Prince of Persia, but the time-shifting ability in this game goes much deeper than the few second backtracking like in the Prince's adventures. Did you ever see the *Twilight Zone* episode where the guy used a stopwatch to stop time in order to rob a bank? Same idea.

Besides, Swift isn't a hulking bad-ass fighter; in fact, he's greatly outnumbered and outgunned, so using the time ability is not only a neat gameplay device, but it's crucial to play the game.

DID YOU KNOW

Laugh at the idea all you want, but Albert Einstein's special theory of relativity says time travel (into the future) is indeed possible. I'd like to use that to see whether the Cleveland Browns will ever win a Super Bowl or whether Robert Jordan's *Wheel of Time* series will ever end.

Unreal Tournament 2007
The Tournament That Never Ends

Image courtesy of GameSpy.com.

DOSSIER

Genre: Broadband Fraggers' Heaven **Publisher:** Midway **Developer:** Epic Games
Platform: PC, PS3 (Possibly Xbox 360)

Unreal Tournament versus the 500-pound gorilla known as Quake III: Arena. This was 1999's heavyweight prize fight between two multiplayer-oriented first-person shooters, which ended up as a first round K.O. by the upstart from Epic Games. Quake III didn't know what hit it.

The military guy from early UT games is apparently back again. That's one tough dude to kill!

Since then, the Unreal Tournament series has proved to be one of the most popular shooter franchises on the planet. As you read this, people are fragging their little hearts out online. There is never a lull in the online world of UT.

Although Unreal Tournament 2004 remains exceptionally popular, Midway and Epic are working on yet another update, which isn't due out until late 2006 and it might even spill into 2007, but based on a first look, Unreal Tournament 2007 should be worth the wait.

THEY SAID IT

> "An early decision in the development of UT2007 was to reduce the number of game types. There are definitely fans of the Bombing Run and Double Domination game types, but the numbers of people playing them are very much dwarfed by the numbers playing Onslaught, Deathmatch, and Capture the Flag. We didn't take the idea of cutting those types lightly, but the ability to have our team focus on the more popular game types will ensure those deliver on every level." —**Producer Jeff Morris in an interview with Gamecloud.com**

You Look Maaavelous

Before getting into gameplay specifics, the star of the show is the new graphics engine, powered by Epic's Unreal 3 Tech and a physics engine driven by Ageia's Novodex technology. If those words don't mean anything to you (you aren't alone), all you need to know is that Unreal Tournament 2007 looks *ridiculously* good and has believable physics that allows for cause-and-effect relationships in the gameplay (like blowing up rocks to cause an avalanche). Epic is also trying to use the physics to allow for a less "floaty" game when your character hits an anti-gravity area; the new engine allows for a more realistic setting.

Speaking of realistic settings, Epic is calling its levels *environments* rather than just static levels. The idea being that each environment is a living, breathing thing and not just a hallway, rooftop, or space station. Although we might still see a

space station "level," all the areas will be active—things will be going on. They'll all be believable places in that they serve a purpose of some kind and players will be able to take advantage of some of their functions.

Image courtesy of GameSpy.com.

This doesn't look like your typical UT level, eh?

The detail in the characters, environments, and the vehicles is striking—so much so that UT2007's graphics stood out at E3, which was a show that was nearly all about graphical flare. When you stand out in *that crowd*, you have a pretty game on your hands. Of course, all of this detail may come at a price for PC gamers; I shudder to think what kind of machine you'll need to run this thing.

Conquest

Most game modes from UT2004 are back, except for Domination and Bombing Run (due to a lack of popularity), but a new game being added is called Conquest, which is a team-based game that involves capturing holding positions. Unlike a game like Onslaught, you aren't controlling small control points but larger territories. Conquest should work great with *lots* of players on large maps.

DID YOU KNOW

Midway was originally known as Midway Manufacturing, and began as an independent manufacturer of amusement equipment way back in 1968.

Rise & Fall: Civilizations at War
Time for Your Heroes to Take Command

Image courtesy of GameSpy.com.

Attack of the pachyderms!

DOSSIER

Genre: Wearing a Lot of Hats **Publisher:** Midway **Developer:** Stainless Steel Studios
Platform: PC

Stainless Steel Studios has a history of throwing everything, maybe even sometimes a bit too much, into its designs. A game like Empire Earth, an RTS released back in 2001 that spanned through nearly the entire history of modern man, is a testament to that.

The developer's upcoming strategy game, Rise & Fall: Civilizations at War, isn't quite as encompassing as Empire Earth in terms of covering multiple epochs of history, but it is trying to add several new ideas to the basic RTS model.

THEY SAID IT

"Beyond the simple aesthetics of how each civilization looks, it's also very important for us to capture the historical accuracy of how each civilization waged war. The Persians, for example, fielded these massive armies, the biggest the world had ever seen, but their units weren't that strong and were generally poorly trained. That will be reflected in Rise & Fall. We're bringing these ancient civilizations to life in a way that gamers have never seen." —**Stainless Steel Studios President Rick Goodman in an interview with Totalvideogames.com**

Image courtesy of GameSpy.com.

Cleopatra leads a massive Egyptian army. She is so hot. No really, it's like 140° out there.

History

Rise & Fall is a 3D real-time strategy game set in ancient times when the game's four playable nations—the Romans, Greeks, Persians, and Egyptians—all fielded powerful armies.

The game seems to be a blend of both historical accuracy and artistic license. For example, the nations are modeled accurately in terms of unit makeup and general strengths and weaknesses. The Romans and the Greeks are more disciplined than the Persians, and yet the Persians field massive armies that dwarf the other three nations.

The units (and there are more than 80 in the game) are grouped into formations with statistics for things like moral and other basic military attributes; it even has cool navy combat with ramming, boarding, and so on (something missing from Rome: Total War). As a result of this primer, it's logical for one to assume that it's a no-nonsense historical simulation.

Not so fast. This is equal parts game and history lesson.

Hero Command

If everything else comes together (the AI, interface, and general gameplay) it is the Hero Command feature that will either make the game an RTS classic or a hybrid mess.

Each civilization receives two heroes from history. Caesar, Cleopatra, Nebuchadnezzar, Ramses, and Alexander the Great— these larger-than-life characters are under your control during the game. These powerful heroes carry with them special powers. Ramses, for example, acts like a priest in that he can heal all nearby units and Cleopatra is ridiculously good with a bow.

During the course of a battle, when things start to get hairy, you can go into Hero Command mode, which drops you into a third-person view similar to that of an action game. While in this view you are in complete control of your hero, leading his/her men on the field, attacking enemies—you name it.

You can stay in this mode for only short periods of time, however. In addition, there are Hero Quests during the solo campaign that all play out in this third-person viewpoint.

Will this mode work as advertised? Will it be unbalanced or, quite frankly, kind of silly? (Will Alexander the Great be able to kill 20 Romans with a loose-leaf notebook?) If it works, and if it's as fun as Stainless Steel says, Rise & Fall has the potential to be an excellent game. If not, well, we all know what happened to Caesar, right?

DID YOU KNOW

Rick Goodman was a co-designer for the original Age of Empires. Sheesh, did anyone in this biz not work on that game?

Enemy Territory: Quake Wars
It's Human Versus Strogg in a Battle Royale

Image courtesy of GameSpy.com.

Strogg Land Walkers look sweet....

DOSSIER

Genre: Broadband Fraggers Rejoice, Again **Publisher:** Activision
Developer: Splash Damage/id Software **Platform:** PC

Wolfenstein: Enemy Territory is a hugely popular World War II–era team-based multiplayer shooter. Developed by Splash Damage and released in the summer of 2003, it was originally planned as a retail expansion to Return to Castle Wolfenstein but was later changed to a free download that gamers gobbled up with a spoon. We gamers just *love* free stuff!

This small taste of background info is important because Splash Damage (with some DOOM 3 engine assistance from id Software) and Activision are bringing the Enemy Territory formula to the world of Quake in Enemy Territory: Quake Wars. It's still a ways off from release; in fact, Splash Damage is noncommittal about a firm date other than "2006." But based on what the press has seen thus far, it has the potential to be a fantastic team-based shooter with all the bells and whistles that the powerful DOOM 3 engine brings to the table. (No monsters hiding in closets included...we promise.)

THEY SAID IT

"With most games, you have this huge focus on visuals, which have no real payoff on gameplay except for immersion. Then you have this other focus, which is physics, guns, or whatever the current buzzword is. For us, with the mega-texture technology, these two things suddenly merge. You can have a map that uniquely identifies different traction properties for different surfaces that has a significant effect on gameplay." —**Splash Damage's Paul Wedgwood in an interview with GameSpy.com**

50 Years Later...

The game takes place on Earth roughly 50 years into the future, before the events of Quake II. The Strogg, the alien menace of the Quake games, have started their invasion of the planet and you're either part of the EDF (Earth Defense Force) or the invading Strogg army. May the best team win.

If you're into playing multiplayer shooters in an organized team setting, you should be jonesing to play this. It looks *that* good. If you're more of an isolationist gamer, feel free to pout at your leisure because as of this writing there isn't even a plan to include AI bots for solo play (as in a game like Unreal Tournament). This is a certified online-only experience.

Meat and Potatoes

Because this is a team game (the current plan is to have a max of 16 players per team) planning and organization are the keys to success. It's also one of the potential pitfalls because playing in a pick-up game without any kind of team cohesion

could be disastrous. Each map has a set of goals for each team (destroy a bridge, set up a base perimeter, escort tanks to a certain location...that sort of thing).

Each player also chooses a character archetype. The exact player types are not available yet but you can expect roles such as medic, assault force, soldier, engineer, and so on. The different classes each come with unique skills, just like in other games of this sort (like Counter-Strike and the original Enemy Territory). The weapons and classes for the EDF and Strogg will be wildly different and thus require different tactics. In addition to the classes, there will be various vehicles at your disposal from choppers and tanks for the EDF to huge land walkers and hovercrafts for the Strogg.

This dude is so dead.

Image courtesy of GameSpy.com.

Unlike the old Enemy Territory, this is not a game restricted to indoor, closed environments. Quake Wars takes placed on a huge landscape complete with mountains, lakes, and open space. Think of it like Star Wars Battlefront with a Quake bent. I can't wait.

DID YOU KNOW

Splash Damage, despite the popularity of its Wolfenstein: Enemy Territory downloadable add-on, has never released a fully priced retail game. Quake Wars is its first.

Gods and Heroes: Rome Rising
Is There a Publisher in the House?

Image courtesy of GameSpy.com.

DOSSIER

Genre: Squad-Based MMOG, in Rome **Publisher:** Unknown **Developer:** Perpetual Entertainment **Platform:** PC

Rome is cool. Even without any of the mythological stuff, stories from ancient Rome continue to fascinate in books, film, and on TV. When you toss in all the fantasy-themed material (gods, magic, curses, mysticism, and creatures), things start to get really interesting; it seems like the ideal place to set a fantasy MMOG, which is precisely what Perpetual's Gods and Heroes: Rise of Rome hopes to offer.

Three guys against a Minotaur. Hmm...I'm laying ten bucks on the Minotaur.

As of this writing, things are eerily quiet. The game has received very little media coverage since E3, which for a fairly high-profile MMOG is, admittedly, a bit strange. It was supposed to be released in time for the holiday season, but was pushed back to Q1 2006 with few details given. This doesn't mean that the game will flop, but the lack of buzz is a bit unnerving.

Still, the developer insists things are on the right track and the public beta should have become available by the time this tome hits the shelves.

THEY SAID IT

> "Well, I think the things that we're adding are going to be really different from a lot of... well, from anything that's been done in MMOs. The addition of squad combat, in particular. Also, the god system and things like that are really going to set us apart, I think." —
> **Designer Stieg Hedlund in an interview with IGN.com**

Character Creation

There are six character classes in the game:

Gladiators. A close fighting specialist, a Gladiator can become proficient with a myriad weapons. Example: Kirk Douglas in *Spartacus* or the tall Nubian in *Gladiator*.

Healers. The healer is a walking first-aid station.

Priests. Need Jupiter to pop a cap in some Carthaginian's ass? Call the priest.

Rogues. Your typical wily streetwise Roman thief. Think Eric Idle in *Monty Python's Life of Brian*. That guy had to be a rogue, right?

Scout. Lives outside the city, good with a bow, can small a Minotaur from 100 paces.

Soldiers. A Roman soldier, deadly in combat and highly disciplined, usually. Think Titus Pollo from the HBO show *Rome*.

Gods and Swords

The gods in Rome Rising are quite real, and can be called upon for aid and can lash out when not given proper respect.

DID YOU KNOW

Your character is actually a son or daughter of a particular god, which you can choose during character creation. (What, you thought you were some run-of-the-mill Plebian?) From Jupiter and Apollo to Mercury and Mars—the gang's all here.

Image courtesy of GameSpy.com.

From Minotaurs to Cyclopes...things are not getting easier.

That said, I think the game's main hook, outside the setting, is the squad-based combat, which has never been done in an MMOG (to my knowledge, anyway). During the course of play, you can hire up to eight NPCs to be part of your squad. These NPCs all have varying talents and abilities, just like a regular player. During combat, you battle with your squad by your side and you can issue orders and organize them in formations to best use their particular skills. There are 50 levels in the game and when you reach a high level (as of yet undetermined), you can even recruit creatures to join the group. Because, really, soldiers are great, but there are times when you just need a Cyclops, ya know?

There are, supposedly, more than 1,200 quests in the game and they can be given by Roman Senators, military officers and gods (it's not advised to turn these down). Or you might receive an Epic Quest, which is part of each player's own personal journey in the game.

Even though this is Perpetual Entertainment's first game, Stieg Hedlund, the game's designer, was also the lead designer of Blizzard's Diablo II. Nice game for the ol' resume, eh?

More Games to Keep an Eye On

We Know the Titles...Yep, That's About It

Ridge Racer 6. Evidently this time you have to out-race a 747. No biggie.

Well, you made it to the final essay of this magnificent tome of gaming knowledge. Wasn't it cool? Don't you feel like a walking encyclopedia of gaming arcana now? But wait! There's more! There are dozens of other games worth talking about that are set to come out in either 2006 or 2007. The problem is that a lot of info regarding these games is being kept under wraps. So, dear reader, here's my definitive list of the biggest games to watch for in 2006 that are so far under wraps I couldn't devote a full entry to them.

Franchise Sequels Galore

Perhaps the most high profile game due out this summer is Bungie's Halo 3. All we know about it is that it will be released on the same day that the PS3 ships and that Master Chief is back. Other than that, it's all guesswork.

Irrational Games is working on the "spiritual successor" to System Shock with a game called BioShock; Ridge Racer 6 screams its way onto Xbox 360; Sam Fisher returns again in Splinter Cell 4; Atari and Eden Games will try to scare us out of our wits with Alone in the Dark 5; and id Software will once again return to Castle Wolfenstein, only this time on the Xbox 360.

PSP gamers will also get a taste of eagerly anticipated games like Metal Gear Acid 2, a new Viewtiful Joe adventure, and a tiny version of Katamari Damacy. The Nintendo DS should see another Final Fantasy game, this one called Crystal Chronicles, a new Zelda adventure, and a DS version of Super Monkey Ball. Super Monkey Ball with a stylus? Hmm....

RPG Heaven

Fans of role-playing games should keep an eye out for Neverwinter Nights 2, which is being developed by Obsidian Entertainment, the same people behind Star Wars: Knights of the Old Republic II. Bethesda Softworks is working on the third game of the legendary Fallout series, and BioWare has a sci-fi RPG in the works called Mass Effect. (Keep your ear to the ground for another new BioWare franchise, called Dragon Age.) If you're into RPGs with a Japanese flavor, keep an eye

open for two games from Mistwalker called Blue Dragon and Lost Odyssey, both Xbox 360 exclusives. Finally, MMOG fans should sit tight and wait for the 2007 release of Warhammer Online from Mythic Entertainment (the Dark Age of Camelot people). If you've read this book, you know I can't wait to see this one.

In Sports

Sports fans should get their first taste of college baseball when EA Sports releases MVP NCAA 06 in the spring, which takes the MVP Baseball engine and slaps it inside a college setting. 2K Games will try to revive the Top Spin series when it heads to the Xbox 360 (the graphics for this one already look stunning) and the company continues to play cat-and-mouse with the media about the future of the 2K football series. Who knows? Maybe we'll see an unlicensed pro football game that actually plays like football.

Play Safe Out There!

And there you have it. One big book of gaming that I hope inspires you to greatness! Actually, my hope was that it was both informative and fun to read. Kind of like *Martha Stewart's Hors d'Oeuvres Handbook*...only both informative and fun to read. (To be fair, her four-cheese fondue is no joke.)

I've thoroughly enjoyed being your tour guide through the year in games that was and the year that will be. Let's all do it again sometime; next year, perhaps. So enough reading: Go have some fun! Remember, games are not art, they're games; go play them.

Index

How can we make this index more useful? Email us at indexes@quepublishing.com

How can we make this index more useful? Email us at indexes@quepublishing.com

How can we make this index more useful? Email us at indexes@quepublishing.com

F

How can we make this index more useful? Email us at indexes@quepublishing.com

How can we make this index more useful? Email us at indexes@quepublishing.com

How can we make this index more useful? Email us at indexes@quepublishing.com

How can we make this index more useful? Email us at indexes@quepublishing.com

N

How can we make this index more useful? Email us at indexes@quepublishing.com

How can we make this index more useful? Email us at indexes@quepublishing.com

How can we make this index more useful? Email us at indexes@quepublishing.com

How can we make this index more useful? Email us at indexes@quepublishing.com

How can we make this index more useful? Email us at indexes@quepublishing.com

How can we make this index more useful? Email us at indexes@quepublishing.com

How can we make this index more useful? Email us at indexes@quepublishing.com

X

How can we make this index more useful? Email us at indexes@quepublishing.com

Xbox 360

Y – Z